Personal Finance & Investing

ALL-IN-ONE

FOR

DUMMIES®

By Melanie Bien, Julian Knight, and Tony Levene

Edited by Faith Glasgow

BICENTENNIAL
1807
WILEY
2007
BICENTENNIAL

John Wiley & Sons, Ltd

Personal Finance & Investing All-in-One For Dummies®

Published by
John Wiley & Sons, Ltd
The Atrium
Southern Gate
Chichester
West Sussex
PO19 8SQ
England

E-mail (for orders and customer service enquires): cs-books@wiley.co.uk

Visit our Home Page on www.wiley.com

For general information on our other products and services, please contact our Customer Care Department within the U.S. at 800-762-2974, outside the U.S. at 317-572-3993, or fax 317-572-4002.

For technical support, please visit www.wiley.com/techsupport.

Wiley also publishes its books in a variety of electronic formats. Some content that appears in print may not be available in electronic books.

British Library Cataloguing in Publication Data: A catalogue record for this book is available from the British Library

ISBN: 978-0-470-51510-5

10 9 8 7 6 5 4 3 2 1

FSC
www.fsc.org
MIX
Paper from
responsible sources
FSC® C013604

About the Authors

Faith Glasgow has been writing on finance and property for longer than she cares to remember, and has freelanced since 1998. She has contributed to a wide range of publications during that time, including most of the broadsheets and magazines from *Vogue* to *Investors Chronicle*. Faith lives in London with a small family and a large mortgage, and occasionally muses on the fact that she still has to work for a living, given the reams of advice on how to manage one's wealth that she has dispensed over the years. Sadly, hers is a classic case of 'Do as I say, not as I do'.

Melanie Bien is associate director (head of media relations) at Savills Private Finance, the independent mortgage broker. She was personal finance editor of the *Independent on Sunday* for five years and writes freelance property features for national newspapers, magazines, and Web sites. She has written several books and pamphlets to accompany television programmes on property makeovers and design, and on buying, renovating, and selling property. Her other books include *Sorting Out Your Finances For Dummies*, *Buying a Home On a Budget For Dummies*, *Buying and Selling Property For Dummies*, and *Renting Out Your Property For Dummies*.

Julian Knight was born in Chester in 1972, educated at the Chester Catholic High School, and later at Hull University. He is the BBC News personal finance reporter and writes for the BBC News Web site; Julian is the author of *Wills, Probate & Inheritance Tax For Dummies*, and lives in London with a large mortgage. Before joining the BBC, Julian worked at *Moneywise* magazine and contributed to the *Guardian* as well as many other publications.

Tony Levene is a member of *The Guardian* Jobs & Money team, writing on issues including investment and consumer rights as well as on taxation. He has been a financial journalist for nearly thirty years after a brief foray into teaching French to school children. Over his journalistic career, Tony has worked for newspapers including *The Sunday Times*, *Sunday Express*, *The Sun*, *Daily Star*, *Sunday Mirror*, and *Daily Express*. He has written seven previous books on money matters including *Investing For Dummies* and *Paying Less Tax For Dummies*. Tony lives in London with his wife Claudia, 'virtually grown up' children Zoe and Oliver, and cats Plato, Pandora, and Pascal.

Editor's Dedication

For my beloved Mum and Dad.

Editor's Acknowledgements

Many thanks to the specialists who helped in the updating of complex information in this book, particularly Paul Causton of Steele Raymond, Tom McPhail of Hargreaves Lansdown, and the HMRC press office.

Publisher's Acknowledgements

We're proud of this book; please send us your comments through our Dummies online registration form located at www.dummies.com/register/.

Some of the people who helped bring this book to market include the following:

Acquisitions, Editorial, and Media Development

Project Editor: Daniel Mersey

Content Editor: Steve Edwards

Commissioning Editor: Alison Yates

Text Splicer: Helen Heyes

Executive Editor: Jason Dunne

Executive Project Editor: Martin Tribe

Cover Photos: © worldthroughthelens/Alamy

Cartoons: Ed McLachlan

Composition Services

Project Coordinator: Jennifer Theriot

Layout and Graphics: Claudia Bell, Denny Hager, Heather Ryan, Alicia B. South

Proofreaders: David Faust, Susan Moritz

Indexer: Aptara

Publishing and Editorial for Consumer Dummies

Diane Graves Steele, Vice President and Publisher, Consumer Dummies

Joyce Pepple, Acquisitions Director, Consumer Dummies

Kristin A. Cocks, Product Development Director, Consumer Dummies

Michael Spring, Vice President and Publisher, Travel

Kelly Regan, Editorial Director, Travel

Publishing for Technology Dummies

Andy Cummings, Vice President and Publisher, Dummies Technology/General User

Composition Services

Gerry Fahey, Vice President of Production Services

Debbie Stailey, Director of Composition Services

Contents at a Glance

Table of Contents

Chapter 4: Making the Most of Tax-Free Savings and Investments

Chapter 5: Delving Into Collective Investments 275

Introduction

Welcome to *Personal Finance & Investing All-in-One For Dummies*, your launch pad to understanding the basics of all the financial considerations you face during your lifetime.

Best of all, this book highlights ways to get the most from your money, but it also helps you decide where your priorities lie when it comes to your finances, and gives you the facts up front and honestly. And as your priorities develop and change, all the advice you need is in the same book so you can make the journey from clearing your debts to building your wealth by investing, to setting up a comfortable retirement and a potential nest-egg to pass on to your nearest and dearest. Think of *Personal Finance & Investing All-in-One For Dummies* as your first great investment!

About This Book

If you're trying to figure out your financial future, cure a tax-related headache, invest your money securely, or work out the most sensible way to refloat your financial boat, this book provides an introduction to the most useful areas of financial and investment advice.

You can read further details in other *For Dummies* books or see a financial adviser for personal or more specific advice. If you've read all there is to read in this book but still want more, check out the extra information in these *For Dummies* titles (all published by Wiley):

- *Investing For Dummies* (Tony Levene)
- *Paying Less Tax 2006/2007 For Dummies* (Tony Levene)
- *Retiring Wealthy For Dummies* (Julian Knight)
- *Sorting Out Your Finances For Dummies* (Melanie Bien)
- *Wills, Probate & Inheritance Tax For Dummies* (Julian Knight)

Conventions Used in This Book

To make your reading experience easier and to alert you to key words or points, we use certain conventions in this book:

- *Italics* introduces new terms, and underscores key differences between words.
- **Bold** text is used to show the action part of bulleted and numbered lists.
- `Monofont` is used for web addresses.
- HMRC (you'll see this acronym a lot in this book!) means Her Majesty's Revenue and Customs – you might better know this organisation by it's old name of the Inland Revenue, or simply as 'the tax man' (regardless of gender). We stick to the technically correct term of HMRC.

It's also worth remembering that although we've included up to date financial and investment information at the time of writing, these things do change! Use the facts and figures within this All-in-One as a guide, but if in doubt, seek expert advice on the most up to date information.

What You're Not to Read

You can read this book cover to cover, or skip through just reading the sections that interest you the most. You can also glean plenty of information from this book without reading the sidebars (the grey boxes) – the detail in our sidebars is interesting but not crucial to understanding the rest of the book's content.

Foolish Assumptions

In writing this book we've made a couple of assumptions about you:

- You're not a financial expert and don't want to become one – you don't want finance to dominate your life, but you do want to feel secure.
- You want to know the basics of your financial future or the key to good investment and want access to tips and advice as and when you need them.

✔ You are interested in some or all aspects of personal finance, for example:

- You want to tackle your finances but you don't know the first place to start. You're wondering whether – just maybe – it might be possible to get out of debt once and for all.

- You want to know enough about tax to make sure you are paying the right amount and claiming what is due to you. You also want to know how to make the tax system work in your favour!

- You want someone to help you understand what investing is really about and what types of investments are available. You also want pointers to help you to risk only what you can afford to lose and to make a worthwhile return on your hard-earned cash.

- You've made a conscious decision to plan towards a wealthy retirement and you want to know how to draw up your 'retiring wealthy' plan – and how to follow it through.

- You want to make plans so that your money and property is used to help your loved ones when you die, but you don't know where to start. You feel a little intimidated by all the legal and accountant speak that surrounds wills and inheritance tax, and are looking for a straightforward explanation.

If any (or all) of these assumptions accurately describe you, you've come to the right book.

How This Book Is Organised

We've divided *Personal Finance & Investing All-in-One For Dummies* into five separate books. This section explains what you'll find in each of these books. Each book is broken into chapters tackling key aspects and skills. The table of contents gives you more detail of what's in each chapter, and we've even included a cartoon at the start of each part, just to keep you happy.

Book 1: Organising Your Finances and Dealing with Debt

Book I is the one most people will want to start with – the chapters within run through the basics of sorting out your current financial state. If you're in debt, this Book is for you too, providing hints and tips on grinding down loans and overdrafts.

Book II: Paying Less Tax

It's very difficult to avoid dealing with HMRC; practically no-one escapes the tax inspector's net. This Book is designed to help you pay the right amount for your financial situation. It contains tax-saving tips and then more tax-saving tips; almost everyone can benefit from reading this Book!

Book III: Building up Savings and Investments

Book III is primarily about investing, but incorporates other aspects of planning your financial future, too. Whether you're looking to start saving your money in a high-interest account, find a cost-effective mortgage, or dip your toes into the world of shares and bonds (or even something more exotic), this Book helps you to understand your options . . . and to weigh up the risks against the benefits.

Book IV: Retiring Wealthy

Putting something away for a rainy day is the name of the game in Book IV. The chapters within outline your different pension options, along with details of other ways to save for your golden years. It's never too early to start planning, and this Book aims to give you a head start.

Book V: Protecting Your Wealth For the Next Generation

Two-thirds of people haven't yet made a will and half of us never will. These people are missing out on a golden opportunity to look after their families and frustrate the tax collector. This Book provides advice on putting a framework in place for your family's future for a time when you're no longer around.

Icons Used in This Book

When you flick through this book, you'll notice little icons in the margins. These icons pick out certain key aspects of personal development:

This icon highlights practical advice to get our investing and finance ideas working for you.

This icon is a friendly reminder of important points to take note of.

This icon highlights information that you might not need to know to sort your finances out immediately, but could stand you in good stead for the future or as background knowledge.

This icon marks things to avoid – they could be costly or drop you in deep water with HMRC, the government, or your bank.

Where to Go from Here

If you need emergency surgery to stop your wallet rupturing, head straight into Book I, or if your finances are in reasonable shape and you're thinking about planning for your or your family's future, check out Books IV and V first. You can of course, read through each and every chapter, but why not spend some time browsing through the detailed table of contents to see if anything of immediate interest springs out at you?

Good luck to you, and we wish you all the best in finding the answers to your financial and investment questions. And if it all goes according to plan, can you lend my editor a fiver?

Book I
Organising Your Finances and Dealing with Debt

In this Book . . .

Being good with money is about getting into good habits and understanding the choices you can make. This Book gives you the confidence to understand and plot where your money goes, to know your limits, and to choose the right financial package for a wealthier future.

Here are the contents of Book I at a glance:

Chapter 1

Figuring Out Financial Goals, Financial Budgets, and Financial Advisers

Congratulations! You've decided to get to grips with your finances and start building up your savings and investments for the future. Making sure you are in control of your finances enables you to do what you want – upgrade your car, get on the first step of the property ladder, or start building funds for retirement.

In this chapter we start by giving you the lowdown on working out what your financial goals are and how you can achieve them. We offer advice on clearing your debts before you begin building up your savings and investments, and the importance of seeking independent financial advice. Only when you have the basics under your belt can you ensure your finances work for you – rather than limiting you from doing all the things you want to do.

Looking at the Benefits of Being on Top of Your Finances

Sorting out your money by clearing your debt and building up your savings and investments makes you master of your financial future. It also brings several benefits:

- ✔ **You stop paying expensive fees and charges for being in debt.** Debt is pricey, with high rates of interest and often extra fees and charges. If you are in a lot of debt and pay a significant amount of interest on it, you may find that you simply can't clear what you owe as all your money goes towards servicing the debt and paying the interest. Clearing your debt removes the debt itself and the cost of financing it.

- ✔ **You get rid of your guilt.** Being in debt can be a worry, particularly if it has got out of hand and you can't see any way of escaping the situation. Some people also regard being in debt as a stigma – something to be ashamed of and hidden from friends, family, and colleagues. Any way you look at it, debt is a burden and getting rid of it can be a huge weight off your shoulders.

- ✔ **You feel more confident about the future.** With the state providing little financial support in retirement (see Chapter 2 in Book IV for more on this), you may be concerned about how you are going to make ends meet. But if you have savings and investments spread across a range of funds, pensions, and property, you can rest easy with regard to the future. You may even be able to look forward to giving up work, rather than dread it.

- ✔ **You open up a range of financial options.** If your finances are in order, you can afford to take time off to travel or try a new career. But if you have lots of debt or little in the way of savings, you may not have the option to do what you like. This can make you feel rather resentful.

Drawing Up a Budget

The only way to manage your finances is to draw up a budget that you can stick to.

People who get into debt generally do so because they live beyond their means – spending more than they earn. Drawing up a budget and sticking to it can help assure that this doesn't happen to you. If you're in debt already, following a budget can help you to get out of that situation and develop habits that help you stay out.

In drawing up a budget, record your income and expenditures for a set period – usually a month. You can then calculate how much money you have left over each month after subtracting all your outgoings from your income. This surplus is money you can use to clear away your debts or to start saving or investing.

In Table 1-1, we list common outgoings. Go through this and answer honestly how much you spend on each item every month.

Book I

**Organising
Your
Finances
and Dealing
with Debt**

Table 1-1	Figuring Your Monthly Budget
MONTHLY INCOME	
Salary (after tax)	£..........
Overtime and bonuses	£..........
Any other income	£..........
TOTAL NET INCOME	£..........
MONTHLY OUTGOINGS	
Rent/Mortgage repayment	£..........
Pension contribution	£..........
Gas/electricity/water	£..........
Council tax	£..........
Telephone/Mobile	£..........
Satellite TV	£..........
Food	£..........
Insurance – car/home/other	£..........
Travel	£..........
Clothing	£..........
Entertainment	£..........
Other outgoings	£..........
TOTAL OUTGOINGS	£..........
Balance (Income minus outgoings)	£..........

If the figures don't add up, and you find that you spend more than you've got coming in, all is not lost. Look for ways to economise in certain areas, though be sure you're realistic about what you can achieve: Don't fool yourself into thinking that you will be happy to stay in every single night if you are usually a party animal. It simply won't be possible. While you might not be able to stay in every night, it may be realistic to say you are going to stay in one night a week when you would normally go out. This won't have the same dramatic results as staying in all the time but it will save you money in the long term and you are more likely to stick to this.

Studying How to Save Without Sacrificing

Almost everyone can save some money without sacrificing too much lifestyle. Even small amounts each day can soon mount up. Here are some initial ideas – and how much you can save each week:

- ✔ Give up smoking. A person who smokes 20 cigarettes a day will save £35 a week.

- ✔ Buy milk at the supermarket instead of using home delivery. You'll save £4 a week.

- ✔ Take a sandwich from home instead of buying one at work. You'll save £10 to £15 a week.

- ✔ Go shopping with a list and stick to it. You'll save at least £10 a week – and probably avoid some fattening snacks as well.

- ✔ Ditch expensive cable or satellite TV stations you hardly ever watch. You'll save £3 to £10 a week.

- ✔ Put every £2 coin you receive into a box. When you have £50, put the money into a special bank or building society account.

- ✔ Buy a copy of *Frugal Living For Dummies* (published by Wiley). You'll save a fortune each week!

Think about your lifestyle and then make your own additions to the list, from saving on transportation to cutting out unnecessary mobile phone calls. The point is to see how you can create big savings with some discipline – the same style of discipline you'll need to be a winning investor.

Book I

Organising
Your
Finances
and Dealing
with Debt

Savings quickly mount up thanks to compound interest

Pennies really can turn into pounds and pounds into thousands. And they can grow even faster thanks to *compound interest,* which is interest on interest.

Suppose, for example, that you manage to save £10 a week and put it in the bank. That's more than £40 a month and £520 a year. These sums can start you on an investment habit.

Here's how much various weekly savings would be worth after five years with a very modest

2.5 per cent interest paid each year – some are more generous, adding interest more often.

- £10 a week: £2,733
- £15 a week: £4,099
- £20 a week: £5,466
- £30 a week: £8,199
- £40 a week: £10,932
- £50 a week: £13,665

Establishing Your Goals

Before you can start saving or investing for the future, you need to work out what your aims are. Only if you know what you are saving and investing for can you choose the best products to help you realise your goals. Otherwise, you're likely to end up with completely unsuitable products.

Some of the financial goals you have may include clearing your debts, buying a house, starting a pension or helping out your children.

Most people have short and long-term financial goals. In the short term you might want to buy a new car or pay for a summer holiday, while in the longer term you may be keen to build up savings for retirement. And, you may have more than just your own future to consider: If you have children (or plan to have them at some stage), they may want go to university or need help getting on the housing ladder, and you need to plan to fulfil those goals as well.

Different goals require different investment vehicles so it's important that you work out what you want and then prioritise them. If you are investing for the long term – for retirement, for example – you should invest in equities because, historically, they produce the greatest returns over time. However, they aren't suitable for short-term investment goals because they are extremely volatile – the value of your shares may plummet just when you need the cash to buy your new car. But if you don't need the cash for many years you have plenty of notice as to when you need to sell your shares so can do so when you stand to make a profit. There may well have been times during the years you own them when you suffer losses – at least on paper. But it doesn't matter as potential losses aren't realised unless you actually sell up.

If you are saving for a holiday or new car – investing for the short term – stick to a savings account paying the highest rate of interest you can find. At least you are guaranteed to get your capital back, plus some return: You aren't risking your cash. You won't make the big returns you might have made on stocks and shares but at least you know there won't be any losses either.

Setting Up a Rainy-Day Fund

Before investing for the longer term, you need to set up your own personal emergency (or rainy day) fund for contingencies that you can imagine but couldn't pay for out of your purse or wallet. The fund should contain enough money to pay for events such as a sudden trip abroad if you have close family in distant lands, any domestic problem that wouldn't be covered by insurance, a major repair to a car over and above an insurance settlement, or a vet's bill not covered by insurance.

Here are some additional snippets from experience for you to keep in mind:

- Don't put your emergency-fund money in an account that offers a higher rate of interest in return for restricted access such as not being able to get hold of your money for five years. The problems and penalties associated with getting your cash on short notice outweigh any extra-earning advantages.

- An emergency cash reserve serves as reassurance so you can ride out investment bad times more easily.

- Monitor your potential emergency cash needs on a regular basis. They can shrink as well as expand.

- Know that you'll rarely be able to access investments in an emergency. You shouldn't be put in a position where you're forced to sell.

- Know that your credit card can be a temporary lifeline, giving you breathing space to reorganise longer-term investments when necessary.

Looking After Your Life and Health

None of us knows how much time we have left on this planet. The good news is that your chances of living longer have never been better. Most people nowadays are likely to live to around 75 to 80 years of age. The bad news? You can never forecast when you're going to be hit by a bus or succumb to a mystery virus.

So you should always make sure there is sufficient life insurance and cover against your succumbing to a serious illness or losing your livelihood that you can provide for your family.

Life insurance won't replace you, but it will replace your money-earning capacity.

Always shop around for all insurances. A recent table from *Moneyfacts* showed that a 40-year-old non-smoking man could buy a £100,000 policy covering the next 20 years for £10.80 a month from AA Insurance Services; exactly the same plan from HSBC Life would cost £19.95 a month.

Before buying life insurance cover, decide how much you need. One rule of thumb is four to five times your yearly take-home pay. But also look at any death or illness benefits that come with your job. There is no point in doubling up cover unnecessarily. And know that if you have no family commitments, then life cover is just a pricey luxury.

As well as buying life cover, you can purchase *critical illness policies* that pay out a lump sum if you have a serious illness, such as a heart attack or cancer, and survive for a month. Some policies also pay if you die during the policy period. The same huge range of prices exists, so never, ever go for the first quote you get.

Some policies, known as *permanent health insurances* or *income protection plans,* promise to pay a monthly sum until your normal retirement age if you can't work due to illness or injury. These policies can be expensive, especially for women because insurers think women are ill a lot more often than men.

Always look at all your family and personal circumstances before signing up for a policy. If you don't really need it, then don't buy it. The monthly premiums could be used to help build up an investment nest-egg.

Paying into a Pension Plan

Your pension plan is an investment for your future but with tax relief in the here and now. This means that, if you're a basic-rate taxpayer, you pay £78 for each £100 that you get in investment going into the plan – a pretty good deal. (The basic rate of tax will fall to 20p in the pound from April 2008, meaning that basic-rate taxpayers will have to put in £80 for every £100 that goes into the plan.) Many personal pension plans, including *stakeholder plans* (these are pensions whose costs are limited by UK government rules – almost all employers have to offer one but they don't have to put any contribution into it for you) as well as some workplace-based top-up schemes, technically known as *Additional Voluntary Contributions* or *AVCs,* let you choose from a wide range of investment possibilities both initially and later on and also allow low- or no-cost switching between investment options in the plan.

Those with larger sums and a DIY (do it yourself) attitude to investment can opt for a SIPP (self-invested personal pension) where the holder gets to choose what goes in. You can start a SIPP with anything from £5,000, although £50,000 is a more normal minimum. However, on the downside, the costs can be high and if it all goes wrong, you have only yourself to blame.

If you want to be a less-active pensions investor, look at a lifestyle plan, which most pensions companies now offer. This type of plan invests in riskier areas, such as shares, when you are younger and have time on your side. Later, as you approach retirement, the plan automatically moves you down the risk profile. One way is to switch 20 per cent of your fund into safer bonds starting ten years before you retire. Then five years before you want to stop work, the fund moves again, bit by bit, into a cash fund. You can always override a lifestyle plan if you want.

Taking Care of Property Before Profits

The roof over your head is probably your biggest monthly outlay. And it's also likely to be your biggest investment. So don't begrudge what you spend on it. In the long run, it should build up to a worthwhile asset. (At the very worst, it'll shelter you from the elements!)

Always look at what it would cost each month to rent the same property compared with buying it. Doing so is easier nowadays thanks to the buy to let boom, because you can find rented properties on most streets. If you're paying more in mortgage costs than in rent, the excess is your *opportunity cost* to make gains later if you sell up and move somewhere smaller or to a less-expensive area. This makes it an investment. On the other hand, if you're paying less in a mortgage than renting would cost, look at the savings as another area for potential investment cash.

Your home is your castle

Homes have generally been a good medium- to long-term investment. They've beaten inflation over most periods and more than kept up with rising incomes in most parts of the country.

Some parts have seen spectacular gains. But even in the worst parts of the country, you would've been very unlucky to lose over the long run, even counting the big price falls of the early 1990s.

There's every chance that the future won't show such spectacular gains. But homes should continue to be a good investment and at the very least keep up with rising prices over a period. Putting whatever you can into a house purchase is probably the best thing you can do with your money.

Pay Off Home Loans Early

'Psst! Want an investment that pays up to 80 times as much as cash in some bank accounts but is absolutely safe and totally secure? And what about a 100 per cent guaranteed return that can be higher than financial watchdogs allow any investment company to use for forecasting future profits?'

Sounds like a snake-oil salesman scam, doesn't it? But if your first reaction is, 'You've got to be kidding', then you're wrong. Paying off mortgage loans with spare cash offers an unbeatable combination of high returns and super safety.

To see what we mean, take a look at the following mathematics. In this particular example, we've used interest-only figures for simplicity, although anyone with a repayment (capital and interest) loan will also make big gains. And, again for simplicity, we've assumed that the interest sums are calculated just one a year. That said, here's the scenario:

Someone with a standard mortgage and with £100,000 outstanding at 6 per cent pays £60 a year, or £5 a month, in interest for each £1,000 borrowed. On the £100,000, that works out to £6,000 a year or £500 a month.

Now suppose that the homebuyer pays back £1,000. The new interest amount is £5,940 a year or £495 a month.

Compare the £60 a year saved with what the £1,000 would've earned in a bank or building society. The £1,000 could've earned as little as £1 at 0.10 per cent. And even at a much more generous 3 per cent, it would only make £30 – half the savings from mortgage repayment.

'But you've forgotten income tax on the savings interest,' you rightly say.

Ah, but the money you save by diverting cash to your mortgage account is tax-free. It must be grossed up (have the tax added back in) to give a fair contrast. Basic-rate taxpayers must earn the equivalent of 7.5 per cent from a normal investment to do as well. And top-rate taxpayers need a super-safe 10 per cent investment return from their cash to do as well.

After a payment is made, it reduces this year's interest as well as that for every single year until the mortgage is redeemed. If interest rates go up, you'll save even more. But if they fall, you'll keep on saving and be able to afford to pay down your mortgage even more.

Some flexible or bank-account-linked mortgages let you borrow back overpayments so you can have your cake of lower payments with the knowledge that you can still eat it later if you need to. Alternatively, you can re-mortgage to a new home loan to raise money from your property if you need it.

Seeking Help: Financial Advisers

It is highly likely that you will need advice before buying financial products, particularly if you are inexperienced at saving and investing.

Life-changing experiences, such as buying your first home, getting married, having children, going self-employed, or retiring, often require professional advice. Potentially, you need a lot of money to see you through each of these stages and generating it can be hard, particularly if you are inexperienced in such matters. An independent adviser will metaphorically hold your hand and guide you through the stages. A professional puts distance between himself and your situation so he can assess the situation objectively and recommend the best financial course.

If you've got friends or family who are financially literate, you could ask them for help. But unless they are experienced advisers themselves, and know all the ins and outs of your particular circumstances, they are not in a position to recommend the best products to you. For that you need a qualified adviser.

Considering Advisers

There are three different types of financial adviser: independent, tied, and multi-tied. If you want unbiased financial advice and access to all the products on the market, opt for an independent financial adviser (IFA). An IFA researches the whole market and takes his pick from what's available to ensure that you get the best product for your needs.

Benefiting from independent advice

The big advantage of using an IFA is that you are using a qualified practitioner to find the best products for your circumstances. Your IFA asks you a number of questions about your situation, your financial goals and attitude to risk to ensure he finds the most suitable products.

IFAs are answerable to the Financial Services Authority (FSA), the City regulator. IFAs have to follow FSA rules, so you have the comfort of knowing that your adviser is governed by certain procedures. If he falls foul of these rules, he will be brought to task by the FSA, and may be fined and could even lose his licence to trade. Hence, abiding by these rules is extremely important to IFAs.

When your IFA recommends products to you, he must provide reasons, in writing, as to why he suggested certain funds and investments and not others. This is to avoid the chance of mis-selling, when you are advised to take out products that aren't suitable for you.

Avoiding the pitfalls

It's worth remembering that not all IFAs can offer independent advice on every investment product. One advisory company may offer advice on mortgages from the whole market but be tied to offering investment products from a limited number of companies (see 'Taking a more limited approach' later in this chapter). Make sure the adviser is truly independent in all areas that you might want to buy in before signing up.

Check that your IFA is actually authorised with the FSA: Don't assume this is the case – the unscrupulous have been known to lie about this. Check that he is authorised even if he has been recommended to you by a friend or relative. You can do this by checking the FSA Central Register at www.fsa. gov.uk/register or telephone 0845 606 1234 for further information.

If you sign on with an unauthorised adviser and he loses your money through negligence, you can't claim compensation as you could in the same circumstances with an authorised IFA.

If a firm is authorised by the FSA, and you feel that the advice you have been given is wrong, take up your complaint with the firm in question. If it isn't answered to your satisfaction and you wish to pursue your complaint, contact the Financial Ombudsman Service on 0845 080 1800 or at www.financial-ombudsman.org.uk.

Book I

Organising Your Finances and Dealing with Debt

Finding an IFA

If you've decided to opt for independent advice – even if it means paying a fee to ensure the service is completely unbiased – it defeats the object if you opt for the first IFA you come across. Do your research beforehand and choose an adviser who is most suitable for your needs.

To find an IFA, contact IFA Promotion on 0800 085 3250 or go to www.unbiased.co.uk to search for a local IFA or one that matches your specific requirements. Or you could try the Personal Finance Society on 020 8530 0852 or www.thepfs.org.

Financial advisers are no different from anyone else you employ to help you. You should receive an initial free consultation. Use this time to work out whether potential advisers are organised or haphazard, and whether they listen to what you want or try to impose their views on you.

Treat an adviser like a partner. Most advisers expect you to know nothing, so if you do your homework first, you'll have a good chance of getting what you want rather than their default option.

Most financial advisers like to quiz you about your life, your ambitions, your pension, and, most importantly for them, how much money you may have to invest. Turn the tables on them. At the first meeting, ask as many questions about them as they ask of you. Here are some questions to ask:

- **What's your preferred customer profile?** This is a good early question because some advisers specialise in high-value clients or the elderly or taxation-linked investments.

- **How long have you been in business under your present firm's name?** Avoid someone who has changed jobs too often.

- **How many clients do you have?** A registered individual can't really deal with more than a few hundred clients. Any more than that risks a one-size-fits-all approach.

- **Do you have a regular client newsletter?** If so, ask for back copies from the past three to five years to reflect a variety of investment scenarios.

- **What sort of financial problems or areas of investment do you not want to get involved with?** This is like the first question but from a different viewpoint. It's useful toward the end of the initial conversation. Advisers who say they really can't help in your circumstances should get a plaudit for honesty.

Book I

Organising
Your
Finances
and Dealing
with Debt

✔ **If I sign up, will I get face-to-face advice when I want it or have to phone a call centre?** Many advisers are now cost-cutting by reducing all but their biggest clients to a 'press one for pensions, press two for investment funds' approach.

✔ **What about regular financial checkups?** Ask how often the adviser provides them and whether you must pay extra for them.

✔ **Are you a member of an independent financial adviser network?** If so, ask whether the network just takes care of regulatory and other paperwork or whether it dictates a list of investments. The former is preferable.

Don't forget that you should always make a final check on an adviser via the Financial Services Authority Web site. The site shows not just whether an adviser is registered under the regulatory regime but also whether the adviser has been disciplined.

When you first meet your IFA, the initial consultation is often free to allow you both to get to know each other. Try to assess whether you could see yourself working with this person as you will be expected to reveal lots of personal information about your finances: If you don't get on with or trust your IFA, you won't get the best results and it will be a largely unfruitful relationship. Shop around – if you don't get the right vibes, say 'Thanks but no thanks' and keep on looking.

Taking a More Limited Approach

Some advisers can give advice only on a limited number of products: In other words, they are not independent because they don't have access to the whole market. Such an adviser may be able to advise you on the investment products – pensions, life insurance and unit trusts – of just one company or a specified panel of companies.

We explain how this works in more detail in the following sections.

Tied Agents

An adviser who can only recommend products from one provider is known as a *tied agent*. Most people buy their financial products through tied agents, usually salespeople at their bank or building society.

Just because it's easy doesn't make tied advice the best way to buy your financial products. In doing so, you're limiting your choice so much that you're highly unlikely to end up with the most competitive product – if you do, it will be a stroke of luck rather than the result of sound judgment.

Many banks and building societies employ a tied sales force, which only promotes the often-narrow range of products on sale from that institution. These tied agency firms may carry the same name as the bank or building society – Abbey or Nationwide, for example, or another brand name. So Lloyds TSB sells Scottish Widows and Barclays deals in Legal & General. Some life companies, such as Zurich or Co-op Insurance Services, also sell all or most of their products through tied agents.

The salesperson in the bank or building society is acting on behalf of the product provider. He is not acting in your interests, as an IFA should, and can give no really independent advice. All he can do is provide information about the product you are already interested in buying, or other products provided by his company He can't tell you whether it is the best product for your circumstances, or indeed right for you at all. He can only talk you through the application process and how the product works.

Always ask tied agents what advantages they can offer to make up for the lack of variety. They'd have to promise a really good deal to get my vote.

Getting to Grips with Qualifications

All advisers, whether tied or independent, have to pass the Certificate in Financial Planning (Cert FP) or its predecessor, the Financial Planning Certificate level 3, before they are allowed by the FSA to provide financial advice. Cert FP covers protection, savings, and investment products; financial regulation; and identifying and satisfying client needs. It is the equal of GCSE, a starter-level exam that's not very difficult.

Refuse to pay top-dollar rates for apprentice investment advisers!

Becoming advanced

Advisers can stick with the basic Cert FP or choose to take a more advanced exam. The most popular are the Advanced Financial Planning Certificate (AFPC) and Certified Financial Planner (CFP) licence.

Book I

Organising
Your
Finances
and Dealing
with Debt

If you are buying a pension, look for an adviser with G60; for investments, look for G70 along with the Investment Management Certificate (IMC). If you require specialist mortgage advice, look for a Certificate in Mortgage Advice and Practice (CeMap) and the Mortgage Advice Qualification (MAQ).

Looking beyond bits of paper

Although it's always encouraging if an adviser has lots of qualifications, they aren't the be-all and end-all. It is also important that you get on with your adviser as you could well have to spend a lot of time with him and it's important that you trust him.

It is also crucial that your adviser specialises in the areas which you are keen to invest in. Experience can also be important so find out how long they've been in the business. An adviser who is wet behind the ears may not have enough knowledge to instill confidence in you.

Paying for Advice

During your first consultation, a potential adviser should give you clear information about what services you're being offered and give you an indication of what you will have to pay for it. This will enable you to compare the cost of financial advice and shop around for the adviser who is best value for money.

Your adviser will explain the above by giving you two *keyfacts documents* concerning:

- ✔ **Services:** This document explains the type of advice you are being offered and the range of products offered.
- ✔ **Costs:** This list explains the different ways you can pay for the advice you receive. It also gives an indication of the fees or commission you may have to pay. If you pay by commission, it shows you how this compares to the average market commission.

The new advice regime (introduced in December 2004) makes it easier to understand what you have to pay. You must be given a menu of charges from the adviser when you first seek advice. This will enable you to compare the cost of advice and to shop around for a better service.

There are three main ways of paying for advice, explained in the following sections.

Forking out a fee

Fees are either charged by the hour or as a set price for the whole job. This is known as *fees-only* advice and is the most expensive option, with fees costing anything from £75 to £250 an hour (depending on your location and how experienced your adviser is). You may get the first half-hour free; the initial meeting is often an introductory session where you simply get to know one another better and figure out whether you are happy to work with the adviser.

You have to pay a fee even if you don't end up taking out a financial product. This isn't the case if you pay by commission (see the following section).

If you do pay an hourly fee, make sure you get a rough idea of how many hours' work is required and how much the total cost is likely to be. Ask your adviser for an estimate of how much he might charge you. You can also request that he doesn't exceed a given amount without checking with you first.

If you use an IFA, you can choose to pay a fee rather than commission. Only an IFA has to offer the choice of payment options. Tied and multi-tied agents don't have to offer a choice, although they may decide to anyhow.

Going with commission

If you aren't prepared to pay a fee, or can't afford to, some advisers charge commission instead – and all IFAs must offer this option. The commission is deducted by the product provider when you invest money in a product. As well as an initial commission for setting up a plan, you may also be charged an annual commission on top, which is known as *trail commission*. Check with your adviser whether this applies before signing up.

Combining fees and commission

You don't have to choose fees or commission – you can have a combination of both. Some product providers pay your adviser commission when you buy a product, which he may pass onto you in one of a number of ways. These include passing on the full value of that commission to you by reducing his fee; reducing the product charges; increasing your investment amount; or refunding the commission to you.

Look for negotiation

Imagine this: A widow deposits £100,000 into her savings account after selling her home and moving somewhere smaller. The bank or building society sees this deposit and offers her a chance to improve her income. Half an hour later, she has been sold whatever the bank is pushing that month for those in her situation. The adviser may have earned as much as 7 per cent in commission. That's £7,000 for 30 minutes of easy work. Great money! And no investment risks!

Tied agents and those working for big firms rarely negotiate even if you ask. If you're happy handing out so much of your money for so little work, fine, as long as you're aware of what you're doing.

The alternative is to avoid the non-negotiators and either ask for a commission-sharing scheme or pay for services by time, at a pre-agreed hourly rate, and get a 100 per cent rebate of all commissions.

Expect to pay a minimum £75–£100 per hour, so always ask for an estimate of how long the job will take.

A list of fee-based advisers is available from IFA Promotions on 0800 085 3250 or www.unbiased.co.uk.

Going It Alone

In some circumstances, you may decide that you don't need advice. If you are opting for a simple product, such as a credit card or savings account, you don't need to pay an adviser for help in choosing the best product: you should simply do the research yourself. Likewise, if you're an experienced investor and have plenty of time to devote to your investments, you may not need advice.

The advantages of not using an adviser are:

- **Low cost:** The only money you spend is on phonecalls.
- **Convenience:** You can buy where you like and when you like. You don't have to wait until you've made an appointment or for your adviser to do the necessary research.
- **Broad access:** You can deal with a wider range of firms. You aren't restricted to dealing just with those in your local area.
- **Speed:** You can buy over the phone or Internet, without having to queue to see an adviser in your local bank branch.

You should only go it alone if you know what you are doing. Not taking advice can save you money in the short term but it's also a risky business if you are inexperienced and could cost you in the long run.

Chapter 2

Choosing the Best Current Account for You

A current account is the most common type of financial product: Most people have one. If you're like the majority of account owners, you didn't give much thought to what you want from a current account before signing up for one, which means your current account may be unsuitable for your needs. For example, if you frequently go overdrawn, you don't want an account with expensive overdraft charges, or if your account is usually in credit you don't want one with a poor rate of interest on balances.

The good news is that if you're not happy with your account – for whatever reason – it is easier than ever to switch. The Internet has opened up competition in the current account market with scores of new providers offering attractive products. And new rules mean that banks have to co-operate within days rather than weeks if you express a desire to move an account. In this chapter we show you how to make sure you find the best current account for your particular needs.

Explaining How Current Accounts Work

Unless you are happy to deal in cash all the time, you need a *current account*, which is where your wages are usually paid by your employer so that you can pay bills, your rent or mortgage, and withdraw cash for everyday spending. Banks, building societies, and even supermarkets offer these.

Most people have their salary, state benefits, and tax credits (where applicable) paid into their current account.

You can arrange to pay your bills, mortgage, rent, and so on directly from your account through one of two methods:

- ✔ A *standing order* is an instruction you give your bank to pay a fixed amount, usually each month, to a particular person or supplier. The amount can be changed only if you give instructions to your bank.

- ✔ A *direct debit* is an instruction to pay a particular person or supplier an amount that can fluctuate. The person or supplier informs your bank how much it is taking out of your account that particular month (after informing you).

Most current accounts come with a cash card so you can withdraw money from automated teller machines (ATMs). This card usually doubles up as a debit card so you can pay for goods in shops with the money debited from your account – usually the next day. Most current accounts also offer a cheque book. If you are over 18 you can also apply for an overdraft (see Chapter 4 for more details on these).

We give you more of the specifics of current accounts in the following sections.

Noting interest and taxes

The interest you receive on the balance in your current account is subject to income tax and usually paid monthly. Interest on some accounts is calculated annually.

You receive interest after it has been taxed at 20 per cent (your current account provider deducts interest and pays it to HMRC on your behalf). If you are a basic rate taxpayer this is the full extent of your tax liability, but if you are a higher-rate taxpayer you have to pay 40 per cent tax – the rest is collected via your self-assessment tax return.

If you don't have a job or are on a low income, you don't have to pay tax on the interest you earn. However, you need to inform your bank or building society of your circumstances by filling out form R85, which is available from your current account provider or local tax office.

Considering safety first

A current account is a safe home for your money: The biggest threat to your money is your spending habit! With a current account, you don't assume any stock market risk or stand much chance of the bank or building society going bust and you 'losing' your cash. Even if your bank or building society goes bust, because it is registered with the Financial Services Authority (FSA) and subject to the Financial Services Compensation Scheme (FSCS) you would receive back 100 per cent of the first £2,000 you had on deposit and 90 per cent of the next £33,000 (up to a limit of £31,700).

Only firms registered with the FSA are covered by the FSCS. To check that a current account provider is *before* you open an account, go to the FSA's website (www.fsa.gov.uk) or call the consumer helpline on 0845 606 1234. The majority of banks and building societies in the UK have signed up to the voluntary Banking Code. This sets out the standards for dealing fairly with customers. A copy of the Banking Code is available on the British Bankers Association website (www.bba.org.uk or contact 020 7216 8800).

If you aren't happy with the service you've received from your bank or building society, complain first to the institution concerned. If the problem isn't rectified, contact the Financial Ombudsman Service, which was set up to settle disputes between customers and financial firms, on 0845 080 1800.

The main risk to your money is the rate of inflation, which indicates how much the cost of living is going up. So when the rate of inflation is higher than the interest you are earning on your account, you are losing money in real terms. For example, if inflation is at 2 per cent and you are earning 0.1 per cent interest on your current account, you are losing money. This is why it is worth shopping around for the best rate of interest (see 'Switching your current account' later in this chapter) and ensuring you don't keep huge sums of money sitting in your current account. Move it to a savings account paying a better rate of interest instead.

Paying the charges

You pay no charges on most current accounts if you are in credit, although packaged accounts impose a monthly fee for a range of additional services (see the nearby 'Paying for Packaged Accounts' sidebar).

You may have to pay a fee of £1 to £2 for using 'convenience' cash machines to withdraw money in small shops and service stations, however, and will be charged for special services such as sending money abroad.

Most banks charge for going overdrawn. As well as the overdraft rate, you may also have to pay a monthly or quarterly fee. Many banks offer a fee-free overdraft buffer of up to £500, while others charge as much as 30 per cent for unauthorised borrowing.

You may – or may not – have to pay fees for other services such as requesting a duplicate statement, using an ATM abroad, or stopping a cheque. So, for example, if you travel frequently, finding an account that doesn't make you pay to use an ATM when you're outside the country makes sense.

Book I

Organising Your Finances and Dealing with Debt

Maintaining the ideal balance

There are no restrictions on how long you keep your cash in your account or on withdrawing money from it, apart from the availability of funds and the limit on how much cash you can withdraw from an ATM in any one day (usually £250 or £300).

You may be required to keep a minimum balance in your account, however. Some accounts have tiered rates of interest, so if your balance falls below a certain level you'll earn a lower rate of interest.

Even if your current account does pay a good rate of interest it is not a good idea to keep a big balance in your account. You could almost certainly get a better deal elsewhere in an instant-access mini cash individual savings account (ISA), because returns are tax free. See Chapter 4 in Book III for more on these.

The ideal balance in a current account differs from person to person, but as a general rule you shouldn't have more than you need to cover the month's outgoings. Keeping tens of thousands of pounds in your current account makes no sense because your money can earn more interest in a savings account or mini cash ISA.

Work out how much you need to cover your bills and expenses each month, allow a couple of hundred pounds as a buffer in case of unexpected outgoings (the exact amount will depend on what you feel comfortable with), and put the rest where it will earn a better rate of interest.

Paying for Packaged Accounts

A number of banks provide packaged accounts that offer a range of benefits and services above and beyond your standard current account. Most charge a fee – of between £6 and £15 a month – but not all do: you may end up paying a higher rate on your overdraft instead (if you have one), so check the rates before signing up if you regularly go overdrawn.

A packaged account is worth the fee only if you make use of the perks available. These can include free annual travel insurance, free commission on foreign currency, and free breakdown recovery. But before taking up offers such as discounts on holidays and flights, or preferential deals on savings, credit cards, or loans, shop around to see whether you can find a better deal elsewhere.

If you don't use the perks and can get a cheaper deal elsewhere on other products, think carefully before opting for a packaged account.

Finding the Best Current Account

When opening your first current account, it's easy to opt for the same account your parents have. Or if you are heading off to university and opening your first current account you may choose the one that offers the best perks: such as a free five-year Young Persons Railcard, which gives you one-third off rail travel. Few people give any more thought to it than that. But seeing that a current account fulfils such a crucial role in your finances because most of your cash flows through it at some stage, it's worth thinking about what you want from it before signing up.

Some banks pay extremely poor rates of interest on current accounts and charge extortionate rates of interest on overdrafts, yet those offering the worst deals also have the largest number of customers. The 'big four' – Barclays, HSBC, Lloyds TSB, and NatWest – all pay 0.1 per cent interest on balances (although Lloyds TSB also has an account paying a higher rate of interest as long as you pay in a certain amount each month). Other banks pay more than 30 times this amount of interest.

The big four also charge around 16-18 per cent on authorised overdrafts (although Barclays has some packaged accounts with 9.9 per cent overdrafts). But you can get an overdraft rate of under 8 per cent if you shop around. Yet despite this, some 70 per cent of all current accounts remain with one of the big four banks.

No bank or building society offers the best deal on every single product. One bank may have a fantastic mortgage range but offer a low interest rate on its current accounts. Product providers specialise in certain areas, offering one or two really attractive deals to pull in the punters. Other customers end up paying for this great deal – usually those stuck with an uncompetitive current account.

Check for an introductory offer. Some banks pay a lump sum or charge 0 per cent on overdrafts for a limited period when you open an account. Find out whether you qualify for preferential rates on other products offered by the bank, such as insurance or personal loans.

When scouting financial institutions, discover what other services are on offer, such as the ability to buy or sell shares (see Chapter 6 in Book III for more on this) or free financial advice. If you're keen on being green, determine whether you can get an ethical banking account, which are provided by socially responsible banks that don't invest in companies involved in tobacco, gaming, gambling, or pornography (see Chapter 5 in Book III).

If you think you have been overcharged by your bank, get help on how to claim a refund from Which? (www.which.co.uk).

When choosing a current account, you need to consider how you will use it. We give you information on several issues to bear in mind in the following sections.

Gaining access

Having money sitting in your current account is all well and good, but you need to be able to get to it. Fortunately, modern banking methods offer you a multitude of ways to access your dough, from stepping into a solid building and getting money from a live person to choosing the virtual route of a stand-alone Internet bank (keep in mind that the money is all too real).

In the following sections, we take you through the various access methods and highlight points to consider when choosing a current account to meet your individual needs.

Going automated with ATMs

A growing number of 'convenience' ATMs can be found in shops and garages, which charge you for withdrawing your cash. This is usually a flat fee of about £1.50 or £1.75 – regardless of how much you withdraw. A message flashes up on the screen just before you complete your transaction warning you of this fee. If you don't wish to pay it, you simply cancel the transaction and don't get your cash.

Bank branch ATMs now offer free shared access to consumers' accounts, so you don't have to pay if you use another bank's ATM to withdraw cash.

You should check the maximum amount of cash you can withdraw from an ATM in a single day. This is usually around £300, subject to available funds or an arranged overdraft, but it can vary. If you are likely to deposit cash or cheques into your account, find out whether you can do this via your bank's ATMs to avoid queuing for hours in your local branch.

Scouting locations

A branch close to your home or workplace is useful, even if you prefer to do your banking over the telephone or Internet. There are times when you will need to visit your local branch to collect travellers' cheques or foreign currency, for example, or to pick up some literature about a new account or talk to an adviser. If you don't have far to go, it will be much more convenient.

Writing cheques and using cheque cards

Most current accounts offer a cheque book and cheque guarantee card (which often doubles up as a debit card). However, many people no longer pay by cheque, so there are a number of current account providers – usually online – who don't offer a cheque book (in exchange, you might get a slightly higher rate of interest on balances).

If you do want the option of paying by cheque, make sure the account you sign up for offers this. Check what limit is on the cheque guarantee card – it may be as low as £50, although some accounts go as high as £250.

Clicking through the Internet

The growth of Internet banking has been phenomenal. A number of high-street banks are behind the various Internet banks, although the latter are run as standalone operations. So, for example, Halifax owns Intelligent Finance, Abbey owns Cahoot, and insurer Prudential owns Egg.

Standalone Internet banks offer better rates of interest on balances and over-drafts than high-street banks. They can do this because they have lower overheads (no branches). Instead, you get 24-hour access, 365 days a year. But the accounts on offer are more limited than on the high street and there are times when you might want to speak to someone face to face. With many standalone Internet banks you have to rely on the phone or email, which doesn't suit everyone.

You won't get a monthly statement in the post either: instead, you'll be able to access an electronic statement online. If you really want a paper statement for your records, print this off and file it.

Before opening an Internet bank, check the security it has in place. Hackers often try to access online accounts but are very rarely successful, as extremely sophisticated security systems are employed by the banks. The FSA warns customers to be wary of banks based outside the European Economic Area as you may not be as well protected as with a UK bank. And make sure you don't give your passwords to anyone or write them down.

Banking by phone

Find out whether the bank has a free or local-rate number for telephone banking and what services you can access by phone. This could make a difference if you contact your bank on a regular basis.

Book I

Organising Your Finances and Dealing with Debt

Weighing balances

Many banks require only £1 to open a current account, but some providers insist that you deposit a minimum amount of cash each month, or that your balance doesn't dip below a set amount. If you don't have much cash to spare, steer clear of such accounts because if your balance dips below, say, £250 you may forfeit your interest. Find out whether there are any penalties for not maintaining a minimum balance before signing up.

Accruing interest

If your current account is usually in the black, it's sensible to opt for one paying a reasonable rate of interest – 3 per cent or above – to maximise your returns. However, these accounts often stipulate a minimum level of funding required per month, so do look carefully at the terms. Some accounts pay tiered rates of interest, so the more cash you have in your account, the greater the rate. But this also usually means that such accounts pay a low rate of interest on small balances so they're not worth bothering with. You shouldn't be keeping the large sums of money in your current account that qualify you for the higher rate of interest on a tiered account in the first place.

Terms and conditions

If there is a chance that you might go overdrawn, check what the charges are for doing so. Overdraft rates vary significantly between account providers, so shop around for the lowest one if you need an overdraft and inform your bank before going overdrawn. Unauthorised overdrafts are far more expensive than authorised ones.

It's worth finding out how much you can go overdrawn by if you may need more than a few hundred pounds. Ask whether you can go overdrawn by a certain amount without having to notify your bank beforehand and not have to pay over the odds for this. There may also be an arrangement fee to pay for setting up the overdraft. See Chapter 4 for more on overdrafts.

If you never go overdrawn, you don't need to worry about the overdraft rate – the interest you earn on your balance is far more important.

Watch out for accounts offering additional features such as travel insurance, on which a monthly fee is charged. If you are not likely to get much use from the add-ons, it's not worth paying £10 or more a month for them.

Book I

Organising
Your
Finances
and Dealing
with Debt

Connected accounts

To really make your current account work for you, you can opt for a connected account. This enables you to connect your current account to several products, such as your mortgage, credit card, savings account, and even personal loans you have with the same provider. The advantage of linking your accounts is that your savings and current account balance is offset against your debts, reducing the interest you pay. For example, if you've got £5,000 in your current and savings accounts, and owe £3,000 on your credit card, you won't pay any interest on the debt because your savings cancel it out.

Similarly, if your salary of £2,500 a month is paid into your current account, and this is connected with your £70,000 mortgage, it can be offset against your outstanding debt so you will be charged interest on £67,500. Interest is calculated daily, so even though you won't maintain this balance in your current account for long, and even if you have nothing left in your account at the end of the month, while there is cash in there you pay less interest on your mortgage. This makes a difference in the long run, knocking years off your mortgage.

The big advantage of linking savings with debits is that because you don't receive interest on your savings, you aren't taxed on them either.

Switching Your Current Account

Switching accounts is easier and quicker than ever, thanks to new Banking Code standards. The good news is that you don't actually have to do very much as your new bank does all the legwork. An automated system swaps customer information between banks and building societies. And the revised Banking Code means your old bank has to provide your new bank with details of all your direct debits and standing orders within three working days of being asked for them. All you do is choose the current account you wish to switch to, fill out an application form, and your new bank does the rest.

Completing the application form

Once you decide to switch current account and find one that suits your needs, you must fill out an application form, which you get from your new bank by popping into your local branch, ordering one over the telephone, or downloading it from the Internet. If you download a form, once you've completed it you must print it off, sign it, and return it to the bank. You will be asked for your name and address and details of your existing current account, such as the name and address of the bank it's with, your sort code and account number.

Along with the completed form, you must supply proof of your identity and address. Proof of identity can be a passport or driving licence, while a council tax or utility bill will provide proof of where you live. You can't use the same document to prove your identity and address.

Send important documents by recorded delivery to ensure they're not lost in the post.

Obtaining a list of direct debits

Once your application to open a current account has been accepted, you will be asked to sign a mandate allowing your new bank to ask your old provider for details of your direct debits and standing orders. Once your new bank has this information, it will usually send you the list so you can check it. Ensure that nothing is missing (and that you aren't still making a payment you no longer need to). If anything is missing, contact your new bank or building society to ensure it gets paid.

Your new provider will contact all the companies you have direct debits and standing orders with and give them your new account details.

Your new bank may contact your employer and arrange for your salary to be paid into your new account. Other banks expect you to arrange this. Check whether you are expected to do so. If your bank is taking care of this, it is worth checking that it has or you could face a serious shortfall at the end of the month.

Handling the changeover period

The length of time for the changeover to be completed depends on the banks involved. The Banking Code says your existing bank should provide your account details to your new provider within three working days, but allow six weeks for the switch to be fully completed.

Keep some cash in your old account for three months after you open the new one and don't close that account until everything has been finalised. That way, if any payments do slip through the net, you've got the funds to cover them.

Chapter 3

Covering Yourself with Insurance

• •

• •

*A*lthough we assume it will never happen to us, accidents will happen and illness can strike. Ensuring that you're adequately insured for the unknown makes it easier to deal with the events life may throw at you.

Many people consider insurance to be a waste of money, as you could end up paying hundreds of pounds of premiums and yet never make a claim. But although you could get nothing but peace of mind – which alone is worth the price to some – if you do have to make a claim, you'll be glad you bothered getting cover.

This chapter examines the main types of insurance available, what suits your needs, and how to ensure you don't pay over the odds.

Arranging Cover

Insurance works by offering you cover against injury or loss in return for a monthly, annual, or one-off payment called a *premium*. The insurer calculates your premium by assessing the risk of something happening to you – such as your home being flooded – and what it will cost to right the damage. The higher the likelihood of an event occurring, and therefore of you making a claim, the greater your premium.

Deciding what insurance you need

Some types of cover are compulsory, such as buildings insurance for those with a mortgage or third-party cover for motorists (see the upcoming sections titled 'Safeguarding your home' and 'Making sure of your car' respectively). But the majority of insurance isn't compulsory; it simply brings peace of mind and makes life easier if disaster strikes.

When deciding whether you need non-compulsory cover, consider the impact of something happening to you and whether you could cope if it did. For example, if you were burgled could you afford to replace all your belongings? If not, you need contents insurance.

The cover you opt for is also dictated by what you can afford. Draw up a short list of the insurance you would buy if money were no object and rank it in order of importance, with the cover you have to buy at the top. After compulsory cover, most people opt for life assurance, but this isn't relevant if you don't have dependants (see 'Insuring your life' later in this chapter). Consider your needs as well as cost. When checking whether you've got enough cover, remember that most insurers state a maximum limit they will pay out in event of a claim: Check whether this would cover your loss.

Disclosing information to the insurer

You have to fill out an application form to obtain cover. This involves answering a series of questions, depending on the type of insurance you are buying.

Answer truthfully, even if you know this will bump up your premiums. For example, if you are applying for home contents insurance and the insurer asks if you are a smoker, don't lie and say you aren't if you are. Even though being a smoker increases your risk and your premiums, tell the truth because if you lie, the insurer may refuse to pay out on a claim. It's better to pay higher premiums to ensure you are covered.

If you have pre-existing medical conditions, mention them to the insurer or broker: Don't wait to be asked. It's better to be safe than sorry.

Shopping around for insurance

You can buy insurance direct from the provider, your bank or building society, a supermarket, or broker. You can also buy insurance from the provider of another product (such as travel insurance from your travel agent). For straightforward insurance, direct providers such as supermarkets often offer the best deal. For the best price for less straightforward cover, use a broker with access to hundreds of policies, who can find the best deal for your circumstances. Log onto www.insuresupermarket.com, www.moneyextra.com, or www.moneyfacts.co.uk to search hundreds of policies for the best deal.

If you are struggling to get cover because, say, your home is at risk of flooding, a broker will probably know which providers are most likely to insure you. Using a broker saves you wasting time ringing several insurers yourself only to be told they can't cover you.

Reading the policy carefully

It sounds obvious, but you must read the insurance policy carefully. It sets out the legal obligations on both you and the insurer. Check that it provides the cover you need and ensure you understand the excess – the amount you have to pay your insurer every time you make a claim (see the next section). Make sure you're happy with what is excluded from the cover: If not, try getting this changed. You may have to pay extra to do so but it may be worth it. If you need clarification, ask your insurer.

Deciding on the excess

When you claim on your insurance policy, you usually make a small payment, known as an *excess,* before you get money from the insurer. Some policies have several different excesses, depending on what you are claiming for. For example, if your home has suffered from subsidence in the past, you may have to pay a higher excess on a subsidence-related claim than you would if your laptop was stolen. The standard excess can be anything between £50 and £250, but you can get this raised or removed completely. The higher the excess, the lower your premiums, but don't opt for a greater excess than you are comfortable paying.

Making a comeback if things go wrong

Your policy documents spell out how you make a claim. If you're unsatisfied with the way your insurer handles your claim, inform it in writing. If you aren't happy with the way the insurer deals with your complaint, contact the Financial Ombudsman Service (FOS), which can intervene on your behalf and make a binding ruling. Telephone 0845 080 1800 or log onto www.financial-ombudsman.org.uk/consumer/complaints.htm.

Cutting costs – without skimping on cover

Insurance can be pricey but there are ways of cutting your premiums – without slashing your cover:

- ✔ Pay premiums annually rather than monthly. Insurers offer a discount for this.

- ✔ Don't double up on cover. You can only claim on one policy. So if you take out baggage cover as part of your travel insurance, check you aren't already covered by your contents insurance. Read the small print on your existing cover first before buying any more.

- ✔ Shop around for cover using a broker or comparison Web sites. But don't be guided solely by price; it is important but enough cover is more vital.

Handling Health and Protection

If you lose your job or become ill and can't work, the state provides very little help in making your mortgage repayments. The government provides no financial help until you have been out of work for nine months, and even then what is available is capped and means tested: You must be on income support or jobseeker's allowance, and can't have more than £8,000 in savings. Benefits cover only the first £100,000 of your mortgage, so if you comply with the above criteria but have a bigger home loan, you have to meet the shortfall yourself.

With such a limited safety net provided by the government, it is vital that you take out your own cover in case you lose your job or become ill and unable to work (see 'Preparing for accident, sickness, and unemployment' later in this chapter).

If you need more advice about insurance, and which policies are right for you, contact an independent financial adviser.

Insuring Your Life

The most basic type of cover is *life assurance*, also known as *life insurance*. It pays out a lump sum on your death, which your dependants (usually a partner and/or children under the age of 18) can use as they please – pay off the mortgage, clear debts, or provide an income. The lump sum is usually tax free. It is vital that you take out life assurance if you are the main breadwinner. Be sure, too, that you take out enough cover; otherwise, your dependants will suffer financially after you die.

If you're single, you don't have a real need for life cover unless you have special circumstances, for example you plan to leave your home to a friend or sibling and want the mortgage paid off before they receive it. Life assurance can do this.

When applying for life cover you must complete an application form, giving details of your age, job, and health. Answer these truthfully, no matter how this affects your premiums. If you don't, your policy may not pay out, which could be disastrous for your dependants.

Most life providers can also tack *critical illness cover*, which pays out on diagnosis of certain illnesses, onto your policy for an extra premium, which is quite expensive. This cover can also be bought separately (see 'Covering critical illness' later in this chapter).

We explain the different types of life assurance in more detail in the following sections.

Beginning term assurance

Term assurance is the cheapest form of life protection. It's getting cheaper all the time as people live longer and give insurers less risk of having to pay out.

Term assurance is available from traditional providers such as insurance companies and banks and building societies to retailers. Because competition is fierce, the cost of cover is reasonable: a 30-year-old non-smoking female buying £100,000 worth of level cover for a term of 20 years could purchase cover for £6.80 a month.

Term assurance works like this: You choose the *term* – how long the policy runs for, which can be anything between 1 and 30 years. Many people choose a term that coincides with the length of their mortgage so that their payments are covered if they die before they clear this debt. So if you have 20 years before your outstanding mortgage is cleared, you take term assurance for the same period.

How much the insurer pays out if you die during the term depends upon the type of term assurance:

- ✔ **Level term:** Covers you for the same amount throughout the term of the policy (your premiums also remain the same). As it doesn't take into account the effect of inflation, level term assurance can put your beneficiaries at a disadvantage.

- ✔ **Renewable term:** A renewable term is shorter than a level term – usually five years. You can then renew it if you wish, although you can't increase the sum assured and your premiums rise with age.

- ✔ **Convertible term:** Can be converted to whole of life or endowment insurance without giving further medical evidence of the state of your health. The new policy should cost the same as a normal whole of life or endowment policy based on your age when you exercise this option. This may be worth doing if you don't have much cash initially (so can only afford level term) but have a greater income and more responsibilities, such as kids, later on.

- ✔ **Decreasing term:** The payout sum falls by a fixed amount every year, so by the end of the term you get nothing. However, your premiums remain the same throughout the term, although they are set lower than level term to account for the decline in the sum insured. Popular for covering a repayment mortgage.

- ✔ **Increasing term:** The payout sum, and possibly your premium, increases every year by a fixed percentage of the original sum insured or the retail price index. This ensures there's enough to cover the rising cost of living.

- ✔ **Family income benefit:** Instead of paying a lump sum on your death, your family receives an income until the end of the term. This is paid monthly, every three months, or once a year. You can also have this increase by 3 or 5 per cent each year, but your premiums will be higher to accommodate this.

The downside with term assurance is that your family is protected only if you die during the term. If you take out a policy with a 20-year term and live longer than this, your family won't see a penny of your outlay returned. There is no surrender value either, so if you stop paying the premiums the cover ceases and you don't get back the premiums you have paid.

Just as it is important to make sure you take out enough cover – ensuring the lump sum is big enough to clear all your debts and provide an income as necessary – you must review your policy on a regular basis to ensure you still have enough cover. Do this at least every two years, and when something significant happens, such as you get married, move house, or have children. An independent financial adviser can help decide how much cover you need. While checking that you have enough cover, ensure your premiums remain competitive as well. There are no penalties for switching policy, so do so if you find the same cover for less money – just make sure the new policy is properly in force before terminating the old one.

Getting whole of life insurance

If you want to ensure your family are covered whenever you die – not just during a set term – opt for whole of life insurance. Premiums are higher than for term assurance because the insurer will definitely pay out. Some insurers require you to pay premiums until death; others require premiums only until you reach a certain age, such as 65 or older, but your beneficiaries still get the sum insured when you die. The size of the payment your family gets depends on how long you pay premiums for and the performance of any investments within that policy.

Protecting Your Income

Also known as _permanent health insurance, income protection_ pays out a monthly tax-free sum if you suffer loss of earnings because you are injured or too ill to work. You pay a monthly premium in return. The payout is less than your normal earnings because it is free of tax and the insurer doesn't want to give you too much incentive to stay off work.

Decide whether you need income protection by working out what will happen if you can't work. Your employer may pay Statutory Sick Pay or something more generous. Find out what you're entitled to, as this affects whether you need income protection. If you're self-employed, your income may almost certainly cease so you need some income protection.

The state offers some benefits, such as Long Term Incapacity Benefit, but they don't pay out in the short term, and may be means tested. Find out what you qualify for from your local Jobcentre Plus or log onto www.jobcentreplus.gov.uk.

After you work out how much money you receive if you become sick or injured, think about how much you need to cover your outgoings, such as your mortgage, council tax, and other bills. If you have savings and/or investments, or your employer provides generous sick pay, covering these may not be a problem. But if you can't cope with a loss of income, you need income protection.

You have several decisions to make when buying income protection:

- **Whether you want *own occupation* or *any occupation* cover.** The former pays out if you can't do your normal job, the latter you can't claim on unless you are too ill to carry out any job. The former is more expensive but usually worth having.

- **How long you want the *deferred period* to be.** This is the length of time after your incapacity before you get a payout. The longer it is, the lower your premiums. If your employer will give you sick pay for six months, you could defer your policy to pay out after this, for example. Avoid opting for a longer deferred period than you can comfortably cope with just to reduce your premiums, as it could be a struggle.

- **How long you want the policy to pay out for.** It is wise to tie this in with your normal retirement date. The longer the period, the more expensive your premiums.

- **Whether your premiums are fixed or variable.** If you opt for a *guaranteed* rate, your insurer can't increase your premiums, except in line with inflation, so you get certainty. If your rate is *reviewable*, the insurer can raise premiums to reflect its overall costs, which may mean you have to pay out significantly more than you'd budgeted for. A *renewable* rate means premiums are set for a fixed period, which again buys peace of mind.

Covering Critical Illness

Critical illness cover (CIC) pays out a tax-free lump sum if you are diagnosed with a specific illness or condition, such as cancer, a heart attack, or a stroke. Full details of the conditions covered are listed in the insurer's key features leaflet.

CIC is more restrictive than income protection because the latter pays out a monthly income if you are too ill to work regardless of the illness, whereas CIC is quite limited in the conditions it covers. And receiving a monthly income until you can return to work via income protection insurance may be more useful than a lump sum via CIC, because you may spend the lump sum and be left with no income.

You can arrange for CIC to cover you for a set number of years, perhaps until you clear your mortgage. Or you can opt for a plan without a fixed period.

Most policies charge a regular monthly or yearly premium, depending on your age, sex, health, occupation, whether you smoke, the cover you need, and for how long. It's most important that you disclose the full details of your medical history when you apply, as your claim could be turned down by the insurer if you missed some information out, whether or not the omission was intentional. If you are already seriously ill, you may not be able to get cover or the provider may cover you but not that particular illness. Alternatively, you may be charged a higher premium. You may also have to pay higher premiums if certain illnesses run in your family.

Premiums may increase over the life of the policy or you can opt for a guarantee that they won't.

Preparing for Accident, Sickness, and Unemployment

Also known as *mortgage payment protection insurance, accident, sickness, and unemployment insurance (ASU)* is the most comprehensive and expensive cover available. It pays out for a limited period – usually 12 or 24 months – and you must wait 30, 60, or 90 days before receiving payment. If you take out all three elements, this type of policy is expensive. But you may not need every element: Work out what you require and take out only enough to cover what you need. For example, if your employer provides sick pay for six months, you don't need accident or sickness cover and may need only the unemployment part.

Income protection may be a better option than ASU, as it is cheaper and pays out until you return to work, whereas ASU pays out only for a limited period. You can buy ASU from your mortgage lender but see whether you can find a better deal first by consulting a mortgage broker or financial adviser.

Purchasing Private Medical Insurance

If you have private medical insurance (PMI), you don't have to wait months to be treated on the NHS. You pay a monthly or yearly premium in exchange for cover for the cost of private medical treatment for curable short-term illnesses or injuries, otherwise known as *acute conditions*.

A long list of illnesses and conditions aren't covered by PMI, including drug abuse, self-inflicted injuries, pregnancy, cosmetic surgery, and organ transplants. For a full list of exclusions, check the insurer's key features leaflet. Treatment by accident and emergency isn't covered under PMI as private hospitals don't have the facilities to cope with it.

Accounting for the cost

PMI can be extremely expensive and you should be prepared for your premium to rise each year, usually above the rate of general inflation. The cost is the result of the increasing number of people claiming for private medical treatment and the increasingly sophisticated and expensive procedures available. According to the Association of British Insurers (ABI) a hip replacement – a common procedure – can cost around £7,000, for example.

The number of claims you make doesn't influence your premiums, unless your cover includes a no-claims discount. However, your premiums will increase as you get older because you are more likely to make a claim. A 45-year-old should expect to pay 25 per cent higher premiums than a 35-year-old, according to the ABI. A 65-year-old would pay more than twice the premium of a 45-year-old.

Your premiums depend on your level of cover: A limited policy costs less than a comprehensive one. Most schemes cover in-patient and day-patient treatment, but not all offer outpatient treatment. Consider how important this is to you when choosing a policy.

Declaring your medical history

The most common type of policy requires you to fill out a form with details of your medical history. Your doctor may be contacted for further information and you won't be covered for pre-existing conditions.

An alternative to declaring your medical history is the *moratorium* option, which is offered by a number of insurers. You don't have to fill in a medical history form, but if treatment for a pre-existing condition (something you suffered from in the past five years) is required within two years after the policy starts, the costs are not covered. If you haven't had any symptoms or received treatment for this condition for two years after starting your policy, the insurer covers you as normal.

It is down to you to declare any medical conditions you have suffered from in the past five years if you don't opt for the moratorium. Resist the temptation to conceal this information, as the insurer may refuse to pay out if you make a claim.

Covering Your Home and Belongings

As well as covering your life and mortgage payments, it is wise to cover your belongings in case disaster strikes.

Safeguarding your home

In return for a monthly or annual premium, buildings insurance pays out if the structure of your home and/or its fixtures and fittings are damaged by fire, subsidence, flood, or storm. Premiums are calculated according to your postcode, previous claims history, the sum insured, and the nature of what you are insuring.

If you have a mortgage, this cover is compulsory. Your lender will insist on proof that you have cover before releasing the mortgage, so purchase insurance before contracts are exchanged. If you own a leasehold property, your freeholder – the landlord – is responsible for arranging buildings insurance. You repay him via your service charge.

Take a look at the buildings or contents insurance that you can buy from your mortgage lender. The lender's insurance policies are likely to be more expensive than those of other companies, so shop around. And the bigger your home, the more you'll probably save from searching the market. Some insurers concentrate on more expensive houses, looking at them as better risks than smaller properties. The savings – £200 to £600 per year is possible – can form the basis for future investments.

Taking care of contents insurance

Contents insurance protects you against damage or loss of your moveable possessions due to theft, fire, or flood. For an extra premium, you can get accidental damage cover, which pays out if you spill a pot of paint on the carpet, for example. Consider whether you need this extra protection. You also pay extra for *all risks*: cover for items you regularly take out of the home, such as a laptop or digital camera.

You can get lower premiums by beefing up your security, fitting alarms and British Standard locks. Ask your insurer for details.

Making Sure of Your Car

If you cause an accident, *third-party cover* protects you against liability to other people and their property. You can also get *fully comprehensive* insurance, which also pays out for repairs to your car if you cause an accident as well as for theft and fire damage. There is also an inbetween policy – *third-party fire and theft* – covering you for liability to other people and their property, and if your car is stolen or damaged by fire.

It is an offence to drive a car without third-party cover.

Motor insurance can be expensive, but there are ways of cutting the cost rather than the cover. Premiums are calculated according to your age and driving experience, occupation, and where you live – there is little you can do about these. But you can choose a car with a low insurance group rating; ensure an alarm is fitted; travel fewer miles; and keep it in a garage.

You can also get a discount on your premiums if you build up a no-claims record – usually around 30 per cent for one claim-free year to 60 per cent after four or five years. Discounts differ between insurers, so shop around for the best deal. Some insurers offer a *protected discount policy* to drivers with a good claims record. For an extra premium, you can typically make two claims in a three- to five-year period without affecting your discount.

Travelling under Cover

It's worth buying travel cover before going on holiday. You might be intending to rely on the E111 form, which gives UK residents free or discounted medical treatment in another European country if it has signed a reciprocal agreement for health services. However, it doesn't cover many countries, such as the US, and few EU countries pay the full cost of reciprocal health care.

What's more, the E111 doesn't cover loss of luggage, money, or passport, or expenses caused by flight delays. With travel insurance, you get recompense if your trip is cancelled or curtailed for reasons beyond your control or you have to be repatriated (flown back) to the UK.

You can take out an annual policy or single-trip policy every time you travel. The former is cheaper if you make at least two trips a year. You can buy cover from travel agents or tour operators, but can get a better deal via a broker. Insurers, retailers, banks, and building societies all offer travel cover, so it's a competitive market.

Ensure you have enough cover. If you are participating in winter sports or bungee jumping, make sure your policy covers you before you go. It is often worth having more cover than you need if there's a chance you might undertake a dangerous sport or activity: It could be difficult or impossible to extend your cover once you are abroad.

Chapter 4

Tackling Your Overdraft and Other Credit Nasties

. . . .

In This Chapter

▶ Going overdrawn

▶ Working out whether an overdraft is the answer

▶ Going for a current account with the best overdraft

▶ Changing current accounts

▶ Whittling down your overdraft

▶ Handling store card debt

▶ Steering clear of debt management companies

▶ Consolidating your own debts

▶ Avoiding bankruptcy

. . . .

*E*ven the best-laid plans can go awry, and even the most careful budget-follower can overspend on occasion. One of the easiest ways of spending more cash than you have is to go overdrawn on your current account. But if you do so without asking the bank's permission beforehand, you are likely to get a nasty shock when you receive your next bank statement.

Not only is unauthorised borrowing expensive, it's also unnecessary. With a bit of careful planning, there is no need for an unauthorised overdraft. This chapter shows you what you need to bear in mind before going overdrawn.

Increased competition in the current account market means that if you are already overdrawn, and have been for some time, you may be paying more in charges than absolutely necessary. Shopping around for a cheaper overdraft – and switching current account – is straightforward, will save you on charges, and enable you to clear your borrowings more quickly. In this chapter, we help you choose the best overdraft for your needs and show you how to manage it to best advantage.

Understanding How Overdrafts Work

Going *overdrawn* – also known as slipping into the red, as opposed to the black – happens when you spend more money than you have in your current account. You are using the bank's money instead of your own and are charged interest for doing so. The amount differs between banks and also depends on whether you asked permission beforehand or not.

You can only get an overdraft on your current account; it is not available on regular savings accounts.

Requesting permission

You must ask your bank for permission before going overdrawn: This is known as an *authorised* overdraft. You should do this as soon as you realise that you are getting short of funds and may need some extra cash. Contact your bank: You will have to fill out an application form or put your request in writing. Your bank will decide how big your overdraft can be, according to status and general rules.

Even if you aren't planning on going overdrawn, there's no harm in applying to your bank for an overdraft just in case. You don't have to pay for it if you're not using it and you never know when you might need extra funds in an emergency. If you've already got the overdraft facility set up, slipping into the red doesn't present a problem.

Most current accounts have an overdraft facility so, in theory, you could slip into the red without notifying your bank first. But this isn't a good idea, as *unauthorised* overdrafts usually have punitive interest charges. And you could well be charged other fees on top (see 'Looking at fees' later in this chapter).

Calculating interest

An overdraft is a form of borrowing because you are using the bank's money, so you usually have to pay interest on it. However, you may not be charged interest on an overdraft if your bank is charging 0 per cent for an introductory period, there is an interest-free buffer, or you have a student or graduate bank account.

If your overdraft is authorised, you pay around half as much interest as you would on an unauthorised one – sometimes less. You may still have to pay a fee for being overdrawn, however, depending on the account provider. Table 4-1 compares interest rates between the big four banks – Barclays, HSBC, Lloyds TSB, and NatWest – and shows how much they charge on the amount you go overdrawn, whether it be authorised or unauthorised. Note that although the authorised rates tend to be much lower than the unauthorised ones, they are still rather high.

Table 4-1	Overdraft Interest Rates	
Bank	**Authorised**	**Unauthorised**
Barclays	15.6%	27.5%
HSBC	16.6%	N/A
Lloyds TSB	18.7%	29.8%
NatWest	max 19.99%	29.69%

(Source: Moneyfacts)

Take care not to exceed an authorised overdraft without requesting further permission from your bank beforehand. Otherwise, you could be penalised more heavily than you imagine: Some banks charge the higher, unauthorised rate on the full amount you are overdrawn – not just the portion over and above your authorised limit.

Say, for example, your bank charges 10 per cent interest on authorised overdrafts and 30 per cent on unauthorised ones. If you have a £250 authorised overdraft but go £1 over this limit, you could be charged 30 per cent interest on the full £251 if your bank follows this practice.

It is vital to find out how interest is calculated on your overdraft. If there's a chance you may run up a small, unauthorised overdraft for a short period of time, find a bank that won't penalise you by charging high rates of interest on your total borrowings.

A couple of banks have the same rate on authorised and unauthorised overdrafts, which can save you the agony of paying twice as much interest for going overdrawn without seeking permission first. But there is a considerable difference between what the two banks charge – one (First Trust) charges 9 per cent on authorised and unauthorised borrowing; the other (Alliance & Leicester) 17.08 per cent on both – so you still need to shop around for the best deal.

Looking at fees

Many people don't realise that interest charges on their overdrafts are just the beginning. Many banks charge an array of other fees and charges, which can be buried in the small print. Be wary of these when signing up for a new current account, as one with a low rate of interest may not look quite such a good deal after fees and charges are added.

You may discover that the overdraft with the higher rate of interest and no fees is actually a better deal than the lower rate with lots of hidden fees and charges. For example, one bank may charge 29.8 per cent on unauthorised overdrafts, while another charges 35 per cent. But if the former bank also charges you £25 a day up to a maximum of £75 a month for an unauthorised overdraft, whereas the latter has no additional fees, the bank with the higher rate of interest may work out cheaper in the long run. Take all fees and charges into account as well as rates of interest when making your choice.

Daily charges

If you go overdrawn without authorisation your account provider may charge you a fee for each day you are overdrawn – up to a maximum amount. This is charged on top of the higher rate of interest, which is why unauthorised borrowing can be so pricey. For example, many account providers charge £25–£30 a day for every day you are overdrawn in one month (in some cases up to a maximum of three charges a month). This charge can be imposed even if you are only a few pounds overdrawn.

Item charges

As well as a daily charge, you may get stung with an item charge every time your bank pays a direct debit, standing order, or cheque on your unauthorised overdraft. This can be as much as £35 per item.

Administration or arrangement fees

Some banks charge a fee for setting up an overdraft, so check whether this is the case – and how much it is – before applying. This is usually a 1 to 2 per cent charge with a minimum of £10 to £30. Many banks don't charge such a fee, however, so there really is no need to pay it. Shop around for an account that won't charge you.

Monthly or quarterly usage fees

Some banks pump up the cost of an overdraft by charging a monthly or quarterly usage fee of around £5 to £7 (some refer to this as a management fee) on authorised as well as unauthorised overdrafts (although most banks have dropped the practice of charging this on the former).

Connecting interest and credit rating

You may find that you apply for a current account only to be told that the rate of interest on overdrafts is higher than the advertised rate. This happens when the account provider bases its overdraft rate on your credit rating.

The rate advertised is the *typical* rate, which means you may be charged that amount of interest or a higher rate, depending on how you score in a credit check. For example, one bank offers a typical overdraft rate of 10 per cent (authorised) or 21 per cent (unauthorised), but people deemed to be higher risk are charged between 11 and 15 per cent for an authorised overdraft. (Chapter 5 has more details on how your credit rating is checked and how you can improve this rating, thereby qualifying for a lower rate of interest.)

Deciding whether an overdraft really is the answer

Your current account may have an overdraft facility, but that doesn't automatically mean you have to take advantage of it. An overdraft can be a flexible and convenient way of borrowing, but it might not be the best way of doing so. Table 4-2 weighs up some of the pros and cons of taking out an overdraft.

Table 4-2	Pros and Cons of Overdrafts
Advantages	*Disadvantages*
Easy to arrange: A letter or call to your bank is usually enough to arrange an overdraft or extend it as required.	Too much flexibility: It is easy to slip into the red, and if you do so without seeking authorisation beforehand, you're penalised through heavy charges.
Great for borrowing small amounts of cash in the short term: Some banks even offer a small interest-free overdraft facility, which may be enough to tide you over.	Cost: You may get stung by high rates of interest, plus monthly and arrangement fees if you don't shop around for a good deal. If you exceed your authorised limit, charges are particularly high.
No fixed repayment schedule: You can pay back the money as and when you can afford to do so.	Danger of having a never-ending overdraft: You may have every intention of using your overdraft only in the short-term, but because there is no repayment schedule, you may find it becoming a permanent fixture.

Overdrafts are excellent for short-term borrowing of relatively small amounts of cash. But if you need to borrow money for a long period of time, an overdraft may not be the answer. Even if your overdraft is authorised, you could still pay considerably more interest in the long run than you would on a cheap personal loan. To decide whether a personal loan may be a better choice, consider how much cash you need and how long it is likely to take you to repay it. If you need more than say, £3,000, a personal loan may be a better bet than an overdraft: Some banks may not let you go overdrawn by this amount, for example, whereas it's usually not a problem obtaining a loan this size.

If you are borrowing a sizeable amount of money, a personal loan's structured monthly repayments might make it easier to clear your debt more quickly. See Chapter 6 for more information on choosing a personal loan.

Choosing a Current Account for Its Overdraft

If you regularly go overdrawn, there is little point searching for a current account that pays the best rate of interest on balances. If you are rarely in credit, you simply won't make the most of this facility so there is little point in having it. What you do need is a current account with a cheap overdraft. Historically, overdrafts were an extremely expensive form of borrowing, but as part of their drive to attract new business, many banks are realising that it's not just the rate of interest paid to customers in credit that is important but overdraft rates as well. When looking for an overdraft, avoid the big four banks as they are among the most expensive providers (see Table 4-1 earlier in this chapter). Instead, shop around for another current account offering a good deal on overdrafts: You should be able to find one charging less than 10 per cent interest.

Check out comparison site www.moneysupermarket.com, which lets you compare overdrafts offered by 300 banks.

Fee-free buffers

If you only slip into the red by a couple of hundred pounds a month it might not be necessary to pay any interest or charges at all, as some banks offer fee- and interest-free overdraft buffers. This enables you to go overdrawn by a certain amount – whether it is £10, £50, £250, or even £500 – without charge. This amount varies considerably, so check before signing up for a new current account.

An aid to the forgetful

My (Melanie's) bank lets me go overdrawn by up to £100 every month interest free. It's a handy feature, because even with the most careful budgeting, unexpected expenses can crop up and catch you unawares.

One month a magazine subscription I'd forgotten about — because I pay annually by direct debit — was debited from my account, pushing me into the red. Luckily, I had the £100 interest- and fee-free buffer to call upon, so didn't rack up any costs for my oversight.

If your account has a sizeable interest-free overdraft buffer, resist the temptation to see it as an extra £250 or £500 to spend every single month. Try and think of it as an extra for emergencies instead. Otherwise, you're immediately down by your overdraft amount when your salary is paid into your account, which means you're likely to dip into your overdraft again the following month, leaving you no reserves to cope with a genuine emergency.

Watch out for the distinction between fee-free and interest-free when comparing overdrafts. If a bank is offering a £250 fee-free buffer, for example, you may find you are still charged interest on this amount. However, if it is an interest-free buffer, you won't be charged interest although you may incur a fee. One bank has a £250 interest-free overdraft limit but no fee-free limit, which means you automatically have to pay a flat fee if you go overdrawn at all although you won't have to pay interest if it's less than £2,500. Check the small print and ask the current account provider if you still aren't sure of the difference.

Introductory offers

A few banks charge 0 per cent on overdrafts for an introductory period of up to 12 months to encourage you to open a current account. They place a limit on the size of overdraft you are allowed - typically £2,500. To qualify for such deals, you may have to meet certain criteria, such as agreeing to have your salary paid into your account every month. Check the small print.

Such interest-free limits are not automatic: You must still apply for them, just as you would any other authorised borrowing.

If you are tempted by a 0 per cent overdraft for an introductory period, check what rate of interest you have to pay once this ends, even if it is a long way off. If the standard rate is extremely high, and you haven't cleared your overdraft before you are charged interest at this rate, you may be better off opting for a low standard overdraft rate in the first place.

Switching Current Accounts When You Have an Overdraft

If you have a sizeable overdraft, you may well find that another account provider is offering a cheaper deal. It's worth checking whether this is the case and, if so, thinking about switching bank accounts so that you can benefit from the lower rate.

While banks tend to welcome new current account customers with open arms, they are not usually so keen to have your existing overdraft as well – unless you have a business account or are a recent graduate. But this doesn't necessarily mean that you have to be stuck with a bank charging hefty overdraft rates for the rest of your life.

One way of switching current accounts if you've already got an overdraft is to use funds from a new account to clear your old one. You can then work at reducing the overdraft on your new account (which will hopefully have a lower rate of interest, making it easier to achieve). First, find a new account with a 0 per cent overdraft for 12 months or a lower rate of interest than the one you are currently being charged, at least. Open your new account and withdraw enough cash to clear your existing overdraft: Pay this into your existing current account, before closing this account. It will then be easier to whittle away your overdraft because the rate of interest will be lower (or there might not be any interest to pay at all for a while).

Reducing Your Overdraft

Although it pays to shop around for the cheapest overdraft, in an ideal world you wouldn't go overdrawn in the first place. Borrowing money is an expensive business: Even if you do your research carefully and find the cheapest overdraft available, you still pay out money in interest charges every month. The sensible approach is to work out how you can cut your overdraft and therefore the charges you pay.

If you're slipping into debt, it's easy to bury your head in the sand, ignore the problem, and hope it goes away. But it won't – and such an attitude simply makes matters worse.

If you have savings in a separate account, which you may be keeping for an emergency, you should use this cash to clear your overdraft (or at least reduce it). You are unlikely to be earning as much interest on your savings as you are paying on your overdraft, so it makes no financial sense to clear your debts before starting to build up your savings.

If you don't have savings to call upon, consider taking out a personal loan to clear your overdraft. This may be a good idea if you've run up a big overdraft and are paying a lot of interest on it: Personal loan rates are likely to be quite a bit cheaper. A loan will also replace what could be unwieldy borrowing with a fixed repayment plan, which can be easier to manage and clear.

Once you whittle away your overdraft, make a budget and stick to it. This will enable you to get in control of your spending and ensure you don't slip back into the red. See Chapter 1 for more on budgeting.

Dealing with Other Debts

Cheap overdrafts, credit cards, personal loans, and mortgages have made borrowing much cheaper than in the past, but not all debt is inexpensive. Cards issued by stores have remained largely untouched by the downward trend in interest rates and charges – remaining as expensive as ever. And despite the growing number of cheap personal loans, loan sharks still operate, preying on the desperate.

But debt management companies, expensive consolidation loans, and bankruptcy aren't the answer. In the next few sections we show you where to get free advice and how to get on top of your debt.

Handling Store Cards Smartly

Plastic is a convenient form of spending, but when it comes to store cards it can be extremely expensive. A *store card* is a credit card branded with the name of the store that issues it and is useful to purchase only goods in that store, or chain of stores. Store cards work much the same as credit cards from major companies, although store cards generally have high annual percentage rates (APRs) and often have short interest-free grace periods.

Signing up for store cards

The big incentive to sign up for a store card is a discount on your purchases the day you apply: Up to 10 or even 15 per cent in some cases, which can be quite a saving if you are spending a lot of cash. But if you don't clear the balance when your statement arrives, that initial discount could easily be eaten up in interest because store cards have high APRs.

Store cards are 'sold' to you by sales assistants, many of whom are on commission so the more customers they can persuade to sign up, the more lucrative it is for them. The sales assistant usually fills out the application form on your behalf while you supply your details, then calls to check your credit rating while you wait. If you're deemed a good enough risk, the card is authorised.

The Office of Fair Trading (OFT) is concerned about hard-sell tactics. Although sales assistants never suggest that you take the application form away with you to read carefully before deciding whether to sign up or not, the OFT advises that you do so to ensure you understand what you are getting into. However, if you take the form away you won't get your 10 per cent discount, which may be the only reason you're signing up in the first place.

Paying extortionate rates of interest

The main problem with store cards is that it often isn't clear when you sign up in store exactly what the APR is – the amount of interest you pay. It is rarely clearly advertised, and the rate could mean a nasty shock when your statement arrives because rates tend to be extremely high. And if you don't pay off the balance in full, you could pay a lot extra.

The gap has closed somewhat, but with a few exceptions (most notably IKEA, which charges 12.9 per cent), store cards are still an expensive method of borrowing. While APRs on credit cards have fallen dramatically in recent years, rates on many store cards still hover around 25-30 per cent mark – around 50 per cent more than those on most credit cards. Although the rate drops slightly if you pay by direct debit, in most cases it remains well over 20 per cent.

Making store cards work for you

Book I

Organising
Your
Finances
and Dealing
with Debt

If you can comfortably clear the outstanding amount on your store card when the bill arrives and are a regular customer of that particular retailer, it may be worth using a store card, as there could be plenty of benefits in doing so. Not only do you get a discount on your first purchase, there are usually other perks, such as bonus reward schemes, free catalogues or magazines, and special shopping days, where you can avoid the crowds and shop in peace. John Lewis gives customers 1 per cent of what they spend in store back in the form of vouchers, for example, so if you are a regular customer this could be worth having.

Some retailers have launched credit cards alongside their store cards so you get the usual rewards of a store card for spending on the retailer-branded credit card. The danger is that while the APR tends to be lower than on a store card, it isn't as cheap as some of the best credit cards. And as you aren't restricted to one store but can use it in whatever outlets you like, you could run up more debt on it than you were able to before. Check the APR before spending – and if it isn't that competitive (and you don't clear your balance every month) don't use it at all.

Set up a direct debit to pay the full amount due on your store card each month. Then, if you forget to pay one month – perhaps because you're on holiday – it will be paid regardless so you won't run up any interest.

As well as persuading you to take out a store card, many retailers will try to force you to buy *card protection* and, just for good measure, *card payment protection* as well:

 ✔ Card protection: Covers you if your card is lost or stolen. A single call from you can cancel all your plastic and usually costs around £12 a year.

 ✔ Card payment protection covers your store card repayments if you lose your job or become ill and can't work.

We would avoid both types of cover, as they are expensive and usually a waste of money. Don't be talked into signing up, no matter how persuasive the salesperson is. If you really want some card or payment protection, shop around for a good deal rather than automatically taking out the policy the store card provider offers: There is no obligation to do so and you will find a better deal elsewhere. Make sure you read the small print before signing anything (Chapters 5 and 6 have more details on this type of cover).

Refusing to bow to pressure

Although store cards have high APRs, I (Melanie) know only too well the allure of a 10 per cent discount. I signed up for one in a major department store when I bought a £150 outfit for a wedding because it seemed an easy way of saving £15. However, when I was still standing there 20 minutes later, worrying about my car on the meter and the disgruntled queue building up behind me, it no longer seemed such a good idea.

I passed the credit check though and got my discount. A few weeks later I got a call from the store advising me to take out its card protection plan: For £45 I would get three years' cover. I was told that it was a good idea and everyone was being advised to buy it. I said I wasn't interested and the salesperson grew quite pushy. I was unimpressed and stuck to my guns.

Don't bow to pressure, whether it's over buying insurance – or applying for the store card in the first place.

Clearing store card debt

If you run up debt on your store card that you can't clear at the end of the month, you will be charged a lot of interest – usually from the day you made the purchase, rather than the statement date. It may be cheaper, depending on the amount you owe, to take out a regular credit card with a 0 per cent introductory offer period on balance transfers and switch your outstanding store card debt to the new card. You will be charged a fee, typically 2.5–3 per cent of the balance, for transferring to a 0 per cent offer, but it is a one-off payment and you should have covered the cost in saved interest after two or three months.

The transfer is a simple process: You contact your new card provider with your store card account number and how much you want to transfer. It usually takes a few working days for the payment to be processed.

Once you've transferred your store card debt, use the money that would have gone towards paying off the interest to chip away at the balance. If you haven't cleared the balance by the end of the introductory period (anything from five to twelve months), switch to another card offering a similar deal, and so on until the debt is cleared.

Once you've transferred the debt from your store card, cut it up and write to the issuer closing your account. This will take away the temptation to spend further on the card. Stick to cheaper forms of credit in future.

Avoiding Debt Consolidation Firms

Book I

Organising
Your
Finances
and Dealing
with Debt

It is no coincidence that rising levels of debt have been accompanied by a growth in the number of debt management or debt consolidation companies. Their services are advertised everywhere – from the television to radio and national newspapers, promising to help with all your nasty debt problems. Need £25,000, £50,000, or £100,000 as soon as possible, no questions asked? If you are a homeowner, a debt management company will be happy to oblige.

The reason debt management companies are interested in homeowners is that the companies replace your debts, which are *unsecured*, with a *secured* loan. In other words, the lender can repossess your home if you don't keep up your monthly repayments. This is extremely risky and should be avoided at all costs. (See Chapter 6 for more on the difference between secured and unsecured loans and the risks associated with the former.)

Consolidating debts into one loan

Debt management companies reorganise your debts into one *consolidation loan*. In other words, they take out yet another loan to pay off your existing debt, thereby increasing your borrowing. You make a single monthly payment: This may be lower than your current payments (particularly if your existing debts are expensive), but you pay more in the long run as you take longer to pay it off.

Consolidation loans can be tempting if you owe money to several creditors who all want paying at the same time. Instead of making payments here, there, and everywhere, you only have to worry about one payment. The debt management company plays on this. But some consolidation loans extend your term of borrowing by as long as 25 years. Ask yourself whether you would be happy paying off credit card debt and other bills over such a long period of time.

Work out the total cost of the consolidation loan to see how much it will be in the long run, rather than just the monthly amount. And avoid expensive payment protection insurance, which the lender may try to sell you, as it often isn't worth having and will simply bump up the cost. (Chapter 6 has more on this type of cover.)

Working out the cost of consolidation

One Citizens Advice Bureau client saw his debt quadruple when he took out a consolidation loan for £24,200. This came with payment protection insurance of £4,823, which covered him if he lost his job or became ill and couldn't meet his repayments. He ended up with monthly repayments of £350 for 25 years – a grand total of £105,078!

Be wary of borrowing more money to pay off existing debt. Despite your efforts to improve matters, you may find you make the situation worse.

Looking at high rates and arrangement fees

Unlike consumer groups and charities that help you get on top of your debts for free, debt management companies charge around 15 per cent, plus VAT (at 17.5 per cent) for arranging a consolidation loan. It's no wonder there are so many debt management companies out there: It's a lucrative business to be in right now.

To avoid paying fees to a debt management company, consider whether a consolidation loan is what you need to get out of your debt mess. You may be able to get an unsecured loan with a lower APR than a secured one if you shop around. You can then use this money to pay off your debts, just as you would if a debt management company set up a consolidated loan for you, and make your monthly payment to your new lender each month. Chapter 6 has the lowdown on shopping around for personal loans.

Steering Clear of Loan Sharks

If you're desperate for cash and have a bad credit rating, which makes it difficult to get a credit card, bank loan, or overdraft, you may be tempted to borrow from a loan shark. But don't be fooled into thinking that you can control such a loan and won't go the way of all those other borrowers who fall behind with their repayments and find themselves intimidated and threatened with violence.

Loan sharks are illegal moneylenders who give out quick cash loans, so they are convenient if you need money as soon as possible. But the rates of interest they charge are astronomical – up to 200 per cent in some cases. This would be hard enough to repay even if your finances were in a strong position.

If you are in such a dire position that you are even contemplating using a loan shark, you must seek advice before you do anything else. (Check out 'Seeking free advice' at the end of this chapter.)

Escaping the Debt Trap

Although debt management companies do a good job of persuading you that you really must use their services to get out of debt, this isn't the case. Once you've faced up to your debt problem – the sooner you do this the better – you can take steps to get out of it yourself.

Prioritising your debts

The first step is to prioritise your debts, deciding which ones you must pay first. This helps you separate the urgent debts from the not-so-urgent ones, so you clear the ones that carry the severest penalty for defaulting first.

Priority debts include:

- **Your rent or mortgage:** If you don't pay this, your landlord can evict you or your mortgage lender can apply to a court to have your home repossessed and sell it to cover your debts. Either way, you end up without a roof over your head.

- **Gas and electricity bills:** If you don't pay these, your supply will be cut off.

- **Telephone bill:** Again, the supplier will simply cut you off if you don't pay.

- **Council tax:** You can go to prison if you don't pay up.

Once you've identified your priority debts, see whether there are any areas where you can make savings (perhaps by switching to a cheaper utility supplier, for example).

Don't pay any secondary debts, such as credit or store card bills or unsecured loans, until you have reached agreement with your priority creditors.

Working out your budget

The next step is to work out how much cash you have leftover once you pay your priority debts. Subtract the cost of these from your monthly income: Any money leftover can be divided between your remaining (or secondary) creditors.

If you haven't got a surplus, or enough of one to clear all your bills, contact one of the free advice services (see 'Seeking free advice' at the end of this chapter) for help.

Making savings work harder

If you have any savings or investments, such as a few windfall shares from the demutualisation of a building society, work out whether you could put this money to better use clearing your debts rather than leaving it where it is. If you earn less interest on your savings than you pay on your debts, use this cash to pay some bills. Even if you earn 6 per cent tax free on your savings in a mini cash individual savings account, if you are paying 30 per cent interest on store card debt, it doesn't make sense to keep the savings. Reduce your debt instead – and the interest you pay.

Juggling your mortgage

If you are struggling to repay your mortgage, you could reduce your monthly repayments by extending the term of your loan. Alternatively, you might be able to reduce your payments, and stick to the same term, by remortgaging at a cheaper rate. If you have had the same deal for several years, you could almost certainly save money by remortgaging. Check first whether you will incur an early redemption penalty for switching: This could be the case if you are on a fixed or discounted deal, or have recently come to the end of such an offer.

Even if you do have to pay a penalty, you may still save cash in the long run. Ask an independent mortgage broker to do the calculations for you (Chapter 3 in Book III has more on finding a broker).

While you are remortgaging you could increase the size of your home loan (if you have enough equity in your home to do so), and use the cash you raise to clear other loans or credit card debts. The advantage of this is that mortgage rates tend to be lower than other forms of borrowing, so you pay less interest.

Avoid increasing your mortgage by an unnecessarily large amount, otherwise you could struggle to repay it and could lose your home. Calculate how much you absolutely need to clear your debts and don't borrow more than this. Remortgaging shouldn't be seen as a chance of raising money to fritter away, but only for the serious matter of clearing your existing debt.

Replacing the plastic

If you've got store and credit cards with high APRs and don't clear the balance each month, consider transferring the outstanding debt to a cheap credit card charging 0 per cent for an introductory period. Then cut up the expensive cards so you won't be tempted to use them again.

Alternatively, take out a cheap personal loan. This cash can be used to pay all your debts in return for a manageable monthly payment. This is, in effect, what a consolidation loan organised by a debt management company does, but by doing it yourself, you save on the management charge and don't have to secure it against your home. Chapter 6 has tips on shopping around for a loan.

Contacting your creditors

When you're in debt, it's tempting to stick your head in the sand and pretend you haven't got a problem. The last people you may feel like telling are those you owe money to: Surely they'll pull the rug from under you if you 'fess up? But in actual fact, these are the very people you should be talking to if you have problems.

The sooner you contact your creditors and explain the situation to them, the more sympathetic they are likely to be. Tell them you are having difficulty paying what you owe and offer to pay a smaller amount each week or month. Even if this is only a tiny proportion of your debt, the lender may welcome it as a sign that you are determined to honour what you owe. Most creditors also realise that a court would only order small payments anyway, so they might as well accept your offer.

If you can't repay what you owe because you've lost your job or your marriage has broken down, the lender may be prepared to reduce or freeze your payments until you get back on your feet.

Don't agree to pay back more than you can realistically afford or you will simply be back where you started.

Seeking free advice

When it comes to getting out of debt and the problems it causes, there are numerous companies out there offering to help you, although you must steer clear of debt management companies for the reasons we detail in the previous sections. You should also steer clear of credit repair companies, which promise to improve your credit rating. There is very little they can practically do, and you can do all that yourself – for free. See Chapter 5 for ways on improving your credit file.

A number of organisations offer free advice if you get into debt difficulties. They will negotiate with your creditors on your behalf, so contact one of these before approaching any debt management companies or loan sharks:

- Citizens Advice Bureau: Check your local phone book for your local branch or go to www.citizensadvice.org.uk.

- Consumer Credit Counselling Service on 0800 138 1111 or www.cccs.co.uk.

- National Debtline on 0808 808 4000 or www.nationaldebtline.co.uk.

Going bankrupt

As the stigma surrounding bankruptcy lessens, it is an increasingly attractive alternative to those struggling with debt. It used to be the case that you were automatically discharged from bankruptcy two to three years after the bankruptcy order, but this has been reduced to one year.

By going bankrupt you finally put an end to harassment from your creditors – the people you owe money to – which can come as a blessed relief. Once a bankruptcy order has been made, a third party or trustee – the *Official Receiver* or an *insolvency practitioner* – takes over your estate. Any financial interest you have in your home is transferred to the trustee: He recovers the value of this for the benefit of your creditors. Your creditors contact him and he decides who gets what, once your possessions have been sold.

Once you are discharged from bankruptcy, your creditors can't come after you for any outstanding debts.

However, it isn't as straightforward as all that. Bankruptcy shouldn't be taken lightly because:

- ✒ If you have a home, you could lose it. The administrator will sell your assets, such as shares and investments, as well as property, to raise the cash to pay your creditors.

- ✒ If you own a business this will almost certainly be sold.

- ✒ It is difficult to get a bank account or mortgage when you are a bankrupt.

- ✒ It is extremely expensive. All court and insolvency service fees are taken out of your assets and the Official Receiver also levies a 15 per cent charge on all sums received.

- ✒ If you want more than £250 credit, you must declare that you are an undischarged bankrupt.

- ✒ You can't hold public office or be an MP, solicitor, or accountant.

- ✒ Your name will be published in the local press, bringing unwanted publicity.

Bankruptcy is a last resort. Take advice before declaring yourself bankrupt by contacting one of the debt counselling groups listed in the previous section.

Book I

Organising Your Finances and Dealing with Debt

Chapter 5

Choosing a Credit Card

Credit cards have replaced cash as the most convenient way to pay for goods and services. Part of the reason for the growing popularity of credit cards is that they are becoming far cheaper. With an increasing number of issuers, including petrol stations, supermarkets, and football clubs as well as traditional high-street banks, interest rates are being forced down. Annual fees are thankfully becoming a thing of the past and there is a range of benefits available if you clear your balance every month. In other words, using a credit card is a smart way of keeping track of your spending, not necessarily a sign that it is out of control.

However, not all credit cards have low interest rates, no annual fees, and excellent perks. Some are still rather disappointing, charging interest at four or more times the Bank of England base rate. This chapter shows you how to avoid such cards – and where to seek out the better ones. We also look at how your credit rating affects the amount of interest you are charged on your card – and how you can improve it.

The world of finance is a fast-moving one. Facts and figures can change rapidly, so treat the examples in this chapter as a guide only.

Understanding How Credit Cards Work

A credit card can be used instead of cash to purchase goods or services. It is more convenient than cash because you don't have to go to an ATM to withdraw money every time you need to buy something or carry round lots of cash. However, unlike a debit card you are, in effect, borrowing money as you are spending the card issuer's cash: You pay this back at the end of the month when you get a statement listing your purchases. So if you don't clear the balance, you usually have to pay interest on your outstanding debt – unless you have a card with a 0 per cent offer.

If you have a large balance you wish to chip away at, consider switching to a card charging 0 per cent on balance transfers for 9 or 12 months to give you time to reduce the debt. You will be charged a transfer fee of 2.5–3 per cent, so it depends how long you are likely to take to reduce your balance. Or if you wish to support your favourite charity while you spend, you need a card that donates a percentage of your purchases to a specific charity. If you clear your balance every month, you need a card with perks such as a proportion of what you spend returned to you in the form of cash or AirMiles.

Calculating interest

Every credit card has an *annual percentage rate (APR)*, the interest the issuer charges you on purchases you don't pay off every month. You can use the APR to compare different cards: All issuers are obliged to tell you what the APR is when you apply.

Generally speaking, the lower the APR the better, although the rate of interest isn't important if you always clear your balance (see 'Enjoying the perks of clearing your balance every month' later in this chapter). APRs vary considerably between providers, so shop around for a competitive deal. Credit cards from the big four banks – Barclays, HSBC, Lloyds TSB, and NatWest – are around 12–17 per cent but others are below 10 per cent.

Some cards offer a 0 per cent introductory offer (see 'Sourcing good introductory rates' later in this chapter). If you are transferring a balance, you will be charged a one-off fee, however. Even on 0 per cent cards, you must still make the minimum payment (see 'Making the minimum payment' later in this chapter) or you will be charged a penalty.

Book I

**Organising
Your
Finances
and Dealing
with Debt**

Most credit cards have an interest-free credit period of up to 59 days, depending on the issuer (some interest-free credit periods last just 46 days). However, if you don't clear your balance within the interest-free period, your interest is normally calculated from the date the item is charged to your account – not the payment due date – usually the same day as you made the purchase or a couple of days later at most.

If you withdraw cash from an ATM using your credit card or ask for it from a retailer, interest at a higher rate is charged straightaway – even if you clear the balance when you receive your statement. You're also charged a fee (see 'Withdrawing cash' later in this chapter for more on this).

Figuring out credit limits

Your *credit limit* is the maximum, cumulative amount you can spend on your card. If you try to exceed your limit, your card is refused at the point of sale.

A credit limit of £6,000 is not a monthly limit but the total amount you can spend. So, if you spend £800 one month and don't clear the balance when your statement arrives, your *available credit* is £5,200 (£6,000 minus £800). After you pay back the £800, your full limit is restored.

Credit limits are not set in stone. They vary from customer to customer. Your card issuer calculates your limit by checking your credit file and giving you a credit score. The company giving you a card wants to be assured that you have a regular income and aren't over-committed with other loans, credit cards, and a mortgage. If you score well, you may get a credit limit of thousands of pounds. (Check out 'Considering your credit rating' later in this chapter).

Even if your card issuer grants you a credit limit beyond your wildest dreams, it doesn't mean you should spend every last penny of it. Doing so may lead to debt problems. Your credit limit is simply the card issuer's assessment of what it can comfortably let you borrow. It doesn't necessarily mean you should borrow that much.

Your card issuer reviews your credit limit on a regular basis and may raise your limit from time to time. You can also apply for an increase. You may want a higher limit if you have a particularly low limit or a one-off expense that you have no other way of paying. But if the latter is the case, take care. Borrowing on a credit card can be very expensive (unless you have a 0 per cent introductory offer), so consider whether this is the best method of getting your hands on extra cash.

Card issuers often raise your credit limit whether you ask for an increase or not. Credit card companies do this to encourage you to spend more money. Of course, your issuer dresses it up as though it is doing you the favour, writing you a letter in which you are 'congratulated' on your higher limit. Simply ignore the increase and resist the temptation to spend more just because extra credit is available to you.

Making the minimum payment

Although you don't have to clear your card balance every month, card issuers insist that you pay a minimum amount. This minimum is set out on your statement, either a fixed minimum payment or a percentage of the outstanding balance. It is usually no more than a token amount, so if you owe £600, say, you may be required to make a minimum payment of around £13.

Although it seems such a piddling sum that you might not bother paying it, there is a penalty if you don't pay the minimum amount. If you are on an introductory offer, the rate may be withdrawn and you will be switched to the issuer's standard rate. There is also a charge for not paying the minimum amount: Halifax, for example, charges customers £12.

The minimum payment is never much so you should have no problem paying it. If you are struggling to do so, it means your debts have got out of control and you're unlikely to be able to clear the full balance on your card any time soon, running up further interest. If this is the case, see it as a wake-up call and look at ways of clearing your balance (see 'Sourcing good introductory rates' in the following section).

If you make only the minimum payment each month, you will run up an even bigger balance because of the interest you will be charged. Even if you can't clear the entire balance, try at least to pay more than the minimum each month.

Finding Low Rates

If you regularly use your credit card but rarely or never pay off the full debt each month, the APR is extremely important. You need a card with a 0 per cent introductory rate of interest or a low long-term standard rate.

Sourcing good introductory rates

Many card providers offer 0 per cent introductory deals to new customers for a period of 5 to 12 months. This rate usually applies to new purchases, *balance transfers* (moving an existing balance from one card to another, in which case a transfer fee will be charged), or both. It may even apply to cash advances, although usually this isn't the case.

Find out exactly what charges apply to your card: Claiming ignorance when you've been stung with outrageous interest charges won't change the situation.

The advantage of a 0 per cent deal is that it can help you clear or reduce a large outstanding debt. For example: If you have a £2,000 balance on a card with a standard APR of 14.9 per cent, you may be able to pay only the interest on your debt each month. But if you transfer to a card offering 0 per cent for nine months, you can now clear some of the balance. You may have to pay a balance transfer fee of, say, 2.5 per cent, which amounts to £50. However, if you repay £70 a month (and don't spend any more), you can reduce your outstanding balance by £630 and save £202.55 in interest during this period. Once the offer ends, switch the remaining balance to a card offering a similar deal and continue until the debt is cleared.

If you continue spending on your card, you have to pay back the money eventually – it isn't free. So resist the temptation to run up huge debts simply because you aren't being charged any interest initially. This won't always be the case.

When the introductory period ends, the card reverts to the issuer's standard rate. This could be quite a lot higher than 0 per cent and if you have run up a sizeable balance, you could be stung for quite a hefty interest bill. To get round this, find another card offering 0 per cent on balance transfers and switch your debt to this new card.

If the issuer charges 0 per cent on balance transfers but not on new purchases, be wary of spending on the card or you could run up a lot of interest – at a rather higher rate than 0 per cent. Not only that but if you make any payments, the cheaper debt is usually cleared first – in this case, your transferred debt at 0 per cent – not the higher rate on new purchases.

You can own more than one card; so take out another offering 0 per cent on new purchases for spending.

Pursuing low lifetime balances

If you have serious debt, don't feel that a six-month introductory period is long enough to whittle it down and can't face the hassle of switching again when the offer ends, or if you usually carry some debt over at the end of the month, consider a card with a low lifetime balance. Any balance transferred to the card is charged interest at a low rate – the lowest is around 8 per cent.

While the balance transfer rate may be very competitive, the rate on new purchases might not be quite as attractive: It is usually the standard APR. If this is the case, get a second card for new purchases.

Enjoying the Perks of Clearing Your Balance Every Month

If you clear the balance on your credit card(s) every month, the rate of interest is irrelevant. Instead, look for cards that offer incentives which match your spending habits. Make sure you choose a card that doesn't charge an annual fee and then look for other benefits that provide a worthwhile return. Some schemes are more generous than others, so shop around till you find the best one for you.

Ensure you do pay your balance in full each month – thereby incurring no interest – by setting up a direct debit with your bank for the full amount each month. Then, all you have to make sure is that you have enough cash in your account to cover this.

Getting cashback

Several card providers offer *cashback* – a percentage of what you spend – which is paid to you via an annual cheque or subtracted from the balance on your card. Shop around, though, as cashback deals are thinner on the ground than they used to be. Only a couple of providers offer 1 per cent cashback and this is only for the first £2,000 spent on your card. After this, both revert to 0.5 per cent.

Earning loyalty points and Air Miles

You may prefer incentives such as a number of Air Miles related to how much you spend on your card or loyalty points for using your plastic in certain stores or to buy certain products. If you shop in Marks & Spencer or John Lewis on a regular basis, for example, it may be worth opting for one of their cards.

Going for the added extras

Card issuers sometimes attach a range of added benefits to your plastic, which may be attractive to you if you regularly travel or make purchases on your card. These may include:

- ✔ **Domestic warranty cover:** Protects electrical purchases bought with your card for up to a year after the manufacturer's warranty expires.

- ✔ **Price promise cover:** Ensures you're refunded the difference should you purchase an item and then find it cheaper elsewhere.

- ✔ **Free purchase protection insurance:** Covers your purchases against loss, theft or accidental damage for a limited period.

- ✔ **Free travel accident insurance:** Provides a limited form of travel insurance. Don't assume that this means you don't need to take out travel insurance; check the small print and buy a standalone policy as necessary.

Buying for charity and affinity groups

Instead of receiving something yourself, you may prefer to help a charity or organisation you feel strongly about. These affinity cards are issued in partnership with the charity or organisation, which receives a one-off donation when you first apply for the card or first use it. The initial donation tends to be between £10 and £20. An ongoing donation is also made based on a percentage of your spending – usually 0.25 per cent. The APR on such cards tends to be about average and you are unlikely to find a 0 per cent introductory offer.

Don't be fooled into thinking that cards that benefit charity have charitable terms and conditions. For example, one card has an APR of 142.9 on purchases, which is average, but on cash withdrawals it charges 27.9per cent. Keep an eye on the small print and don't assume anything.

Book I

Organising Your Finances and Dealing with Debt

Avoiding Certain Credit Card Activities

To use your credit card effectively, you need to watch out for hidden charges and stick to your debit card when making cash withdrawals. The following sections point out some credit card pitfalls to avoid.

Paying annual charges

Many card providers used to charge an annual fee for owning a credit card, though this practice has declined as the market has become more competitive. However, some providers still charge a fee, arguing that you get value-added goods and services in return. But in most cases, these aren't worth what you pay, particularly if you never use these services.

Withdrawing cash

It is never a good idea to withdraw cash using your credit card, as a *cash advance* is very expensive, with providers charging high rates of interest and fees. Even if your issuer is offering 0 per cent on new purchases and balance transfers on your card, this usually doesn't apply to cash advances. Most issuers charge a percentage of the amount withdrawn – 1.5 to 2.5 per cent, with a minimum charge of £2.50 to £3, every time.

The APR on cash advances is often far higher than on new purchases or balance transfers. For example, Bank of Scotland One Visa charges 9.9 per cent on purchases and 22.95 per cent on cash withdrawals. However, some providers such as Egg and Bank of Ireland charge the same on cash as on purchases. Be warned – on cash advances you are charged interest from the date of the transaction – there is no interest-free period.

Buying credit card protection

Another waste of money, credit card protection is offered by issuers for an annual fee of around £12–£15. If your card is lost or stolen, this protection ensures that you aren't liable if your card is used fraudulently before you have a chance to cancel it, as long as you aren't responsible for the loss or theft. But the same is true if you don't have this protection.

Have credit card, won't necessarily travel

If you thought using your card to withdraw cash in the UK is expensive, wait till you hit foreign shores. If you withdraw cash abroad, you're charged a *loading fee* – typically 2.75 per cent of the amount withdrawn. (This loading fee is also charged when you make purchases abroad using your card.) On top of this is an added ATM charge – around 2 per cent of the amount withdrawn (minimum £2). The problem is that you probably won't be aware of these charges until you receive your card statement back home and get a nasty shock.

Credit cards do have their advantages abroad: They are fairly safe, as fraudsters can't use them easily, and they are quick and simple to replace if they are lost or stolen. But to save money, stick to a debit card when withdrawing cash, preferably the Nationwide Flex account, which imposes no charges at all for withdrawing cash abroad. Or at least limit the number of withdrawals you make using your credit card.

Card protection can come in handy if you have several cards, and they're all lost or stolen at the same time – one call cancels them all. But if you can just as easily make the calls yourself: Keep a list of all the issuers' numbers near the phone so if you need to cancel your cards, you can do so quickly and easily, without paying for unnecessary insurance.

Protecting Your Purchases

If you purchase goods or services costing between £100 and £30,000 using a credit card, you are protected under Section 75 of the Consumer Credit Act 1974. Both the supplier and your card issuer are responsible if there is a problem. So if the supplier goes bust, for example, you should be able to get a refund from your card issuer.

Only credit cards are covered by this protection. It doesn't apply to debit cards, so think carefully before making a purchase on one of these, as you may be better off using your credit card.

Considering Your Credit Rating

When you apply for a credit card or any other form of loan, the lender checks your credit rating and assigns you a credit score before granting the card or loan.

If you have no previous credit history (no mortgage, other credit cards, or loans), have county court judgments (CCJs) against you, are in arrears or default, or are self-employed, you may find it difficult to get a credit card. Some card issuers specialise in such cases but charge a higher rate of interest than the typical rate. If you use such a card properly and repay at least the minimum amount each month, you can build or rebuild your credit rating before switching to a card with a more attractive rate.

Working with credit scoring

With credit scoring you are awarded points depending on your answers to questions on the card application form. The questions help the issuer assess how big a risk you are. How many points you earn determines whether the issuer lets you have a card at all and, if so, what your credit limit is.

If you don't have a high enough score, the issuer does one of the following:

- ✔ Refuses your application outright.

- ✔ Offers you a lower credit limit than you hoped for. You may be able to apply for a higher credit limit after you prove that you can repay what you owe.

- ✔ Charges a higher rate of interest. The advertised rate is not necessarily the one you receive. Many lenders treat the advertised rate as a *typical* rate and decide what to charge you according to your credit score. The riskier you are deemed to be, the more interest you have to pay. Check whether your rate can be reduced once you prove that you can meet your repayments.

If you fail the credit score, the issuer doesn't have to explain why. Scoring systems are commercially sensitive, so issuers prefer to keep them under wraps. Anyway, if you knew what answers they were looking for, you may fill out your application form accordingly so it wouldn't be a fair assessment.

While it may not go into details, the issuer should give you a general indication of why you failed the credit score, if you ask. Do so, as this may help you with further applications.

Correcting mistakes on your file

Book I

Organising
Your
Finances
and Dealing
with Debt

Credit card issuers check your credit file by applying to a credit reference agency. If you have a good credit history – haven't been declared bankrupt and have no CCJs against you – this helps your application.

Credit reference agencies hold all sorts of information on their files, including:

- ✔ **Public record information:** The UK electoral roll is used for checking names and addresses, CCJs, and bankruptcies and repossession orders.

- ✔ **Credit account information:** Includes information such as whether you've kept up to date with other payments and other borrowings you have, such as loans and credit cards.

- ✔ **Search information:** Every time you apply for credit, a *footprint* is recorded on your file. If you make a lot of applications over a short period of time, you appear desperate for credit. The card issuer will wonder why: Are you over-committed or committing fraud?

It is worth obtaining a copy of your credit file so that you can check it for errors and correct them. The Data Protection Act 1988 gives you the right to correct inaccurate information held about you. If you spot a mistake, contact the reference agency to find out how to remove or amend it. A note of correction may be added to your file.

To order a copy of your file, contact the three main agencies: Callcredit, Equifax, and Experian. You can get a copy of your file online; Experian makes no charge, Equifax charges £15 and Callcredit £9. You will need:

- ✔ Your full name and current address
- ✔ Date of birth
- ✔ Any addresses you have had in the past six years
- ✔ Whether you've changed your name in the past six years

Details for the three agencies are:

- ✔ Consumer Services Team, **Callcredit** plc, PO Box 491, Leeds, LS3 1WZ. Telephone 0870 060 1414 or www.callcredit.co.uk

- ✔ Credit File Advice Centre, **Equifax** plc, PO Box 1140, Bradford, BD1 5US. www.econsumer.equifax.co.uk

- ✔ Consumer Help Service, **Experian** Ltd, PO Box 8000, Nottingham, NG1 5GX. Telephone 0870 241 6212 or www.experian.com

Plenty of credit repair companies promise to clean up your credit file or help you obtain credit. Avoid them. These companies charge expensive fees but are limited in what they can do because only genuinely incorrect information can be removed, which you can do yourself using the information in this section.

Failing credit scoring

If you fail the credit score, it doesn't necessarily mean that no issuer will let you have a credit card. Issuers use different criteria in assessing whether to lend to you or not, and some may give more points to certain aspects of your score than others.

You could try other issuers to see whether they will consider your credit card application. But remember, each application is recorded on your credit file, so if you try several issuers to no avail, you harm your credit rating.

If you do fail, it may be the case that you are over-committed. Look candidly at your debts to assess whether this is the case. If it is, work out how you can cut back on the debt you already have before taking on even more. This will enable you to pass the credit score next time, as well as manage your debts more easily.

Chapter 6

Weighing Up Personal Loans

* *

In This Chapter

▶ Deciding whether a loan is the answer

▶ Investigating loans and how they work

▶ Searching for a loan that suits

▶ Ensuring you don't get stung on insurance

▶ Managing repayment problems

* *

No matter how good you are at managing your finances, from time to time you may need to borrow money. This may be to cover the cost of a big outgoing, such as a new car or kitchen for example, where the alternative is years of saving. In such a situation, you may want to consider a personal loan.

Redemption penalties for repaying a loan ahead of schedule and expensive payment protection insurance lie in wait to trip up the unwary. In this chapter we show you what to look out for when choosing a loan to avoid spending more than you absolutely need to. If you are looking for a mortgage, you won't find the necessary information in this chapter: You need to go to Chapter 3 in Book III for that.

Figuring Out When a Loan Makes Perfect Sense

If you need at least a couple of thousand pounds in the medium term to buy anything from plastic surgery to a new kitchen or a cruise, a loan can be a good choice. Loans are useful because:

✔ **You can borrow more than you can on a credit card or overdraft:** You can take out a personal loan for any amount, usually between £500 and £25,000. You may even be able to borrow more than this via a secured loan (see 'Taking out unsecured versus secured loans' later in this chapter for more details).

✔ **The rate of interest is normally fixed:** You know exactly how much you have to pay back over the term of the loan, making it easy to budget.

✔ **You know when the debt will be cleared:** Loans have a fixed repayment schedule, unlike an overdraft or credit card where you pay the money back as and when you can. If you lack the discipline to do this, a loan could be the answer.

✔ **A loan is easy to arrange:** Loans can be arranged through the post, over the telephone, or via the Internet. There is no need to make an appointment to see your bank manager. The money is sent to you by cheque or transferred to your bank account within days.

✔ **Your borrowing is limited:** You get a specified amount of cash – you can't keep dipping in and taking more, as you can with an overdraft or credit card.

As long as you can afford the monthly repayments and shop around for the cheapest deal you can find, a loan can be a good choice for borrowing money.

Deciding When a Loan Is Not a Good Idea

A personal loan isn't always the ideal way of borrowing money. You might want to think twice if:

✔ **You need to borrow only a few hundred pounds:** The smaller the sum you borrow, the higher the rate of interest you pay. Borrowing an amount under £1,000 is extremely expensive in terms of interest charges. Most lenders also have a minimum that you can borrow: If you need less, you may find yourself taking out a bigger loan simply in order to get the money in the first place. This isn't a wise move. You may be better off borrowing smaller sums on a credit card or extending your overdraft instead of opting for a loan.

✔ **You can repay the money in a couple of months:** The shorter the loan's term, the bigger your monthly repayments, so work out whether you could afford them if you take a loan out for just a year or so. If there's a chance that you'll be able to clear the loan even sooner, you may be charged a redemption penalty for doing so (see 'Watching out for early redemption penalties' later in this chapter). If this is the case, you may be better off borrowing on a credit card with a 0 per cent introductory period for several months instead. This may be enough time to repay your borrowings – without having to pay any interest at all. (See Chapter 5 for more on credit cards.)

 ✔ **You're borrowing £20,000 or so to improve your property:** If you already have a mortgage, it might be cheaper to ask your mortgage lender to extend your home loan rather than take out a personal loan particularly if you need money to build an extension or otherwise fix up your home. Although interest rates on personal loans have fallen, they still tend to be higher than mortgage rates (the cheapest loan is around 6 per cent compared with mortgage rates of less than 5 per cent). So you pay less interest if you increase your mortgage instead. This may also be easier to arrange than a personal loan because you already have a relationship with the lender.

Think carefully before extending your mortgage and overburdening yourself. Your home is at risk if you can't keep up the repayments on it, whereas if you take out an unsecured loan to pay for your extension, your home is safe (even if you default on the loan payments). Don't gamble with the roof over your head.

Book I

Organising Your Finances and Dealing with Debt

Understanding How Loans Work

You can borrow between £500 and £25,000 on a personal loan. Some lenders let you borrow quite a lot more than £25,000 if you opt for a secured loan (the next section addresses secured and unsecured loans). You choose the repayment period, which can be anything from six months to seven or even ten years.

Repayments are monthly, usually by direct debit from your bank account. If you opt for a flexible loan, you may be allowed to overpay or make lump-sum payments in order to clear the debt more quickly. However, generally speaking, lenders charge a penalty if you pay off your loan early.

Taking out unsecured versus secured loans

There are two main types of loan available: unsecured and secured. The former offers the lender no security, the latter offers the security of your home. So if you fail to keep up the repayments and have a secured home, the lender has a claim on it. We explain this in more detail in the following sections.

You might opt for a secured loan if you have a poor credit rating, but you may be able to find a cheaper, unsecured loan if you are prepared to shop around instead.

Unsecured loans

Most personal loans are *unsecured*, which means that the lender has no security for your debt. If you fail to make your repayments, the lender doesn't have the automatic right to seize an asset, such as your home. The lender can pursue you through the courts for an unpaid loan, however, so you aren't totally off the hook if you don't pay up.

Unsecured loans of up to £25,000 are governed by the Consumer Credit Act 1974, so are also known as *regulated loans*. This is not the case with secured loans, which aren't covered by the Act. The Act strictly regulates how money is lent and ensures that the lender must give you seven days to change your mind about taking out a loan.

Secured loans

On *secured loans*, your assets, such as property or investments, provide the lender with some security. If you default on your repayments, your lender can take you to court and demand repossession of the property you used to secure the loan.

If the loan is secured against your home, and your home is still mortgaged, the loan is known as a *second charge loan*.

Secured loans have a lower APR than unsecured loans because they are less risky from the lender's perspective. They are also easier to come by for this reason.

Secured loans are not regulated by the Consumer Credit Act, so make sure you read the terms and conditions extremely carefully before signing the credit agreement, as it is binding. The lender is not obliged to give you seven days to change your mind, as is the case with unsecured loans.

You can usually borrow more on a secured loan as the lender is taking on less risk because it knows it will get its money back if you default. Most lenders offering secured loans will let you borrow up to £50,000 – although some may let you borrow up to £100,000. However, if you need to borrow this much, consider remortgaging instead, as you should be able to get a cheaper rate.

The term of a secured loan can be longer than a secured loan – up to 25 years in some cases. You will be charged a penalty for repaying the loan early, so check with the lender what this is before signing on the dotted line.

Book I

Organising
Your
Finances
and Dealing
with Debt

Deciding on the term

You can choose how long you want to pay off the loan within the minimum and maximum terms on offer. The longer the term of the loan, the lower your monthly repayments (so if you opt for five years rather than two you pay less each month) but the more you end up paying in the long run. You pay more interest and make more payments over a longer term.

Consider the term of the loan carefully. If you need cash to pay for a dream holiday this summer, for example, do you really want to still be paying it back in four years' time? But whatever term you choose, make sure it is realistic: Don't overstretch yourself with massive monthly payments just to clear the loan within a year if there's no way you will be able to cope.

Working out the interest

The lender charges interest on the amount you borrow, known as the *annual percentage rate (APR)*. This is usually a fixed percentage, but may be variable. Every loan has an APR, which you can use to compare deals to find the cheapest one. How much you borrow, for how long, and the lender's perception of your chances of repaying it all affect the APR you are charged.

The advertised APR can be misleading. This headline rate is usually the best deal available. To qualify for this rate, you may have to take out the biggest loan that the lender offers, which may be far more than you need. Borrow a smaller amount and you are likely to be charged a higher APR. However, this shouldn't be seen as an excuse for taking out a bigger loan than you need.

Whether your interest rate is fixed or variable can make quite a difference to your repayments, so ensure you understand which type you are signing up for:

- ✔ Fixed rate: Interest is the same throughout the term of the loan, no matter what happens to the Bank of England base rate. This enables you to budget, as your monthly repayments are always the same.

- ✔ Variable rate: The APR rises or falls in line with changes to the base rate. Your monthly repayments are therefore not fixed, which makes budgeting harder. However, if the base rate goes down, and the APR on your loan falls accordingly, your repayments are lower than if you'd opted for a fixed-rate loan. However, the reverse can also happen if rates increase, so you are taking a risk. If this would be a struggle for you, opt for a fixed-rate loan.

Some lenders charge a lower APR if you apply for a loan over the Internet rather than the telephone, post, or in a branch. Find out whether this is the case: If it is, apply online if you can.

Calculating the total cost

In order to compare loans from different providers, find out exactly what the lender charges for the amount of cash you want to borrow. Otherwise, the comparison is meaningless. The lender may simply provide you with the monthly cost, rather than the full amount. Check how much you pay in total to compare with other providers and work out whether it's a good deal or not.

It's worth doing the sums yourself so you know exactly how much you are paying in the long run. Then you can consider whether it *is* such a good deal. For example, if you want to borrow £5,000 over three years, you may find two lenders charging you £150.89 and £168.68 a month respectively. The latter may not seem that much more and you may well be able to afford the extra. But if you consider how much extra you will pay over the term of the loan, you might think twice: £5,432 on the first loan and £6,072 on the latter. That's a difference of £640 – a significant amount.

Watching out for early redemption penalties

A low APR is important when choosing a loan, but you should also watch out for early redemption penalties, also known as *early settlement charges*, which can push up the overall cost.

Some lenders, not all, charge a redemption penalty if you clear your loan ahead of schedule. This comes as a shock to many borrowers: According to the Department of Trade and Industry, 62 per cent are not aware that early settlement charges apply if they repay their loan ahead of schedule.

Some lenders charge a redemption penalty of one or two months' interest but, under changes to the Consumer Credit Act, lenders are no longer able to charge more than one month's interest. While this is encouraging, you are better off selecting a lender who doesn't charge a redemption penalty: Several lenders have scrapped this practice. When shopping around for a loan, make sure you ask lenders whether they charge a redemption penalty.

You may be charged a higher APR for taking on a loan with no early settlement charges, but if there's a chance that you might repay your loan ahead of schedule, it's still worth considering.

Aiming for flexibility

Most loans are fixed, so you borrow a set amount over a certain period and pay the same amount each month to clear the debt. But there are a smaller number of flexible deals available, allowing you to overpay or pay a lump sum to clear your debt early (without penalty).

You may also be able to take a repayment holiday (which means you don't have to make a repayment for anything up to several months). You can do this at the start of the loan or at an agreed date during the loan. But you must arrange this with your lender: You can't simply stop making your repayments without warning.

Even when you take a payment holiday, your outstanding balance continues to accrue interest. This may result in higher monthly payments to ensure that your debt is still repaid over the term of the loan as agreed at the outset.

With a flexible deal, you don't have to take all the cash in one go. Instead, you may also be able to withdraw funds from the account on a rolling basis, as long as you stay within your credit limit. So you apply for the full extent of the cash you need in the first instance and then take it as and when you require it.

Finding the Best Personal Loan

Long gone are the days when you had to put on your best suit, polish your shoes, and make an appointment to visit your bank manager to grovel for a loan. Nowadays, you can apply online in a matter of minutes and receive the cash within hours.

Shopping around is also easier than ever if you have access to the Internet, as there are a number of sites which enable you to compare the cost of products. Check out www.moneyextra.com, www.moneyfacts.co.uk, and www.moneysupermarket.com for more details. Most of these sites have links direct through to lenders, so you can click on a button and up pops an application form immediately. It couldn't be simpler, so think carefully before taking the plunge and committing yourself to something you can't really afford.

If you don't have Internet access, keep an eye on loan adverts and 'best-buy' tables in the quality weekend newspapers for the cheapest deals. You can get loans for under 7 per cent, so anything around this mark is good value. If the APR is in double digits, it should be avoided.

If you are buying a new car or kitchen, the retailer will probably try to persuade you to take out its finance deal. This may be tempting as it saves you the bother of searching for finance, but it is unlikely to be the cheapest solution. You're better off searching for a cheap personal loan instead.

The advantage of arranging a loan before making your purchase is that you will be, in effect, a cash buyer as far as the retailer is concerned. You should be able to drive a bargain and perhaps get a discount, as well as saving interest on the loan.

Applying for a Loan

After choosing the loan you want, you have to complete an application form. The application asks for details of your existing financial commitments and income. The lender uses this to assess whether you can afford to take on the loan and repay it. If you are married, both you and your spouse must be named on the application form: The lender insists upon this.

The lender also contacts credit reference agencies to obtain a copy of your credit file. Your credit file indicates whether you have any outstanding county court judgments against you, are bankrupt, or have a history of defaulting on debts. (See Chapter 5 for more on your credit file and obtaining a copy to check this information.)

Lenders also use credit scoring, enabling them to work out what category of borrower you are, according to your personal circumstances (see Chapter 5 for more details). This enables it to work out what APR to charge you: The higher risk you appear, the higher the APR will be.

When the lender is happy with the result of its checks, it offers you a loan. It usually takes only a few hours or days to process an application, depending on the lender. If the lender isn't happy with its findings, you may be refused a loan.

As well as being a great place to search for a loan, the Internet also provides the easiest way of applying to borrow cash. And because fewer administration costs are involved, lenders tend to offer a lower APR if you apply for your loan online rather than via the post, in person at your local branch, or over the telephone.

If you've had difficulty repaying credit in the past, you may have a bad credit history. This history is unearthed when you apply for a new loan and the lender runs a credit check on you. As a result, your application may be turned down.

It's not only people with bad credit histories who are refused credit. If you don't have a credit history because you've never had a credit card, loan, or mortgage before, the lender won't be able to figure out whether you are a good risk or not. How can the lender tell whether you are going to make your repayments every month if you haven't done this before? If you're self-employed you may also find it more difficult to get credit, or if you've changed jobs recently. And moving around frequently doesn't look good either.

If any of these apply to you, don't give up just yet. A number of lenders specifically target people with bad credit histories or those who have difficulty getting a loan. If you apply to one of these lenders, you increase your chances of success but you also have to pay a higher APR – because you are perceived as being higher risk. This could be more than twice as much as the cheapest loan on the market, so the extra cost can be considerable.

Even if you do pay a higher APR initially, you may not always have to pay over the odds. Once you build up a payment history, it has the same effect as rebuilding your credit history (or creating a new one). This will go on your credit file, so when you apply for credit in the future it will count in your favour and you should be able to qualify for a standard loan with a lower APR.

Alternatively, if you are having difficulty getting an unsecured loan and are a homeowner, you can opt for a secured loan. Because the lender has the added benefit of security – in other words an ultimate claim to your property if you default on your repayments – it is more likely to consider lending you money. (See 'Taking out unsecured versus secured loans' earlier in this chapter for more details.)

Avoiding Payment Protection Insurance

When you take out a personal loan, you must sign a binding credit agreement. This commits you to making the repayments each month, even if you lose your job, or become ill or sick so you can no longer work. To protect yourself, you can take out a form of insurance called *payment protection* to ensure that your repayments are still made – even if you personally can't afford to do so. Some policies also clear your debt if you die leaving an outstanding loan, making life easier for your dependants.

Working out the cost

While you may think this cover is vital, it is expensive and largely unnecessary. To make matters worse, many lenders conceal the true cost by automatically adding the cost of cover to the loan, whether you request it or not. The danger is that you assume you have to take it out, which is nonsense. And you also don't appreciate exactly how much the insurance is costing you.

Do the sums to find out the true cost of cover. For example, if you borrow £5,000 over three years with payment protection, it could cost you £171.39 a month (for a 6.4 per cent loan from Northern Rock). But if you opted not to take out the cover, your monthly repayments would be £152.65, a saving of £18.74. Over three years, the insurance would cost you £674.64.

Checking the small print

Both the level of cover and cost of protection vary considerably between lenders, so check individual policies so you know exactly what is included – and what isn't. Most policies don't let you claim immediately after you are out of work: There is usually an excess period of 60 days or longer before you can make a claim. Decide whether you could cope without an income for this period of time. If you can't, shop around for another policy which doesn't have such a long excess: A number of providers have an excess of 30 days, for example.

Loan payment protection can be comforting, but it is also usually extremely expensive, particularly if you buy cover from your loan provider. Standalone payment protection policies offer much better value for money. For example, if a person borrowing £5,000 over three years from Northern Rock at 6.4 per cent shopped around for cover instead of buying it from the lender, they could pay £6.16 a month for insurance from a broker via an online search at www.moneysupermarket.com. This is a saving of more than two thirds, amounting to a saving of over £450 over the term of the loan.

Deciding whether you need cover

You may wonder whether this insurance is just another method devised by the industry to make money out of you, or if it is worth having. Much depends on your personal circumstances and whether you have other savings or investments, which could be used to clear your loan if you lose your job or can't work.

If you're seriously worried about losing your job, think about whether now is the best time to take on extra borrowing. Perhaps it's wiser to wait until the situation is clearer and you know where you stand with your employer.

Check whether you already have some cover for sickness or accident – perhaps from your employer. If this is the case, you don't need to purchase further cover: You may only need the unemployment element. There is no point doubling up on cover, as it will just cost you more than you need to pay.

 If you're self-employed, there's little point taking out this cover because it usually only pays out if you wind up your business – not if you don't have any work on. Don't waste your money.

Taking Action If You Are Struggling with Repayments

If you have problems meeting your loan repayments – and have no payment protection – resist the temptation to ignore the problem and hope it goes away. Ask your lender for advice: The earlier you get in touch and explain the situation, the more understanding the lender is likely to be.

 If your home is secured against your loan, it is particularly important to seek help as soon as possible. Otherwise, you are at risk of losing the roof over your head.

If you don't feel you can speak to your lender for whatever reason, a number of organisations provide free advice and will contact the lender to negotiate on your behalf. Try your local Citizens Advice Bureau (details in your local phone book). Alternatively, try the National Debtline (www.nationaldebtline.co.uk) or the Consumer Credit Counselling Service (www.cccs.co.uk).

 Steer clear of debt management companies that organise your debts into one monthly payment for a fee. Try the free advice services instead of going down this route, particularly if it is just your loan you are having trouble repaying. (Chapter 4 has more information on debt management companies.)

Book II
Paying Less Tax

In this Book . . .

This Book is your essential practical guide to paying less tax. Covering everything from sorting our your self-assessment forms, to mastering PAYE or working for yourself, follow the advice within this Book and you could make some serious savings.

Here are the contents of Book II at a glance:

Chapter 1: Understanding Tax Basics

Chapter 2: Dealing with Self Assessment

Chapter 3: Taxing Family Situations

Chapter 4: Understanding Tax When You Work for Someone Else

Chapter 5: Working for Yourself Can Be Less Taxing

Chapter 6: Taxing Your Savings and Investments

Chapter 1

Understanding Tax Basics

*T*he truth about taxes is that they pay for the services the government provides such as education, the National Health Service, and the police. Lower taxes mean either the government provides fewer services so you get less, or it has to borrow money in order to provide the same services. If it borrows, interest rates go up so your mortgage, credit card and any other loans cost you more. Simple, isn't it!

The UK has one of the world's most complex tax systems. But that bold statement only holds true for some people some of the time. Provided you earn around the average amount and don't get income from a second home, investments overseas, a spare job, an at-home business – or any of a number of other sources – and aren't concerned with what happens to your money and assets after you die, you need never come into direct contact with HMRC. Your employer or investment broker will make sure you pay your tax liabilities.

However, if you're better-off than average, worse-off than average, have much in the way of savings, have children, are retired, are saving up for a pension, run a business, make profits buying and selling things, have spare-time work, or hope to leave reasonable amounts to your family after you die, then you have to interact with HMRC.

Even if you don't currently need to have direct dealings with HMRC, the UK's all-powerful tax organisation, you'll need to understand the tax system sooner or later. If you buy one investment, or have a child, or get a workplace perk such as free or subsidised private medical insurance cover, you have a reason to interact with HMRC.

This chapter starts with an overview of how the tax system works.

Laying Out the Basics of the Tax System

We bet you thought tax was tax! But there's a huge variety of ways the state takes what it needs from the taxpayers who provide the wealth that pays for all those hospitals, schools, and roads. So here's a list of the taxes that can involve you as an individual:

- **Income tax** is levied on what you earn at work or the profit you make if you are self-employed. You also have to pay it on the returns you make on savings. Surprise: state benefits such as the basic retirement pension are counted. Income tax levels are currently at 0 per cent, 10 per cent, 20 per cent, 22 per cent, and 40 per cent.

  As of April 2008, the Treasury has decided that income tax levels will be simplified – the 10 per cent rate will disappear altogether and the basic rate will be reduced to 20 per cent. Those losing out are expected to be single people and those without children on smaller incomes (£5,000 to £15,000), who do not qualify for higher benefits and tax credits designed to help families.

- **National Insurance** is a tax on those who work and the people they work for. Both employee and employer have to pay. There are special rules for the self-employed. Surprise: You can pay national insurance even if you don't earn enough to pay income tax. The rates are very complicated but most people pay 11 per cent across most of their earnings from work. (Chapter 4 in this part explains national insurance in more detail.)

- **Capital gains tax** is payable on the profit you make when you sell certain assets such as shares and properties. Surprise: There's no tax to pay if you sell something with an expected useful life of 50 or fewer years. So you'd have to pay on selling an Old Master but not on a piece of Britart that probably won't last so long (try thinking dead sheep pickled in formaldehyde.) You could lose up to 40 per cent of your profits to capital gains tax (which is addressed in more detail in Chapter 6 in this part).

- **Inheritance tax** is paid on what you leave behind when you die. Surprise: one great way of reducing the tax is to spend, spend, spend, while you are living. There's just one rate – 40 per cent – but Chapter 4 in Book V points out ways to avoid paying any.

✔ **Corporation tax** is a tax on company profits. Surprise: There is a zero per cent rate.

✔ **Value added tax (VAT)** is added by most businesses every time goods change hands or they go through another process. The end result is a sales tax on many items and services you buy. Surprise: Millions of pounds were spent on a legal case to decide whether a Jaffa Cake is a cake or a biscuit. Cakes are tax-free, biscuits are taxed. The current VAT rate is 17.5 per cent and Chapter 5 in this part has more on VAT.

✔ **Council tax** is paid on your residence whether you own it, are buying it, or are renting it. Surprise: Two can't live as cheaply as one as there are rebates if a property has only one adult occupant rather than two or more. What you pay depends on where you live and the value of your property.

✔ **Stamp duty** is paid on most property transactions and on most stock market deals. Stamp duty ranges from 1 per cent to 4 per cent depending on the value of the property. Surprise: The tax does not go up evenly. Sell a house for £499,999 and you pay £14,999.97. But if you get £500,001 for the same property, the tax goes up to £20,000.03.

Book II

Paying Less Tax

Considering Tax and Your Family

Single people without dependants or partners have an easier tax life than most. The rest of the population has to juggle roles as parents, grandparents, or children. Many may have to deal with their own parents and their own children at the same time.

Family tax-saving pointers to consider include:

✔ **Deciding whether to marry:** Thanks to independent taxation, women's tax lives are no longer subordinate to their husband's tax concerns. Crazy as it sounds, there are still lots of occasions when married people can do better out of the tax system. Civil partnerships carry the same tax status. Try Chapter 3 in this part for information on whether to tie the financial knot or not.

✔ **Passing assets between spouses:** Swapping savings accounts between the two of you can save a lot in tax. But do you trust each other that much? And what happens if you divorce? Chapter 3 is better than a visit to a matrimonial guidance agency.

✔ **Working out the best way for children to pay less tax on savings accounts:** It should be easy. But it all depends on where the money came from. Turn to Chapter 3 for childhood tax issues.

✔ **Looking at employing partners and children in family businesses:** This is fine as long as the work's real and the rates you pay are sensible. Chapter 5 in this part has more details.

✔ **Arranging the best way to take advantage of capital gains tax exemptions:** Two can sell more cheaply than one if you follow some simple rules. Take a look at Chapter 6 in this part.

✔ **Taking advice on how to deal with the tax benefits of pension payments:** Simplification has made pension planning easier, but there are still pitfalls to watch out for. Look at Chapters 2 and 3 in Part IV.

✔ **Knowing how to deal with your pension when you take it:** There's a basic choice for many which can mean paying more or less tax for the same income. It all comes down to how you invest retirement cash as Chapter 2 in Book IV shows.

✔ **Calculating tax bills in retirement:** Just because you stop work doesn't mean your relationship with HMRC changes. It can get more complicated.

✔ **Realising that the old saying about the inevitability of taxes and death is correct:** Items such as your home and certain savings and investments that escape tax while you are alive will be caught for possibly even more tax after you die. Turn to Chapter 4 in Book V for tips.

Running through the Tax Year

A number of key dates and deadlines run through each year. Some involve your employer sending various forms that you will need to incorporate on your tax return; others involve deadlines for claiming credits.

The tax year starts on 6 April each year. Whatever the reason for that date (the nearby 'What a silly date!' sidebar shares some theories), HMRC realises that most people are paid monthly, so it works on the basis that 31 March is the end of the year for many employees. But 5 April as a year-end still applies to many investment-related matters such as individual savings accounts or capital gains tax. However, more up-to-date tax systems such as value added tax (VAT) use the standard calendar.

When 5 April is a weekend, or a Bank Holiday (such as Good Friday or Easter Monday) fund management firms publicise any special arrangements on last-minute individual savings accounts (ISAs) because if you don't use your ISA in the tax year, you lose it forever. Some investment firms bring the staff in on a weekend or Bank Holiday. But whatever day of the week 5 April falls on, it is the date on the paperwork that determines which year counts for tax-free benefits or taxable transactions.

What a silly date!

No other nation has such a daft tax-year date. No one is too sure why this date was chosen. But here are some possibilities:

✔ Some think it was because the Christian calendar features Easter as a starting time. This also reflects pre-Christian Europe, when the end of the winter snows and the start of plants growing marked the beginning of the year.

✔ Another theory is related to the historical use of the Feast of Annunciation of the Virgin Mary on 25 March – nine months before Christmas. The feast day, called Lady Day, was the start of the religious year, and when the church was paramount, the start of the secular year as well. When Britain moved to the Gregorian calendar in 1752, 11 days were added to 25 March as the tax authorities wanted to maintain a full 365 day tax year.

✔ Some say 6 April came about because of the largely rural nature of the UK when income tax was introduced during the Napoleonic wars. April gave farmers a chance to work out how much they had earned over the whole year. It also gave landlords a fortnight or so after they collected quarterly rents on March 25.

✔ In pre-railway Britain, the April date gave taxpayers the chance to send in details of their income in the summer when the roads were easily passable by stage coaches.

Each tax year follows a set pattern:

✔ **6 April:** The self assessment return form for the tax year which has just ended is sent out to those who previously received a return, to those who have declared they should in future have one, and to anyone else HMRC thinks should get one. The form is also available online for downloading and printing. You can electronically file a return via the internet from this date should you wish. See Chapter 2 in this part for information on the form itself.

✔ **31 May:** The deadline for receiving form P60 showing your previous year's earnings from your employer. This is the latest date you can get this.

✔ **5 July:** The deadline for tax credit applications backdated to the start of the tax year. This is a use-it-or-lose-it benefit – you cannot go back further than three months. Chapter 3 in this part has more information.

✔ **6 July:** The deadline for receiving form P11D or form P9D from your employer. These forms give financial details of the value of any fringe benefits such as a company car or a medical insurance scheme your employer provided over the previous tax year. Chapter 4 in this part explains benefits-in-kind.

✔ **31 July:** The final date for sending in the second interim instalment of tax due for the tax year which ended in the preceding April. This only applies to some who file self-assessment returns, usually the self-employed or those with large investment incomes.

✔ **30 September:** The filing deadline if you want HMRC to calculate your tax due under self assessment. It is also the last date if you want HMRC to collect any tax due out of your future Pay As You Earn (PAYE) deductions via a tax code change (but see 30 December as well).

✔ **5 October:** The deadline for informing HMRC that you had new sources of income such as self-employment earnings during the previous tax year. You risk having to pay a penalty if you don't notify HMRC of changes in your tax status by this date. This is also the deadline to report new sources of capital gains over the preceding tax year.

✔ **30 December:** The notification deadline for employees who file tax returns over the Internet (known as *e-filing*) to opt for tax due up to £2,000 to come out of their regular income via a PAYE tax code change.

✔ **31 January:** The big date! It's the final day for filing the self-assessment return. And it is the day for the first interim payment on the current tax year as well as the final, balancing payment, for the tax year that ended the previous April. In the past, HMRC has stretched January 31 by one or two days when it falls on a weekend.

✔ **1 March:** The automatic surcharge starts for those who failed to comply with the January 31 deadline. This is in addition to the automatic fine levied on February 1.

✔ **5 April:** End of the tax year.

To qualify for tax savings, you have to take care of a number of financial and investment transactions *before* the end of the tax year. These are use-them-or-lose-them allowances.

New forms are sent out again on April 6 and the whole cycle starts all over again.

Filing dates change for tax returns issued after April 2008 (covering the tax year 2007-08 and subsequent years). From then on you'll have to be quicker returning your self-assessment form. The new deadline for paper-based filings will be brought forward to 30 September (so, for example, 2007-08 returns will have to be filed by 30 September 2008), though if you file online you will still have until 31 January of the following year.

Keeping Good Personal Records

Keeping good records can help you save on tax. It is often only when the tax year is finished that you realise you could have claimed for something or that tax deducted at source should not have been. Having the paperwork to hand simplifies everything. Additionally, you should only make a claim for tax relief on an item such as a personal pension purchase if you have the paperwork as a back-up.

Keeping only some of the required records can be almost as bad as keeping none at all. It won't take a genius at HMRC to spot suspicion-raising gaps. This may sound really, really basic, but it is far easier to have a regular day once a month to get on top of the paperwork than let it all pile up over a year. If there's not a *Keep Your Home Tidy For Dummies,* then the For Dummies publishers should get around to commissioning it! (But we're not putting ourselves forward to write it.)

Book II

Paying Less Tax

Identifying who needs to keep records

Everyone should keep financial records. Even if you don't have to fill in a self assessment form, you should still maintain good record keeping.

Failing to keep records; paying fines

You can be fined up to £3,000 for each year when you fail to keep the required records. This amount is intended as a deterrent. It is only used sparingly. You will usually receive a written caution for a first offence unless you have deliberately destroyed records you are known to have had. In this latter case, you can expect the full fine and some more for other offences that may be uncovered.

Your failure to show records is more likely to result in the tax inspector refusing to allow you to claim tax relief. Small or spare-time businesses may be barred from deducting legitimate expenses, for example.

Don't forget, HMRC can uncover bank interest payments as well as details of payments in and out of your bank accounts if it has to.

But HMRC is aware that it can sometimes be difficult for an individual to approach an employer for paperwork, especially if the employee has left. In some circumstances, it can approach your employer, or former employer, for records on your behalf.

Keeping records goes beyond tax

Obviously, proper record keeping makes it easier to fill in your tax form or less costly if you employ an accountant on your behalf. But record keeping goes beyond keeping straight with HMRC.

The discipline can help you see when you are spending too much or getting too little from your investments and savings. You may also find it easier to get loans if you can show full proof of earnings and other income.

If your earnings are low enough, you may be able to claim a rebate of the tax taken from the interest on your bank accounts. And look on the bright side: You may be a basic rate taxpayer at the start of the tax year, but who knows? Your mediocre share portfolio might soar in value so you sell out at a huge profit leading to a capital gains tax liability. Or you might get a big pay rise that takes you into the top-rate zone when you'll need to fill out a form and declare all your savings and investment returns. Or you might scoop the lottery!

People who use an accountant to file their tax forms still need to keep records themselves. Many accountants and tax professionals limit their help to processing the figures you give them. You need records for that.

But even if your tax form filler is willing to take a big pile of paper and create some order out of your chaos, make sure you take photocopies of everything as well as insisting on the return of the originals. And expect to pay an awful lot for this.

Sorting out what to keep

Record keeping should start from the viewpoint that you only recycle paperwork that you know you won't need. Keep everything else, starting with anything that says *Keep This*. Bank statements, wages slips, and paperwork from investment firms are all vital.

Pension information is important to keep, including records showing how much you paid in to personal pension plans. If you are retired, keep details of pension payments you receive whether from company schemes or insurance companies.

Save statements from the Benefits Agency about your State Pension or any other taxable social security benefit.

Keep records of payments you make under the Gift Aid scheme for charitable giving.

When you give money or assets away to reduce the impact of inheritance tax, receipts or similar proof can come in handy if HMRC decide to query the reduction in your capital.

Holding onto work-related paper

Keep forms your employer gives you such as the P60 form showing end-of-year earnings. If you are out of work, or you have changed jobs, the P45 you were given when you left your last workplace becomes a vital document to show your earnings up to that date. Likewise, keep information on redundancy or other termination payments.

Book II

Paying Less Tax

Some other employment-related records to keep include

- ✔ The P11D (or P9D) which shows your payments-in-kind from your employer. *Payments-in-kind* are perks such as a company car, gym membership, and private medical insurance.

- ✔ Details of any bonuses you earned. These can include 'prizes' for achievements such as visits to 'conferences' in exotic locations.

- ✔ Records of any share incentive schemes operated by your employer to which you subscribed.

- ✔ Evidence of expenses paid by your employer for use of your own car. In addition, if you use your own vehicle or pedal cycle for work travel you can claim for the cost of fuel, and something towards other expenses such as maintenance and vehicle depreciation, but you cannot claim for commuting. So keep records. Chapter 4 in this part has more details.

Keep evidence of payments made to professional bodies if you claim membership fees.

If you are lucky enough to get benefits such as expensive gifts or foreign travel (a supplier-sponsored golfing weekend at St. Andrews, for example) from an organisation other than your employer as part of your work, keep those records because there is a chance you may be taxed on them as a perk of your employment even if your own boss did not pay for them. (Don't worry, you can ignore items of negligible value such as diaries or pens or calculators or paperweights with a value of less than £25. And non-monetary gifts costing no more than £250 in total over a year are also outside the tax net whether given to you or your family provided they are not linked to any specific services you have supplied.)

Travelling for work

Most employers pay your expenses when you have out-of-pocket costs such as travelling on behalf of your firm or organisation.

But there may be cases where your employer does not refund expenses which you have had to incur as part of your work. In that case, keep a record of mileage details if you drive (including dates, destinations, parking fees and tolls); foreign travel itineraries including tickets, hotel receipts, credit card statements, and cheque stubs.

Your employer will probably require you to keep these proofs anyway to show the money is a refund of expenses and not an attempt to pay you without an Income Tax or a National Insurance deduction.

Certain professions have specific record-keeping duties:

- ✔ If you're a sub-contractor in the construction industry, save certificates of tax deducted under the special scheme for people like you.

- ✔ If you receive tips, keep records of any amounts you receive that are not entered elsewhere.

Securing interest and investment information

You may want to save bank records for your own uses, but you do not need to keep records of personal bank accounts where no interest is paid to you unless you are also running a spare-time business. Records you do need to keep include:

- ✔ Interest statements from banks and building societies. You can keep your bank statements and building society passbooks as additional back up.

- ✔ Contract notes that show how much you paid for shares or investment trusts or unit trusts. These will be needed for capital gains tax calculations if you decide to sell them.

- ✔ Details of dividends on any foreign shares from which tax has been deducted.

- ✔ Dividend statements from shares. You must also include those where you receive extra shares instead of a cash dividend.

- ✔ Interest statements from bonds and bond funds.

Deciding how long to keep tax records

You must retain personal investment and savings-related items for one year after the final 31 January date for filing a self assessment form. So the records for the 2007-08 tax year that you use to fill out the self assessment form due by 31 January 9 must be kept until 31 January 2010.

HMRC cannot challenge your records or ask you to produce them after that date unless it alleges fraud or other criminality and opens a formal investigation into your affairs. HMRC can open an investigation whenever they suspect wrongdoing – there's no time limit on this. But you need only worry if you are seriously concerned about facing tax evasion charges.

Keeping some records for far longer

Records of items you purchase which can incur a capital gains tax if you sell them later on at a profit should be retained until you dispose of them, unless, of course, the entire capital gains system is replaced – which is very unlikely! These items include shares, unit trusts, investment trusts, other investments such as hedge funds, works-of-art, stamp collections, and antiques.

Saving some records your whole life

Documentary evidence of trusts should be kept for as long as the trust is in force. With some trusts set up for Inheritance Tax purposes working to a seven or ten year timetable, the paperwork has to be retained for that time period even if there are no assets left in the trust.

Records of disposals and gifts that can eventually reduce your estate for Inheritance Tax on your death are important to your heirs. So keep records of the amounts and the recipients for seven years after they are made. After seven years, the gifts drop out of tax contention, provided you are still alive.

Retaining Business Records

Running a business involves noting every transaction from the very first day. You record transactions under two basic headings:

- ✔ **Income** is for money that you take in for your goods or services.
- ✔ **Outgoings** are what you spend on acquiring stock, materials, or items required to run the business such as a telephone, stationery or a computer.

Retain utility and other bills for your home if you operate the business from your family property so you can claim the proportion of the total you use in your business. The same 'proportionality' of costs applies if you use the same vehicle for private and for business use.

The simplest way of establishing how much you use your car for business is to keep a note of business-related mileage and work this out as a proportion of the annual mileage. The tax authorities appreciate it is not possible to get this precisely right as urban and motorway driving tend to have different costs so no one expects figures down to several decimal points. But you can keep accurate records of parking fees or toll road costs.

You must file away any statements for bank accounts you use in your business even if they are personal accounts as well. Here HMRC may want to check transactions, not just any interest received. You must, of course, be able to show which entries on your statement are for your business and which for your personal use if you have one account for these two purposes.

Asking for receipts

Keep as many receipts and other items of proof of purchase as you can.

Obviously, you can't ask for a receipt if you put coins in the slot for a call related to your self employment. And the same applies to other small cash items such as the local evening paper that you might buy for the small ads, particularly if your business is buying old bikes, doing them up, and selling them on.

HMRC accepts that you cannot always get written proof of expenditure. But they still expect you to make a note of all such expenditure as soon as possible. List the amount, where you spent it, and why.

To save yourself hassle, use these tips:

- ✔ If you cannot or don't want to use a mobile, buy a phone card and get a receipt rather than put coins into public call boxes. Call boxes can be cheaper for many calls than mobile phones while credit calls involve paying more in most situations.

- ✔ Use a regular newsagent who can hand out a monthly receipt for the newspapers you buy.

- ✔ Get receipts for taxi fares and train tickets, and keep your bus tickets.

- ✔ Photocopy receipts from shops. Many use thermal printers and the ink fades rapidly. Even if you copy them, retain the originals, even if they become virtually illegible.

Remember that HMRC is run on increasingly commercial lines. It does not wish to enter protracted correspondence or arguments over a 90p bus fare. (And nor should you!)

Keeping business records for a long, long time

You have to keep personal financial records for one year past the final 31 January filing date. With business records, including spare-time earnings, you need a much larger filing system. Businesses have to keep records not for just one year past the final filing date but for five years.

Your records for the 2007–08 tax year form the basis for the self employment section on the self assessment form due to be filed by 31 January 2009. You must then keep this paperwork a further five full years after the final filing date so you only get to send the documents to the recycling bin after 31 January 2014. That's four years after you're allowed to throw personal stuff away.

When you dispose of an item such as machinery, a car, or a computer that you use in your business, you need to show how much you paid for it so that you can finalise your accounting, irrespective of whether you make a profit or a loss. Keep records of these capital items as long as you own them and then for the statutory five years after you don't own them anymore.

The same rules apply to assets such as a work-of-art your business might buy in the eventual hope of selling it on at a profit. Your paperwork will help establish a capital gain or loss.

Ensuring a part-time business follows the rules

When the tax folk are not busy checking your tax returns, they are out and about reading classified ads in local papers, noting down details from newsagents' notice-boards, and having a good look at who's trading what on internet auction sites.

They're not interested when you sell the bicycle your child has grown out of. Or when you get rid of your student books online. Or when you get on the Internet and try to auction that stuffed donkey your aunt brought you back from Spain. But if they see you offering to buy unwanted two-wheelers from

Book II

Paying Less Tax

local families and then selling them on at a profit, or regularly dealing in books which you acquire to sell for gain, or advertising for unwanted souvenirs to sell them to someone else's favourite aunts at prices less than they would pay in souvenir shops on the Costa del Sol, then the tax authorities will be interested.

There is nothing wrong with some spare-time buying and selling, or doing a bit of work on the side, provided you keep records and declare any profits.

You need to keep records even if your spare-time business *turnover* (sales in plain English) stays below £15,000 and lets you file a short form of accounts. Why? Unless you are a good record-keeper, how else do you know about your turnover figure and how do you prove it to the tax authorities?

Managing Your Record-Keeping

Record keeping does not have to be expensive. Simple filing systems and the use of easy-to-obtain account books may be all you need. But a number of computer programs, such as Quicken or Microsoft Money, can help you as well.

Many people find using a computer easier than keeping hard-copy paperwork. But while this can lead to quicker calculations and speedier finding of information, HMRC insists you keep the hard copy as well unless you store the originals as microfilm records or use an optical imaging system. The taxman needs to be sure that computerised images are kept in a tamper-proof form and fully reflect the originals.

Always keep original copies of all records. If the original goes missing, it is not the end of the world providing you can re-create it from the original source. However, banks and many other financial companies may charge you for duplicate copies.

Chapter 2

Dealing with Self Assessment

. . . .

In This Chapter

▶ Looking at the form

▶ Completing the basic return

▶ Calculating the right amounts

▶ Sending in the paperwork

▶ Paying what you owe

. . . .

*F*illing in your self assessment form (or, officially, your *tax return*) is an annual chore. And it could be followed by having to send a substantial cheque to HMRC. Painful.

This chapter doesn't give you hints on how to reduce your tax bill. Nor does it show you how to answer all the questions, most of which are self-explanatory anyway. Instead, it points out common errors that could derail your tax return, involve you in fines, interest and penalties, and possibly an investigation.

Managing the Mechanics of the Form

In these sections, we look at who gets the self assessment form (or forms for a few), what they have to do with the form, and what happens if they don't fill it in.

Getting the forms

Around one in three taxpayers is sent a form automatically each year at, or just after, the start of the tax year on 6 April. These are people that HMRC believes should get a form because they:

- ✔ Have earnings from self-employment or are in partnerships
- ✔ Are top-rate taxpayers or are approaching the cut-off point for basic-level tax
- ✔ Are company directors
- ✔ Have more than one source of income
- ✔ Have earnings from overseas
- ✔ Are pensioners with a complex income mix
- ✔ Own substantial land or property
- ✔ Regularly have capital gains or losses from investments.

This is not an exhaustive list. And you may find the reason that you were sent a form no longer applies – perhaps you moved from self-employment to employment or spent all your savings. You do not have to send in a completed form if you do not owe tax.

HMRC is trying to cut down on the number of tax-payers who receive forms each year. It is experimenting with simple forms for those who only have the odd item to declare and taking around one million people out of the tax net altogether as it is more efficient to use PAYE to collect any extra tax an individual might owe.

However, if you wish to, or have to, communicate with the taxman, you can always ask for a form or download one from the HMRC Web site at www.hmrc.gov.uk.

If you go for the traditional paper-based method when you submit your tax forms, you are likely to receive three documents from HMRC. These are:

- ✔ **Tax Return:** Everyone has to complete this as it provides the basic information for your self assessment (around 10 pages).
- ✔ **Tax Return Guide:** This booklet offers substantial detail on how to fill in the return (around 36 pages).
- ✔ **Tax Calculation Guide:** This helpful guide enables you to work out the amount you owe (or are owed as a rebate) with no more technology than a pocket calculator (around 16 pages).

    HMRC does not send out the Tax Calculation Guide to everyone. You may not receive one if you have previously filed over the Internet or sent in forms based on a recognised computer program.

There are also supplementary pages that cover such areas as employment, share option schemes, self-employment, partnerships, owning land or property, receiving foreign income, receiving income from trusts or estates, capital gains and losses, and being not resident in the UK for tax purposes. HMRC normally sends supplementary pages you used previously. In many cases, these pages are bound together with your basic form. (The upcoming 'Seeing about supplementary pages' section talks about these pages in more detail.)

These supplementary pages are designed to cover some 99.9 per cent of needs. But if you're in doubt, or have a source of income that should be taxed that doesn't seem to fit any of the supplementary pages, you can make use of the additional information section on the form. You can always write a letter, as well, if you need to communicate with HMRC for any reason.

It is your legal duty to fill in a form if you have to. It is not an excuse to say you did not receive one. Or that you left it all up to your employer to sort out. Or that you thought an accountant would do it all for you. If you are in any doubt, apply for a form by telephoning HMRC Order Line on 0845 9000 404. You can also fax your request to 0845 9000 604 or download the form from the internet at www.hmrc.gov.uk. And don't forget to send it in. If you have not received a tax return and have further tax to pay, you must tell HMRC by the 5 October following the end of the tax year.

Your local tax office can provide you with the form and other material in Braille, large print, and audio format. You can also communicate with HMRC in Welsh. There is a Welsh language helpline on 0845 302 1489.

The standard forms are also available to print or use on screen in the many tax return computer program packages on sale.

Discovering you don't have to fill in a form

If your total earnings are from one employer under PAYE, you only have to fill in a form if you are a top-rate tax-payer. If you have an ordinary job and no extraordinary income, you pay tax through the PAYE system on a regular basis. So you don't have to fill in a self assessment form or pay anything extra at tax time.

If your total income, including investment income and savings interest and the value of any workplace perks such as a company car or company health scheme, leaves you firmly in the basic-tax rate zone (or lower), you do not have to fill in a form. The only exception is where you have other sources of taxable income from which tax was not deducted at source.

If you believe that your only need to contact the tax inspector is to ask for a rebate of previously paid tax, you can either fill in a self assessment form or, more simply, ask for form R40, which is a claim for repayment. R40 is also available as a download from www.hmrc.gov.uk/forms/r40.pdf.

Keeping records

Self-assessment works on a file now, check later procedure. This means you file your self-assessment return, then HMRC checks it. So saving the records of your finances is really vital. You have to keep paperwork for one year after the final filing date (31 January) after the end of the tax year (ending the previous 5 April). This is extended to five years if you are self-employed. Chapter 1 in this part has complete details of what you have to save and for how long.

Filling In the Return

If you're like most taxpayers, you can ignore around four fifths of the form. If you do not tick the 'yes' box to any section, you can move on. You do not have to write in 'not applicable'. HMRC's gadgetry is trained to recognise blank pages.

Avoiding the most common self assessment errors

You'd be surprised at what some people forget to do; ensure you don't make any of these common mistakes:

- ✔ Failing to sign the form – it's your responsibility.
- ✔ Failing to tick all the mandatory boxes.
- ✔ Failing to provide complete information about any repayment due you.
- ✔ Failing to tick your choice of repayment. You can opt to have repayments sent by cheque or repaid through PAYE (if you're an employee). And if you're feeling generous, see the next tip.

- ✔ Failing to tell HMRC where any repayment should go. You have to remember to put in details such as bank account numbers.

- ✔ Failing to tell HMRC to whom any repayment is to go.

  You can have a refund sent directly to a charity.

- ✔ Failing to complete the correct supplementary pages (see the 'Seeing about supplementary pages' section) or to attach all the supplementary pages.

- ✔ Entering weekly or monthly amounts in an annual box – this applies especially to pension payments.

- ✔ Recording the capital in your savings account as well as the interest in the interest box on the form.

The Tax Return Guide is not the easiest document to use. Although not a legal document, it is written like one in many parts and is full of Inland Revenue jargon. But you can call HMRC's helpline and get someone to translate it (and more) into everyday language. The telephone number is 0845 9000 444. With patience, you can make the Tax Return Guide, combined with the Tax Calculation Guide, work for you. You may still need a pocket calculator (or a good ability with long multiplication and division).

Listing income and credits

The basic tax return is designed to gather information about certain income including interest you earn from National Savings, bank, and building society accounts. You also need to provide information about interest from unit trusts and dividend income from trusts and investments.

If you draw a pension or receive Social Security benefits, HMRC wants to know about them. Remember state pensions and contribution-based job-seeker's allowance are taxable.

You also need to report any miscellaneous income, which can include small amounts of casual earnings, royalties, and commission you might get from selling for mail-order companies. In many cases, it's easier to record details by filling in a supplementary section. The basic form lists all the supplementary sections, which range from employment and self-employment to Lloyd's insurance names and foreign investment income.

Book II

Paying Less Tax

The form also has space for you to list items you can claim as tax credits. These include:

- ✔ **Personal and stakeholder pension contributions.** Don't record these contributions if your only pension payments are through your employer as relief should occur automatically through PAYE.

- ✔ Venture capital trusts.

- ✔ Tax-deductible contributions to trade union and friendly society sickness and funeral plans. You cannot claim for standard trade union membership fees.

- ✔ Gifts to charities.

- ✔ The Blind Person's allowance.

- ✔ The Married Person's allowance, which applies only if at least one partner was born before 6 April 1935.

You should not put pence into any box when you fill in the form. You can round down income and gains (items you owe tax on) to the nearest pound. Equally you can round up credits and deductions (items that HMRC owes you) to the nearest pound. This can sometimes lead to slight differences between boxes on the form. And it can save a few pounds!

Going into savings and investments

You should get an annual return for each UK savings account you have. This report shows the amount of interest, the amount taken off for taxation at source, and what you are left with. Investments such as shares, unit trusts, and investment trusts include similar information with each dividend payment. But if your investment does not pay dividends, you don't receive any such information.

Less than obvious areas to note include:

- ✔ **Purchased life annuities:** The annuity provider give you a certificate to show what proportion of each payment is tax-free.

- ✔ **Relevant discounted securities:** Items under this heading can include retail price index-linked UK government stocks, zero-dividend split capital investment trust shares, and some stock market index-tracking bonds which offer a minimum guaranteed return irrespective of the performance of the shares in the index.

> ✔ **Scrip dividends:** A scrip dividend is an offer of shares in place of cash. You should show the cash equivalent in the correct box. *Dividend reinvestment schemes,* in which you choose to have any dividends automatically go to buying new shares instead of getting cash, do not count as a scrip.

Don't forget to count investment trust shares under the 'dividends from companies' heading, but not dividend distributions from UK authorised unit trusts and UK authorised open-ended investment companies (OEICs).

Making friends with the blank page

Book II

Paying Less Tax

You can use the blank box at the end of the form to tell the tax inspector about items you are not sure about. By showing your doubts at this stage, you can probably head off trouble later on.

You can also use this space to confess to any items you have estimated because, for one reason or another, you do not have the paperwork to hand.

Always over-estimate tax due if there is any doubt. You cannot be penalised if you overpay your tax and then receive a refund. Underpayment is a different matter entirely.

Seeing about supplementary pages

The basic form, with details such as your name and address and your national insurance number, is only the starting point. Most people have to fill in extra pages known as *supplementary pages.* These cover what makes you different as a tax-payer – you're employed or you're self-employed or you have overseas investments, for example. In fact, in many cases, the supplementary pages are the most important! They are part and parcel of the self assessment form so you can't avoid them.

The supplementary pages, in order of HMRC reference numbers, are:

> ✔ **Employment (SA101):** Fill this in if you have to file a self assessment return and were employed under PAYE on a full-time, part-time, or casual basis. This category also includes agency work and 'IR35' work where you provide your labour through a company. Ask HMRC for special pages if you are a paid minister of religion.

✔ **Share schemes (SA102):** On this page, you record the options granted and options exercised under a number of employee incentive schemes. You do not need to fill this in if you were in an Inland Revenue approved scheme such as Save As You Earn and have met all the conditions.

✔ **Self Employment (SA103):** In addition to those who get some or all of their income from self-employment, you will need to fill this section in if you are a buy-to-let landlord or provide furnished accommodation in your home where you also offer meals, such as in a bed-and-breakfast. You need to complete a separate SA103 for each business you have. So if you work for yourself as a builder but also rent out properties, you have to complete two forms. If you invested your money into a Lloyd's of London insurance underwriting syndicate, there are special extra pages.

✔ **Partnership (SA104):** There are two versions of this form. The short version covers the standard situation in which you earn money from a partnership whose trading income is the only or main source of money coming in. The full version covers more complicated situations. Most partners can use the short version but if you are not sure, ask for the full version. All partners are jointly responsible for completing the partnership's returns.

✔ **Land and Property (SA105):** This section covers income from land and property in the UK, including furnished holiday lettings, but excluding buy-to-lets.

✔ **Foreign income (SA106):** This is a catch-all section for all sorts of income produced from sources outside the UK. It includes offshore bank accounts, investments, and insurance policies. It does not matter if the income has already been taxed at source by the overseas tax authority, you still have to fill in this section. There are a number of tax treaties between the UK and other countries that sort out what you pay in the source country and in the UK. Filling in this section enables HMRC to know whether you have more to pay or whether you qualify for a rebate.

✔ **Trusts (SA107):** If you are a beneficiary of trusts or settlements (but not the bare trusts used often by grandparents and others to give money to those under 18 who (or whose parents) have to account for any tax due themselves), you need to complete this page. You should also use this page to record regular income from a deceased person's estate, but not for one-off payments from a legacy (these are not taxed). If you receive an income from an income-producing asset such as shares you inherited, include the income in the standard return along with any other investment income.

✔ **Capital gains (SA108):** If you disposed of assets liable to capital gains tax worth at least four times the capital gains tax annual allowance, you have to fill this part in even if you don't have to pay any tax. In 2007-08, the allowance is £9,200 so the reporting level is £36,800. You also fill in these pages if you have a loss.

✔ **Non-residence (SA109):** This part is for people who earn income in the UK but are not regarded as UK 'tax citizens' (the proper phrases are 'not resident', 'not ordinarily resident', or 'not domiciled'). It can also apply if you are resident in the UK for tax purposes but also a tax resident of another country with which the UK has a 'double taxation' agreement.

Looking at the employment pages

You have to fill these in if you are a top-rate taxpayer or a director (even if you own the majority of the company's shares).

Book II

Paying Less Tax

You do not necessarily have to enter any more than the name of your employer and the amount of pay you received (noted on your P60).

Considering the self-employment pages

You will need a separate set of forms for each form of self-employment. For instance, if you drive a cab as a self-employed driver by day, but earn a living as a freelance entertainer by night, you have two totally different forms of self-employment.

You also fill in these pages if you provided accommodation with a service attached such as regular meals or nursing. Buy-to-let is included under 'investments'.

You have to fill in the capital allowances section, where applicable, no matter what your turnover. This is where you can claim *depreciation* (the declining value of cars, plant and machinery, and some buildings) against your profits.

In general, you can write off 40 per cent of the value of most items in the first year, followed by 25 per cent of the balance in each successive year.

You need only show turnover (sales), expenses against turnover and the resulting profit or loss if your turnover is under £15,000. You still have to keep records and accounts, however, to show HMRC if your return is subject to additional checking. The £15,000 level has remained unchanged for many years. If your turnover exceeds £15,000 you have to show a more detailed breakdown of costs and tax adjustments as listed on the form.

If you received small or one-off earnings and you have no expenses to set against the sum, you might put these under 'other income' in the main pages. This might include a single payment for writing an article for a magazine or for selling a patented idea to a firm.

Counting the Ways of Doing the Sums

Even if you get professional help with your self assessment form, you still have to assemble all the paperwork needed. But you can find assistance at no cost. The following sections tell you how to figure out your bottom line as far as tax liability goes.

Filing early

Filing a paper tax return before 30 September gives you the option of asking HMRC to calculate your tax. The calculations, of course, depend on you filling in the return correctly. You're told how much to pay or whether there is a repayment coming your way by the following January 31. You can, if you disagree with HMRC's figures, rework them yourself or hire an accountant. But the reality is that this 30 September option is generally only used by those with relatively simple tax affairs.

If, for some reason, your tax form was sent to you late, the window for asking HMRC to do the sums extends to two months after the return was sent to you.

Using purpose-built software

You can put all your details into a number of computer programs. These then lead you into the right additional sections and work out what you owe (or are owed).

HMRC Web site `http://www.hmrc.gov.uk/individuals/index.shtml` has a list of software providers with kits that work. There are packages such as Quicken and Microsoft Money that include tax form software amongst other financial applications. Expect to pay around £10 for the most basic downloadable software.

Some programs don't support all the supplementary pages although most do. So check the 'Seeing about supplementary pages' section earlier in this chapter for the reference number of the pages you need before buying.

Filing Your Form

Self assessment depends on a strict annual timetable with deadlines reinforced by fines, interest and penalties. These dates can be stretched by a day or so year-by-year to avoid bank-holidays and weekends.

The four basic dates in each tax year are:

- ✔ **6 April:** New forms available.

- ✔ **30 September:** The final date to submit your form if you want HMRC to calculate your tax.

- ✔ **30 December:** The final date for Internet filing if you owe less than £2,000 and want the payments taken out of your regular salary through PAYE.

- ✔ **31 January:** The deadline for returns to avoid automatic penalties and interest.

Book II

Paying Less Tax

Paying a £100 penalty for filing a day late can easily undo all the tax-saving work you have done over the past year. Get your payments in on time! The deadline for paper-based returns will be brought forward from January 31 to the previous September 30 from April 2008 onwards.

Posting your form

Around 90 per cent of self assessment taxpayers use some form of paper-based return. You can send it in through the post – you have to pay the postage – or you can hand deliver the forms to your local tax office (even if it is the office that handles your affairs). If you post it, ask for proof of posting. If you hand it in, ask for a receipt. Many tax offices stay open from 8.30 a.m. to 8 p.m. on deadline day.

Submitting your form online

You can file electronically, and more and more people do so each year. HMRC is a big online filing enthusiast. Large companies and accountancy firms already do much of their communications online. The system is much better after a sticky start a few years ago when the process was hit by criticism and crashes. HMRC's reputation was damaged some years ago when it offered a £10 rebate for online filing (good) and then made it so difficult that even downloading the basics took hours (bad).

There is no longer a £10 rebate. And it still takes seven days between register-ing and receiving, by post, an ID number and a separate unique activation PIN number. This expires if you forget to activate it within 28 days of receipt so you have to start all over again if you forget.

But the service is improving. You get automatic calculation without having to buy a software package that only lasts for one year. The system guides you through the questions and automatically steers you away from parts of the form that are not relevant to you.

Repayments are faster than with paper-based filing. And you have until 31 December 31 (rather than 30 September) to file if you want any tax you have to pay to be collected through PAYE.

The disadvantage is when you are cut off by your service provider in the middle of filling up a section! – don't forget it can still take some time to fill in the form. You can, however, take your time over the filing and go back to it in a new online session. You do not have to get it done in one go.

Print out a hard copy anyway, just to be sure. If you have some idea of your potential tax bill first, then you will see if you have done anything silly such as turning a £5,000 spare-time earning into £500,000 or £5!

Paying on Account

The self assessment tax system works with two formal payment dates a year. On 31 January you have to pay anything still outstanding from the tax year which ended on the previous 5 April, plus half your likely tax bill for the year which will end on the forthcoming 5 April. So on or before 31 January 2008 you should have paid any outstanding balances for 2006-07 plus half of what you are likely to owe in 2007-08.

The final payment date for the other half of the period 2007-08 is 31 July 2008. If it turns out that these two payments are not enough – a situation that may happen if your earnings are rising – you make a third and final payment on the following 31 January.

You do not have to make payments on account if 80 per cent or more of your income tax bill (but not capital gains tax) is covered by tax deducted at source – PAYE and automatic deductions from savings interest are common deductions. It's up to you to work this out. It is best to ignore this concession if you are a 'borderline' 80 per cent case.

There is no interest benefit if your payment arrives early (but at least you know you've done it and won't get penalised!)

Asking for a reduction in payments

If your tax liability for this year is likely to be significantly lower than the previous year, you can ask for a reduction in your payments on account. Otherwise, you could end up paying more than you need until it is corrected in the following year's tax return.

You can claim a reduction on your payments on account on a tax return, or by writing to HMRC. You must give valid reasons to back your claim. HMRC adds interest to your repayment, but the rate is far lower than the interest they charge you if you owe them money.

Book II

Paying Less Tax

Adding up the potential penalties

You face an automatic £100 penalty if you fail to get your return in by 31 January. And there is a further £100 if you have still not filed by the following 31 July. In addition, there is a 5 per cent surcharge on tax unpaid on 28 February, and a further 5 per cent if it is still unpaid (plus interest on the first surcharge). This is a painful sum!

Penalties cannot be greater than the tax owed. If you discover you owe nothing or are due a rebate, the 31 January deadline does not apply.

Some people who cannot fill in their form properly make an estimate and then pay over more tax than needed. If you pay more than you owe, you cannot be fined. You can claim any excess back later.

Chapter 3

Taxing Family Situations

. . . .

In This Chapter

▶ Changing your tax life when changing your marital status

▶ Making the most of your married state, tax-wise

▶ Weighing up the pros and cons of cohabiting

▶ Splitting up and sorting your taxes

▶ Being a tax-payer from the day you're born

▶ Expressing generosity to children

▶ Cutting back on tax bills

▶ Applying for tax credits

. . . .

*L*ife is full of choices. And none are more significant than those we take in our personal life. This chapter looks at how you can legitimately arrange your tax affairs and those of your family to pay less tax.

You don't have to follow all the tips. In many cases, you won't be able to. Marriage is not for everyone; nor does the married/unmarried partnership divide apply coherently across the tax board. In some cases, husband and wife are two different people entirely; in others, they are treated as an indivisible unit. And in still other cases, they are considered in exactly the same way as an unmarried couple. Then there's the issue of children, who are potential taxpayers from the moment they are born, but also receive some special tax breaks.

Getting Married

HMRC does recognise marriage as an institution. But don't expect too much, too easily, tax-wise from your wedded bliss. The days of tax relief on marriage are long gone except for those where one partner was born before April 5, 1935. And even that is not worth a great deal in hard cash terms.

Where marriage counts most is in *capital taxes* such as capital gains tax and inheritance tax.

Married women became tax persons in their own right in 1991. Before that, they were their husband's tax chattels with few rights. This 1991 move, known as *independent taxation,* actually increased the scope for tax-saving moves. (We provide the details in 'Maximising the Tax Benefits of Marriage' later on.)

You no longer get any income tax saving through a married couple's allowance unless one, or both, of the partners was born before 6 April 1935. (If this applies to you, see 'Looking at what's left of the married couple's allowance' in the next section.)

Don't forget to amend your will ahead of marriage as wills automatically stop on marriage. You don't have to wait until after the honeymoon for this. You can write a new will in anticipation of your forthcoming status change.

The married couple's allowance (MCA) was abolished for the majority of married partnerships in 1999. But it still remains for those relationships where at least one of the partners was born before 6 April 1935.

MCA is a tax relief so a married couple who qualify pay less tax than a similar couple who are not married.

Seeing who can claim the MCA

The 6 April 1935 date is a fixed cut-off date, so the number of people eligible to apply for MCA diminishes each year.

The MCA goes by default to the husband. But couples can request that half, or all, of the basic amount be transferred to the wife. The wife can insist on half even if the husband says no. The decision to transfer half, or all, of the allowance must normally be made before the start of the tax year.

As the basic allowance counts against all income, it is more useful to the higher earner. It would be gesture of mere sexual politics if a non-earner insisted on their share of the MCA.

Figuring out the allowance

The MCA has two elements:

> ✔ The **basic amount** is given as an allowance against taxable income irre-
> spective of income levels. This is currently £2,440, though it can change
> each year if the Treasury so decides. Divide that figure by the ten per
> cent tax allowance and it's worth £244 in cash terms.

> ✔ The **age-related amount,** which, like the additional age-related personal
> allowance, can be clawed back by the taxman if the income of one partner
> falls in a higher tax band. In 2007-08, age-related MCA starts to disappear
> once the husband has an income in excess of £20,900. Sexist or what!

The MCA has two levels – one for couples in which the older partner was born
between 6 April 1930 and April 5 1935 and a more generous tax relief level
that applies for the tax year when the older partner reaches 75 years of age.

If that sounds complicated, don't worry. The difference between the two
rates is not great. The lower MCA paid to the under 75s is worth a tax
allowance of £6,285 a year while the higher level is £6,365.

To get the allowance, couples have to earn enough to cover the amount.
Then, because the tax level for the allowance is just ten per cent, the maximum value in cash terms the lower level is £628.50 while the higher level is
worth just £7 a year more in hard cash terms at £636.50. Not worth getting
old for!

Connecting MCA and the age allowance

What's left of the MCA after the basic amount has been paid out (see the previous section) is subject to the age allowance trap, which affects older couples with higher-than-average incomes whose extra age allowance benefits
are chipped away once their income hits a threshold. Earnings caught in the
trap are taxed at 33 per cent instead of the basic 22 per cent.

When your income reaches £20,900 (for the 2007-08 tax year), the age-related
element starts to fall away by £1 for every £2 your total income exceeds this
level until it disappears entirely.

Maximising the Tax Benefits of Marriage

If you are married, use your marital status to save tax. No one will thank you for forgoing the tax-saving opportunities we tell you about in this section.

If you want to get the best out of marriage and tax, you and your partner need to trust one another financially as well as in the usual ways. The strategies listed here generally require that couples either divide their assets up between themselves or that the better-off partner hand them over to the other.

Probably the biggest tax benefit of marriage is that you can pass ownership of money and other assets between the pair of you without tax hassles. Marriage can, for some couples, be worth £1,000 or more in tax savings each year. Of course, not every couple is able to save this sort of money. You need to have enough savings first of all to make it worthwhile switching the ownership from the higher-paid partner to the lower-paid one.

There are no limits to any moves of money between spouses. The tax inspector seems to forget independent taxation of women and go back to a former age when a husband was responsible for the taxation of all the income-producing assets his wife possessed.

When assets are shared out, the division has to be real. The partner who gives something away cannot demand the assets back or have the income from them paid to her or his bank account. The new owner must have absolute ownership and control, including the right to sell.

Sorting out your tax allowance

Each partner in a marriage, along with every other taxpayer, has a personal income tax allowance. This stands at £4,895 for the 2005–06 tax year.

Some people don't have sufficient earnings from work and from interest on savings accounts to use up their personal allowance. If this is the case for you, but your spouse earns enough to use up all his or her allowance and then some, it makes sense for your partner to transfer income- or interest-producing assets to you (or vice versa if the financial situation is reversed):

✔ Geeta earns £25,000 a year from her job, and the total of her income puts her in the 20 per cent tax band, so the £2,000 interest she is paid on her savings account costs her £400 in tax. Her husband Vijay has no income of his own. Geeta can transfer all her savings to Vijay so that he can reclaim the interest and the household is £400 better off.

✔ Patrick earns £50,000 a year and is a top-rate taxpayer. The £5,000 he earns from his £100,000 savings account loses £2,000 (40 per cent) to the taxman. His wife, Rachel, earns £20,000 a year and has no savings of her own. She is a basic-rate taxpayer for whom the 20 per cent savings rate applies. If Patrick gives all his savings to Rachel, they would save £1,000 a year, the gap between 20 per cent and 40 per cent of the £5,000 interest. But Patrick needs control day-to-day over some of the money so the couple agree to joint ownership. The result is Patrick now pays £1,000 tax on the £2,500 he earns in interest while Rachel pays £500 on her portion. The couple is now £500 better off.

Swapping your assets

Each partner in a marriage has their own capital gains tax annual allowance. capital gains tax (CGT) is payable when you make a profit in selling or transferring an asset to someone else but using the allowance lets the seller have that amount of any such gain tax free.

Keeping an investment portfolio in just one partner's name means a couple can make use of only one capital gains tax allowance. But dividing up the assets potentially liable to CGT, as married people can do freely, doubles the potential tax savings by giving two CGT allowances to use instead of just one.

Book II

Paying Less Tax

Being partners at work as well as at home

Couples, whether legally married or not, who have their own business can transfer income from that business between themselves to make the best use of tax allowances and the advantages of lower tax rates.

HMRC is targeting husband and wife teams to ensure that any monies moved between the two in order to reduce their overall tax bill is wedded in reality. Where both partners are on the payroll, both have to do work to the commercial value of the payments they receive. And the earnings must be paid to the partner concerned.

Sending it to a bank account in that partner's sole name is a wise move.

Also, provided it is a real job, a spouse (or unmarried partner) can employ their lower tax-rated other half. The wages paid are subject to PAYE and PAYE record keeping unless the amount is below the national insurance minimum. Higher pay amounts, though still below the national insurance pay level, qualify for benefits such as the state retirement pension and, in particular, for the state second pension. (Chapters 2 and 3 in Book IV talk about pensions.)

In some cases, sharing out stocks and shares in this way also reduces the income tax payable on dividends. Chapter 6 in this Book has the lowdown on dealing with capital gains tax.

Inheriting each other's assets

When a husband or wife dies, the surviving partner doesn't pay any inheritance tax on any transfer of assets between themselves whether during their lifetime or in a will. Inheritance tax is not levied on anything that passes between spouses. Chapter 4 in Book V on inheritance tax has more details of what to do and what to avoid doing.

Taking a stake in a pension

Spouses can invest up to £2,808 a year into a stakeholder pension for their other halves, irrespective of the partner's income. This contribution qualifies for automatic tax relief at the basic 22 per cent level, taking the real value invested into the pension plan up to £3,600. This limit seems to be fixed in stone, it does not rise each year. The pension company does all the paperwork and increases the payment into the pension scheme in line with this tax relief.

Cohabiting instead of Marrying

Current UK law does not recognise common-law marriages between a man and woman, although cohabiting couples are treated as though they were married for various means-tested tax credits. The tax-planning opportunities given to married people are denied to couples who are not married.

There is, however, nothing to stop you making a gift of an asset to someone to whom you are not married. The risk is the inheritance tax that would apply if you failed to live seven years from the date of making the gift.

Unmarried couples who buy assets together are treated as though each one owned half the value on a disposal so both face any tax liability.

If you live together in unwedded bliss, make sure you each have written a will to ensure the fewest tax hassles should one of you die.

Planning recognition

The Civil Partnership Act (which came into force in December 2005) allows lesbian and gay couples who register their relationship to enjoy the same tax breaks as heterosexual married couples. Much legislation has been amended for this, including the pension rules for the civil partner of a future prime minister. The *fiscal* (the posh word for tax) advantages for UK-registered civil partnerships include:

✔ Property including cash and investments passing between civil partners are exempt from all taxation. Any such transfers will be free of capital gains tax.

✔ Employee or pension benefits offered to heterosexual partners by an employer or the state are equally offered to same-sex partners in a civil partnership (but there may be difficulties with some older pension schemes where one partner joined before the civil partnership).

✔ Rules applying to married couples who are both controlling directors of a small company are extended to same-sex couples.

✔ No inheritance tax is paid on assets passed on if one partner dies.

Book II

Paying Less Tax

Breaking Up

A large number of marriages end in the divorce courts. But don't expect any sympathy from HMRC. There is no longer any tax relief on maintenance payments or Child Support Agency payments.

The law says that divorcing couples remain spouses until the decree absolute brings the relationship to an end. HMRC has other ideas. It only allows tax-free transfers between spouses if they have lived together for at least part of the tax year during which the asset changed hands. A couple who separated (formally stopped living together) on 30 April 2007 can transfer assets without tax hassles until that date and for the rest of the tax year ending on 5 April 2008.

We know it's tough, but if you're heading for divorce, plan ahead. Transfer assets while you are still living under the same roof or at least during the current tax year.

Sorting out the tax bill

Under present tax law, husband and wife or civil partners are counted as one for capital gains tax and inheritance tax that can complicate the financial picture of a divorcing couple.

Ex-partners who transfer assets such as shares or property between themselves to even up the financial position as part of a divorce settlement can face an unexpected tax bill. If the partners didn't live together during the tax year, the profit made by selling an asset may be subject to a hefty capital gains tax.

Paying and receiving maintenance payments

Payments you make for maintenance to a former spouse, and payments for the upkeep and education of a child of a former relationship until they are 18, or while they are still in full-time education, don't count for inheritance tax calculations if you die.

Any maintenance money you receive for whatever purpose, including maintaining a child, is tax-free whether it comes from a former spouse in this country or abroad.

Becoming a Taxpayer

As you celebrate the birth of your child, someone else is celebrating too. The taxman is ready to count your infant as a new taxpayer. But it's not all one way. Along with being a potential taxpayer, your child also has tax-saving possibilities. And for most parents, that new-born will take them into the sometimes arcane, and often complex, world of child tax credit.

HMRC says that childhood officially stops at the age of 16, not the usual 18, age of majority, as in other legal matters. This applies even if the child is still at school or college. You do not need to register your child with HMRC before the age of 16, but once they reach 16 they're given a national insurance number and start paying national insurance.

So be prepared to persuade your offspring to take action to formalise their taxpayer status on or around their 16th birthday. If their overall income is still low enough to qualify for tax-free status on their interest earnings (if they have any) they need to sign HMRC form R85.

An under 16-year old becomes a taxpayer if they earn enough to pay income tax or realise profits from sales or investments that are eligible for capital gains tax.

In reality, most children's income is limited to the interest that they're paid on savings accounts. But that does not stop them (or rather you as parents) from filling in a tax form and claiming the tax back on any interest on savings.

Either you, as parents, or your child on reaching 16, has to reclaim any tax deducted from interest-earning bank accounts or investments. Preferably, you tell the bank or building society that your child is not a taxpayer so the interest can be paid gross in the first place. The most usual method of reclaiming tax is by using HMRC form R85. Any savings institution can supply this form and will often pre-print the details for signature to save time.

For most children, there's a substantial, tax-saving flipside of gaining tax-payer status as soon as they are born because they also gain use of the annual personal tax allowance from that very same time. This initial tax-free income amount, £5,225 in 2007-08, can be set against any earnings from part-time jobs as well as interest earned on savings and investments. The taxman lumps everything together whether it comes from savings or hard work delivering newspapers.

Giving Money to Children

As a parent, you can give your children as much money as you want to give them. But HMRC is not stupid. It knows that many parents would happily hand over all or some of their money to their offspring in an effort to dodge tax. Don't think you can just switch money from your own savings to an account you opened for your child to avoid income tax on the interest.

HMRC distinguishes how it treats tax on the interest on gifts of money from parents. The interest, or other returns on these gifts, is considered to belong to the parent, not to the child.

You can give your over-18 offspring as much as you like without income tax worries because, unlike the under 18s, they count as legally adult. However, you can't ask for it back as the money has to be really given away and not just parked in your child's bank account to dodge tax.

The age thing can be confusing and annoying. HMRC starts to treat children as taxpayers when they reach 16 but they are only independent beings when they are 18.

Giving money as a non-parent

There is no limit on how much grandparents, aunts, uncles, godparents, cousins, any other relation or family friends can give to children. Once they have handed over the money, it becomes the child's property, leaving the child liable for tax on the interest. The generous relation no longer has to worry about paying tax on the gift.

Taking advantage of the small amount exemption

Even HMRC has a nice side and grants parents a special exception: You can give away sums to your children and not worry about being taxed on the interest, providing the annual interest on the all savings accounts does not top £100 per parent per child. It doesn't matter whether your children are natural, adopted, legitimate or illegitimate, or whether you live with your children – the exemption still applies.

Within the £100 level, the interest is taxed as belonging to your children, so they can reclaim tax deducted on it by the building society or bank (always assuming their total income falls within the personal allowance) using form R85.

Your children, or you as parents or guardians, can also reclaim half of the tax deducted if your or their income falls within the ten per cent tax band. Ten per cent taxpayers are allowed to reclaim the difference between their rate and the 20 per cent standard savings rate deduction. But make the most of this while you can, as the 10 per cent tax band will be abolished after April 2008.

With interest rates at five per cent, each parent can give each child £2,000 and stay under the £100-interest limit. If rates fell to 2.5 per cent, then the capital could go up to £4,000. But if interest levels rose to ten per cent, the gift limit would fall to £1,000 – the parent would have to ask for a refund!

One parent can give the other money to give to their child to generate up to £100 a year in interest.

The £100 is a concession, not a tax relief given as of right. Once interest tops this figure, even to £101, the entire sum is taxed as if it belonged to the parent. The only exemption to this rule is if a 16- or 17-year old marries! But that's a drastic way of paying less tax.

Keep records of where the money comes from for each account your child has. It is easiest to have one designated 'pocket money account' rather than mix up sums from you as parents with those from others. This way your child can prove to HMRC the source of each pound on which interest is earned. Of course, if your child spends all the pocket money you give or keeps it in a piggy bank, then HMRC is not concerned at all.

To keep your parental contributions in line with HMRC requirements, keep these tips in mind:

- ✔ Make sure any money comes evenly from both parents wherever possible to maximise the amount that cam be given.

- ✔ Explore tax-free savings such as some National Savings products.

- ✔ Remember that once a child reaches 18 – or gets married – the £100 rule ceases.

- ✔ Don't be tempted to give cash to a grandparent so the grandparent can appear to make a gift to the child – HMRC can track money.

- ✔ Go for riskier investments such as certain types of shares where the capital grows and there is little or no income. Part IV explains more on this.

- ✔ You can invest up to £25 a month on a child's behalf into a *friendly society plan,* a special form of insurance policy. But costs are high and can often outweigh the tax savings. Also, the minimum contract length is ten years. So, like all other tax tips, think twice to see if the tax savings are really worthwhile.

Saving Tax by Giving Wisely

As a parent, you can beat the £100 rule (see the previous section) by investing money in savings schemes that do not pay income or that are not liable for income tax. These tax-free savings include:

- ✔ **National Savings Children's Bonus Bonds:** You can buy these for children up until they reach 16. They have to be held for five years and pay a fixed interest rate during that time. To get the maximum benefits, they need to be held for the full five-year period. If you cash them early, you're subject to interest-rate penalties.

- ✔ **National Savings Certificates:** These come in two varieties. You can choose between fixed interest (for two or five years) and index-linked bonds whose value depends on inflation as measured by the retail prices index. Index bonds come in three and five year varieties.

- ✔ **Premium bonds:** These give you the chance of winning £1 million without ever having to worry about losing your initial money. If you invest the maximum £30,000 or a sum approaching that, the law of averages says you should get some small winning tickets every year to give you an income.

- ✔ **Friendly society plans:** These plans are intended for regular savings of up to £25 a month for a minimum of ten years. Savings grow in a tax-free environment.

Investing in single premium insurance bonds

The special tax treatment of *single premium life insurance bonds* can enable you to give money to your offspring but avoid paying tax as these bonds do not pay any income and therefore don't affect your child's personal allowance.

Insurance bonds can be complicated, so always discuss whether they are right for you and your child before buying a bond through your financial adviser.

Generally you need to start with at least £1,000 and sometimes £5,000. Parents who are top rate taxpayers get the most advantages from these bonds.

HMRC is currently looking for ways to stop parents benefiting from the capital gains tax allowances of their offspring. But provided the children keep the investments until they are legally grown up at 18, HMRC can't do anything about the gains as they belong to the new adult. And in any case, the capital gains tax rate on assets held for over three years reduces each year after the third year until the tenth year. We deal with this taper process and other capital gains tax issues in Chapter 6 in this part.

Setting up a trust

A *trust* is a legal device that gives property and other assets, including cash, to a beneficiary without giving the lucky recipient full control. For most tax purposes, the gift of a trust has to be irrevocable. If you give money or property away to a child, you can't ask for it back or set conditions where it will bounce back to you.

A trust is a way of passing money to your children but preventing them from getting their sticky fingers on the cash. Most trusts are set up through wills or by gifts during someone's lifetime. Some trusts also offer tax savings because those giving money into the trust are then able to use the child's tax allowances.

Trusts can also differentiate between assets, such as shares or property, and the income they produce. So you can leave the income from a portfolio to one person and the capital assets to another person on the first person's death.

You might, for instance, want to help your child if they run into personal difficulties with a regular cash income. But the last thing you want to do is to give that child control over the capital assets that produce the income. A trust could serve this purpose.

Or you might own a substantial parcel of shares in a private firm. If you left them to your family, some might try to sell, creating problems for those wanting to hold on. A trust structure where ownership and control are separated from the income could solve the difficulty.

Alternatively, you can use this device to help your offspring through college and university but then ensure they have to use their own efforts for the rest of their lives rather than live off the trust fund monies.

However, the Chancellor introduced a major shake-up of the taxation of trusts in 2006; as a result, trusts are much less attractive than they used to be as a means of protecting assets while passing them on to the next generation. We look in detail at trusts, the new tax regime, and the situations in which they may still be useful in Chapter 5 of Part V.

Getting Money for Children

Government-financed help for families comes in many similarly named benefit schemes. *Child benefit* is paid to all, irrespective of income. *Child tax credit* is paid to most families but at a uniform rate unless the household income is substantially below the national average. Children's tax credit no longer exists and the *Child Trust Fund* started in 2005!

We talk about the various programs in the following sections.

Benefiting from child benefit

The parent, nearly always the mother, of every child qualifies for a fixed *child benefit.* This is currently £18.10 a week for the first (or only) qualifying child and £12.10 a week for each subsequent child. Many mothers choose to have it paid monthly into their bank accounts.

Child benefit is paid tax-free to parents no matter what their own tax rate. It does not have to be declared on any self assessment tax forms.

Child benefit is paid until the September after the child's 16th birthday but extended a further two years, up to 1 September after the child's 18th birthday, if she or he is still in full-time education. Strangely, this means a child born on 1 September has a whole year's more child benefit than one born on the day before, 31 August. Family planning or medical techniques to delay a late August birth are outside this book's brief!

Claiming child tax credit

Child tax credit is paid to parents of children under 16 whose income is low enough to qualify. In other words, legally speaking, child tax credit is means-tested. But the great majority of parents receive the income boost because the maximum joint-income ceiling for the credit is quite high. It is paid through salary slips – either by reducing the income tax taken or by giving back money if your tax payment is lower than your credit. See 'Counting your income for child tax credit' later on for information on who qualifies.

Child tax credit sums are not taxed and do not have to be declared on tax forms.

You have to apply for child tax credit. You do not get it automatically even if HMRC or your employer knows your income is below the threshold.

You can claim by

- ✔ Asking your local tax office for a claim pack and returning the paper form.

- ✔ Going online at www.hmrc.gov.uk/taxcredits.

- ✔ Calling the child tax credit helpline on 0845 300 3900 – calls are charged at the local rate.

The money is usually paid directly to a bank or building society account controlled by the parent (generally the main carer). Although HMRC has improved its act since the early days of the credit when it was making many errors, you can still end up with the wrong amount.

Use these tips to ensure you get the full amount due to you:

- ✔ Remember to submit a claim form on your new-born baby as soon as possible (if you qualify). Children under twelve months qualify for higher payments.
- ✔ Check that older children still in education are continuing to qualify for a payment.
- ✔ Report all falls in earnings at once where this either brings you into the child tax credit payment zone or gives you eligibility for the higher payments under the childcare element of Working Tax Credit (a way of boosting earnings for the lower paid through their wage packets).
- ✔ Realise that you can only claim retrospectively for three months. So if you forget to fill in the forms, your claim can only be backdated by three months.

Book II

Paying
Less Tax

Counting your income for child tax credit

Child tax credit is calculated and administered by HMRC. It adds up the incomes of both partners in a two-parent household, whether they are legally married or not, providing they are responsible for a child or children. It looks at the facts of the relationship where there are two parents rather than legal niceties such as marriage certificates. This brings child tax credit into line with other means-tested benefits but runs counter to the independent taxation of married (and unmarried) women.

To determine whether you qualify to receive child tax credit, you (and your partner, if any) add up all your income from employment, self-employment and taxable interest and dividends on investments. You do not count income from Individual Savings Accounts, tax-free National Savings, the rent-a-room scheme, or maintenance payments from former partners. You can also ignore contributions to an approved pension scheme, and any donations you pay in to charity via the Gift Aid or Payroll giving schemes for good causes.

Only those partners whose joint incomes add up to £58,175 or more a year (and that's increased to up to £66,350 when there is a child less than one year old in the household) will find that their claims do not go into payment.

It's always worth acclaiming tax credits. Many people who qualify get nothing because they don't bother to claim.

How much you get is normally based on your income for the previous tax year. But if your income has fallen substantially, the amount you receive may be based on the current year. You do not have to be working to claim child tax credit.

You have to tell HMRC if your income increases by more than £2,500 a year. Any increase less than that is ignored although it will be counted in the following year as the start point for your family income. This buffer zone is designed so you don't have to report every single change and so that HMRC doesn't have to bill you for overpayments.

HMRC can recover overpayments – in some cases after they have been spent! So if your income rises because one earner moves from part-time to full-time work, or an older child leaves school and starts working, you must report these changes within a month.

You must tell HMRC if your circumstances change in any of the following ways:

- ✔ You marry or become part of a couple who live together as husband and wife.
- ✔ You stop being part of a married couple or a couple living together as husband and wife.
- ✔ Your childcare costs go down by £10 a week or more.
- ✔ You stop paying for childcare.
- ✔ You or your partner leave the country for more than eight weeks (12 weeks in certain circumstances).
- ✔ You are no longer working 16 hours a week (for part-time workers).
- ✔ You are no longer working 30 hours a week (for full time workers).
- ✔ You cease to be responsible for a child (for example if they leave home) or a child or young person no longer qualifies for support (for example if a child over 16 leaves full-time school or college, or goes to university).

If your income is low, you can qualify for a higher rate of child tax credit and if you are working you may also be able to claim for Working Tax Credit. The exact figures depend on how many children you have, whether there are one or two claimants, and other personal details. For more information on means-tested benefits, try a local council money-advice unit, Citizens Advice, the Child Poverty Action Group, or look at www.direct.gov.uk.

HMRC can refuse to pay child tax credit if it considers you work or provide a service at a level which is less than the going rate. This is to prevent people (including the self-employed) artificially depressing their income so that they qualify for the credit.

Calculating how much you get

Most parents receive at least £545 a year tax-free no matter how many children they have. Parents with a child under 12 months are usually entitled to more. In HMRC jargon, the first £545 is known as the *family element* and the extra for a child under one year (also currently £545) is called the *family element, baby addition.* On top of this there is a *child element* of up to £1,845 per year in 2007-08 (with additional payments for disabled and severely disabled children). This is paid for each child in the family.

Table 3-1 shows how much those on various income levels with various numbers of children are eligible to receive in child tax credit each year. The table shows key earning points and credit amounts in the 2007-08 tax year – the amounts are subject to change.

Book II

Paying Less Tax

Table 3-1	Working Tax Credit & Child Tax Credit Awards		
Annual Income (£)	*Annual Award (£) One Child*	*Two Children*	*Three Children*
Not working	2,390	4,240	6,090
5,000	5,825	7,675	9,520
9,000	5,130	6,980	8,830
10,000	4,760	6,610	8,460
15,000	2,910	4,760	6,610
20,000	1,060	2,910	4,760
25,000	545	1,060	2,910
30,000	545	545	1,060
40,000	545	545	545
45,000	545	545	545
50,000	545	545	545
55,000	210	210	210
60,000	0	0	0

Table 3-1 assumes children are over 1 year old and not disabled. Households with a child under the age of 1 year old can have an income of £66,000 and claim tax credits.

HMRC website has a calculator you can use at www.taxcredits.hmrc.gov.uk to make a dry run to see if you qualify. The sum it produces (if any) is the amount between the date you log on to the site (deemed to be the day of claiming) and the end of the tax year.

Someone claiming on 6 December, for instance, would get a third of the sum in the table above as there are four months (one third) left of the 12 month tax year. This is worked out on a day-by-day basis so it can still be worthwhile claiming a few days before the end of the tax year.

For help and advice with tax credits call HMRC's confidential helpline on 0845 900 3900.

Gaining a trust from the government

The government introduced a Child Trust Fund in 2005. This fund gives a £250 special bonus to every child born on or after 1 September 2002. Children born between the start date in 2002 and the introduction of the scheme in 2005 will find their trust fund earns up to £27 in extra interest depending on when the child was born.

Children born to families on lower incomes may qualify for a top-up of a further £250, for a total £500 (with the corresponding extra interest to those born between 1 September 2002 and the starting date for payments). To receive this additional sum, parents must be means-tested by HMRC, although it will go automatically to those children whose families already claim Working Family Tax Credit and certain other state benefits. Further payments (£250 or £500) are made when the child reaches the age of seven.

The money is free of all taxes both to the children themselves and to their parents.

The fund grows in a special tax-free Child Trust Fund for each child, to which anyone – including parents, grandparents, and friends – can also contribute, provided all contributions added together do not top £1,200 per year.

The great advantage of the Child Trust Funds is that they enable parents to give the equivalent of £100 a month to each child without worrying about their own tax position. It also gives children an extension to their tax-free allowance.

As a parent, you are able to select how the money is invested from a range that includes shares and bonds as well as risk-free savings. You have a year from the birth of your child (or the official start of the scheme) in which to make the investment. If you do not take this opportunity, HMRC will invest the money on behalf of your child into one of a number of selected funds.

Neither you nor your children are able to withdraw the trust fund until your child reaches 18. But once that age is reached, there are no restrictions on taking the money out or on how it is spent. Alternatively, at that point the fund can be 'rolled over' into an Individual Savings Account (ISA) where it can continue to grow indefinitely, free of tax.

Receiving help with childcare costs

If your income is low enough to qualify you for Working Tax Credit, you may also be able to claim help with the costs of childcare. If there are two parents, both must work at least 16 hours a week unless one is incapacitated, in hospital, or in prison.

Childcare help amounts to 80 per cent of the actual costs up to an actual cost maximum of £175 per week for one child and £300 a week for two or more children. In cash terms, this equals a maximum £140 a week for one child and £240 a week for two or more children.

The childcare provider has to be registered or approved. This can include pre- or after-school clubs as well as nurseries and registered childminders. It can also include carers who come to your home, such as au pairs and nannies. HMRC conducts spot checks to look at whether the claimed childcare actually happens, as well to as to verify the qualifications of the carers.

Don't try getting your mum or dad or the child's older brothers and sisters to do the caring and then expect some government help. Family members are excluded from the scheme unless they are registered childminders looking after the children of other people as well, or they own a registered nursery.

You might have a low income (or make a loss) when starting out in self-employment. So even though you expect to earn high sums eventually, you might be able to claim for this extra childcare help and additional child tax credits at the beginning of your self-employment. If you have set up a company of your own, you might qualify for a higher level of child-related credits and childcare help if the income you receive from the company (whether as dividends or salary) is sufficiently low. HMRC looks at your total earnings in the last complete tax year before the year in which you claim.

Chapter 4

Understanding Tax When You Work for Someone Else

*T*he vast majority of working people work for someone else. We show you why that's good news as the Pay as You Earn (PAYE) tax system makes life easy for employees. It leaves many with nothing more to do tax-wise. It's the boss who has to do most, and sometimes all, of the work. And it's the boss who has to pick up the tab if something goes wrong, even if the employee profits. Amazing.

So if employment is so simple, why bother with this chapter? The reason is because you have choices. We give you the lowdown on your tax coding, show you many tax savings, ranging from cycles to computers, and explain how you can take a share in your employer's business. That help comes with assistance from your friendly tax inspector. Naturally.

Delving into the Mysteries of PAYE and Its Codes

PAYE (Pay As You Earn) is a tax-collecting system in which your employer deducts income tax from your pay packet and sends the money on to HMRC. It is run in parallel with the national insurance deduction scheme.

It's up to employers to collect both PAYE and national insurance on a monthly basis. This responsibility extends to casual labour and to other individuals, such as IT contractors, who prefer to be self-employed.

Your PAYE tax code tells your employer how much tax to deduct from your pay packet. If the code is wrong, you can end up paying too much or too little tax. The code consists of two parts – a number followed by a letter. The number gives HMRC and your employer an indication of the amount of your allowance; the letter shows what type of tax allowances you're claiming. This knowledge is of most use when tax allowances change.

Your PAYE code should take in a number of elements. Besides your personal allowance, which will increase if you are 65 or over, you may be able to claim on other expenses such as pension payments, certain job-related expenses and professional subscriptions. In addition there are a number of other allowances you may be able to claim such as payments to a friendly society for death benefits or the blind person's allowance for you or your spouse if she or he does not earn enough to benefit. You're charged for perks such as a company car, private medical insurance, and most state benefits such as the state pension and jobseeker's allowance.

You should also receive extra tax relief if you donate to Gift Aid and you are a top-rate taxpayer. Although, if you give more to Gift Aid than you have paid in income tax or capital gains tax, then the nice people at HMRC will claw back tax relief on the charitable donation through the coding system. That's not very charitable!

Finding out what the numbers mean

The tax code number is your tax-free allowance divided by ten with fractions ignored. If you have the full personal allowance (£5,225 in 2007-08) your code is 522. Someone over 65 but under 75 has a £7,550 basic allowance, giving them a 755 code if they have a full personal allowance.

Your allowance may be reduced if you have taxable perks or receive taxable sums from investments or a spare-time job.

Someone starting with the full 522 code with a £1,000 valuation of their car benefit will end up with £4,225 in allowances or a 422 code. Add in £500 tax due on spare-time earnings and £500 in tax on savings and investments not deducted at source and the code falls to 322.

Looking at the letters

The second part of your tax code consists of a letter or combination of letters. These give those concerned with your PAYE status a quick indication of the general level of your tax allowances. They mainly help when the government announces changes to tax allowances.

The following list tells you what the most commonly used letters represent:

- ✔ **L:** The basic personal allowance.

- ✔ **P:** The allowance for those aged 65 to 74.

- ✔ **V:** The allowance for the 65-to-74 age group plus the married couple's allowance, which you qualify for if you're married and were born before 6 April 1935.

- ✔ **Y:** The personal allowance for those aged 75 or over.

- ✔ **A:** The basic personal allowance plus one half of the Children's Tax Credit. It's used if you pay the basic tax rate and share the Children's Credit with your partner.

- ✔ **H:** This is similar to A; it's the basic allowance plus *all* the Children's Tax Credit.

- ✔ **K:** The code used when the total allowances you are due are not as great as the total deductions. The preceding number is negative: the higher it is, the more you pay.

   Someone who is due the personal allowance starts off with £5,225 (in 2007-08) or code 522. If they have a car benefit worth £4,000, medical insurance worth £505, extra savings tax of £500, and spare time earnings worth £2,000 in tax, they end up with £7,005. Subtract that from £5,225 and they end up with a negative K code of 178 to reflect the £1,780 they owe. It works out the same as if they earned £1,780 more than their salary without any deductions.

- ✔ **T:** The code you get if you ask the Inland Revenue not to use any of the others. You may, for instance, not wish the wages department to know about your other sources of income. It's also used for some special cases.

- ✔ **OT:** No allowances at all but tax deducted normally otherwise at the highest rate applicable to your earnings. Used usually when you have a second income source that uses up all your allowances.

> ✔ **BR:** The code indicating that all your income is taxed at the basic rate, currently 22 per cent.
>
> ✔ **DO:** This is generally used if you are a high earner who has more than one job and have been fully credited with your allowances elsewhere. Every pound you earn is taxed at the top rate, currently 40 per cent.
>
> ✔ **NT:** Used when no tax is to be taken from your income.

If you have two jobs, it's likely that all of your second income will be taxed at the basic or higher rate, depending on how much you earn. This is because all of your allowances have been used against the income from your main job.

Checking Your Deductions

Everything you earn from your employment, whether called wages, salary, commission, bonus, or even, for vicars, a stipend, is known as an *emolument* in tax-speak. It does not matter whether you are paid weekly or monthly or whether you're paid in cash, cheque, or straight into a bank. All emoluments are subject to PAYE.

So too, are many pension payments from past employers and other schemes. You can't necessarily escape PAYE by retiring. Many pension payers lump in the state pension into the overall payment. That way, it is added in and subject to PAYE. But if all you have is the state pension, you don't pay any tax as your earnings are below the tax threshold.

Payments of expenses and perks (technically known as *benefits-in-kind*) are not in PAYE even if they are taxable. The second half of this chapter deals with tax issues related to perks.

Checking your pay packet

All tax and national insurance deductions made by your employer should be accurate to the last penny. But you should check your pay cheque to see that nothing is wrong, especially when you start a new job or receive a salary boost (or reduction). There is always the chance of data being incorrectly input into the computer program or a small business employer getting confused with the PAYE manual.

Meeting your national insurance obligations

Employers have to deduct national insurance where appropriate at the right amount. And they have to pay their own contribution. Failure to do so can bring similar penalties to failing to send a PAYE cheque.

Your boss should deduct national insurance at the time they issue your pay packet. They cannot normally chase you later if they forget.

Paying in

When national insurance started in 1948, everyone in employment paid a stamp at a flat rate. This payment provided you with certain benefits such as a retirement pension and payments during periods of unemployment. Today, national insurance is effectively a tax on earnings from employment until you reach the state retirement age, currently 65 for men and 60 for women. You won't get anything more by offering to pay more through PAYE!

Many benefits are tied to certain minimum payment rules that required you to contribute for a minimum number of weeks each year at the lowest level applicable to that year.

Because national insurance is under the control of HMRC, it comes under the purview of this book. After all, you need to know what you can claim and hence increase the amount you receive from the state in return for your tax pounds when you are in need.

What you pay as an employee depends on what you earn, but for most people the combination of basic rate income tax with National Insurance takes 33p from every additional pound they earn after their personal allowances and the 10 per cent tax band. (This will fall to 31p in the pound when the basic rate of tax is cut to 20 per cent in 2008-09.)

By comparison, top-rate taxpayers lose 41p from every extra pound they earn above the 40 per cent tax band. This is because the main 11p in the pound stops before the top tax band. The only extra national insurance anyone in the top band has to pay is a one per cent surcharge, making 41p in the pound in all. *Surcharge* is just another name for tax. And you don't get any benefits from it.

Arriving at a ball park figure for take-home pay

Following the steps in this sidebar gives you an estimate of how much money you'll take home each month: This formula is designed to work across tax years as it pays no attention to minor changes in personal allowances. It ignores pensions, the 10 per cent income tax starter rate, workplace charitable donations, and other deductions. But it works surprisingly well for people earning up to around £32,000 a year, which is more than 80 per cent of the employed population. Chapter 2 on self assessment shows you how to come up with an exact figure for the year. This rough formula should work with your monthly salary slip.

1. Subtract £5,000 a year from your gross salary.

   As an example, start with a salary of £23,000 a year gross. Subtracting £5,000 gives you £18,000.

2. Divide what's left by 12 to give a monthly figure because you're paid once a month.

   Dividing £18,000 by 12 gives £1,500.

3. Take away one third of this new figure – 22% for income tax and 11% for national insurance.

   A third of £1,500 is £500; subtracting that gives £1,000.

4. Add back the £5,000 you took off at the start but divide it by 12 to turn it into a monthly figure. This sum roughly equals the money you have to spend, known as *net pay*.

   £5,000 divided by 12 gives you around £400. Adding that to the £1,000 in Step 3 gives you £1,400, which is roughly the amount your employer should deposit in your bank account each month.

From April 2008, the national insurance upper earnings limit will be brought into line with the point at which people start to pay the top rate of tax.

Taking out

Some state benefits are linked to national insurance, but generally to amounts based on the minimum weekly payment rather than what you might actually have paid. A *minimum payment* is the lowest level that can be taken for one week in any one tax year. But because some benefits are expressed as so many times the equivalent minimum, these can tot up faster if you pay more on higher earnings. The maximum is usually around five times the minimum, so if you pay the highest possible amount, you gain the benefit five times faster.

You have to claim many of these benefits as they are not paid automatically. Rates, which can be complicated, change from time to time. You can get more information from the HMRC Web site at www.hmrc.gov.uk, at local advice centres, or from charitable organisations such as Citizens Advice and the Child Poverty Action Group.

The benefits include:

✔ **Bereavement allowance:** Paid for one year to widows and widowers over 45 who were below pension age when their spouse died. The dead spouse would have to have paid the equivalent of 25 minimum payments.

✔ **Contribution-based jobseeker's allowance:** Paid to those who are out of work up to a maximum of 26 weeks. You need to have earned enough to have paid the equivalent of at least 25 payments of the minimum weekly amount in any tax year plus at least 50 payments of the minimum weekly amount in each of the last two complete tax years as an employed person before your unemployment started. National insurance paid as a self-employed person does not count.

✔ **Incapacity benefit:** Paid to those with long-term illnesses or disabilities. The contribution requirements are similar to those for the contribution-based jobseeker's allowance but the self-employed can apply.

✔ **State retirement pension:** Currently paid to men at age 65 and over and to women age 60 or over. (The age for women will rise to 65 by 2015 on a stepped changeover from April 2010 onwards. This affects women born after April 5, 1950. It will be gradual so that a woman born in 1952 will have to wait until she is 62, one born in 1954 will have to wait until she is 64, while all of those born after April 5, 1955 will have to wait until they reach 65.) Either you or a late spouse (or former spouse) must have paid 52 times the minimum contribution in any tax year. And you have to have paid at least 52 times the minimum weekly contribution throughout your working life although you are allowed to miss out one year in every ten. If you don't meet these minimum requirements, you may get a percentage of the full amount depending on how far you fall short.

✔ **Widowed parent's allowance:** Paid to widows and widowers with children. The contribution rules are similar to those for the state retirement pension.

Book II

Paying Less Tax

If you have a period away from work, check with HMRC to see if you can have your contributions credited (usually for family care duties) or if it is worth your while buying Class 3 voluntary contributions to maintain your record.

The Class 4 contributions paid by the self-employed do not qualify for any benefits at all as this is a pure extra tax-raising exercise.

Noticing when your employer gets it wrong

Along with basic PAYE deductions, employers have a duty to check on any expenses paid without a tax deduction. For instance, someone who normally works in Manchester and is sent to London for the day can claim travelling expenses. But someone who is normally based in Manchester and is told to work in London for six months cannot claim travelling costs.

There are obviously many grey areas. But unless an employer can show the PAYE error was made in good faith (usually a polite way of saying the employee or someone else tried to pull a fast one), then the employer has to pay up.

Employers sometimes tell casual staff who demand full-time staff benefits that they will report them to HMRC for keeping their self-employed status. But any boss that does that will shoot themselves in the foot. HMRC's attitude will be that the amount paid is net and the employer will be liable for tax and national insurance on top of the money already paid.

There are very few, and very special, circumstances when the employer can go back to the employee and ask for extra tax money. Always check with an accountant, Citizens Advice, or a trade union before agreeing to such a deduction from your pay packet. Bust bosses have been known to loot pay packets before disappearing!

Pleading confusion or ignorance is not a defence for the boss. Employers who fail to pass on PAYE deductions face interest charges and penalties.

Part time, casual, and contract workers have to pay PAYE and national insurance in just the same way as those on normal full-time contracts. From the government's point of view, there is no difference. HMRC is clamping down on firms that try to pay casual and contract workers on a self-employed or freelance basis as a tax dodge.

Losing or Leaving Your Job

A tiny number of those who lose their jobs every year end up featured in one of those newspaper 'finance-for-failure' stories that dissect once high-flying executives of major companies who collect millions after they are sacked for being useless. Don't shed too many tears for them. They are rich enough to hire lawyers and accountants to help minimise any tax take.

For mere mortals who lose their jobs due to changing economic circumstances or shifting employer needs, post-termination life is likely to be a bit less rosy. In these sections, we tell you how to cope successfully with the tax issues.

Don't forget to claim jobseeker's allowance if you are out of work but trying to find a new job. You pay for this benefit through your tax and national insurance payments, so don't ignore it. At £59.15 a week for six months it's not a fortune. But it will help pay for stamps to send off application forms and expenses in going to interviews.

The magic figure for payoffs, redundancy, or termination payments (or whatever the current euphemism may be) is £30,000. The first £30,000 of any redundancy payment is tax-free. This £30,000 includes any statutory amount you receive under the Employment Protection (Consolidation) Act 1978, which is tax-free anyway.

To calculate the statutory amount if you're between the ages of between 20 and 63, you multiply your weekly pay up to £270 by one-and-half times the number of years you worked. So if you worked ten years and earned £250 a week, you would be entitled to 15 times (1.5 × 10) your £250 giving you £3,750.

The statutory payments are not that high and cannot reach the £30,000 tax free limit. Many about-to-be-former workers manage to negotiate higher non-statutory amounts. Additional amounts should normally be paid tax-free providing:

Book II

Paying
Less Tax

✔ You have been in the job for at least two years.

✔ Payments are made to all employees in the same situation and not just to a select few or part of the group.

✔ Payments are not excessively large in relation to salaries paid and length of service.

   This point can be contentious. But it's designed to stop bosses paying you very little while you are working there and then sacking you with a huge redundancy payment.

The sum of £30,000 has remained unchanged for many years. But, under a complicated formula, the £30,000 exempt figure can be increased if your employment included a spell overseas. This is rarely applicable but the HMRC Web site (www.hmrc.gov.uk) has the complicated details.

If your redundancy payment tops £30,000, the excess is taxed as income in the normal way.

If you have to leave a job through illness, disability, or injury, try to negotiate a payoff. It will normally be paid tax-free.

When you leave an employer for whatever reason (including a voluntary resignation when quitting may be a blessed relief), you receive form P45 to take to your next job. The P45 details your earnings in the work you are leaving and helps your new boss with the PAYE computation. Check your P45 to make sure any termination payment you receive isn't included.

If you are in your fifties or older, make sure that any redundancy payoff, or golden handshake, is structured so that HMRC cannot claim it is effectively an early retirement sum and then hit the amount with a tax bill. Early retirement can include people near their normal retirement age leaving jobs to take care of aged relatives.

Taxing Those Little Extras

Your employer can provide you with a wide range of extras ranging from private healthcare plans to company cars to workplace parties to the occasional free breakfast if you cycle to work.

If you receive perks from your employer (a company car and healthcare scheme are probably the biggest), you most likely have to pay tax on their value. This value is added to your regular earnings. So, someone with a £25,000 salary and £3,000 in taxable benefits-in-kind is treated as though they earn £28,000.

Workplace perks split into three categories: those that are taxed, those that are tax-free, and the essentials – expenses which are free of income tax because they are 'wholly, exclusively, and necessarily in the performance of your duties.'

HMRC always talks about taxable charges. These are not as big as they sound. The *taxable charge* is not what you pay but a factor added to your other income and then taxed at your highest rate. So someone paying 40 per cent tax on their income who has a perk with an annual £10,000 taxable charge value has to find 40 per cent of that sum (or £4,000) in cash when it comes to finalising their tax bill for the year.

In normal speech, you never hear the word emoluments but it's an important word in tax-inspector-ese so watch out for it. *Emoluments* are the total value of all you get from your job including the worth of all the perks. And because the value of these perks counts for your overall taxable emoluments, they can push someone from the basic-rate tax band into the top-rate tax band. A tax-payer on £35,000 a year is within the basic zone; add in £5,000 worth of taxable benefits such as a company car and the top slice of their total emoluments is taxable at 40 per cent.

Don't turn your nose up at a perk just because it is taxable. Employers can often negotiate far better deals than you can as an individual on benefits such as healthcare plans because buying for hundreds or thousands gives them bulk purchasing power. In any case, if you bought the benefit personally, it would come out of your taxed income.

Taxable perks are known in the tax trade as *P11D benefits* after the HMRC form your workplace gives you once a year if you receive any taxable perks.

The P11D lists reports the amount it cost the employer to provide the benefit less any amount you contribute yourself from your taxed salary (we talk about the special rules for company cars and vans in the next section). Some employers, for instance, offer gym membership but insist that the employee pays a percentage to show that they are serious about exercise.

Perks on which you have to pay tax are listed on this form. You can either pay the amounts through the self assessment system or elect to pay for them through PAYE (Pay As You Earn) deductions from your regular salary if the annual tax on the perks is no greater than £2,000. If the tax tops £2,000, you have to pay separately through the self assessment system every six months. So, if this fits you, you need to put cash aside (or have a helpful bank manager!).

Book II

Paying Less Tax

Travelling to and for Work

One of the biggest costs of working is getting there in the morning and coming home at night (or vice versa if you work shifts). Your boss may help you with some of these expenses.

Your employer can provide tax-free help, including the cost of hiring cars and hotel bills, if your normal travel arrangements are impossible due to a rail strike.

Counting the cost of a company car

The company car is Britain's biggest employer-provided benefit. Its popularity dates from years of *tax breaks* (special tax relief for special situations). And though many tax advantages have been eroded, a company car remains a potent, if taxable, status symbol.

You no longer have to visit clients in both Land's End and John O'Groats at the end of the tax year to boost your proportion of business to private mileage. You're taxed as long as you can use the car privately, no matter what the proportion is.

Working out the tax

The annual taxable benefit of most workplace-provided cars depends on two factors:

- The car's full list price including the full value of any accessories (excluding a mobile phone and anything to help drivers with disabilities). Any discounts, or extras such as 'free' hi-fi upgrades, air-conditioning or metallic paint that a private buyer can obtain, are ignored. So the taxable value is likely to be more than the cost would be to you as an individual.

- The car's CO_2 (carbon dioxide) emissions. The greener the car, the less you pay. The Inland Revenue computes a factor deriving from carbon emissions to give a percentage of the car's original cost. The taxable amount can range from 15 per cent of cost for the cleanest cars up to 35 per cent for the least atmosphere-friendly vehicles. This figure gives the taxable value.

There are special rules for older cars, and other vehicles which do not have an emission figure. Those who drive valuable vintage cars are now assessed on the vehicle's current market value if it is over £15,000 and not the original list price. So, there's another loophole gone!

Under the present rules, the maximum value of any car for these calculations is £80,000. Going over this only applies to a few people but it's useful to know if you are really ambitious about that Ferrari, Lamborghini, Bentley, or Rolls-Royce!

Considering other ways to pay for driving

In many cases, you might be better off negotiating a pay rise and giving up the company car benefit. Employers can pay you a tax-free and national insurance-free amount for every mile you drive on workplace duties in your own car.

This is currently

- 40p per mile for the first 10,000 miles
- 25p per mile for each subsequent mile
- 24p per mile for motorcycles
- 5p per mile extra for each passenger carried on work-related journeys

If you are reimbursed for mileage at less than these rates, you can claim the balance (but not the 5p per mile passenger extra) against your taxable income. For instance, if your employer gives you 30p per mile for 1,000 miles, you have a 10p a mile shortfall so you can claim £100 against your taxable income.

A number of lease packages effectively duplicate the company car experience by including insurance, repairs, regular maintenance, depreciation and other expenses in an overall monthly sum.

Alternatively, you can just go out and buy a cheap second-hand car or, if you want, a really flash sports car. Or you can decide you do not need a car at all.

The sums involved can be horrendously complicated with every case different, but if your employer is willing to swap your company car for extra cash (there is no obligation to do so), ask your personnel department or a benefits consultant to work out the sums for you.

Checking what counts as business mileage

The big exception to business mileage is the daily commute from home to work and back again. The Inland Revenue defines regular commuting as travel to a location you report to on 40 per cent or more of your working days.

But if you have to go for work purposes to a location that is not your normal place of work, you may be able to claim business mileage on this *triangular travel.* (We bet you thought triangular travel was when you tried to sail against the wind!)

Suppose you live in London and regularly commute to your workplace in Brighton. This is not business mileage. But if you're told to go to Birmingham for the day, this mileage would count. You can not, however, count somewhere directly between London and Brighton such as Gatwick Airport. Nor would it count to anywhere within 10 miles of the normal journey.

You can also claim costs involved in *site travel,* in which you have to go to and from a location that isn't your official place of work. You may also be able to claim tax relief on *subsistence costs* such as buying yourself a midday meal when you are not at your normal workplace. You can't do this forever, however. After 24 months, HMRC says the site is now your normal workplace.

Fuelling concerns

You have to pay an additional tax charge for private petrol provided free-of-charge. This is calculated by multiplying the CO_2 percentage (see the previous 'Working out the tax' section) by £14,400. So if the percentage is 20, the tax charge for petrol is £2,880. For a basic-rate tax-payer, the after-tax cash equivalent is £633; it's £1,152 at the top rate.

The charge is the same whether you take 2 litres or 2,000 litres, so once you've paid it makes sense to use as much free petrol as possible.

Your employer can give you tax-free fuel allowance if you pay for fuel used for business travel. This ranges from 9p per mile for smaller diesel cars (under 2,000cc) to 16p a mile for larger petrol cars (over 2,000cc). There are lower rates for cars using the cheaper liquid petroleum gas where rates range from 6p to 10p a mile.

Cycling – two wheels are better

The government is keen on green commuting. And it's willing to subsidise pedal-pushers through the tax system. In general, any cycle benefit has to be made available to all employees from the most senior to recent school- or college-leavers.

Employers can provide cycles, cycling equipment, and cycle facilities such as bike sheds and showers to employees without employees incurring any tax or national insurance liabilities.

Having the tax collector help buy your bike

Whether it's a boneshaker costing under £100 or a top-of-the-range model at £4,000 plus, you can get a new bike and all the extra bits such as locks, lights, and pannier racks with help from HMRC.

It's called the Green Transport Plan. You persuade your employer to either buy or lease the bike (which is chosen can depend on your boss's tax and cash position). There are specialist firms that do all the paperwork. But a good local dealer will be able to do this as well, especially if it means selling a few dozen machines!

The employer then loans the bikes to the employee in return for a monthly amount, deducted from their salary. The employee's gross earnings are cut (which can have pension and mortgage application repercussions).

The employer can reclaim the VAT so a £270 bike immediately becomes £40.20 cheaper (and that's not counting doing a deal with the bike shop because so many extra bikes can be sold). That brings the cost down to £229.80. Employers then arrange a repayment period, perhaps over 24 months. So the employee sacrifices £9.57 a month.

The £9.57 is free of employee's national insurance and income tax, for most people equal to 33 per cent. So the real cost is £6.39 a month or £153.36 over the 24 months. This includes interest-free credit worth perhaps £20 on the bike's original selling price. All in all, you have so far paid around half the real cost (it would be even less if you were a top-rate tax-payer).

After two years, the employer sells the bike to you. This will normally be a nominal sum – perhaps £20 in this case.

You are supposed to use the bike for commuting but commuting also includes where you use the train for long distances while riding at either end. You can also use it for leisure purposes.

Amazingly, this benefit also extends to electric bikes so you don't have to be that athletic to apply.

Employees can use these bikes for journeys to work and for some leisure use. HMRC knows that deciding on who cycles where and why is just about impossible, so in reality, you're free to use a work-provided cycle whenever you like.

Those who use their own bicycles for business use can claim a 20p a mile tax free 'approved mileage allowance payment' from their employers. If the firm pays less, or nothing at all, you can claim that 20p per mile mileage allowance relief via your employer, through writing to your tax inspector, or on your self assessment form. So if you cycle 1,000 miles a year and receive nothing from your employer, you can deduct £200 from your taxable income. However, you can't claim the 20p per mile if your bike is being bought under the Green Transport Plan (see the sidebar 'Having the tax collector help buy your bike').

Employers who encourage staff to cycle by holding cycle-to-work days can provide a tax-free breakfast to those who pedal on up to six days a year!

Book II

Paying Less Tax

Getting Non-Transport Perks

There is a huge variety of benefits employers can give as part of an overall remuneration package. The following sections talk about many of them.

Housing: from the vicarage to the lighthouse

If you are offered low- or no-rent accommodation as part of your overall pay package, expect to pay income tax and national insurance on the benefit. However, in certain situations, your housing benefit is tax-free. Such circumstances may be because:

- ✔ You have to live in the housing to fulfil your duties properly. You may be a caretaker, or a gamekeeper who needs to be close to the birds you're looking after. This exemption also includes lighthouse-keepers, and many staff members of boarding schools such as housemasters and mistresses.

- ✔ Living in on-site housing helps you perform your duties better or such accommodation is customary. This may include some farm-workers in the first category and vicars in the second. It can also include pub managers and caravan-site managers.

- ✔ You have to live in specific accommodation due to a special security threat to you. This can include members of the armed forces and those in the diplomatic service.

The tax freedom only extends to the rent. You can be charged a P11D-style amount on the value of furniture and equipment within the house. This is usually calculated at 20 per cent of the market value of the furniture when it was first installed. So any charge would be negligible if the furniture was second-hand.

Paying for childcare

Firms can offer childcare (such as a nursery or a pre-school or after-school club) free of national insurance and income tax providing:

- ✔ It is not in a private home.
- ✔ It meets local authority guidelines.
- ✔ It is concerned with care rather than education – it must be a nursery not a school.

A new scheme from April 2005 allows employers to pay up to £50 a week free-of-tax and national insurance towards childcare arrangements other than those listed above. These can include registered childminders.

The money will normally be in the form of vouchers or go directly to the child-care provider. This scheme must be made available either to all employees or all employees at a particular location – employers can't offer the benefit just to a few people.

Realising other tax-free perks

Your firm can provide an amazing range of perks tax-free designed to keep you happy.

Enjoying your lunch tax-free

Providing a free or subsidised canteen or staff restaurant is a tax-free benefit. It does not have to be on the premises but if it is elsewhere, it must be in a separate part of the outside restaurant or hotel from where the general public is barred. Higher paid staff can have a separate room as long as the food they get is no better than that served to others.

Employers can provide luncheon vouchers up to the amazing value of 15p a day tax-free for each working day. The sum has stayed unchanged for some 40 years when it was three shillings in pre-decimal money (15p in decimal money) and you could buy a proper meal for that sum! It's worth about £7.50 for a basic rate taxpayer a year. So it's just about enough for half a pint and a sandwich for two to toast the Inland Revenue's continuing generosity!

Playing games tax-free

Free or subsidised sports or social facilities such as football fields or a darts club do not count as a taxable perk. But company membership of health clubs or other outside fitness venues is taxable under the P11D mechanism unless those facilities are available to employees only.

Making calls and paying less tax

Private use of mobile phones supplied by your employer escapes the tax net altogether (but only for one phone or PDA).

Moving home with Inland Revenue assistance

You can receive up to £8,000 a move from your employer and not pay tax on it when your company forces you to relocate or when you take up a new job which compels you to move home.

The tax-free expenses can include removal costs and the legal and other expenses of any house purchase that fails. You do not have to sell your old home.

Profiting from the suggestion box

Unless it is part of your normal job to come up with brainstorming ideas, you can get tax-free cash if suggestions made into schemes are adopted. The amount is related to the financial gain to your employer. The limit is an award of £5,000 – anything above this is taxable. You can also have up to £25 tax-free if your suggestion is a bright concept but is not implemented.

Enjoying a party

Your employer can spend up to £150 a year per employee on staff parties. This does not have to be a Christmas party; it can be any time of the year for any purpose. Your boss can also hold a summer and a winter party and split the cost between the two. The party must be generally open to all staff or all staff on a certain site; it cannot be open just to senior executives. This sum does not cover the cost of inviting any outside guests.

Getting your gold watch tax free too

Long service awards are tax-free as long as the recipient has at least 20 years with the same employer and there has been no similar gift in the past 10 years. The gift can be worth as much as £50 for each year of service. It cannot be in cash.

Taking financial advice

You can have up to £150 worth a year of financial and pensions advice tax free when it is provided by your employer.

Free eyesight tests and glasses

Health and safety legislation demands that employers offer regular eye checks to staff who use computer screens. This is a tax-free benefit, as is any fixed amount you are given towards buying glasses. This is usually enough to purchase a basic pair of spectacles.

Explaining Expenses: The Wholly, Exclusively, and Necessarily Rule

The self-employed have substantial freedom in deciding the expenses they can set against earnings, and so remove them from the income tax net. Not so, those who work for others. They have to convince the tax inspector that any expenses they receive from their employers are 'wholly, exclusively, and necessarily in the performance of their duties.'

These are very strict guidelines. Pass them, and the money your employer gives you is tax-free. Fail them and you face tax and national insurance on the amounts, just the same as if they were part of your salary packet. There is, of course, nothing to stop your employer picking up the tax bill on your behalf.

Examining expenses that qualify

There is no tax to pay on:

- Travelling expenses when you are ordered by your employer to make the journey.
- The cost of meals when you are away from home on business.
- Travelling to a temporary workplace for up to 24 months.
- Personal expenses when you are away from home on business of up to £5 a night in the UK and £10 a night elsewhere.
- Payments of up to £2 a week for expenses when you have to work at home.
- The cost of two return journeys a year for your spouse and children to a location outside the UK if you have to work overseas for a continuous period of at least 60 days.
- Medical treatment if incurred overseas when on business.

> ✔ The cost of entertaining customers, contacts and clients. Earlier attempts by HMRC to split the bill so the guest's food and drink was tax-free while you paid tax on your consumption resulted in a farce as hosts claimed they had one glass of water while guests tucked into big meals, and bigger bottles of wine.

Eyeing expenses you pay tax on

Here are some examples of claims when tax inspectors were not convinced of wholly, exclusively, and necessarily.

✔ Ordinary every day clothing

✔ Travelling costs to work at a normal site

✔ Costs of domestic help at an employee's home

✔ Meal expenses paid out of meal allowances

✔ Phone line rental costs when the phone is not used wholly, exclusively and necessarily for work (but claims for fax lines at home have been more successful)

✔ Courses to improve your background knowledge of the subject – for instance, an architect cannot claim a tour to see the architecture of Ancient Rome.

✔ Costs incurred by a teacher in keeping a room at her home for marking work

✔ Diet supplements for professional sports people

✔ Newspapers read by journalists – these may be 'wholly and exclusively' for work but HMRC will argue that there are not 'necessary'.

Book II

Paying Less Tax

Special deals for special jobs

HMRC allows you to deduct the cost of subscriptions to various professional organisations that are essential if you are to continue with your work. In some cases, only part of the amount is allowable as the balance covers non-essential items such as lobbying. There is also a long list of flat-rate deductions that can be claimed by people in various manual jobs requiring special clothing or tools. But don't get too excited. The sums are relatively small, have not been updated since 1996, and the cash savings are small. Most employers in these industries arrange for automatic deductions so you may not have to claim.

HMRC's *Extra Statutory Concessions* booklet has a complete list with full descriptions including unusual jobs such as artificial limb makers (they get £90 but £115 if the limbs are made of wood – don't ask why!) You can download this booklet from the HMRC Web site at www.hmrc.gov.uk or get it from your local tax office. It's quite a hefty publication so if you print if off from the Web site, make sure you have about 150 sheets of paper.

Offering Share Schemes – Who and How

Many employers operate schemes that give employees a chance to share in the firm's ups (and sometimes, regrettably, downs) by offering them a share stake in the company.

In a *share scheme,* the company's directors offer employees an opportunity to invest in the company by buying shares in the firm or by offering options to buy shares. An option is a sort of one-way promise. If the shares go up, you can take up the option but if they go down or you can't afford them, you can tear up the option and not suffer any penalty.

Different share schemes have differing rules on how much you can put in, what your boss can add, when you can take your investment out and how much (if any) tax you pay on any profits you make. So read on, and if your employer has shares, you should find a plan that's suitable.

Your employer can offer you a *share incentive plan* (SIP) and a *Save As You Earn* (SAYE) scheme at the same time, entitling you to extra benefits.

Working out who offers what to whom

There is no obligation on employers to offer a share scheme. Companies that offer their staff share plans reckon it is well worth the cost of issuing the shares as employees tend to be more motivated, work harder, and remain loyal when the carrot of a big pack of shares with tax benefits is dangled a few years in front of them.

Schemes are most common in large quoted companies. Schemes are rarer in smaller companies where the shareholder list is likely to be restricted to members of the family that owns the firm. There is no bar against overseas companies offering access to their foreign-quoted shares to their UK employees.

With the lone exception of free share incentive plans (SIPs), these schemes must be available to all employees whether full- or part-time and however exulted or lowly their salary level or job status. In Save As You Earn schemes and some SIPs, the firm can impose a qualifying period of up to five years' work for the firm, providing it applies equally to everyone.

Treasuring the tax savings

Company share schemes can be worth over £1,000 a year in tax savings. Most of these incentive plans include tax saving possibilities. The exact amount of tax savings depends on how much you go in for and what happens to the shares. You get the tax savings at the end of the scheme period. And, of course, the shares have to go up for you to realise any tax savings at all.

To get tax advantages, share schemes have to be properly structured. A straight gift of shares from your employer counts as a taxable benefit. You will have to pay tax based on the shares' market value on the day you receive them. If you pay part of their worth, you will be taxed on the gap between what you paid and their stock market value.

Saving with a Save As You Earn Scheme

Save As You Earn (SAYE) is the most popular share incentive scheme. Through a SAYE plan, employees contract to save a set amount from £5 to £250 out of their pay packet each month for a set period of time – three or five years. A further option is to leave the money in the account for a further two years after the fifth year.

Be sure you are comfortable with the amount you agree to pay into an SAYE account. You cannot increase or decrease the amount during the term of the plan. Decreasing or permanently stopping payments ends the plan.

You are allowed to delay up to six monthly payments during your SAYE plan. This extends your contract by the number of missed months. Once you go beyond six missed payments, the plan is terminated.

You may have the choice of saving for three years, five years, or seven years. In the latter case you save for five years and then leave the money saved for another two years. Employers can offer a choice of these periods (and many do), or you may only have one option.

The money you pay into your SAYE plan every month goes into a special SAYE account with a bank or building society, chosen by your employer. It earns tax-free interest and a tax-free interest-related bonus.

You do not acquire any shares yourself with each monthly payment. But you can buy them with the proceeds of your SAYE account at the end of your SAYE period at the pre-set option price.

When you start a SAYE plan, the company sets the share value anywhere in a range between the current stock market value or 20 per cent lower. This is your starting price. You compare the price at the end of the scheme with this to see if you have made money on the shares. If not, walk away. You pay no income tax or national insurance on these undervalued shares.

You can have more than one scheme with your employer providing your monthly contribution total does not exceed £250. Many firms have regular offers, each with a different option price, to reflect ups and downs in the stock market.

If your SAYE scheme works out well and you take up the shares, why not use another tax saving plan to protect further growth against capital gains tax? You can do this by transferring your shares into an Individual Savings Account (ISA). There is an annual tax year limit of £7,000 on all money put into an ISA. So if you have used your allowance for other investments or savings, you can't put your share-scheme money into it. And even if you have already put just £1 into a mini-cash ISA, your annual shares limit falls to £4,000 (but the rules will become less restrictive from April 2008). There are strict rules about not exceeding your ISA limits. If you do it accidentally, you have to pay any tax you otherwise avoided. (Turn to Chapter 4 in Book III for full details about ISAs and the changes due in 2008.)

Sharing a SAYE success story

Suppose the shares of your company trade at 100p when you start. You are given an SAYE option at 80p, the maximum 20 per cent discount.

You save £100 a month for five years which, including the tax-free interest, gives you a fund of £6,610. This will buy you 8,262 shares, no matter what has happened to the price of the shares over the period of your contract. I'm ignoring the 40p left over.

If the price of the shares is over 80p, you can make a profit by exercising the option with the money in the account and then selling the shares. This profit will be liable to capital gains tax on the amount between the present value and the option price. But don't forget you have an annual zero rate allowance. And you don't have to sell. You can keep all the shares for the future or sell some to make the best use of your annual CGT allowance.

Discussing Share Incentive Plans

Share Incentive Plans (SIPs) offer more (sometimes much more) in the way of tax-saving benefits than the SAYE plan we explain in the preceding sections. SIPs used to be called All Employee Share Ownership Plans, with the whimsical acronym Aesops, but SIPs is pretty jaunty in its own right.

Share incentive plans come with higher risks than SAYE schemes. You buy actual shares from the start instead of accumulating options. The shares you buy are not like options you can abandon if the stock market price falls. So if the share price goes down, you will take a loss.

You do not receive the shares when you are awarded them. Instead, they are held by trustees in a plan for three to five years, depending on the specifics of the scheme. If you leave the firm, other than for disability or death, you may forfeit your tax-saving arrangement (see the earlier 'Treasuring the tax savings' section).

Share prices in your company may fall along with share prices generally in the stock market no matter how hard you and your colleagues work! There is no tax compensation if you have to sell out at a loss.

Share incentive plans come in three flavours: free shares, partnership shares, and matching shares. Which type you receive is up to your employer. Some go for the free shares route; others will take the partnership (and possibly matching shares) road.

Keep full records of all SIP share transactions for five years. You can face an income tax charge if you withdraw your shares from the plan within five years of joining it.

Getting something for nothing with free shares

Free shares are obviously the best deal because they cost you nothing. Unlike other work-related perks, there is no income tax or national insurance to pay. And as employers can give up to £3,000 in any one tax year, that's worth up to £999 in tax benefits for basic-rate taxpayers and up to £1,230 for top-rate payers.

You can receive free shares according to performance measures, salary, or length of service. These targets must be publicised ahead of your signing up for the scheme and cannot be changed midway. And the highest performance linked handout cannot be greater than four times the non-performance figure.

Book II

Paying Less Tax

Turning a SIP into a SIPP

No, this is not alphabet soup gone mad, just a way to take your share incentive plan (SIP) investments and transfer them directly to a *self invested personal pension* (SIPP). Doing this turns each 78p of SIP shares into £1 of SIPP for a basic- or lower-rate or non-taxpayer. A top-rate taxpayer can turn 60p of SIP into £1 of SIPP. The SIPP provider has to be happy with accepting the shares so they will probably have to be equities in stockmarket quoted companies. Once within the SIPP, they can be sold without tax concerns.

This SIP to SIPP transfer must be made within 90 days of withdrawing the shares from your employer's plan.

This is an all-employee scheme so it must be available to everyone in the company, including part-timers. But firms can set a qualifying limit of up to 18 months employment before letting someone join.

These shares are held on your behalf in a trust. If you leave the firm within three years of your starting the scheme then you generally lose your rights to the tax benefits on free shares. If you take your investment out of the plan between the three and five year period, you may face a tax charge on the difference between the value on the day you acquired them and the day you took them out of the plan to spend the proceeds. The exact rules depend on the company and the way it has set up the trust. But you cannot lose your tax savings if you have to leave through injury, disability, illness, retirement, or redundancy. And, if you die, your heirs can make use of the tax savings.

Going into partnership with your employer

Partnership shares in a SIP give you the chance to back your firm with your own cash. You buy shares at market value with money that is free of income tax and national insurance deductions. There is an annual limit of £1,500 (or 10 per cent of your gross pay after pension plan contributions, and any workplace charitable donations if this is lower). The £1,500 maximum is worth up to nearly £500 for basic-rate taxpayers and up to £615 for top-rate taxpayers.

If you withdraw partnership shares from the trust within three years of joining the plan, you pay tax based on the market value at the time you take the shares, not the original value which may, of course, be lower or higher. After five years, you can take them out of the plan and sell them without any income tax worries.

As long as you keep your shares in the plan, they grow free of capital gains tax bills.

Going Beyond Approval

A number of employee share incentive schemes are deemed 'not approved' by Inland Revenue, yet are still worth consideration in certain circumstances. Being *not approved* means that, unlike approved schemes in which all the rules are laid out, precise details are not checked out by HMRC. These schemes are generally offered by small companies and are intended to help retain key staff members.

Getting a reward for enterprise

Enterprise management incentives (EMIs) can add up to big tax savings for employees, usually senior staff, in smaller companies.

Firms with assets worth up to £30 million can give share options worth up to £100,000 per employee in the scheme. Options are not shares; they're a promise you can buy a set number at a pre-set price on a future date.

The options can be issued at or below market value. Most are issued at market value; this allows the recipient to cash in the options without paying income tax or national insurance on their value.

The only tax charge is capital gains tax. But this is only paid when the shares are sold. And it can be managed by selling shares over a number of years, so making use of several annual exemptions.

Picking out particular employees with a CSOP

A CSOP is a *company share option plan*. It can give employees selected by the firm the right to buy shares worth up to £30,000 on the day the option is granted. Provided the options are held for at least three years the only tax will be income tax on the gain, if any, between the option price and the value of the shares on the market on the day the option is exercised.

Chapter 5

Working for Yourself Can Be Less Taxing

According to the Federation of Small Businesses, around four million people in the UK work for themselves. But whatever the exact head-count, HMRC taxes all these businesspeople. This chapter looks at dealing with the tax authorities as the owner of your own business instead of as an employee in someone else's.

Doing your taxes correctly can put your new firm on the road to success; messing them up is a sure-fire road to commercial oblivion or even bank-ruptcy. In this chapter we show you the tax advantages of self-employment and steer you away from some of the dangerous pitfalls.

Defining the Terms

Most people who strike out on their own, even if they go on to become multi-billionaires, often start as *sole traders* – the technical term for working for yourself, being a one-person band, or working as a freelancer.

For some, being self-employed means running a full-time business complete with commercial plans, business bank loans, staff, and public-liability insurance. If that's you, then, one day, you may hope to be a really big company and even float the company on the stock market. Lots of quoted companies started off as ventures run from an entrepreneur's dining room table.

Some sole traders offer the skills they have, such as plumbing, management consultancy, car mechanics, or writing books about money, directly to the client or end-user. Most of these businesspeople will never be big firms but they enjoy the freedom (as well as the responsibilities) of self-employment.

And for a growing number, it's all about part-time boosts to their earnings from a paying job that can be anything from regular wheeling-and-dealing on online auction sites to being a buy-to-let landlord.

Some small businesses decide to become companies rather than sole traders. But whatever category you are in, you are in business. And that puts you firmly into the tax-paying net even if you already pay income tax because you work full-time for an employer.

Meeting HMRC's standards for self-employment

HMRC applies basic tests to determine whether you are really self-employed rather than working for someone else. Pass them and you can be on the way to tax savings! The standards are that:

- ✓ You work for more than one customer – and preferably several.

- ✓ You work from your own premises, or, if you don't, you work from several locations. If you're a writer, for example, you probably work from your home; however, if you're a plumber, you travel to your customers' premises.

- ✓ You're in control of what you do and the hours you work. You must be able to turn down work you do not fancy, and you should set your own prices.

- ✓ You have a business address – often your home – from which you carry out some business functions, if only message taking.

- ✓ You supply and maintain your own vehicles, tools, computers, and/or other items of equipment needed for your trade or profession.

- ✓ You correct bad work in your own time and at your own expense.

- ✓ You are legally liable for your mistakes.

Some businesses have acquired a reputation for turning people whose main function is selling their labour into self-employed workers when they should be employed under PAYE. Some examples are computer consultants who work for one company, sub-contract builders who work for others on sites, and hairdressers who rent the chair and basin space in the salon. HMRC makes big (and usually successful) efforts to deny such people self-employed status and the tax savings that can go with it.

Delving into the grey area: Sole trader or simple seller?

Book II

Paying Less Tax

Most know when they start as a sole trader. They do work for customers in return for a commercial rate of reward. But there is a grey area where you may not know if you are trading or simply selling something.

One activity HMRC is targeting is selling via online auction. Proceeds from these sales are not, as some believe, always outside the tax net. Nor are car boot sales. Tax inspectors look for evidence of trading.

If you buy goods, either from wholesalers, or from other auctions, or from junk or charity shops with the intention of selling these things on at a profit, you are *trading* and so face a potential tax bill.

If you're clearing out the loft or spare room and have a one-off sale as an alternative to carting the lot to the charity shop or dump, then you are not trading, so there are no tax hassles. Although, should you find a Picasso in your loft and sell it for wads of money, you can face a capital gains tax bill on the proceeds! (See Chapter 6 in this part for more on capital gains.)

It is your responsibility to register so find out about your status if you are in doubt. You cannot argue against a fine or penalty by saying you did not know or that you were waiting for HMRC to contact you.

Testing your wings whilst staying employed

These days, HMRC insists that the newly self-employed register within three months of starting up their activity. But in practice, someone on PAYE who earns a one-off payment, perhaps for contributing to a publication or a one-off consultancy payment, does not need to register as self-employed although the remuneration they receive for this must be declared for tax. No absolute rules govern this – if you're unsure of your status, register with HMRC just to be safe.

Formalising Your Status

Just as no job is complete until the paperwork is done, neither can you start a business without filing forms with HMRC and deciding when your tax year runs. The following sections tell you what you need to do.

Registering your new business

The self-employed have to register as such with HMRC. This procedure includes making arrangements to pay National Insurance contributions which you will probably have to make. The upcoming 'Scanning National Insurance' section covers this issue.

You can register by:

- **Calling** a special helpline on 0845 915 4515. It's open between 8.00 a.m. and 8.00 p.m. seven days a week (except Christmas Day and one or two bank holidays).

- **Filing** form CWF1. Find it in HMRC leaflet PSE1 *Thinking of working for yourself?* Or download it online at www.hmrc.gov.uk/forms/cwf1.pdf or register online at www.hmrc.gov.uk/startingup/register.htm.

Failing to register within three months of starting self-employment can bring a £100 penalty. In some cases, the business's exact start date may be debatable so it is best to register as soon as you can.

Larger penalties can be imposed if tax is paid late because an unincorporated business failed to register by October 5 of the following tax year in which it was set up.

Choosing your tax year carefully

Most businesses have an accounting year that runs alongside the tax year from 6 April to 5 April, though you may find it more convenient to use 31 March as the end date for your tax year. If you use 5 April or 31 March as the last day of your year, you're opting for *fiscal accounting,* so-called because your business year is the same as the tax, or fiscal, year. Fiscal year users account for tax by the 31 January following the end of their year.

You can use any other date for your year-end. Choosing a different date can give you longer to file and more time to keep the tax earning interest in the bank, which sounds like a great tax saving idea. However, while many accountants still recommend choosing a different date, there are drawbacks.

Filing your first two returns

If you don't opt for a fiscal year-end, you have to meet extra requirements when filing tax returns for your first two years of operation. Your first year's tax bill is based on profits, if any, from the start of trading until the next 5 April – even though that's not the year-end date you chose. So, depending on when you start your business, your first tax bill may cover a matter of a few days or a whole year.

Taxes for the second year are based on either the 12 months trading that ends on the date you chose in that year or your first 12 months of trading. You have to use the second option if the selected year-end date is less than 12 months after the start of the business.

Jessica starts her business on 1 August 2007 and decides on a 31 July year end. She makes a regular £2,000 a month profit. Under the start-up rules for the first two years, she has to account for her business from her 1 August 2007 start-date to 5 April 2008 on her 2007–08 tax return due in by 31 January 2009. She has to declare profits of £16,000 for these eight months because her selected year-end date is less than 12 months from the start of her business.

So far, so good. But her second year-end date is after her first twelve months of trading, so she has to account for the full twelve months from 1 August 2007 to 31 July 2008. Her profits here will be £24,000. Now for the really bad bit, which sounds like something out of *Alice in Wonderland*.

Even though Jessica has had to pay tax on her first eight months, she also has to pay tax on the first year. Now these overlap to a big extent. So although she has only 12 months of trading to earn her money, she is assessed for 20 months of tax payments. On her £2,000 a month profits, she has earned £24,000 but she has to pay as though she has earned £40,000 (that's 20 months or 12 months plus 8 months).

Of course, no one who is self-employed has exact months like that all the time. But we selected the same amount each month to make a complicated overlap a little simpler.

Lessening the effects of overlap

Having to pay tax on profits you haven't yet made is known in the tax trade as *overlap*. And you ignore it at your peril. For most small businesses, overlap is something to avoid. The answer is to align your business year with the tax year.

You can change your accounting year-end during the life of your business to lessen the effect of overlap if you need to. You can elect for a year-end change by notifying HMRC on a self assessment form or sending your tax inspector a letter.

If you don't cure your overlap while you are in self-employment, you only get your excess tax payment back when you cease trading. Such an event can be many years in the future, and the overpayments you made on starting will not be adjusted for inflation or changing tax rates.

If you have to borrow extra cash because paying overlap tax takes cash out of your business, you can claim the interest against a future tax bill.

Those setting up a business where the costs of the first year or so of trading are likely to be greater than their earnings obviously need have less fear of overlap as there will be no profits to tax.

Signing on for and paying VAT

Whether you are a self-employed sole trader, a partnership, or a limited company, you have to register for VAT once your annual sales top a threshold amount (£64,000 in 2007-08) determined by The Chancellor of the Exchequer. This threshold tends to rise each year roughly in line with inflation. (For the current VAT threshold, go to HMRC website at www.hmrec.gov.uk.) You also need to register if your earnings in any one quarter are such that, multiplied by four, they would exceed the threshold.

The VAT threshold is determined by *total sales* – not total profits. You can make a loss and still need to be VAT registered.

Once you register for VAT, you have to charge VAT on all the work or goods you supply to customers (other than VAT-exempt goods and services) and account for these amounts. But then you can also deduct VAT on goods and services you have to buy in for your business.

Most goods and services are charged standard rate VAT, now 17.5 per cent. But some items are different. Supplying electricity to people's homes has a 5 per cent rate. More importantly, a number of everyday items largely fresh food, children's clothes, books, magazines, and newspapers have a special 0 per cent rate. This is called *zero-rating*. You must be VAT registered even if all the goods you supply are zero rated, providing your sales top the VAT threshold.

Register with HMRC within 30 days of being aware that you will exceed the threshold. Failing to register brings a fine which is the greater of £50, or 5 per cent of the VAT owed, if registration is made within nine months of when registration should have taken place, 10 per cent where it is between nine and 18 months late and 15 per cent in all other cases. All these figures are on top of the VAT itself.

You can register for VAT even if your sales are below the threshold, and you may actually save tax by doing so. If you buy a £100 item for your business as a non-VAT trader and pay VAT on it, you have £117.50 (£100 plus 17.5 per cent VAT) to set against your profits for income tax. As a basic rate taxpayer with a 22 per cent rate (20% from April 2008), that cuts your bill by £25.85 as you can take off 22 per cent, so the asset costs £91.96. But if you were registered for VAT, you would reclaim the £17.50 *input* (the technical VAT term for anything you buy in for your business) and still have £100 to set against profits. Taking off 22 per cent gives a £22 tax reduction. In this case, the actual cost is £78. So, registering for VAT can be useful if your main clients are organisations that can reclaim VAT themselves.

VAT-registered businesses supplying goods and services to private individuals are at a disadvantage to their non-registered counterparts as they have to boost every bill by 17.5 per cent. If you supply goods or services, you may be able to keep below the annual VAT threshold by supplying labour only and getting your clients to buy the goods needed themselves. For instance, a decorator can ask a customer to buy the paint and wallpaper from the local DIY store. The customer still pays VAT on these items but not on the decorator's labour, which can be a substantial part of the total decoration cost.

Paying the VAT bill

The VAT return asks for two figures: your *output* – the amount you take in for selling goods or supplying services shown on your invoices to customers – and your *input* – the value of goods or services you buy in to help carry out your business shown on invoices you receive from suppliers.

In the past, you had to report your output and input on a quarterly basis. Accountants charged substantial sums for dealing with this work even for relatively small businesses. Some businesses, though, like the discipline of quarterly returns which make sure they get on top of their affairs and don't leave things to fester for up to a year.

But you can ease the VAT paperwork burden (and accountancy bills) through one of the following three options.

- ✔ **Cash accounting:** You pay tax according to what actually happens in your business. With this method there is no need to go through the complicated business of reclaiming VAT on a bad debt. You still pay quarterly.

- ✔ **Flat rate scheme:** This plan is aimed at businesses with taxable sales of up to £150,000 a year. In following this scheme, you bill customers in the normal way at 17.5 per cent. But instead of paying this amount, less your input, you agree a percentage of your turnover with Customs and Excise and pay it. This percentage varies from 2 per cent for food and children's clothing retailers up to 13.5 per cent for builders and contractors who only supply their labour. You don't have to figure out your outputs and inputs, so it's a lot simpler, but you can end up paying more than you would have had you claimed for your inputs. To join, submit form VAT 600 (FRS), which you can download from the HMRC Web site at www.hmrc.gov.uk. You pay quarterly and can swap back at any time if your inputs rise (making the flat rate a bad deal). You can also claim VAT on any capital expenditure worth over £2000 excluding VAT.

✓ **Annual accounting:** This system is used for businesses with turnovers of up to £660,000 a year. You make one VAT return a year but make nine monthly interim estimated payments. The annual return allows you to balance your monthly payments either with another payment or asking for money back if you have over-estimated your sales. This is just like the way many pay for gas and electricity – 11 fixed amounts plus a balancing payment in the final month.

Deregistering for VAT

If your sales fall to below the VAT threshold (£64,000 in 2007-08) you can opt to deregister. This drop takes you out of the VAT net. But you don't have to deregister.

If you anticipate that your business downturn is temporary and if charging VAT does not harm your relationships with customers, stick with it if you can stand the paperwork as you'll only have to re-register when your sales go up again. And keeping a VAT number means you can continue to offset all the VAT on goods and services you buy in.

Keeping Accounts to Keep Everyone Happy

Here's a scary thought: The biggest single cheque you'll ever write out may well be to HMRC. In this section, we show you how to minimise your tax bite legally. And, in keeping with this book's theme of making sure that you don't give up all the tax you've saved by sending it all back, and, even worse, paying penalties, we focus on how to stick to the rules.

You need to keep records of transactions, not only to make your business run smoothly but in order to fill out your self assessment return. You can make use of a number of computer packages available for both record keeping and accounts. And consult *Starting a Business For Dummies* by Colin Barrow (Wiley) for tips on setting up an accounting system.

You have to keep records of your business for five years following the final filing date for your trading year. Someone with a trading year ending on 31 March 2008 will file by 31 January 2009 and needs to keep the paperwork (or computer records) until 31 January 2014.

Filling out Schedule D can pay dividends

Self-employed people have to fill in the basic self assessment tax form and also the self-employment pages (downloadable from HMRC at www.hmrc. gov.uk/sa/index.htm or available via HMRC helpline, telephone: 0845 9000444). (Chapter 2 offers help with the self assessment form.)

If you are self-employed, you will end up being taxed under what the taxman and accountants call Schedule D. Being on Schedule D can make your personal bank balance happier, most importantly because you can claim many expenses against what you earn (see the following section).

Those who work for someone else on PAYE can claim business expenses against tax only if those expenses are 'wholly, exclusively, and necessarily' incurred in carrying out their contract of employment. That definition is really tough to meet. But when you are on Schedule D, the 'necessarily' part of the PAYE definition goes. The reason? No outsider can define 'necessity'. Do you actually need to advertise your services in one particular way? Do you necessarily need a new vehicle when you can do the work using a clapped-out pushbike? Is your computer over-specified and do you need one at all?

All these choices are open to big companies and small companies alike and all the expenses can be set against the company's tax or your personal self-assessment form.

Counting your credits

You have a lot of freedom as a self-employed person. You can choose how you'll carry out your business and money spent wholly and exclusively for your business can be set against your earnings.

The tax authorities are not idiots. Don't try putting the costs of a Rolls-Royce down against tax claiming it is a vehicle you use 'wholly and exclusively' for your business, unless, of course, you run a wedding limousine hire firm.

HMRC is always on the lookout for exaggerated expenses, but you don't have to exaggerate to minimise your tax bill. Just make sure you deduct everything you're legally allowed to, including:

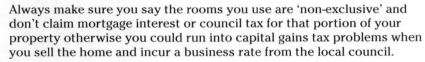

- ✔ The administrative cost of running the business against your earnings from it. This sounds elementary, but many people with start-ups or those who have a small business on the side still have the mindset of working for an employer who picks up all the costs of running the business. All those little items such as postage stamps, fuel, mobile and fixed telephone charges, and even heating and lighting for your workplace add up over a year and are legally deductible.

- ✔ The cost of equipment including computers, machinery, and other big items. We explain how to deal with big items in the next section. Cars have rules of their own and are covered in the next section.

- ✔ Bank charges on business accounts and interest on loans for your business.

- ✔ A proportion of the costs of running your home if you use part of your property as a base. There are no specific rules for this. It's a question of common sense. If you have a house with six rooms and use one fairly regularly for your business, then look at your domestic bills and take a sixth-part.

    Obviously, if you use other premises solely for business, then you can deduct all the costs.

    Always make sure you say the rooms you use are 'non-exclusive' and don't claim mortgage interest or council tax for that portion of your property otherwise you could run into capital gains tax problems when you sell the home and incur a business rate from the local council.

- ✔ Accountancy and legal fees and the costs of debt collection.

- ✔ Pension contributions can count against self-employment earnings.

- ✔ Publications, stationery, postage, wages and other costs of employing people, insurance, travel, subsistence, gas, electricity, water – all the way down to the batteries in your calculator.

Accounting for big business items

Big expenditure items such as plant and machinery, cars, and computers are not counted against your profits in the same way as the goods and services you buy in to make your business work. With these big items, you can claim capital allowances against your profits. A *capital allowance* is a proportion of the purchase cost that you can set against profits each year as long as you own the item. The result is that tax relief against the expenditure made on these items can be spread out over several years.

The following list explains capital allowances for major items:

- ✔ **Plant and machinery,** you can claim 40 per cent of the value in the first year, and then 25 per cent of the balance each following year. So something costing £1,000 has £400 (40 per cent) offset against tax in the first year, and 25 per cent of the £600 balance, or £150, offset in the second year. The starting figure is £450 for the next year, and goes down by a quarter each year.

- ✔ **Cars** qualify for a 25 per cent capital allowance each year with a limit of £12,000 on the value of the car. Using this ceiling, the maximum allowance in the first year is £3,000, then 25 per cent of the remaining £9,000 (£2,250) and so on.

    Low-emission vehicles benefit from a 100% allowance for the first year. The vehicle manufacturer will tell you if your vehicle qualifies as less noxious – printing the rules in full would take up a large part of this book.

Capital allowances are available against the actual cost of the asset. You set the costs of any bank loan or other financing against business expenses.

You cannot claim capital allowances greater than your profits. But there is nothing to stop you claiming less than your maximum and then carrying the remaining amounts into a subsequent year.

Claiming extra help as you start up

Money you spend before you start can be counted against your profits once you set up. This expenditure may include the money you paid for a computer and other machinery you already possess and the cost of feasibility studies into your hoped for business. These sums will normally be counted against your first year's profits. But if you make a loss, you can count them against the next year (and so on for a total of four years if you fail to make a profit).

Accounting for loss making

With the best will in the world, your self-employment could result in a loss. In such a case, you have two tax options, which we explore in the next two sections.

Deducting the loss from other taxable sums

Provided you have earnings from a PAYE job, a pension, from dividends or interest, or from taxable capital gains, you could set your loss off against these amounts. This is a good route for a self-employed person whose business is part-time. Someone earning £20,000 from a PAYE post, and losing £2,000 on their business would end up with a tax bill based on £18,000.

If you make a loss in any of the first four years of a new business, you can offset this loss against tax on your salary in the three years preceding the establishment of your business. You may have to prove you intended to make profits during this period; Tax inspectors look out for loss-making 'hobbies' whose main function is to dodge tax.

You have to inform the tax inspector within 12 months following the 31 January after the end of your loss-making business year.

Subtracting the loss from future earnings

If your losses exceed your taxable sums, you can carry forward the loss against future profits. You can do this for as many years as you need – there is no limit. But you have to tell HMRC within five years of the 31 January following the end of the tax year in which your personal accounted year finished.

In most cases, it makes sense to offset your losses against earnings, dividends, interest, and capital gains from elsewhere. But if you expect your self-run business to be very remunerative in the future and take you into the top tax band, then consider subtracting early losses from future earnings.

Scanning National Insurance

As a self-employed person, profits you make from your business are added to other earnings, pensions, dividends, and interest for income tax. National Insurance is different. There are special rules for the self-employed and two sets of payments you may have to make.

Complicating the classes

National Insurance comes in four classes, numbered one through four. Class 1 is for employed persons. The self-employed have to look at Classes 2 and 4, which we do in the next sections. And in case you're wondering, Class 3 is voluntary – it's paid by people who do not work but who wish to keep up their record to qualify for the state retirement pension and other benefits.

Class 4 is collected through the annual self-assessment return. It is the only national insurance to be collected in this way. Most people pay Class 1 via their salary packet while Class 2 and Class 3 are paid usually with a direct debit.

Paying Class 2

As a self-employed person you have to pay a fixed £2.20 a week (in 2007-08) in National Insurance. This maintains your payment record for the state pension and health-related benefits – but not Jobseekers Allowance.

If your earnings from all self-employment is below the Class 2 threshold (£4,635 in 2007-08), you are exempt from Class 2.

Paying Class 4

Class 4 National Insurance is effectively an additional tax on the self-employed. It does not provide any benefits, but that doesn't mean you don't have to pay it if your profits (what you take in less your costs) are at least £5,225 in a year. If your profits are below that figure, you don't have to worry about Class 4.

But if you do have to pay, it is currently (2005–06) charged at 8 per cent of your taxable profits from £5,225 a year to £34,840. The 8 per cent stops there. But there's a 1 per cent surcharge on all sums above that. So if your profits were £44,840, you would pay 1 per cent on the £10,000 above the upper profits level.

Putting a cap on national insurance

Someone with a mix of self-employment and employment could end up paying Class 1, Class 2, and Class 4. The bad news is that many pay more in national insurance for the same amount of income if it comes from a variety of sources, such as self-employment and employment, than they would if it all from one source. The good news is that there are ceilings on payments.

If all your income comes from being self-employed, then you cannot pay more than £2,483.60 (in tax year 2007-08) in Class 2 and Class 4 together. HMRC Web site (www.hmrc.gov.uk) or your local tax office can give details of future rates. And if you have earnings from employment as well, there is a chance you have paid a lot more than you should when you add up all the sums from your job and your self-employment. Check with HMRC if you think you may have overpaid.

None of these limits includes the 1 per cent national insurance surcharge on earnings over £34,840.

If you know, or reasonably suspect, that you will hit the overall National Insurance limit, you can apply for Class 2 and/or Class 4 payments to be deferred until you know the outcome of the year's earnings pattern. You should do this before the start of the tax year but HMRC, which runs the National Insurance collection, often allows later applications.

Hiring Helpers

Being a sole trader doesn't mean you have to work on your own. It's a tax definition, after all. You may need to pay for help on a part- or full-time basis or to hire someone to help out every now and again. If you have family, you may want to make the most of the tax advantages you can reap by employing them. The next sections tell you how to look at employees as tools to lower your tax.

Employing your family

You can employ your family in the business and thereby take advantage of the lower tax rates your spouse or children may fall under to reduce your household's overall tax bill.

You do have to keep a few rules in mind, though:

- ✓ You have to hire your relative to do real work at commercial wage rates. You cannot get away with paying a small child £100 an hour for taking telephone messages!

- ✓ Local authorities have rules on children working. This will not apply to a few hours' working in the home. But if you want to employ a child under 16 in other circumstances, always check with the council first.

- ✓ Family members who earn more than £100 (in 2007-08) in any week must make national insurance payments. As the employer, you also have to pay national insurance on their behalf, in the same way as you would for any other employee. This is called the *national insurance lower earnings limit*. Accountants call it the LEL.

Your teenage children might have no income to offset against their personal allowance. Or you might be a top-rate tax payer and have a partner whose maximum is at the basic or lower rate.

You set up a computer repair service working from a small shop. Your 16-year old helps you at your premises for four hours a week at £5 an hour. That's £20 a week – say £1,000 a year allowing for holidays and some overtime. You can offset the £1,000 against your profits. And, if your teenager has no other income, he or she does not have to pay tax at all as the £1,000 is well within the personal allowance limit. Had you done the work yourself and not used your child, the £1,000 would have been taxable as profits at up to 40 per cent so the household would only have £600 instead of the full £1,000.

You have to pay the money for real, of course. HMRC can ask for the audit trail to see how the payment goes from your business to the family member concerned.

Book II

Paying Less Tax

Establishing a partnership with your partner

If you and your spouse or partner are both involved in running a business, it could be worth exploring a partnership structure. There are legal concerns such as each partner being liable for debts incurred by other partners. For tax reasons, it is best to have a partnership contract which sets out how profits will be shared.

Starting a Business For Dummies by Colin Barrow (Wiley) sets out who should and who should not set up as partners. You need to work out whether you are better off with a partnership but, more importantly, whether your relationship could stand it.

HMRC is on the lookout for phoney partnerships, established solely with the aim of reducing a couple's overall tax bill. If you have a business partnership with your spouse, you may have to show that both work in the firm and both contribute work according to the proportion of the profits you each earn. This is a measure to prevent couples sharing profits on a 50-50 basis to use up tax allowances of the non-worker when only one works.

Paying employees

If you hire employees, you are in the same situation as any other employer. You have to sort out any PAYE tax and national insurance contributions they owe.

Giving Up Work

Stopping work is easier than starting. You should inform HMRC if you intend to stop working in your business. And if you were caught by overlap, now is the time to claim it back. Your final accounts can also take care of what happens when you sell plant, machinery, vehicles, or stock.

The reality of self-employment is that most businesses cease entirely when the self-employed person retires or goes back to working for someone else. A few businesses have a future value.

Chapter 6

Taxing Your Savings and Investments

Save right and you pay no tax. Save wrong, and up to 40 per cent of what you make goes to the tax authorities. But saving for tax-breaks can be an investment disaster.

In this chapter we show you how tax works on your nest-egg from basic savings to big risks. The lesson? There are no correct answers. It all depends on you, your family, and what you need.

And don't forget, some financial advisers have their own agenda. They want you to buy investment packages from them. They know putting 'tax-free' in the biggest typeface available will pull in loads of commission-paying punters. That doesn't mean it's good for you. Be warned.

Taxing Interest

Suppose you have £1,000 in savings. You find an account which pays 5 per cent – and you're proud of yourself because that's a comparatively good rate at the time. You reckon you don't even need a calculator to work out that you're going to earn £50 in interest for the year. You get top marks for arithmetic. Your old maths teacher would be proud of you. But if you think you can budget to spend that £50 at the end of the year, think again.

The stated annual interest rate, whatever rate it might be, is the rate your money earns – the *gross interest* amount – and indicates the sum you would get if there were no such things as taxes. However, the final amount that actually gets paid to you, or gets paid back into your account, is the gross interest amount minus the income tax HMRC takes for taxes. This final amount is the *net interest*.

The following sections talk about how this system works.

Paying tax without effort (or intent)

Under long standing arrangements, the bank or building society you invest your savings with automatically diverts some of your interest to HMRC. You may be able to prevent this – see 'Recovering money with form R85' later on – but for the great majority, tax comes off willy-nilly.

From your point of view, this automatic deduction can save you a lot of bother paying the tax later. And by taking it away before you can spend it, this method prevents the embarrassment of having to scrimp, steal (metaphorically, anyway), or borrow to find the money at tax time.

From HMRC's point of view, this tax-gathering process is super efficient. The bank or building society does the Revenue's work for it. It knows that this deduction makes it impossible for savers to 'forget' about paying.

You must keep all the paperwork, including any notices you get from the bank or building society, which shows interest paid. In some cases, this comes in the form of an entry in a savings passbook. You must keep this for a minimum of 22 months after the end of the tax year.

Shelling out at the special savings rate

Currently, the tax rate on savings is 20 per cent, a nice round sum (as well as just a little less than the basic tax rate). Most basic rate taxpayers need do no more – they need not fill in any forms or pay any more tax. But the statement your bank or building society sends shows your interest in two parts. The bigger amount is the net interest your account is credited with; the smaller amount is the tax deducted. Adding the two back together again produces the gross interest. Table 6-1 shows how various interest rates affect £1,000 in savings.

Table 6-1	Interest and Taxes on Savings of £1,000		
Interest Rate	*Gross Interest*	*Tax Deducted*	*Net Interest*
6%	£60	£12	£48
5%	£50	£10	£40
4%	£40	£8	£32
3%	£30	£6	£24
2%	£20	£4	£16
1%	£10	£2	£8
0.5%	£5	£1	£4
0.1%	£1	£0.20	£0.80

Doing the sums yourself

For most basic rate taxpayers, the deductions in Table 6-1, which turn gross interest into net interest, is the end of the matter. But HMRC concerns itself with all your income, not just your savings. So, before you breathe a sigh of relief and think that the savings rate deduction is all you have to worry about, you need to do some arithmetic.

Your savings interest, added to other sources of income (such as employment earnings, self-employment or pensions) can push you into the top tax bracket, which currently starts at £39,825 for someone with a standard personal allowance. The personal allowance is dealt with fully in Chapter 3 in this part.

Top taxpayers, and those whose interest from savings pushes them into the 40 per cent tax bracket, have to pay more income tax on their savings earnings. If this applies to you, you do this by declaring your savings interest income on the self-assessment form and then paying the extra tax on the due dates or via PAYE (Pay As You Earn) if the sum is small enough. The self-assessment form is considered fully in Chapter 2 in this part.

The process works like this: You add the gross interest from all your interest-bearing accounts to all your other earnings and then you calculate the top rate – 40 per cent – of this amount. Remember, the bank or building society has already deducted tax at the 20 per cent special savings rate and the self-assessment form makes allowance for this deduction.

For example, if your income from your job in 2007-08 is £37,000 then it is well within the basic 20 per cent rate tax band, and comfortably below the threshold of £39,825 for paying 40 per cent. However, if you're lucky enough to win £100,000 on the lottery (lottery winnings are tax-free) and you invest the money in a safe, sensible bank account earning 5 per cent (or £5,000 gross interest) then your bank deducts 20 per cent (£1,000) of the annual gross interest leaving you with £4,000 net to spend.

And if you think that's the end of the matter, think again. You have to add the gross interest sum (even though you receive only 80 per cent of it) to all your other earnings. Unfortunately the total now pushes you into the higher 40 per cent rate band. So, when you file your self-assessment form be prepared to pay tax over and above the amount already deducted at source. And make sure that you read the next section on how bank and building society interest impacts on top rate taxpayers.

Adding your £5,000 gross interest to your work earnings of £37,000 gives you a total £42,000, assuming you have no other source of income. So everything over and above £39,825 falls into the top tax band. In this case, you have to pay extra tax beyond the standard rate on the sum of £2,175 – the difference between the £39,825 where the 40 per cent top rate starts and your £42,000 total income.

You have become a higher rate taxpayer. As 20 per cent of the difference has already been taken off by your savings provider you need to find a further 20 per cent that, in this case, works out at £435.

Making the most of joint accounts and sharing savings

Many people have joint accounts with spouses or partners to simplify their household finances. The notion that a married woman was dependent on her husband for tax returns died in the early 1990s. Now each holder of a joint account is considered a separate person. And the rule is that each signatory to an account earns an equal share of the interest. So, if there are three signatories, the account is divided three ways.

Each partner must work out if they qualify for gross interest in their own right. For example, if the total gross interest earned is £200, divide that by two and add the resultant £100 to each holder's income to see if they can ask for a rebate.

HMRC doesn't care if you qualify for the rebate and your partner does not. Nor does it matter if one of you qualifies completely and the other one only partially qualifies because their earnings are a little above the cut-off point set at the personal allowance level. As far as HMRC is concerned, you each have your own account with your share of the total interest.

Married couples have the absolute legal right to transfer savings between themselves without any taxation consequences. So it makes sense to put as much savings as possible into the name of the partner with the lower tax rate. So, if one spouse is a non-tax-payer in their own right, or pays the lower ten per cent tax rate (see 'Looking at people in the ten per cent band' later in this chapter), or pays the basic rate tax while the other partner is taxed at a higher rate, then transfer savings to the partner with the lower income. Doing this can, if your savings are large enough, save you several thousand pounds a year.

So if one partner has £10,000 worth of savings producing £500 interest a year gross, she or he will pay £200 in tax if taxed at 40 per cent. By transferring the £10,000 to a non-tax paying spouse, the interest can be paid gross, saving £200.

HMRC treats transfers as gifts and counts interest or other income from such transfers as income for the recipient, not the giver.

Tax savings can add up if you and your partner arrange things correctly. For example, if one partner is a higher rate payer and the other a basic rate payer, and the higher rate payer earns £500 gross interest, then this amount is reduced to £300 with the 40 per cent tax rate, handing over £200 to HMRC . Transferring the same capital, and the £500 gross interest, to the basic rate taxpayer reduces the tax rate to 20 per cent or £100 – a saving of £100.

The same neat bit of arithmetic and the same £100 savings occur if one partner is a basic rate payer and the other is a non-taxpayer. The basic ratepayer has 20 per cent or £100 deducted. The non-taxpayer suffers no such deduction (thanks to the wonderful R85, see the upcoming 'Recovering Money with Form R85' section) or can claim the £100 back later.

But take care, having savings in one partner's name has several ramifications, and not all of them work for every couple:

✔ Only the partner in whose name the account is can access the money.

✔ The extra interest may push the new account holder into a higher tax band, making the transfer a waste of time.

✔ Each partner has to trust the other financially! There's no point transferring your life savings to your partner only to have him or her spend it all or run off with your wealth! Read *Relationships For Dummies* by Kate M. Wachs (Wiley) to find out more about the effect that arguing about money has on domestic bliss. It's probably the biggest single cause of partnership stress and break-up.

Looking at people in the ten per cent band

People with incomes just over the tax-free band do not go straight to the basic rate. Instead, there is a small slice of income (£2,230 in 2007-08), which is taxed at 10p in the pound (although this starting rate will be removed from April 2008 and the basic rate will be reduced to a flat 20 per cent).

Given the current ten per cent tax band, it would be unfair to tax someone at ten per cent on earnings and 20 per cent on savings. So if your total income ends up in the 10 per cent zone – if you're under 65, that embraces the £5,225 to £7,455 earnings range a year for 2007-08 – you can reduce the 20 per cent savings rate to 10 per cent.

You can reclaim in two ways: You can use a self-assessment form, though it's improbable that you would need one as your tax affairs are unlikely to be that complicated if you income is this low! Or you can reclaim via form R40 – a more likely route as it's much shorter and easier to fill in than the self-assessment form!

An example may help make this clear. Say Maria's only income is bank interest from her savings in one account. In 2007-08, she earned £6,000 gross, which was reduced to £4,800 net after the 20 per cent tax deduction. The gross amount, however, is higher than her personal tax allowance of £5,225 so she cannot fill in form R85.

Using R40 (see the forthcoming section 'Getting money back with R40'), she claims

✔ Gross bank interest £6,000

✔ Total income £6,000

✔ Less personal allowance of £5,225

✔ Equals taxable income of £775

Maria must pay ten per cent on the £775, or £77.50. But she paid £1,000 through having it deducted from her savings account, so she gets back £922.50 (£1,000 less her tax bill).

Asking for a Tax Rebate

It's not all one-way traffic. Although HMRC always has its tax-raising eye on the 20 per cent of bank and building society interest you earn, it does not have an absolute right to the money. This is in sharp contrast to the deduction of tax on income earned from dividends on shares (dealt with fully later in this chapter) where the deduction of tax rights are absolute.

Literally millions of savers can apply to get £1 in every £5 of their interest deduction reversed and, legally, keep all the interest. In other words, you keep the gross interest amount instead of the net figure after 20 per cent is paid to HMRC.

The following sections tell you whether you qualify and how to apply for a tax rebate.

Checking your rebate qualifications

A large proportion of people who can apply for a tax rebate do not. They needlessly hand over cash that's theirs by right. Sadly, these people are often those who can least afford to pass up cash. They are on low, or no income at all, and it is because their earnings are so low that they can escape the tax net.

Even HMRC has a conscience about this. Every so often, it mounts a publicity campaign for people to check whether they are receiving their full entitlement from their savings interest.

The main groups who qualify for tax rebates include pensioners, non-working spouses, and children. Broadly speaking, anyone with a low income can avoid paying tax on savings interest.

The basic rule is that if your gross interest from all your interest paying accounts plus all your earnings from employment or pensions (including state pensions but excluding any pension credits) total a sum below the personal allowance level (see Chapter 3 for information on allowance levels), then you should be paid gross interest rather than net on your savings. So, if you're under the age of 65 and have an income of less than £5,225 in 2007-08, you qualify.

Recognising reasons people don't ask for their own money back

Check to see whether the reasons (or excuses) savers let the tax authorities end up with several hundred millions in extra tax each year apply to you:

- You had no idea that tax was automatically deducted and that this situation can only be prevented by filling in a tax form.

- You thought that tax did not apply to you as your income was so low.

- Your bank or building society did not explain your rights.

- You knew about the deduction but you thought the amount was too small to bother about.

- You were frightened to apply.

- You do not like filling in forms.

- Your previous arrangements to receive interest gross stopped because you reached 16.

- You had a period on no or low pay a few years ago but you now earn good money. Those in this position can apply for a rebate for up to six years in the past.

- You have a joint account with a spouse or partner and your other half is a high earner.

If any of these points apply to you, now's the time to get applying.

Savings firms such as banks and building societies don't sort your tax out for you automatically – they don't know your overall tax position unless you tell them about it. So, even with the best will in the world on their part, you have to start the ball rolling. The upcoming 'Recovering money with form R85' section tells you how.

Recovering money with form R85

If your total earnings from work and interest on savings falls below the personal allowance level, this section tells you how to claim your tax rebate.

The easy way of ensuring that you keep all the interest you earn is by filling in the very wonderful form R85. You can get this from a bank, building society, or from HMRC. You can print it from HMRC Web site at www.hmrc.gov.uk.

In filling out form R85 and sending it to HMRC (your bank may do this for you), you're saying that your total income is below the tax-paying level, and therefore the bank or building society is authorised to pay you gross interest. You only have to fill in one form for each particular bank or building society but you must list separately and in full all the existing accounts you have with each financial institution. If you open a new account, or take your money out of one account and transfer it to another with the same bank or building society, make sure you fill in a new R85.

Your R85 declaration continues from tax year to tax year until you rescind it by telling the savings institution that you no longer qualify. You can also rescind the form by informing your tax inspector. You need to do this when your income grows to tax-paying levels. The one exception to this rule is for children reaching 16 – the special rules for youngsters' savings are considered in Chapter 3 of this Book.

 The best way to get form R85 is to ask for it when you open an account at a bank or building society. Many savings firms give you an R85 ready-printed with details such as your name and address, that of the bank or building society, and the account number so all you have to do is sign it. By doing this, you get paid gross interest from the very start.

Book II

Paying Less Tax

Getting money back with R40

If you failed to fill in form R85 (see the preceding section) – perhaps your expected income fell so you became a non-taxpayer, or you simply forgot to ask for the form – don't worry. The tax is not lost.

Using repayment claim form R40 (available at your local tax office or as a download from HMRC Web site at www.hmrc.gov.uk, or sometimes at a bank or building society), you can ask that your overpaid tax be refunded.

 Using R40 is a little more complicated than filling in form R85 and depends on your keeping good records of how much interest you earned in each account as you will need to list this. You may need to ask the bank or building society for a duplicate certificate of tax deducted or a copy of your passbook.

You do not need to send this paperwork to HMRC along with the form but you must be able to show the claim is genuine – a number of claims are checked.

With R40, you have to put down all your income including interest from savings to show that some, or all, of your interest falls into the tax-free band.

Getting money back up to five years later

You have five years from 31 January after the end of the tax year for which you are claiming to file for a refund of taxes you have already paid. It may come as a surprise that you can go back on what you might have thought was a closed book, but HMRC does not consider it odd for people to go back all these years. So if you realise in January 2008 that you paid tax unnecessarily, you can ask for your money back for all the years back to 6 April 2001.

To do this, you complete form R40 (see the preceding section 'Getting money back with R40') and send it to the relevant Inland Revenue office. In some cases, you may need to ask for seven R40 forms as you have to fill in one for each tax year in which you believe you overpaid.

R40 claims are dealt with by five special Inland Revenue offices. The office that handles your R40 claim may not be the one nearest your home. For example, residents of some London postcodes have to deal with an office in Leicestershire while some other Londoners have to send their forms to Glenrothes in Scotland. But don't worry about this – your local tax office has the list.

Considering a Trio of Taxes

Putting money into stocks and shares – the main investments quoted on the London stock exchange and other stock markets across the world – has soared in popularity over the past two decades or so. But whether your portfolio is worth £100 or £100 million, each investment you make has tax implications, and, unfortunately, the different ways of making (or, if you're unlucky, losing) your money on the stock market all have their own tax rules.

Some gains and losses, and regular payments, such as dividends, have to be declared on self assessment tax forms. Others can be ignored. Some investments have advantages for those in the top tax bracket whilst some give benefits for those who pay no tax at all – and others treat all investors identically.

Three taxes can hit your investment return – Stamp Duty, income tax, and capital gains tax. The next sections talk about each in turn.

Doling out Stamp Duty

Stamp Duty doesn't apply to philatelists – it's basically a tax you pay on legal transactions. And, because buying and selling stocks is a legal transaction, you pay Stamp Duty on your stock market investments.

Stamp Duty, technically called Stamp Duty Reserve Tax, is one of the oldest taxes around. Documents literally had (and often still have) government revenues stamps embossed or stuck onto them.

Forking out small amounts frequently

Stamp duty is no respecter of people. You pay the same percentage on the day you buy whether you're dealing in a £100 or £1 million lot of shares. The basic rule is that every time you buy a share the government charges you 0.5 per cent as stamp duty. You can't avoid it on transactions where it applies. And you can't ask for it back.

The more often you buy shares, the more stamp duty you pay overall. For frequent traders those 0.5 per cent slices really add up. You may need to make 5 per cent or 10 per cent gains each year just to overcome stamp duty deductions.

The good news is that you don't have to do anything to pay stamp duty. The stockbroker charges you when you buy shares (and that includes investment trusts whether you purchase them from a stockbroker or through a special savings scheme).

Licking stamp duty

Some stockmarket and other financial transactions don't attract stamp duty. These include:

- ✔ **Cash accounts,** including National Savings and mini-cash ISAs.

- ✔ **Bonds,** whether issued by the government or a company.

- ✔ **Derivative funds,** which are funds based on stockmarket performance but do not own actual shares. Instead, they invest in complicated vehicles called futures, options, swaps, and swaptions (please, don't ask!). The most common form is the stock market guaranteed fund where you are promised at least your money back no matter how far the stock market may fall.

- ✔ **New shares** issued by a company in an initial public offering (often called a *flotation*).

- ✔ **Exchange Traded Funds,** which are special investments based on a parcel of shares such as the *FT-SE100 Index* (the *Financial Times* Share Index covering the top 100 UK public companies, usually referred to as the Footsie) and traded on the stock market.

- ✔ **Contracts for difference, spread bets, traded options, and warrants,** which are specialist ways of buying into shares, often designed for very short-term investment or professional share punters. *Investing For Dummies* by Tony Levene (Wiley) has details of all of these.

- ✔ **Gifts and transfers of shares,** which includes transferring shares out of your name to someone else, such as a family member; transferring shares under a will; and transferring shares on a divorce settlement.

Declaring your dividends

Dividends are payments from shares, unit and investment trusts, which, investors hope, are not only regular (usually twice a year) but also rise over time to reflect the company's (or trust's) growing fortunes. Dividends are taxable as income.

The good news is tax on UK share dividends is deducted before you get it. If you are a basic rate taxpayer, you don't have to do anything else. Non-taxpayers and ten per cent taxpayers don't need to do anything either. But there's bad news here: You can't reclaim the deducted tax under any circumstances. Even though it's called a tax credit by HMRC, we refer to it as a deduction to save confusion.

Top-rate taxpayers have to declare dividends on their self-assessment form and have the cash ready to pay the gap between the 40 per cent rate and the tax deducted.

Whether you get income from unit trusts, investment trusts, or individual shares, look at the date the dividend was declared and ignore the period for which the dividend applied. A 10p a share dividend for the year ending 31 December 2006 declared on 1 May 2007 and paid on 1 June 2007 counts as part of your 2007 – 08 return, not the 2006–07 calculation.

If you invest for long-term growth in shares that pay low or no dividends, you'll pay less income tax. But don't forget these shares tend to be riskier. And you can get hit for capital gains tax on your profits (see the upcoming 'Dealing with capital gains tax' for information on that subject).

Don't forget if you are near the top of the basic rate ladder – earning around £36,000 a year – your dividends can push you into the top tax bracket. For instance, if you earn £36,500 and have £3,500 of dividends you'll be over the £39,825 (in 2007–08) basic rate tax limit for a person aged under 65.

The sums can be complicated. So either use self assessment software or get your form in before 30 September so HMRC will do the calculations.

Receiving dividends from foreign shares

Dividends from stocks traded in foreign markets can be tough to deal with. You may have to convert dividend payments into sterling as well as account for them separately.

You need to fill out the *foreign income* pages of the self assessment form. The UK has '*double taxation agreements* with most foreign countries. The effect of these agreements is to cap the tax due on foreign-sourced income so you are no worse off as a result of possibly being taxed twice.

Re-investing dividends

Many stock market companies have schemes by which shareholders can opt to receive new shares to the value of their dividends rather a dividend cheque. Even if you choose this option, you still have to declare the value of the new shares and any balance carried forward in cash because it is not large enough to buy a share. You're liable for tax on re-invested dividends in just the same way as a cash dividend.

Dealing with capital gains tax

Capital gains tax (CGT) is paid on profits you make on selling a number of assets including shares and properties (but not the house you count as your main residence).

Counting the things that don't count

You pay capital gains tax on a lot of profitable items, including shares and buy-to-lets. The following list reminds you of some items that aren't subject to CGT, even though they may produce income or make you money when you sell them:

- ✔ Your only or main home (not counting anywhere you rent). If you have more than one property, you can choose which one is out of the CGT net – it will usually be the more valuable. Unmarried couples can each have a home provided they live in them.

- ✔ National Savings including Certificates and Premium Bonds.

- ✔ UK government bonds (gilts) and most corporate bonds.

- ✔ Bank accounts and deposits.

- ✔ Personal Equity Plans (PEPs) and Individual Savings Accounts (ISAs).

- ✔ Life insurance policies (but these have internal CGT charges so you pay effectively whether you want to or not).

- ✔ Investments in forestry and woodlands.

- ✔ Classic cars.

- ✔ Tangible moveable property with an expected life of 50 years or under (this may cover some of the more controversial artworks such as sharks and sheep pickled in alcohol!) and all tangible moveable property worth under £6,000.

- ✔ Profit from selling your own medals for valour.

- ✔ Shares held on behalf of employees in share incentive schemes up to the date the employee gets full ownership.

- ✔ Shares in special schemes such as the Business Expansion Scheme, the Enterprise Investment Scheme, and Venture Capital Trusts.

You pay CGT only when you sell an asset – keep it and you have nothing to pay or declare.

The CGT bill is calculated at either 20 per cent or 40 per cent of the gain. Which rate you pay depends on your other income for the year. Your CGT bill is added to your other taxable income and you pay accordingly. If the grand total keeps you in the basic rate band, you pay 20 per cent. Otherwise, you pay at 40 per cent. You could, of course, pay part in the basic band and part in the top band.

Someone who earns £20,000 salary and has capital gains of £10,000 has a total of £30,000 in income, which is well within the basic tax-rate band. This taxpayer is liable for 20 per cent taxation, or £2,000, on the £10,000 capital gain part of their income. A £40,000 earner – already in the 40 per cent band – who makes the same £10,000 gain ends up with £5,000 at the 40 per cent end of the tax world and has to pay £4,000 to HMRC.

Reducing your CGT bill

You can do a lot to reduce your bill – perhaps all the way down to nothing – by remembering a few CGT basics:

- ✔ You're entitled to an annual free slice – the first £9,200 (in 2007-08) of capital gains is tax exempt. Keep in mind that this exemption is good only for the current tax year. You can't go back and make claims for past years. It's a use it or lose it deal. The amount usually changes from year to year – so far it has always increased.

- ✔ You pay only if you make a profit. You can deduct costs such as stockbroker commission and any legal expenses connected with property or share purchases. And don't forget to deduct selling costs as well.

- ✔ The longer you hold on to a taxable asset, the less you have to pay as a percentage of the gain (see the 'Cutting the tax with rising prices and the falling taper' section later in the chapter for more on this).

Swapping shares to claim the tax exemption

You are not allowed to sell a share and then buy it back the next day (or within 30 days) to create a gain so that you can use your free slice. But you can sell one share and buy another, perhaps one with a similar profile such as selling Bank A and buying Bank B. You don't have to be a stock market genius to know companies that are similar to each other tend to go up and down together.

One half of a married couple can sell shares to use the free slice, leaving the other half to buy the shares at the same time. But this has to a genuine transaction with each side paying the stockbroker costs involved and not merely a paper change of ownership or a precise swap. It doesn't work if the shares were jointly held in both names. Selling and repurchasing shares in this way establishes a new, higher, starting price for subsequent calculations.

Another great way of using the annual exemption to the best effect is to spread sales of shares over two tax years – sell half on 5 April and the rest on 6 April if you can. Doing this enables you to claim the tax exemption for two years.

Using your married status to best advantage

A married couple can split assets such as shares and each can set £9,200 against their gain. And if one partner pays top-rate tax while the other pays a lower rate, then it's worthwhile transferring the assets to the lower-rate taxpayer.

Married couples can transfer assets between themselves without taxation worries.

Book II

Paying Less Tax

Cutting the tax with rising prices and the falling taper

To figure your capital gains liability, you add the original purchase price and any associated fees and selling costs together and subtract them from the final sale price.

CGT works by subtracting the original purchase price and any costs from the final sale price to give the tax liability. And until April 1998, that could be further adjusted to take account of inflation. If you bought before April 5 1998, your starting figure is now the inflation-adjusted cost of your asset between the date of purchase and April 1998.

A buyer of shares in ABC Enterprises for £10,000 in January 1987 would find there was a 65 per cent increase in the cost of living by April 1998. So the new starting price for the shares would be £16,500 (a 65 per cent gain).

HMRC publishes a table of CGT indexation allowances on its Web site at www.hmrc.gov.uk.

But inflation is nowadays far lower. A new scheme came in force in April 1998 – the CGT taper. So from April 1998 onwards, you have to move the taper system we describe here. So you can find you have to do two sets of sums; one for the asset up to April 1998 and one for the subsequent period.

Here's how the taper works. The taper reduces your taxable gain on most assets after you have held them for three full years from the date of purchase. You then cut 5 per cent off the profit for each year until ten full years are passed and you reach a 40 per cent deduction. It only applies to non-business assets. The taper for business assets is far shorter.

Assets bought before 17 March 1998 get a bonus year. They earn 35 per cent after eight rather than nine years, for instance, and hit the final 40 per cent one year earlier.

Looking at the Tax Implications of Investing

It's obviously important for you to know where your investments stand in the tax pecking order. It's vital you don't get trapped in an investment whose special tax status is just plain wrong for your circumstances.

There is one even more essential rule: Never, never, never invest your money on the basis of any stated tax advantages. There are many investments that offer special tax treatment that they push as 'tax savings' or 'tax freedom'. But a government-backed tax-favoured status is not a guarantee of profitable performance. And if your investment fails, HMRC will not ride to your rescue and restore your losses.

Saving hassle with unit and investment trusts

A portfolio of shares managed by a professional organisation such as a unit trust (often called an open-ended investment company or OEIC) or investment trust is a great idea for the tax saver. Such investments can save tax, and just as importantly tax hassle.

The manager of a unit trust takes care of paying stamp duty for you – otherwise it would be charged at 0.5 per cent of the purchase price. How do they do that? They build it into the price they charge for a unit. But you do pay stamp duty as a separate item when you buy into an investment trust, even on regular savings schemes in which you invest as little as £20 a month.

And investment trusts and unit trusts don't pay capital gains tax on profits they make a-wheeling and a-dealing. So the managers can swap and change portfolios without worrying about tax. So when does the capital gains tax hit you? Only when you sell the units or investment trust shares yourself.

You may still have to pay capital gains tax, but you have some control over when and whether you pay as you only become liable when you sell the unit or investment trust.

You only have to put down one entry for each trust on your tax form each year, even if the trust itself holds hundreds of different shares.

Buying bonds

Bonds are loans to companies and governments. A bond is essentially a promise to pay a set sum of interest (known as a *coupon* if you want to be technical) every six months and to repay the face value of the bond on a set date in the future. The face value may be more or less than you paid for it.

Bonds, which are traded on the stock exchange, are pretty simple to deal with from a tax perspective – they act like cash accounts. The regular payments on most UK bonds, including government stocks (known as *gilts*), are paid with the basic savings rate (20 per cent) already deducted. So if you're a basic-rate taxpayer, you don't need to do anything more (unless the payment nudges you into the higher rate). Those who don't pay tax and those who pay at the 10 per cent rate can reclaim all or part of the deduction. Higher-rate taxpayers have to pay the difference between the 20 per cent rate and the 40 per cent rate.

Some bonds, including those from the government, are *low coupon,* meaning that the regular payment is lower than normal. The payment is lower so the tax you have to pay is less. But you don't lose out – you get a bigger bonus when the bond matures, and that gain is tax-free.

The opposite also applies. You can pay more than the face value of the bond because you want a higher income. But when it matures and gives you less than you paid, you can't offset the loss.

The dividends on War Loan bonds and government stocks bought through the National Savings Bank Register are paid gross without deducting any tax, which is good news for non-taxpayers who don't want the hassle of reclaiming.

Examining the benefits of ISAs

It can be worthwhile looking at Individual Savings Accounts (ISAs) if you're investing in shares or bonds. But ISAs (and their predecessors PEPs or Personal Equity Plans) are not as worthwhile from the tax point of view as they once were.

ISAs give you freedom from paying income tax on dividends and Capital Gains Tax on profits. The flipside is that if you make a capital loss on an ISA (and millions have done just this!), you can't claim it against gains elsewhere.

Book II

Paying Less Tax

And, thanks to the complications of the tax credit on shares (see 'Declaring your dividends' earlier in this chapter), basic-rate taxpayers now do not get any rebate on dividends. If you're a basic-rate taxpayers, the only benefit with a shares ISA is not facing a capital gains tax bill. But you still gain from tax relief on bond funds you bought into.

With an ISA, you don't have to do anything. The ISA management company you use deals with all the tax hassles on your behalf. You don't even have to tell the taxman about your ISA.

Higher-rate taxpayers may still benefit from investing through an ISA, though, because they pay no additional tax on the investment. Why? Well, as you don't list ISAs on your self-assessment return, there can't be any additional tax to pay.

Put in cash terms, a higher-rate taxpayer investing the maximum £7,000 allowed in the 2007-08 tax year for ISAs into shares, or unit or investment trusts, with a typical 3 per cent yield, will be about £53 better off inside an ISA than outside one (assuming there is no extra ISA cost).

The government has made ISAs a permanent fixture on the savings landscape, and as of April 2008 the overall limit will rise to £7,200. For more about the changes to the ISA regime, see Chapter 4 in Book III.

You can get more out of your ISA whatever your tax level if you stick to bonds and bond funds. There is no dividend tax credit arithmetic to worry about. If you put £5,000 into a bond fund yielding 10 per cent, you get the full £500 each year whatever your tax rate. Outside an ISA, a basic-rate tax-payer would lose £100 of that in tax while a top-rate tax-payer would have to pay £200 of the £500 in 40 per cent tax to HMRC. Funds that hold both shares and bonds must have at least 60 per cent in bonds to qualify for this treatment.

Rewarding risk takers

A number of schemes investing in high-risk assets have special tax saving characteristics. We go through them in the following sections.

Taking AIM

AIM stands for *alternative investment market,* a vehicle for trading shares in smaller companies – although a few of the companies are now very big. The companies are listed in newspapers and you buy and sell shares through stockbrokers in the normal way.

But as far as HMRC is concerned, shares invested in AIM are on a different planet. Because they are not fully listed, HMRC considers them *unquoted* (even if they're quoted everywhere!). Trading in unquoted shares is to your advantage. AIM assets count as business assets rather than shares. And business assets have a super-fast taper. Hold them for just one complete year and the capital gain tax is cut by 50 per cent. Sell them after two years and your taper relief is 75 per cent. This means the 40 per cent taxpayer has an effective 20 per cent rate after one year and just 10 per cent after two years.

The same rules apply to shares listed on OFEX, the even further off-the-main-stock-exchange market. OFEX stands for *off-exchange* because the shares are not traded on the London Stock Exchange.

AIM and OFEX shares are far more volatile and more likely to make losses than blue-chip stocks. To repeat a warning we made earlier this chapter, NEVER invest just on the basis of potential tax savings.

Venturing ahead with VCTs

Venture capital trusts (VCTs) are investment vehicles that invest in small, usually start-up, companies. VCTs offer big tax incentives for investors prepared to back a fund of unknown, untested, and generally unprofitable companies. The hope is that, while many will flop, a few will become the Microsoft, Google, or Ryanair of the future. VCT promoters claim the few winners will more than make up for the failures and the go-nowheres.

If you are willing to accept these risks, plus the high charges in many funds, HMRC will help you on your way – you can invest up to £200,000 per person in a tax year into a VCT. You must hold the shares for at least three years.

Here's what you get for your courage:

- ✔ 30 per cent tax relief when you buy a new VCT issue (they come out every year usually around November to January). You get this rate even if you're not a top rate payer, provided the tax you paid at least equals the rebate.

    Suppose you pay £6,000 in tax this year as a basic rate payer. The £6,000 is 30 per cent of £20,000 so you can invest up to £20,000 into a VCT and get up 30 per cent back – up to the £6,000 you paid in tax.

- ✔ Tax freedom is given on dividends paid out both to new holders and to those who purchase existing shares. You don't even have to put the dividends received down on your tax form.

- ✔ No Capital Gains Tax liability when you sell – hopefully at a profit.

Book II

Paying Less Tax

If you don't want to venture into the totally unknown, AIM-listed shares count as VCTs as well. Fund managers create AIM funds to take advantage of this loophole. (See the previous section for more on AIMs.)

Sheltering gains with EIS

If you made a capital gain in the past three years and are willing to take a big risk with that gain to avoid paying capital gains tax, then maybe the Enterprise Investment Scheme (EIS) is for you.

EIS investors put their money into one small company that often has no track record, let alone a profit or dividend. What they get in return is a shelter from their CGT bills from the previous three years. If you're rich enough, you can put in £200,000 a year! There is no minimum, but most EIS companies don't accept less than £1,000. And you can, of course, put your money into a number of EIS companies each year if you wish.

So, if you have £20,000 of capital gains tax to pay, you can put £20,000 into EIS companies, hold the money there for the required three-year minimum and watch your CGT bill evaporate.

On top of offsetting your CGT, you get 20 per cent income tax relief on all EIS share purchases. Add the possible 40 per cent CGT saving to the 20 per cent income tax credit, and you get 60 per cent – so you are only risking 40p for each £1 you invest. If you make a profit you do not pay any CGT on the gain. But obviously, you can't have it both ways! If you make a loss (and this is ever so likely) you cannot offset this against gains elsewhere.

Taking account of losses

You don't really want to read this bit, and we hope you never have to make use of the information here. But life has been tough on the stock market since early 2000, and there are a lot of ways to lose money as well as to gain it. This section talks about dealing with losses.

The one bright spot in selling shares for a loss is that you can set that loss against capital gains you make elsewhere – either now or in the future.

You can use part of your losses for the current year and hold over the balance – there is no time limit.

You can't, however, use the indexation on assets bought before April 1998 to create a loss. *Indexation* is adjusting the starting price of your asset for inflation. It applies only on assets up to April 1998 when the capital gains tax rules changed. In theory, you could create a loss by using inflation. For example, if you bought a share in 1990 and its price remained unaltered until April 1998, the effect of inflation would be that you would have an asset whose real value had dropped.

Shares in companies that are worthless because they've gone bust can have their uses! You have to tell HMRC the shares have a *negligible value.* Negligible may sound like a few pence – it really means nothing. So, if you paid £10,000 for shares in a company that went bust, you have £10,000 worth of losses to offset against £10,000 of gains elsewhere. Taking £10,000 out of the equation can save up to £4,000 from a future tax bill if you're a top-rate taxpayer.

Looking at the Basics of Insurance

Life insurance policies (we should say *assurance* but that's just for the really pernickety) have been, and still are, sold under various guises. With *term insurance,* you pay a fixed amount each month for a set period. If you die within this period, the policy pays the promised amount. *Critical illness policies* work in the same way but pay out if you are diagnosed with one of a number of serious medical conditions.

But here, we're mainly concerned with various life insurance plans that are really investments dressed up as policies. These often have complicated tax conditions. You can purchase a wide range of policies including endowments, maximum investment plans, whole of life plans, with-profits bonds, friendly society plans, single premium life funds, guaranteed income bonds, flexible whole of life, and insurance savings plans.

To help you understand life insurance lingo, we explain some of the basic terms and in the following list:

- **Beneficiary:** The person who gets the proceeds of the policy.
- **Endowment:** A mix of protection cover with investment.
- **Insurance-linked investment fund:** More of an investment than insurance. These funds exploit tax loopholes to offer gains to some taxpayers.
- **Insured:** The person covered under the policy.
- **Premium:** The amount you pay each month or as a lump sum into a policy.
- **Surrender (a policy):** To give up a policy before its maturity date or the death of the insured.
- **Trust:** An often complicated legal device that can take your money out of the tax net.

Evaluating Endowments

Millions own *endowments,* a combination of life cover and a savings plan. If you die during the policy's set period, your family receives a guaranteed minimum amount. It can be more if the investment portion did well. And if you survive beyond the set period, you receive a sum of money that reflects how well (or how badly!) the investment portion fared over the period.

Just how much of the money you pay in is devoted to the life cover and how much to the insurance company's costs, commissions, and profit margins is rarely revealed in any form let alone made clear. But all sales people preach perfect clarity on one item – especially when they try to sell an endowment as a way of repaying a mortgage. They all say the amount you get when the policy matures is 'paid to you tax-free.'

The sales pitch is true. If you buy an endowment and keep up the payments, you have no tax to pay at the end when the insurer sends you a cheque. That's only half the story, however. The rest of the story is something the sales folk don't mention. While the proceeds are tax-free to you, the fund itself is taxed. The life insurance company has to pay tax on the money it invests for you. All the dividend income and interest the fund earns on its investments are taxed. And when the fund makes a gain on selling an investment, there's more tax to pay.

How is this worked out? Don't ask! It's extremely complex, in a formula called the 'I-E basis' which takes in investment income and capital gains before subtracting the insurer's costs. If this book was two or three times the length, it would still only scratch the surface of this subject. And even then, it wouldn't help too much as the detailed rules seem to be constantly changing.

Cutting Away the Complexity of Life Insurance Taxation Rules

A life insurance company's internal taxation is quite complex and the taxation has an impact on your investment savings. So there are some broad-brush rules for investment-oriented life insurance funds. Generally, a fund is taxed on

- ✔ Income it gets from share dividends, bonds, bank deposits, and property.
- ✔ Capital gains on any profits the fund makes on selling shares, property, or other taxable assets.

Whatever the level of tax an insurance fund pays out, you can't reclaim it. Under no circumstances. Never. It does not matter if you were a non-tax-payer during part of the policy term or even throughout the entire term of the policy, you can't get anything back. The same applies if you paid tax at a maximum ten per cent. I bet the salesperson never mentioned this!

If you're a non-taxpayer, avoid insurance-based funds like the plague. Your savings will end up being diminished by taxes you may not know exist and which you would never have paid outside the insurance plan.

Checking out whether policies qualify or not

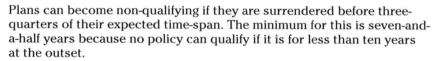

Book II

Paying
Less Tax

Many tax ramifications hinge on whether a policy is *qualifying* or *non-qualifying*. Knowing technical terms helps ensure that you maximise any tax savings and minimise tax spending when you cash in your investment policy. Your knowledge will also impress the seller, making it less likely that you are mis-sold. Generally speaking, qualifying policies are better, especially for top-rate taxpayers.

Requirements for a *qualifying policy* are:

- ✔ It must be for a minimum 10 years. They can be for longer, typically 20 to 30 years.

  Plans can become non-qualifying if they are surrendered before three-quarters of their expected time-span. The minimum for this is seven-and-a-half years because no policy can qualify if it is for less than ten years at the outset.

- ✔ Premiums have to be paid regularly according to the schedule. That's usually monthly and must be at least once a year. There are special rules if you miss out a few payments and need to catch up later on.

- ✔ The guaranteed sum payable on death must be at least 75 per cent of the total premiums paid in if the policy buyer is aged 55 or under when the plan is purchased. That percentage goes down by 2 per cent a year for the over 55s.

If a policy does not fit the above rules, it is a *non-qualifying policy.*

Jumping tax hurdles

If a qualifying policy matures or is paid out on death or because it is triggered by one of the listed medical conditions in a critical illness plan, the policy-holder does not need to pay a penny in tax.

In some cases, top-rate taxpayers have to pay tax when they cash in a policy. If you cash in a lump-sum plan, such as a with-profits bond in full or in part, or fail to keep up a regular payment plan for at least seven and a half years and then ask for the policy's current value back, you may owe tax.

You can realise tax benefits if you're a top-rate payer when you take out a policy but drop back to the basic tax level when you cash it in. Likewise, you're disadvantaged if you buy investment-linked insurances as a basic-rate taxpayer and cash them in when you are a top-rate payer. We explain this in 'Slicing from the top' later in this chapter.

Top-rate taxpayers may find that they pay less tax overall if they invest in insurance funds than if they use unit or investment trusts or invest directly into stocks and shares. Why? The typical rate an insurance fund is charged internally is lower than the 40 per cent top-rate tax and capital gains tax.

If you surrender it before three-quarters of its stated term, a qualifying policy becomes a non-qualifying policy. Clever insurers have found a partial way around this. Instead of giving you one policy for your money, they give you a cluster of mini-policies, perhaps as many as 100. If you need some of your money before the policy term is up, you only need to cancel a few mini-policies, resulting in fewer tax hassles.

If you still pay into a life insurance policy that was bought before March 13 1984, you get life assurance premium relief (LAPR) at 12.5 per cent of the amounts you pay in. The insurance company accounts for this automatically so there is no need to claim. If you pay in £10 a month on paper, the insurer will only take £8.75 from your bank account. You get this up to a maximum of £1,500 a year or one-sixth of your total income, which is an awful lot of insurance! And you get it whatever your personal tax rate. But if you extend or increase the policy, you don't get the LAPR on the extra.

Looking at Lump Sum Insurance Bonds

The *lump sum insurance bond,* sometimes called a *single-premium investment contract,* is a non-qualifying policy. It does not have a fixed life or any of the other attributes of a qualifying policy. So you have to be careful, otherwise you could find yourself on the end of an unwelcome tax bill.

The life cover is usually limited to 1 per cent more than the *underlying value* (the value of the investment less the commission and other charges deducted upfront) of the fund. And as life insurance companies start off by slicing off anything up to 7 per cent of your premiums in fees and commissions, they can easily afford to give you back 1 per cent if you die.

If you intend emigrating or returning to your country of origin, always tell the financial adviser what you are going to do and which country you intend moving to. Australia, New Zealand, and South Africa are among the nations whose very different tax systems can hit UK insurance bond holders with a double whammy. They can pay tax on the UK bond and then find they have to pay more tax in their new country.

Taking a regular income

Insurance bond holders can take a regular payment from their policy to give themselves an income. They pay no personal tax on it, no matter what their own top-tax rate is. But they must follow these rules.

- ✔ You can withdraw no more than 5 per cent of the original investment sum each year for a period of 20 years. HMRC sees this as taking your own money back.

- ✔ If you miss out on a year or years, or took less than 5 per cent, you can catch up. Someone who missed the first annual withdrawal of 5 per cent can take 10 per cent in the second year. An investor who took 1 per cent in the first five years has a 20 per cent sum to carry forward to year 6. Again, the idea is that the original investment sum, not any gain, is paid back tax-free.

- ✔ If you breach the 5 per cent rule, or want all your money back, you enter the wonderful world of top slicing. (See the upcoming 'Slicing from the top'.)

If you take from 5 per cent upwards in a year (and you don't have unused previous years you can catch up on), or you cash in the insurance lump sum investment completely, you have to do some arithmetic. First you have to calculate the profit, which is either the amount over the 5 per cent per year, or, if you want all your money back, the excess over what you paid for the policy in the first place.

Older taxpayers caught in the age allowance trap can profit from the 5 per cent withdrawal rule because this does not count as income.

Here's some really good news. Because the fund pays tax internally, using an indecipherable formula or two, there is no more tax to pay if you are a basic-rate tax-payer.

But no good news comes without some bad. The profit is added to your other income to check whether the total falls into the top tax bracket.

The following examples show how the tax liability falls in various situations:

- ✔ Your income is £10,000 and your insurance gain is £5,000. The total £15,000 is well within the basic-tax band so there is no tax to pay.

- ✔ Your annual income is £30,000 making you a basic-rate taxpayer. Your insurance gain is £20,000, which puts your total income at £50,000. You have to pay tax on the amount over the basic level (£39,825 in 2007-08). You can use the top slicing method described in the next section.

- ✔ Your annual income is £50,000 and your insurance gain is £30,000. The entire insurance gain falls within the top-rate tax band. But the policy is treated as though 20 per cent has been paid to accommodate basic-rate payers, so you only have to find the other 20 per cent, not the whole 40 per cent.

Slicing from the top

Now for some better news, again. This section looks at *top-slicing,* which is a way of making your withdrawals from lump-sum insurance bonds less liable to a tax demand. Top slicing is not too easy. But bear with us. It gets better, the longer you leave your money in the fund. And if it applies to you, then it could save you a lot of tax payments.

Take someone earning £19,825 whose bond has produced a £40,000 gain over 10 years. Adding the income to the gain gives £59,825 so £20,000 falls in the top tax rate. You would expect this person to pay tax at 40 per cent on this £20,000 profit in the highest tax band, equalling £8,000.

Wrong. The fund is tax-free at the basic income tax level, as 20 per cent has already been paid internally. So you might expect to pay 20 per cent on the gain, equalling £4,000.

Wrong again. The tax collector knows it would be really nasty to take 10 years' worth of growth and hit the holder for it in one year. There is, instead, a wonderful but little known process called top slicing. With top slicing, the gain is divided by the number of years the insurance bond has been in force, in this case 10.

So divide the total £40,000 gain by 10 to give £4,000. Add that £4,000 to the holder's other income for the year, (in this case £19,825) and the total is £23,825 that falls well within the basic-rate band. The result is that no extra tax is payable.

Being aware (and wary) of costs and commissions

Always ask your financial adviser or bank for as much information as possible on the costs you will incur in buying an insurance-based investment compared with a similar investment outside the insurance policy wrapper. You can find these expenses outweigh any tax benefits.

Someone investing a £10,000 lump sum into a low-cost investment such as an investment trust or an exchange-traded fund with an upfront 1 per cent in costs and growing at 7 per cent after annual fees will have £20,513 after 10 years, ignoring tax.

Another person investing a £10,000 lump sum into an insurance-based fund where the upfront fee is much higher at 6 per cent, but otherwise growing at the same rate, will have £19,530 at the end of ten years.

You need to sit down with the adviser to see if those higher costs are worth it in your particular situation. Remember that lump-sum insurance bonds can cost you as much as 7 per cent in upfront commission.

Now suppose the bond holder had a £37,825 income. Add the £4,000 to that, making £41,825, and half (£2,000) falls into the higher rate (starting at £39,825 in 20070-08). Only that top half is hit for higher-rate tax at 20 per cent with the result that overall, the tax rate falls to 10 per cent. Apply that new rate to the £40,000 and the charge is £4,000.

If the entire sum had fallen within the top rate, the holder would have had to pay at 20 per cent, gaining nothing from top slicing.

Top slicing can also work if the bond is partially encashed beyond the 5 per cent annual tax-free withdrawal.

Top-rate taxpayers who expect their income to fall back when they retire or downshift their work can combine the 5 per cent rule with top slicing to cut down on tax bills. While they are earning high amounts, they can take the 5 per cent tax-free withdrawals to give themselves a regular income, saving on the extra tax they would have had to pay on income from other investment types. But when their earnings fall to basic tax rate levels, they can cash in the bond, use the top slicing rules, and pay less tax (or none at all) because all or part of the gain now falls into the 20 per cent basic savings tax band.

Top slicing on cashing in a bond does not apply in calculating whether you can apply for children's tax credits or whether you qualify for the extra age allowance given to the 65 plus age group. In these cases, you add in the complete gain to your other income for that year.

Eyeing Guaranteed Bonds

Guaranteed income bonds (or GIBs) pay a fixed sum annually or monthly for a set period after which you get your initial investment back. A variation is called a guaranteed growth bond, in which the income rolls up to increase the eventual payout rather than being distributed. Either way, the rate you see quoted is tax-free for basic-rate taxpayers. Top-rate taxpayers have to pay extra (see the earlier 'Slicing from the top' section).

Gains, if any, from high-income bonds linked to stock market indexes are also treated in the same way.

Going Offshore with Your Money

You don't have to buy insurance-style investments issued in the UK. If you live abroad or are thinking of living abroad, you may want to consider a tax haven policy. These usually come from offshore offshoots of well-known UK insurers who have set up offices in places such as the Isle of Man, Jersey, Guernsey, and Luxembourg for this purpose. Investments in policies with these tax haven companies mount up without any tax charges.

Looking at the legalities

There are no restrictions on any UK tax resident moving their money offshore. You can invest where you like, what you like, and how you like.

If this were as far as it went, then no one would bother paying UK tax because we would all ship our investments offshore. But life is never that easy. You have to tell HMRC about any gains you make on offshore bonds in the same way as if the bond were onshore.

To make sure you do, the tax authorities are working to ensure that many off-shore life companies (including almost all those with onshore business in the UK) send in an annual return showing who has encashed what. This is part of a new European Union crackdown on cross-border tax evasion, which means that insurers (and other financial institutions) have to report gains whatever the laws on policyholder confidentiality say in the country where the insurer has its legal home. So no cheating.

Weighing up costs versus savings

Unless you wish to court illegality by tax dodging, or you want to invest in an esoteric asset not available in the UK, there may be no point in going offshore if you are a resident in the UK for tax purposes. Costs are usually higher, and you will be hit for taxes just as if you had dealt with a UK-based company.

But if you work offshore and then return, there is a big plus point. The gain is reduced proportionally by the number of years you were not resident in the UK. An offshore bond-holder who cashes in after 14 years but who spent seven of those years overseas, has the gain halved for tax computation purposes. Of course, if you never come back or cash in the policy entirely before you return to the UK, you're liable only for local taxes (if any) where you were living.

 If you intend moving permanently to another country, it can be worth using an offshore bond as it will roll up without any tax. You then cash it in when you set up your new home. But always check first on the tax rules in the country you want to go to.

Book II

**Paying
Less Tax**

Book III
Building Up Savings and Investments

'Just think – with our own house and mortgage,
we'll be as carefree as these lambs.'

In this Book . . .

*I*f you're thinking investing is only for the super-rich, think again! This Book shows you how to make sound, sensible investment choices whatever your budget. Detailing shares, bonds, property, and the best savings accounts, we also cover alternative investments for the more experienced and adventurous investors.

Here are the contents of Book III at a glance:

Chapter 1

Squaring Risk and Return

- -

In This Chapter

▶ Working out risk and reward theory in practice

▶ Deciding the level of gains you want

▶ Calculating what you could get

▶ Knowing about the advantages of diversification

▶ Keeping an eye on how time works for you

- -

*W*hen we walk down the street or drive a car, we're aware of risks. We know, for example, that we might risk life and limb crossing a road when the Red Man symbol is displayed. And we know that our safety (not to mention driver's licence) is threatened if we drive 60mph in a 30mph zone.

Granted, if we run helter-skelter down the street or drive recklessly down the road, ignoring everyone and every rule, we might arrive more quickly at our destination. But the faster we go and the more corners we cut, the greater the chance of losing everything. So we generally take simple precautions to avoid risks. That way, we make some progress through life.

But what if we never took risks at all and, instead, wrapped ourselves in cotton wool? If we only walked on perfectly kept, deserted fields and drove on empty roads at exactly 20mph? We'd simply not get anywhere, and our lives would be boringly empty. We'd make no progress through life. We'd be taking the risk of missing out on something interesting and perhaps profitable.

The same can be said about investing. Investment risk is no different from the risks of daily life. There are steady-as-you-go investments that give a moderate rate of return with perhaps the occasional loss (after all, even the most careful driver can have a bad experience). There are hell-for-leather investments that can offer massive returns or huge losses. And there's the investment equivalent of surrounding yourself with layers of cotton wool – where nothing will happen at all.

In this chapter, we examine investment risks – specifically, the benefits and drawbacks of various investment possibilities and ways to increase your odds of successful returns.

Examining Two Investing Principles You Should Never Forget

Here are a couple of clichés that sound banal but should be carved in mirror writing on every investor's forehead, so she or he can read them first thing each morning when facing the wash basin:

- ✔ There's no gain without pain. This means that in your daily life, you have to move out of the couch potato position to achieve.

- ✔ You have to speculate to accumulate. If you don't take some chances with your money, you'll never get anywhere.

Financial markets – indeed, all of capitalism – work on these two principles.

Here's an example to help you see the importance of these two philosophies. Suppose that you're running a company and need £10m to expand your firm into a new product. You could borrow the money from the bank knowing that you'll pay 10 per cent interest a year whether the new venture works or not. If the new venture fails, you still have to pay the bank its £10m plus interest even if it means selling the rest of the business. But if your business goes on to be a winner, the bank still only gets its £10m plus interest while your fortune soars.

Alternatively, you could raise the cash through an issue of new shares, where the advantages for you are no fixed-interest costs and, if the project is a flop, your investors suffer rather than you. They could lose all their money. That's the risk they run. But if the venture is a success, the shareholders receive dividends from you and see the value of their stake rise due to everyone demanding a share of the action. You shared the risk with others, so now they get a slice of the reward.

Now suppose that no one had taken any risks. You decided not to expand into the new product. The bank manager vetoed all loans. And the share buyers sat on their hands and kept their money under their beds. There'd be no pain – no one would lose – but there'd also be no gain for you, the bank, the investors, or the wider economy.

Absolute safety means little or no reward

The most secure place to keep your money is in a low-interest guaranteed account from the government's National Savings & Investments department. In certain circumstances, this is a good place for some of your money. But unless you have very good reasons, you risk losing out on potentially better investments.

Putting your money in such an account also presents a second danger. When you protect a piece of china in cotton wool and bubble wrap, you expect it still to be there years later, but money is different. Its buying value erodes each year due to rising prices. You'll go backward in real terms if all you do is put all your money in the safest possible home. And the longer you look at investing your money, the truer that becomes.

Suppose that two people coming back from the Second World War in 1945 each had £100 to invest. One person invested the money in a basket of shares, each with an uncertain future,

and the other person put the money in super-safe UK government stocks. Both investors told their family and friends that they'd re-invest all the dividends and interest they received.

By the end of 2002, the investor who went the safe route had a fund worth £3,668 according to figures from Barclays Capital. But when inflation is taken into the calculation, the £100 is only worth £150. And it took until 1996 before that original £100 regained its value in terms of what it would buy.

The shares investor did better. Although some of the original investments failed, more did well. Despite the pain of a roller-coaster ride at times, the investment showed big gains. On paper, the £100 became £65,440. Rising prices and recent falling stock markets took their toll, but speculating did produce an accumulation. Adjusted for the cost of living, that original £100 became £2,689.

Granted, all these potential participants could've argued that they'd taken a risk-free stance with their cash. But had they? No. They'd taken the very severe risk of missing out on something positive. They didn't speculate. They didn't accumulate.

Determining the Return You Want from Your Money

The starting point of any risk-reward assessment is to determine the return you want from your money. The harder you want your money to work, the more risks you need to take.

You may want your money just to maintain its buying power – to keep up with inflation. Or you may want to see it grow in real terms by a relatively small amount – just enough to keep ahead. Or you may want some aggressive growth to fund a pet project. Suppose, for example, that you have a 10-year-old child who's been given a £10,000 lump sum by an adoring relation who had one proviso: The money must be spent on university education when the child reaches 18.

The most basic education costs £10,000. But most will need more – especially if they wish to study for a post-graduate qualification. So what rate of return over the eight years would you need to produce the result you want? Inflation, which erodes your target figure in real spending terms, investment fees, and taxation have been ignored here to simplify the figures:

£10,000: 0%

£12,000: 2.31%

£14,000: 4.3%

£16,000: 6.05%

£18,000: 7.62%

£20,000: 9.05%

£25,000: 12.14%

£30,000: 14.72%

£35,000: 16.95%

£40,000: 18.92%

The higher figures are more than what you're likely to earn on your money unless

✔ You're prepared to take big risks, including losing your original capital.

or

✔ Inflation returns with a vengeance so you appear to obtain substantial gains even if they don't translate into real spending power at the shops.

To show you how your money could grow, we want to give you recalculated figures using the official rates for salespeople from the Financial Services Authority (FSA). The FSA first instituted these rates, which are adjusted from time to time, to prevent unscrupulous salesfolk from coming up with the first growth rate they could think of and then multiplying that by their phone number (and yours as well if they really fancied earning extra commission that day). The current rates are 7 per cent for untaxed investments such as pension plans and Individual Savings Accounts (ISAs), and 6 per cent for taxed investments such as unit trusts, life assurance savings bonds, and investment trust savings plans.

The FSA's official rates aren't what they seem. No one ever earns the full rate, so you can't just assume 6 per cent or 7 per cent as the likely targets. Instead, the quoted rates are cut back by costs and commissions so firms have to show actual returns adjusted for these expenses. That means you get less. Here's an example. The paperwork for a £100 investment would show £106 at the end of the year at 6 per cent. But a 1 per cent cost structure brings it down to £105.

So take a look at the recalculated figures to see how long it would take your £10,000 to grow assuming a 6 per cent annual return:

£10,000: No time

£12,000: 3 years and 1 month

£14,000: 5 years and 9 months

£16,000: 8 years and 1 month

£18,000: 10 years and 1 month

£20,000: 11 years and 10 months

£25,000: 15 years and 9 months

£30,000: 18 years and 10 months

£35,000: 21 years and 6 months

£40,000: 23 years and 9 months

Investments are for the medium to long term – from five years upward. So over this timeframe, what can you expect? The following sections tell you.

The likely return from shares

Anyone reading newspaper headlines since early 2000 can be forgiven for believing that shares only go down – that they're a surefire way to waste your cash. But anyone who had read the same newspaper headlines up to the end of 1999 could equally be forgiven for believing that shares only go up – in big leaps.

Shares are volatile, but over the very long term, the whole of the last century, a basket of typical equities has produced average annual gains of around 12 per cent before tax.

Using different start and finish dates can produce almost any other figure you care to think of. But however you cut it, the trend in share prices is upward provided that you're patient. No one would bother to take the inherent risks with shares if he or she didn't expect to make greater gains than with bonds, property, or cash over the longer term.

The return from shares comes in two forms, although neither is guaranteed, let alone even promised:

- Dividends
- Capital gains

Dividends are the way companies have of returning part of the profits they make, or the reserves they've built up over good years, to the part-owners of the firm. That's you, the shareholder.

These are small amounts compared to your initial investment. But if reinvested into more shares, they can boost your holding. A 3 per cent annual dividend after any tax reinvested would add around 40 per cent to your shareholding after 10 years.

The beauty of dividends is that you should get them whether share prices as a whole are going up or down. Dividends are regular, and a company cutting out or missing a payment is a very bad sign indeed.

The second return from shares is that the capital goes up. Is this a sure thing? No. But should it happen? Yes.

Adding Capital Gains to the dividend produces the likely annual gain. A typical share offers a 3.7 per cent dividend. And a reasonably well-run company should be able to produce about 5 per cent a year growth on top of inflation, which is now around 2.5 per cent a year. Add all this up, and your shares should produce around 11 per cent a year.

What you get from a share depends on the exact price you paid. If you bought at the top of the market and the share subsequently halves in value before returning to the 10 to 11 per cent I suggest, it could take the best part of a decade before you're back on the growth track.

The likely return from bonds

Are you an avid reader of Victorian novels? If so, you know that the heroines always know the value of the hero's (or villain's) fortune by turning his lump sum wealth into so much per year. And the figure selected is always 5 per cent because this was the long-term return on investments the Victorians expected.

And how do heroines of Victorian novels always know this? Because in Victorian days, most money went into bonds. Those from the government were the safest. Those from railway companies and iron works were riskier. So although the Victorian novel heroine may not be able to recognise all that much of the world around her, she is at home with the finances on bonds.

Nothing much has changed now that inflation is once again moderate. As a result, her 5 per cent isn't a bad long-term guess for today. You'll get a little less if you head for the super-safety of UK government bonds, or *gilts* as they're known in the money trade. And you'll get a percentage point or two more if you aim for *corporate bonds,* bonds issued by commercial companies raising loans.

But how do you get the 8, 9, or 10 per cent on offer from some bonds and bond funds? Easy! You just aim at bonds – known as *junk bonds* – from firms that have a dodgy track record. In addition, the bonds of some countries have junk status because the country's underlying finances are a mess. Nations from Latin America are often likely guilty parties.

If you're willing to take the risk that they'll miss a payment or, worse, fail to give back your capital on time or at all, then you may be rewarded for your bravery by the potential doubling of your return over safe bonds. But although you may end up with more, you may equally get your financial head blown off in a crisis.

Book III

Building Up Savings and Investments

Investors who like to sleep at night should look at bonds paying out a maximum of 6.5 to 7 per cent. Bond fund purchasers should go no higher than 5.5 to 6 per cent. Why the gap? Because the fund carries an annual fee, typically 1 per cent, which must be paid out from somewhere! And it's usually from the income on the bond.

The likely return from property

According to the Nationwide Building Society, the average price of a property throughout the UK was around £175,500 in Spring 2007. Back in 1997, the price stood at £56,000. Go back to 1987, and it was just under £41,000. And three decades or so ago in 1977, it was £12,400.

But for purposes of this discussion, leave aside what you might make from your own home because you have to live somewhere, don't always have much choice on where you live, and would be paying rent if you weren't buying. Instead, think in terms of commercial property.

Professionals invest in commercial property, such as factories, office blocks, and shopping centres. You can't go out and buy a business park unless you have tens of millions and the ability to manage your investment. But you can tap into commercial property through a number of funds.

What you get from a property investment comes from two sources. One source is the rent tenants pay you. You won't get this straight into your pocket, though. You'll have to find management costs, repairs, interest on borrowings, and tax.

The second source is the hoped-for gain in the underlying value of the buildings. Add the two together, and you get the full return.

Since 1971, the overall annual returns from property have only declined in four separate years according to figures from experts Investment Property Databank. One year was 1974, when a financial crisis occurred in the UK. The other three years were during the economic downturn at the start of the 1990s. In addition, during a handful of other years, property failed to keep up with inflation.

In present-day conditions, you can expect to earn around 7 to 9 per cent a year averaged over long periods. So you can expect more from property than from bonds but less than from shares. However, you don't need to repair a bond, have security guards for bonds, or worry about a bond going out of fashion. And properties come with more expenses.

Commercial property is different from domestic property. Figures for the two seldom go in tandem.

The likely return from a cash account

Don't expect much too much from a cash account. In return for the security, you'll do well to get around 3.5 to 5 per cent from a bank or building society. You may get a lot less. You should only invest in cash for safety, never for the long term unless it is of paramount importance that you know exactly what you will have in the future to meet a known financial need such as a child's education.

Since 1971, cash has only been the best performing asset type during two years – 1974 and 1990. And both years, the financial system was in trouble. Cash was the worst place to put your money during 10 separate years. And over almost any long period, cash has been easily out-gunned by bonds and property, and it's been beaten out of sight by shares.

The building society or National Savings is the starting point for any calcula-tion of whether a risk could be worthwhile. There's no point investing in a speculative enterprise if the best you can foresee is a fraction of a percentage point above the bank branch.

Leaving medium- to long-term money in a current bank account is a guaran-teed loser. Rates can be as low as 0.1 per cent, and yes, that's before tax on this virtually invisible return at 20 per cent for most people and 40 per cent for the better off. Inflation means your money is worth less each year.

The government inflation target is 2.5 per cent (though it currently stands at above 3 per cent), so your money needs to earn that much after tax to stay level. For a basic-rate taxpayer, that means a headline rate of around 3.2 per cent when inflation is on target, and a top-rate taxpayer needs 4 per cent just to go nowhere. Shopping around and being prepared to accept restrictions on withdrawals should produce around 5-6 per cent.

What happened to the 10 per cent rates on bank and building society accounts of a decade or so ago? They disappeared along with high inflation. A 10 per cent rate when prices are rising at 12 per cent equals a guaranteed annual loss – even before taxation. At least a 5.5 per cent savings account when inflation is 2.5 to 3 per cent offers the chance of slight gains.

The likely return from other assets

Investors have seen spectacular returns from gold, diamonds, works of art, and even special shares offering guaranteed tickets at the centre court at Wimbledon for the All-England championships. Others have made big money out of racehorses, vintage wine, and stamp collections.

But all these ventures demand a whole lot of specialist knowledge combined with a whole load of luck. Fans of this sort of thing tend to flag up the good times and ignore the bad years.

Figures are fairly unreliable because you're always comparing apples with bananas. A painting by Pablo Picasso may double in value over a year, but that doesn't say anything about a Salvador Dali or even other works by Picasso.

Many illegal investment schemes have been offered in areas such as stamp collecting and fine wines. These schemes offer big gains for supposed small risk. The authorities have shut down some of these ventures but usually not before hapless investors have lost their savings.

Hedge fund returns are all over the place. Much depends on what the fund sets out to do. Some go for maximum returns. Others aim at protecting your money.

Increasing Your Chances of Successful Returns

Risk and reward, risk and regret can't be separated. You must take risks and put your head above the cash investment parapet if you want to win.

Now turn risk on its head and call it opportunity. It's really the same thing, but now you have a positive phrase. You can increase your chances of success by diversifying (not putting all your investment eggs into one basket) and being patient.

Plenty of factors affect your chances of success

Suppose that you acquire shares in ABC Bank and XYZ Insurance, perhaps as a result of free share handouts. Obviously, you have to work out whether the opportunities in each company are worthwhile. But for now, you need to consider the bigger picture altogether. No company is an island, and none lives in a vacuum. Plenty more factors can enhance your opportunities or increase your chances of making a mistake:

- **Currencies.** Foreign exchange markets can have an impact on your investment. They have a habit of moving in slow trend lines, although they jump about at the umpteenth decimal place all the time. Each day, even each minute, exchange rates can go either way by very small amounts. There are no investment straight lines!

- **Interest rates.** You may invest in a brilliant company, but if interest rates go up, it will be less attractive because the cash they need from the bank for expansion will cost them more. Rising interest rates are bad news for almost everyone other than holders of cash.

- **Stock markets.** When share prices are generally booming, even badly run companies do reasonably well. And when share prices are falling, the best organised firms with the greatest prospects tend to lose out.

✔ **Inflation.** Nope. Not car tyre pressure but rising prices. Inflation can be good for some sectors, such as retailers, because it takes the pressure off, meaning they don't have to run perpetual sales and price cuts.

✔ **The economy.** You can't really beat it. If it looks good, everything shines; when it turns down, only a handful of assets manage to hold their heads up.

Diversification is your best friend

Diversification is putting your eggs in many baskets. So if you trip up and choose a poor investment, you still have some capital left to help your finances recover.

Understanding the multi-layered approach that professionals use

Professional investors consider what the fund they manage is supposed to achieve. If the fund's main role is to provide a regular pension income for those whose retirement needs it has to meet, the fund goes in the main for safer assets, such as bonds, property, and cash. But if the fund advertises itself as a route into, say, higher risk Far Eastern share markets, it must be restricted to these investments, although the fund may have a small percentage in cash to give it the flexibility to move around stock markets.

Those running a fund with a wide remit, such as a life-insurance-with-profits fund (the basis of many retirement and endowment plans as well as the cornerstone of investment bonds sold to older people), work out their asset allocation as percentages of the whole fund between the main asset classes, including shares, bonds, cash, and property.

Within each of those asset areas, they then buy a wide range of investment assets. The idea is not to be caught out if one area catches a cold. Within property, for example, a fund manager may buy some office blocks, shopping centres, and industrial premises. Within shares, a well-diversified fund manager may have holdings in the UK, the US, mainland Europe, and the Far East.

Wide-remit managers then further subdivide. Say, for example, that a fund manager has holdings in the UK, the US, mainland Europe, and the Far East. Regarding the fund focusing on UK shares, the fund manager may decide to have a percentage in different stock market company sectors, such as bank stocks and engineering companies.

Only after looking at all those various things do fund managers look at individual shares, deciding to hold pharmaceutical company A rather than B.

Book III

**Building Up
Savings
and
Investments**

Note that those running narrowly focused funds may not bother with sectors. And they concentrate even less on wider factors. But they still diversify so that they don't have too much riding on one fund. They know that companies can fall apart very quickly. (Two examples are Polly Peck in the late 1980s and Marconi in the 1990s.)

Concentrating too much on one or two investments is a mistake. Another mistake is not looking at all your wealth. If your pension fund is riding on UK shares, then you should consider other points in your own investment strategy for money under your direct control.

Spreading your money in practice

Suppose that someone gave you £1,000 in 1971. In addition, assume that you managed to avoid the temptation to spend it all (it's big money as after adjusting for inflation, you would need £9,000 now to have the same spending power) and invested it instead. And, to simplify matters, say that you had a choice of just four investments – cash at the building society, UK government bonds, a commercial property portfolio, and the UK stock market. The results would have been widely different depending on how you had invested that money. Our timeframe is well over the span of a generation, so plenty of ups and downs have occurred. They are all well documented by Barclays Bank offshoot Barclays Capital in an annual number-crunching exercise whose figures we use here.

If you had put all your money into one area and left all the income and capital gains to grow back in your fund, your £1,000 would've been £13,750 in the building society by the end of 2002. Putting your money into government bonds would've given you a more respectable £31,800. Property would've fared even better – around £37,500. And despite the shares crash from early 2000, an equity portfolio would be valued at £58,100.

Now had you been really cautious and divided your money into four equal parts for our four asset classes, you'd still have a considerable £35,300, or nearly four times the amount you would've needed to keep up with inflation.

But what if you had been a real speculator, believing that you knew the best of the four each January 1 for the following 12 months? If you had perfect foresight, your £1,000 would've grown to £1.33 million. Yippee!

And, finally, what if you had got it wrong each time, picking the following year's disaster zone? You would have £543 after inflation, little more than one-twentieth of what you started with. What would've bought a new car in 1971 was just about enough for a medium-priced bike by 2002!

By the way, as you're assessing all the preceding figures, keep in mind that all those figures ignore tax and the cost of moving money from one asset to another. These factors would've lessened all these returns.

Over that timeframe, cash was the best asset in only two years and the worst in 10; the government stock portfolio was a superstar in five years and the worst in eight; property was the best 10 times and the worst six; shares were the best in 15 separate years but the worst in eight.

Note that the great outperformance in shares wasn't gradual. It came in fits and starts. During eight of the 32 years, the index made 25 per cent or more gains. But bad years were really bad – down as much as 50 per cent in the very worst 12-month period. And if you scratch those figures more closely, you find that the big gains in equities were concentrated on just a relatively low number of days in that period. If you missed them, you would've fared no better than with your money in the building society.

Patience is your pal

To be a good investor, you need to have a good strategy and good diversification, but to be a savvy investor, you also need patience and time. Your investments may need years to mature. There may be more days when your investments go nowhere or down than when they rise. But when they do increase, it can be by substantial amounts over a short time.

Your own time horizons determine the risks you can afford to take. Investment is not a short-term punt on financial markets. It requires at least five years, preferably longer. Short-termism can also increase your costs and your tax bill.

Chapter 2

Saving for a Rainy Day

* *

In This Chapter

▶ Working out how much cash you need for emergencies

▶ Searching for the best rates

▶ Deciding what type of account you're after

▶ Protecting your savings

* *

Saving seems to have gone right out of fashion, with the average UK household in debt to the tune of almost £8,800 (excluding mortgages) and rising in February 2007. Debt appears to be far more tempting and dangerous, while boring old saving doesn't excite in the same way as getting what you want, right now. Saving is looking increasingly old-fashioned while debt is rather cooler.

However, in an emergency, it's far better to rely on savings than your credit card or overdraft to see you through. If you need money here and now, it's far easier to get hold of cash sitting in a savings account, rather than having to arrange credit at short notice.

In this chapter we look at the importance of building up an emergency pot of savings, which you can use to pay for any emergency that arises – repairs to your car should it fail its MOT or to replace the boiler when it packs in.

Dealing with an Emergency

If you don't have cash put by for an emergency, your options may be limited should one arise. Your disposable income is unlikely to generate enough of a surplus to pay for this, given the other demands on your incomings each month.

You may be able to extend your overdraft, slap the cost on a credit card, or take out a personal loan. But these all cost money and may take time to arrange. The overdraft rate will depend on your lender but could be very high, particularly if you forget to ask permission for extending it first. Even shopping around for a cheap credit card may be difficult if you need the money immediately: It takes a couple of weeks at least for your application to be approved and processed. And taking out a personal loan for just £1,000 will cost you a lot in interest.

When you're desperate, you're more likely to opt for higher rates of interest than you would normally when you've got time to shop around for a competitive deal. And if you've already maxed out on your credit, you may find you simply can't get your hands on the extra cash that you require.

The big advantage of having emergency savings is that it negates the need to take out pricey payment protection insurance or income protection. If you have enough cash to see you through several months with no income, you don't need to have cover for that period. Or if you do opt for income protection, you can arrange for an excess period to kick in after your savings run out – whether it is one, three, or six months. (See Chapter 3 in Book I for more on these types of insurance.)

Looking at Savings Strengths

It's worth having a few grand stashed in an easily accessible place to cover emergencies. Common sense dictates that at some point you'll encounter an unforeseen expense; research says the average cost of such expenses is £3,000.

Making sure your rainy day fund is easily accessible doesn't mean shoving it under the floorboards though: The smart way to save this cash is in an instant access savings account paying the highest rate of interest you can find – preferably tax free. Your savings vehicle must also be risk free, such as an instant access savings account rather than an investment in the stock market, so that nothing can happen to your money.

The interest your rainy day savings earn is a bonus, not the main reason to have such an account. The key is to be able to access your cash in an emergency – interest is a nice little extra. Beware of keeping thousands of pounds in this account because finding the best rate of interest will become more of an issue. Only keep enough for a rainy day and invest the remainder more wisely elsewhere.

Avoid using your current account to build up a fund for emergencies. You may be tempted to dip into it for everyday expenses, which could mean you don't have enough money left when you are faced with a real emergency. Current accounts don't pay the highest rates of interest either: You will earn a better return in a savings account. Keep your current account for day-to-day bills and expenses.

Clear any debts before you start saving, because you pay more interest on your debt than you can earn on your savings. It makes no sense to have a few hundred pounds earning 5 per cent interest in a savings account when you are paying 30 per cent interest on your store card. Clear your debts first.

Making sure your money is easily accessible

There's no point saving up emergency cash if you have to give the bank a month's notice before you can get your hands on it. The whole point of an emergency fund is that you're able to access it in an emergency, so aim for an instant access account that enables you to get the cash the same day or in a couple of days at most (if it is an Internet account).

Building societies were the traditional choice for savings accounts, but you are likely to find a better deal from one of the newer providers, such as a telephone- or Internet-based account. These often come with cash cards so you can withdraw your cash from an ATM without hassle, or you can transfer money to your current account where you will be able to access it.

Minimising risk

If you leave thousands of pounds lying around at home, you are at risk of being burgled. Lock it away in a savings account so you don't lose it or are tempted to spend it.

It is important that you don't take on any risk with your emergency savings. A deposit-based savings vehicle is perfect for this purpose because it guarantees your capital back when you need it, preferably with some added interest on top.

Stock market investments may grow more quickly over time than cash, but steer clear of equities when it comes to your emergency fund. Your aim shouldn't be to generate the biggest return possible but to keep your money safe. Stash it where you aren't going to lose any of it, and that means a bank or building society account.

Deciding How Much You Need to Save

A reassuring amount of cash for one person may not be nearly enough for another. Your personal situation largely dictates how much cash you need in your emergency fund. The amount depends on your resources and how much you can afford to put by, as well as your responsibilities and how much you need to cover your usual outgoings. For example, if you are single and in your twenties, renting a flat with no dependants, you are likely to need much less cash in an emergency than if you're the main breadwinner for a spouse and four children, with a large mortgage and two cars.

Most financial advisers suggest stashing enough to cover between three and six months' worth of outgoings in an instant access savings account. Tailor the amount to suit you and your family's needs.

If you are self-employed you may need more cash put by because you won't qualify for sick pay, as you would if you were employed. It may also be worth taking out some income protection to cover you if you can't work. (See Chapter 3 in Book I for more information.)

Finding the Best Savings Account

Just because your emergency cash is easily accessible in a low-risk deposit account doesn't mean that you can't earn a decent amount of interest on it. The vast majority of savings accounts are variable, which means that the rate of interest loosely reflects movements in the Bank of England base rate. And with the base rate at over 5 per cent at the time of writing – its highest level since 2001 – the return on savings looks increasingly attractive.

In the past, you had to tie your savings up for a year or more if you wanted to get the best rates. But that's no longer necessary: You can get an attractive rate of interest and no restrictions on accessing your money – good news for generating returns on your emergency fund.

Saving with a monthly account

The best way of building up emergency savings if you are starting from scratch is to get in the habit of putting a small sum of cash aside every month. A monthly savings account can discipline you into doing this by requiring you to make a deposit each month – no excuses. This is a set amount, somewhere between the minimum and maximum amounts set by the account provider.

You can't invest a lump sum, so if you have surplus cash one month you still can't put away more than your set monthly limit.

What access you get to your savings with a monthly account depends on the provider, so check the small print before opening one. Some are instant access, which is what you need, while others have notice periods or a fixed term, which is not what you need.

Monthly savings accounts often have bonuses, which you earn once you've made enough deposits or paid a certain amount of cash into your account. The bonus often also depends on you not making any withdrawals from your account or less than a certain amount. But as you don't know when you are going to need to make a withdrawal or how many you might have to make, you might not want these restrictions.

If you're building up an emergency savings fund from scratch, rather than signing up to a monthly savings account, why not pretend that's what you've got? Open an instant or easy access account and then decide on a realistic monthly amount that you can afford to save. Then, set up a direct debit from your bank account to your savings account for this amount of cash, ensuring it is transferred over the day after you get paid. That way you won't miss it, you are making regular contributions, and you don't have any of the restrictions of a monthly savings account.

Opting for a mini cash individual savings account

The advantage of a mini cash Individual Savings Account (ISA) is that you can build up your interest free of tax. Make sure you opt for one that is easy access and doesn't require that you give notice before accessing your cash, as quite a few of them do – particularly those paying the highest rates of interest. Also, make sure the provider doesn't require you to maintain a minimum balance, as you may need to drop below this on occasion should you withdraw some cash from your account.

There is currently a £3,000 limit on the amount you can invest in a mini cash ISA in any one tax year (6 April to 5 April the following year). And you can only open one type of ISA each year, so you can't invest in two mini cash ISAs or a maxi and a mini in the same year . However, from April 2008 the ISA rules are changing, with the removal of the distinction between mini and maxi ISAs. Instead, it will be possible to hold up to £3,600 in cash in an ISA, and also to switch cash holdings into stocks and shares (and vice versa) if you want. See Chapter 4 in this Book for more details on ISAs.

Watching out for notice periods

Some of the accounts offering better rates of interest require you to give notice – of anything from a week to 30, 60, or 90 days – if you want to withdraw your cash. If you don't give this notice, you are likely to be penalised by losing the same amount of interest as the notice period. In other words, if you have to give 90 days' notice to get your money and you don't, you lose 90 days' interest.

If you need your money in an emergency you won't be able to give the required notice, resulting in a loss of interest. So steer clear of notice accounts when saving for a rainy day.

Notice accounts also tend to require a minimum balance of several hundred pounds, which may be difficult if you need most of your fund in an emergency. If you fall below the minimum amount, the account may be automatically closed.

Choose an account that lets you have your cash when you need it without notice or having to pay a penalty. The best choice is an *instant access* or *easy access* account, also referred to as a *no notice* account. These tend to have a minimum investment of as little as £1, which can be useful if you need to withdraw most of your cash in an emergency, and handy when you are just starting to build up your emergency fund.

With an instant access account, your money is available on demand; with an easy access account you can get your cash within a few days. You will earn less interest on these accounts than you would with a notice account, but it may be worth it for not having to pay a penalty when you want your money.

Considering the impact of bonuses

Some account providers cynically propel themselves to the top of the 'best buy' tables by offering a tasty bonus for the first 6 or 12 months after you open an account. This can make the rate highly attractive, but it's important to remember that it won't last forever. Once the bonus period ends, the account may look far more ordinary and no longer competitive.

Only opt for an account offering a bonus if you are prepared to move your cash once the bonus runs out. If you don't want the hassle, opt for an account which is regularly near the top of the best buy tables and has a good rate of interest all year round – not just because it is offering a bonus.

Realising the advantage of tiered rates

Some savings accounts have tiered rates of interest, so the more you save the better the rate of interest you receive. This can mean a significant amount of interest if you have a few thousand pounds stashed in your emergency account. But remember, if the balance falls (perhaps you have to withdraw some cash to pay for some emergency repairs) the amount of interest you earn will also fall.

Fixing the rate and the term

Fixed-rate accounts usually pay a higher rate of interest than variable easy or instant access accounts. But this higher rate comes at a cost: With a fixed-rate account you have to invest a certain amount of money for a set period of time – usually one to five years.

Most providers don't allow any withdrawals before the maturity date, which rather misses the point of emergency savings. If you are allowed to make withdrawals, you will have to pay a penalty. And you usually can't add to your balance during the term, so it's not a place for building up your emergency savings. Steer clear of such products in this instance.

Offsetting your savings

If you've got a mortgage, you can use an offset account to build up your emergency savings. Instead of earning interest on your savings, you reduce the amount of interest you pay on your home loan. You pay interest only on the difference between your savings and mortgage debt, reducing the length of your mortgage term.

For example, if you have a £150,000 mortgage and £3,000 in your emergency savings account, offset against your home loan, you only pay interest on £147,000 (and earn no interest on your savings). But as your repayments are calculated on the £150,000 loan, you will be overpaying each month (if you don't ask your lender to reduce the payments accordingly) so you pay off your mortgage more quickly.

Because the interest on your mortgage is likely to be higher than what you can earn on your savings, an offset account makes a lot of sense. And you can still access your savings whenever you need them, without notice, so it's ideal for a rainy day fund.

Book III

Building Up Savings and Investments

Shopping Around for the Best Deal

As with any financial product, it's important to shop around for the best deal available. Although your bank will offer a savings account, this is unlikely to offer you the best rate of interest: Indeed, it is far more likely that this will be one of the worst rates on the market, particularly if you bank with one of the 'big four' – Barclays, HSBC, Lloyds TSB, and NatWest.

Once you've picked the account with the most competitive rate, don't just rest on your laurels and pat yourself on the back for being astute. Review your account and the rate of interest it is earning on a regular basis – at least once a year – to ensure you are still getting a competitive deal. There may be new accounts offering better rates of interest, or other providers may have increased their rate of interest while yours hasn't.

Log onto www.moneysupermarket.com to use its free savings calculator: You tap in how much you have saved up and the rate of interest you are currently earning – you will then be told how much extra interest you could earn elsewhere.

If you do decide to switch to another account paying a better rate of interest, check that you won't lose interest or pay a penalty for doing so. If you do have to give notice, make sure you give enough before moving your money. There is no point losing interest in order to move to gain interest: It defeats the whole object.

Logging on

The best rates for savings accounts are to be found online. The Internet is also the easiest place to research the best savings deals. Although strictly speaking such accounts are not instant access, because you can't get your hands on your money immediately, they are easy access, which is almost as good.

When you need to access your cash, you can arrange for it to be transferred to your current account, so you can withdraw the cash from an ATM, write a cheque, or use your debit card. Some online accounts also come with a cash card, making it even easier to get your money because you don't have to transfer it anywhere first.

Use comparison sites such as www.find.co.uk, www.moneyfacts.co.uk, www.moneyextra.com, or www.moneysupermarket.com to find the best savings account for you.

Telephoning and posting

Any savings account that isn't operated from a branch is more likely to have a tasty rate of interest than one that is. This is because the overheads are reduced: Having operators in a call centre dealing with applications and enquiries helps keep costs down.

Check that access isn't a problem when signing up: If you get a cheque in the post once you make a withdrawal, this could take a week or so to arrive, which isn't as convenient as being able to get your hands on the money immediately.

Look at 'best buy' tables published in newspapers or finance magazines, and online at sites such as www.moneyfacts.co.uk, for the best postal and telephone savings accounts.

Accessing savings via a branch

The most immediate type of account is the one where you can walk into a branch and come out with your money. But you will sacrifice interest for this convenience because of the overheads incurred in running a branch network. Thus, such accounts rarely pay the highest rates of interest.

Book III

Building Up Savings and Investments

Safeguarding Your Savings

As you're saving for an emergency you will want to be assured that your cash is safe. Thankfully, most UK banks and building societies are stable institutions, but there is a safety net in place in case the worst does come to the worst and the provider of your savings account goes bust.

The Financial Services Compensation Scheme protects you if your provider goes into liquidation or out of business. You won't get all your savings back, but you will get a significant proportion of them. Expect to get:

- ✔ 100 per cent of the first £2,000 you lose
- ✔ 90 per cent of the next £33,000 you lose

The maximum amount of compensation you will receive is £31,700 – far more than you should have in your emergency savings account at any rate!

Chapter 3

Choosing a Mortgage

In This Chapter

▶ Figuring out how much money you need

▶ Looking at the different types of home loans

▶ Getting a grasp on rates

▶ Searching for the right deal

▶ Steering clear of unnecessary expenses

*P*roperty is an excellent investment, enabling you to kiss goodbye to grotty rental accommodation and throwing money down the drain on rent, while at the same time investing in something that is likely to increase in value over the years.

But there is no escaping the fact that getting on the property ladder for the first time is hard. Many people have to delay their first property purchase because they simply can't afford to buy any younger. The average age of a first-time buyer is 33, according to the Halifax, the UK's biggest mortgage lender, as would-be buyers spend their twenties trying to clear student debts and struggling on low incomes. (*Buying a Home on a Budget For Dummies* by Melanie Bien offers valuable advice on creative ways to get on the property ladder.)

This chapter helps you work out how much cash you need to get on the property ladder and what you can realistically afford.

Working Out How Much You Can Afford to Borrow

Before you can actually buy a property, you need to work out whether you can afford to do so. Affordability can be a big problem, most notably for first-time buyers. Most people need a *mortgage* to buy a property – a loan from a bank or building society. Lenders calculate the maximum you can borrow based on how much you earn. But what the lender is prepared to lend you and what you should borrow are two different things.

Mortgage lenders have relaxed their borrowing criteria over the past couple of decades, with much bigger home loans now available. But that doesn't mean you should take on the biggest mortgage you can. Keep in mind that you have to repay it. Even if you can cope initially, you may struggle if you lose your job, for example. If you are overstretched, even a small change in circumstances can prove catastrophic.

Even if you can't afford to buy on your own, there may be other ways of realising your goal by buying with friends, a sibling, or persuading your parents to help out. See *Buying a Home on a Budget For Dummies* by Melanie Bien for loads more useful advice.

Multiplying your income

Typically, you can borrow three or three and a half times your annual income if you buy on your own, or two and a half times your joint income if you hook up with someone else. So if you earn £30,000, you should be able to get a mortgage for £90,000 to £105,000, depending on the lender, if you buy on your own. If you buy with your spouse, who earns the same as you, you could borrow up to £150,000.

Unfortunately, these income multiples won't get you very far. The average price of a property in the UK in March 2007 was £194,362 according to the Halifax (though averages do vary from one source to another), and there's no sign of a reversal in the upward trend at the time of writing. Unless you have a large deposit – perhaps an inheritance from a relative – you won't be able to bridge the ever-widening gap between property prices and how much you can raise.

In an effort to help borrowers make up the shortfall, some lenders have increased their *income multiple* to four, five, or even six times income. But think carefully before taking on such a big loan if it is offered to you. Make sure you are happy with the repayments and can cope if interest rates rise. Don't overstretch yourself.

Coping without a deposit

With more than 7,000 mortgages available from over 100 lenders, there's bound to be one out there that suits you – even if you haven't got a big deposit or don't earn hundreds of thousands of pounds every year.

There are several 100 per cent mortgages available and some lenders even let you borrow up to 125 per cent of the value of the property. So even if you haven't got a deposit, it doesn't necessarily mean you can't get a mortgage.

Realistically, it could take you several years to save up a 5 or 10 per cent deposit, depending on how good a saver you are and other demands on your wallet. In such circumstances, it could make sense to borrow a greater proportion of the purchase price now, rather than put off buying for a few years while you save up several thousand pounds for a deposit. If you delay your purchase in a rising property market, you could find prices increasing to such an extent that you're priced out of the market yet again.

The problem with not having a deposit (or having a very small one) is that you won't get the cheapest mortgage rate. You qualify for the best deals if you have a sizeable deposit, because lenders regard you as being lower risk than someone without a deposit. A number of lenders also charge a *mortgage indemnity guarantee (MIG)* – a one-off insurance premium typically charged if you borrow more than 90 or 95 per cent of the value of the property. See the 'Watching out for MIG' section later in this chapter for tips on how to avoid paying this charge.

Another response to rising prices is the introduction of loans spread over longer than the traditional 25 years. A quarter of lenders offer mortgages running 40 years or more. Such arrangements reduce monthly payments, but be warned – you could be still be paying off your home loan after you have stopped working.

Calculating How Much Cash You Need beyond the Price

Book III

Building Up Savings and Investments

The cost of buying a property largely depends on the purchase price, which reflects its location, size, features, age, and condition. The price is also partly dictated by demand: The more interest among prospective purchasers for that property, generally speaking, the higher the price.

As well as the purchase price, there are several other extras to consider, which bump up the final bill. We discuss these in more detail in the following sections.

Looking out for the lender's fee

Most mortgage lenders charge a fee of some kind when you take out a home loan. This charge may be referred to as one of several things, such as an application, arrangement, or completion fee. It can be anything from £300 to £1,000, and can be added to the loan rather than paid for up front. There may also be a booking fee, which is usually in the region of £50 to £100, which is the cost of reserving the funds to enable the lender to offer you a particular rate.

Some mortgage offers with the lowest rates of interest carry the highest arrangement fees. However, this may still work out cheaper in the long run than paying a lower arrangement fee and higher rate of interest. Ask an independent mortgage broker to do the sums for you: See 'Seeking advice' later in this chapter for more details on finding a broker.

Paying a mortgage broker

The best way of finding the right mortgage for you is to use an independent mortgage broker. This saves you time and money, because as long as the broker is truly independent he will have access to all the deals on the market so will be able to source the most competitive one for your needs. He will also handle the application form for you and speed up the lender if you want to complete sooner rather than later.

Brokers are paid by commission, a fee, or both. Those who are paid by commission receive several hundred pounds from the lender who provides your mortgage. If the broker charges a fee, you have to pay: Prices vary but expect to pay up to 1 per cent of the purchase price for this advice. Whether you choose to pay a fee or use a broker who receives commission depends on personal preference and what you can afford. But make sure you are clear which you are opting for at the start of your relationship.

Commissioning a lender's valuation and survey

The lender will insist on a valuation of the property to confirm that the property is worth the amount you are borrowing. If you default on your repayments, the lender can cover its costs by selling your property. Expect to pay around £250–£350 for the lender's valuation.

The valuation tells you nothing about the condition of the property: To ascertain this, you must pay for a survey. Although a basic survey – the *homebuyer's report* – costs between £300 and £500, it's worth it because it tells you whether there are problems such as subsidence or dry rot. If there are, you can either pull out of the purchase or try to negotiate a lower purchase price with the seller. Either way, you make an informed decision, which isn't the case if you don't know the full extent of the problem.

Home Information Packs

From 1 June 2007, anyone putting their property on the market must have a pack available for prospective buyers. The pack has to contain an *Energy Performance Certificate*, which shows how energy efficient the property is, and various other documents which previously would have been gathered by the buyer's solicitor, including an index of contents, a sale statement, searches, and evidence of title. Sellers also have the option of providing a *Home Condition Report* (HCR), along the lines of the conventional Homebuyers Report, but (following pressure on the government from the anti-HIP lobby) this is has not been made a compulsory part of the HIP.

The idea is that by providing this information up-front, the buyer will be able to make a more informed decision and reduce the risk of pulling out at a later stage. But many people believe that without the HCR, sellers will be forking out £400 to £1000 for a pack that is of little real value to buyers.

You can commission a HIP from a specialist pack provider, or from your estate agent or solicitor; other providers such as IFAs or even supermarkets may also start to offer HIPs. Alternatively, you can put your pack together yourself.

More information on HIPs is available online at www.homeinformationpacks.gov.uk.

A more detailed (and expensive) survey is the *full structural survey*. This generally costs between £500 and £1,000 (in some cases more) but if you are buying a very old or unusual property it is worth considering. If a problem emerges later on that the surveyor didn't pick up, you may have grounds for compensation.

Book III

Building Up Savings and Investments

Settling legal fees and disbursements

There is a lot of complicated legal work involved in the transfer of property from seller to buyer and it is advisable to use a solicitor to represent you, particularly if you are purchasing a leasehold property, as this is much more complicated than buying a freehold property.

Some people take on their own *conveyancing* or legal work but it is complicated and time-consuming. If you get it wrong the consequences can be great, so save yourself time and money in the long run and use a solicitor.

Solicitors don't come cheap: Fees vary, so shop around and get a couple of quotes. Expect to pay £450–£700 plus VAT (17.5 per cent) if you are purchasing a £200,000 property, though you may be able to get much cheaper quotes (under £300) from online flat fee conveyancing services. If the property is leasehold, expect to pay another £100–£150 plus VAT to cover the extra work involved in checking the lease. Legal fees are payable on completion, along with the cost of *disbursements* – the searches your solicitor carries out on your behalf. Until June 2007, various searches were carried out by the buyer's solicitor to check, for example, that the property had planning permission before it was built and that the seller was legally able to sell it. After this date, local authority, water and drainage searches become the responsibility of the seller as part of the Home Information Pack (see the sidebar 'Home Information Packs'), although buyers in some areas (for example those prone to flooding or with a lot of mines in the vicinity) may want to carry out additional searches.

Sending in your stamp duty

Stamp duty is an unavoidable tax payable to the Government on completion of your property purchase. How much you pay depends on the price of the property:

- Nothing if it costs less than £125,000 (or £150,000 in certain disadvantaged areas)
- 1 per cent on properties between £125,000 and £250,000
- 3 per cent on properties costing more than £250,000 and less than £500,000
- 4 per cent on properties costing more than £500,000

Your mortgage doesn't cover the stamp duty: You need to raise these funds yourself, so remember to budget for it.

Eenie, Meenie, Miney, Mo: Choosing the Right Mortgage

The first step to choosing a mortgage is to understand the different types available and how they work.

Whether you opt for a *repayment* or *interest-only* mortgage (explained in more detail in the following sections) depends on your attitude to risk. Monthly payments are higher with a repayment loan but you get peace of mind because you are guaranteed to pay the capital back in full by the end of the mortgage term (as long as you keep up your repayments). With an interest-only mortgage you have to set up an investment vehicle which you contribute to monthly: This type of mortgage usually means lower monthly repayments but there is no guarantee that the investment vehicle will raise enough cash to pay off the capital. You must decide whether you are happy to take a gamble on the roof over your head – in effect, this is what you are doing with an interest-only home loan.

Before taking out this type of mortgage, definitely seek professional advice.

Understanding repayment loans

The only way you can guarantee that all the capital is paid back at the end of the mortgage term is to opt for a *repayment* loan. You pay back a slice of the capital (the amount you borrow) each month, plus interest – what the lender is charging you for borrowing this cash. If you keep up the repayments, at the end of the term you've paid off all the capital and the property is yours.

Going interest-only

With an *interest-only* mortgage you pay just the interest on your mortgage each month. You repay none of the capital until the end of the mortgage term. If you don't have enough cash to pay back all the capital in one hit, your lender could repossess your home and sell it to recoup its outlay.

You must set up some sort of investment vehicle to raise enough cash to clear the capital due at the end of the mortgage term. We talk about the various options in the following sections.

Endowments

Endowments – a combination of savings vehicle and life assurance – used to be the first choice of homeowners with interest-only mortgages, but with some people being mis-sold these and many policies under-performing, they are now unpopular.

With an endowment, you make monthly payments into the fund, which is run by a life company. It invests in stocks and shares, property, gilts (government bonds), and cash. An endowment policy tends to run for the same length of time as your mortgage – the idea being that it matures when you need to pay back your mortgage capital. Because it includes life assurance, the mortgage capital is paid off if you die before the policy matures. But if you outlive the policy there is no guarantee it will raise enough cash to clear the mortgage.

Book III

Building Up Savings and Investments

You must choose between a with-profits and a unit-linked endowment. A *with-profits endowment* may produce annual bonuses, depending on the investment performance of the fund. You can't get these until the fund matures, when you may also get a one-off terminal bonus, again based on the performance of the fund.

With a *unit-linked endowment*, your monthly premiums buy units in a managed fund run by a life company and are invested in the stock market. The number of units you hold increases over time as you pay more premiums and the value of these fluctuates in line with the investment performance of the fund. The problem with this type of investment is that the value of your endowment could drop considerably if the market plummets just when you need your money.

Stocks and shares can go down in value as well as up. Don't gamble on the roof over your head unless you have enough cash in reserve to cover any potential shortfall in your endowment.

ISA mortgages

You can use an individual savings account (ISA) as a repayment vehicle to back interest-only mortgages. Chapter 4 in this Book has more details on how these work, but the main advantage is that returns are tax free (unlike the returns on an endowment) so your money grows more quickly.

For the purpose of repaying your mortgage capital, you need an equity ISA. Cash won't produce good enough returns to pay off your mortgage. The problem with using an ISA is that you can take out only one maxi stocks and shares ISA a year and can invest a maximum of £7,000 (in 2007-08, rising to £7,200 from April 2008).

You can invest monthly into an ISA mortgage offered by a lender or build up a personal portfolio of ISA investments, which you choose yourself. The latter option is probably better as your ISAs will be run by several professional fund managers rather than a mortgage lender being responsible for your cash.

The advantage of an ISA is that you know exactly how much your investment is worth. ISA investment charges also tend to be lower than endowment fees: You may have to pay an initial charge of up to 5 per cent and annual management fees of around 1.5 per cent, compared with the high set-up costs of endowments, which eat into investment performance in the early years. ISAs are also more flexible: It's easy to switch investments if your fund is underperforming and stop or re-start payments. You also have more say over where your money is invested.

When it comes to repaying a mortgage, too much flexibility is a bad thing as there's a risk you could end up with less money than you need. Plus, stocks and shares ISAs are as vulnerable to stock market fluctuations as endowment policies so there's no guarantee they'll raise enough cash to pay off your mortgage. Linking your mortgage to an ISA is extremely high risk and only really suitable for experienced investors and higher-rate taxpayers, who can make the most of the tax breaks.

Pension mortgages

Another way of maximising tax breaks and paying off the capital on an interest-only mortgage is via a pension. However, if you're a member of your employer's occupational pension scheme, you can't have a pension mortgage.

With a *pension mortgage*, you pay money into a personal pension every month. You also pay premiums into a life assurance scheme (which ensures your mortgage is paid off if you die ahead of the policy maturing).

At retirement, you get a tax-free lump sum – up to a quarter of your pension pot – which you use to pay off the capital you owe your mortgage lender. You purchase an *annuity* with the remainder, which is a guaranteed income for the rest of your life. Because you can't get hold of your cash lump sum until you retire, pension mortgages tend to run for much longer terms than endowment home loans – sometimes as long as 35 or 40 years.

Pensions are highly tax efficient: Every 78p a basic-rate taxpayer (60p for higher-rate taxpayers) invests in their pension is topped up to £1 by the Government (this means that the Government contributes 22p to a basic-rate taxpayer's pension and 40p to a higher-rate taxpayer's). This means higher investment returns than you get from an ISA or endowment because more money is going into your pension fund.

Pension mortgages may be tax efficient but they are stock market linked so they are also risky. They are also very complicated so really only suit sophisticated, self-employed, or higher-rate taxpayers. If this isn't you, give them a wide berth.

There are no guarantees that a pension mortgage will raise enough cash to pay off the capital you borrow from your lender. You will also have a smaller pension pot at retirement with which to buy an income because you will be losing a chunk to clear the mortgage. It's hard enough saving for retirement without taking a large chunk out of your pension pot. The performance of the stock market and the skills of the fund manager handling your money decide how much cash you eventually get. To minimise risk as much as possible, keep a close eye on investment performance: If it's not on track to pay off your mortgage, consider alternative arrangements to cover the shortfall.

Book III

Building Up Savings and Investments

Combining repayment with interest-only

It is possible to combine interest-only and repayment deals. Mortgages that let you pay just the interest on your loan in the early years before switching to a repayment deal (to ensure you pay back all the capital by the end of the term) are particularly useful for first-time buyers who struggle with lack of funds in the early years of their mortgage. You get cheaper payments for the first two years or so because you only pay interest – none of the capital.

Watch out for a big jump in your monthly repayments once you start paying back the capital as well as the interest because it could be considerable. Get an idea of how much it will be from your lender or broker and budget for it accordingly.

Understanding Rates

Once you decide on the type of mortgage you want, you must choose what rate to go for. Your choice depends on your circumstances and attitude to risk. We explain the various rates in the following sections.

Avoiding the standard variable rate

Each mortgage lender has a *standard variable rate* (SVR). This is its benchmark, which it uses to calculate all its mortgage deals. The SVR can move up and down with no notice at all: When the Bank of England raises or cuts the base rate – the base interest rate, which it increases or decreases when it thinks this is necessary for the economy – most lenders adjust their SVR accordingly within minutes.

You can take out a mortgage on your lender's SVR but it won't be the cheapest deal. Opt for a fixed or discounted rate instead – they're usually a couple of percentage points below the SVR.

Even if you opt for a fixed or discounted rate, don't forget about the SVR as your mortgage reverts to this once the offer period comes to an end – unless you switch to another deal. If you stay put, your mortgage repayments could dramatically increase so shop around for another deal.

Opting for a fix

With a *fixed-rate mortgage* your repayments are guaranteed for a set period of time, no matter what happens to the base rate. A fixed rate provides certainty: Most people opt for a two-, three-, or five-year fix but you can also fix for one, 10, 15, 20, 25, 30 or even 40 years. Make sure you are comfortable with the length of your fix, because if you want to move house and switch your mortgage before the term is up, you could pay a penalty.

With a fixed rate, if the base rate rises you're laughing but if it falls you don't benefit. And if the base rate falls several times during your fixed term, you could end up paying a lot more than you would have done if you'd opted for a shorter fix.

The longer the fixed rate, the higher the rate of interest: two-year fixes are cheaper than five-year deals because the lender is taking on less risk.

Plumping for a discount

Discount rates tend to be a couple of percentage points below the lender's SVR. Lenders usually offer discount rates over two, three, or five years: As with fixed rates, generally the shorter the term, the lower the rate. The big advantage of discounts is that they are also usually lower than the lender's fixed-rate deals – at least initially. You also benefit from any cut in the base rate if interest is calculated daily on your mortgage because it is directly linked to your lender's SVR.

Book III

Building Up Savings and Investments

Here lies the problem: If the Bank of England increases the base rate, your mortgage payments increase. And if there is a lot of volatility in the base rate, your mortgage payments could fluctuate dramatically from month to month, making budgeting difficult. Opt for a discount rate only if you can afford to be wrong; in other words, if you can cope with an increase in your mortgage repayments. If you can, you'll get a better deal than on a fixed rate – at least initially – plus you benefit from any cuts in the base rate during the discounted period.

Checking out capped rates

With a capped rate, you know the absolute maximum you have to pay each month, just as you do with a fixed rate. However, as there is no lower cap, you could end up paying less interest than you would on a fixed-rate deal, depending on what happens to the base rate. Your initial mortgage rate is set lower than the cap: It can rise but only as high as the cap. If the base rate is raised again after the cap has been reached, your mortgage repayments won't be affected. Capped rate deals are usually offered over three, five or 10 years.

Because the rate is capped rather than fixed, it can fall, allowing you to take advantage of cuts in the base rate. This makes a capped rate attractive because you can benefit from the best of both worlds.

Capped rates tend to be higher than fixed-rate deals. There is also less choice as fewer lenders offer them.

Tracking the base rate

A *base rate tracker mortgage* follows movements in the base rate, tracking a margin of, say, 1 per cent above it. So if the base rate is 4.75 per cent, the interest rate on such a tracker is 5.75 per cent – until the base rate changes. The big advantage is that your lender can't widen the margin and charge you more than this set margin above the base rate, so you know where you stand.

Flexibly does it

A number of mortgages have *flexible features*. This means you can vary your monthly repayments, overpaying if you've got spare cash and thereby paying your mortgage back more quickly, reducing the interest you pay. You can also underpay if you're short of cash, or even pay nothing at all, as long as you have built up funds in your mortgage 'account'. If you have overpaid by several hundred pounds you can take payment holidays, but you can't miss a payment completely if you haven't built up anything in reserve.

Interest is calculated daily, rather than monthly or annually, which makes a huge difference to the total amount you pay over the term of your loan. As soon as you make a payment, the money gets to work reducing your mortgage debt and the interest you pay.

Flexible mortgages are handy if you are self-employed or your income fluctuates. When you are flush you can pay more than you need to so that when finances are tight you can miss a payment or two – and not incur a penalty.

Watch out for the rate of interest on flexible deals as it can be higher than on fixed or discounted offers. If you don't use all the flexible facilities, it might make sense to avoid a flexible deal: Most borrowers are only interested in your ability to overpay. Many standard mortgages allow you to overpay up to 10 per cent of your outstanding loan each year without penalty. Such a mortgage may work out cheaper than a fully flexible deal.

Many lenders offer substantial discounts on tracker deals for six months or more as an incentive. So you could be offered 1 per cent off the base rate, giving you a very attractive payable rate of 3.75 per cent if the base rate is 4.75 per cent. And if you opt for a short-term tracker there might be no penalty to pay at any time so you can switch to another deal without charge when the discount period comes to an end.

As with a variable deal, tracker mortgages go up and down – there is no certainty. And as they usually track *above* the base rate, you will pay more than if you'd opted for a fixed or discounted deal. You may be better off opting for a fixed or discounted rate instead.

Offsetting your mortgage

One way of reducing your mortgage interest is to opt for an offset or current account mortgage (CAM). An *offset mortgage* lets you use your savings to reduce the interest you pay on your mortgage. The way this works is that you open a savings account and/or current account with your mortgage lender. Although your savings and current account are kept separate from your mortgage debt, the amount you have on deposit is offset against the amount you owe on your mortgage to reduce the interest you pay. So if you owe £60,000 on your mortgage, for example, but have £12,000 in savings and, say, £500 in your current account, you're charged interest at your mortgage rate on £47,500 (your £60,000 mortgage minus the sum of your deposits of £12,000 and £500). You can also offset your family and friends' savings against your mortgage.

A CAM lumps your mortgage, current account, savings, and even credit cards and personal loans together in one account rather than keeping everything separate. Even a small amount of money can make a big difference to the interest you pay: for example, if you take out a £100,000 mortgage over 25 years at 7.5 per cent interest, and spend all your salary each month except £100, which stays in your account, you'll pay off your mortgage six years and nine months early, saving £40,263 in interest. The residue of money left in the account every month might not seem much but the key thing is that it eats away at your debt.

Because the interest on offset mortgages and CAMs is calculated daily, you pay what you owe on that day. So if you have just been paid, it doesn't matter that you will soon spend all that cash; for several days, your entire pay packet is offset against your mortgage. In the long run, this enables you to repay your loan more quickly.

Critics of offset mortgages and CAMs argue that they are so flexible there is a danger that undisciplined borrowers won't pay their mortgages off on time. For example, some CAM providers will lend you the difference between your mortgage (say, for example, £62,000) and the value of your house (say, £150,000). So, in this example you could get your hands on a further £88,000 to spend how you wish. Other CAM providers limit the amount you can borrow. If you are not disciplined and are likely to give in to temptation, steer clear of a CAM and opt for a fixed or discounted deal instead.

Offset mortgages and CAMS are a great way of reducing your interest payments, and competition has helped to bring interest rates more into line with conventional deals, but they still tend to be rather higher than fixed or discounted deals. So unless you have several thousand pounds in savings to offset, you won't save money in the long run. Lenders have started offering fixed rates on offset mortgages, making them more attractive, but watch out for penalties during the offer period.

Cashing in on a cashback mortgage

When you take out a *cashback mortgage*, you get a cash lump sum from your lender. The amount varies from a flat fee of a couple of hundred pounds to a percentage of the amount you borrow (as high as 10 per cent of the mortgage). You can do what you want with this cash – buy a new sofa, pay off your credit card, or even take a holiday if you need a break from the stress of moving.

You don't get something for nothing, and this is particularly true with cashback mortgages. They tend to be expensive in the long run because the cashback is an advance that you pay back over the mortgage term. So £6,000 cashback on a £100,000 mortgage is the equivalent of borrowing £106,000 because you pay interest on this additional loan over the entire mortgage term. The rate of interest also tends to be higher on a cashback mortgage than on a standard fixed or discounted deal.

Early redemption penalties are common on cashback mortgages, which could effectively lock you in for five to seven years. Check the small print before signing up.

Instead of taking out a cashback mortgage, choose a competitive standard fixed or discounted home loan and get hold of the cash another way. You could opt for a personal loan with the lowest rate of interest you can find, extend your overdraft, or apply for a credit card with a 0 per cent introductory period. Not only will you get access to a few hundred or thousand pounds, you can pay it back over a couple of years, rather than 25, and so pay less interest. You can also choose from a wider range of mortgages, rather than limiting yourself to just those offering cash back.

Finding the Best Mortgage

The bank you have your current account with may offer you a mortgage, but think twice before automatically applying for it. It is unlikely to be the best deal. You need to shop around and find the mortgage that best suits your needs and circumstances. There is so much competition, with thousands of loans offered by scores of lenders, that there is no room for misplaced loyalty.

Seeking advice

The easiest and most foolproof way of finding the best mortgage rate is to use an independent mortgage broker. There are three types of brokers:

- Brokers who can only sell products from one provider.
- Brokers who can advise on products from a handful of lenders.
- Brokers who can advise on the best deal available from the entire marketplace.

Before choosing a broker, ask how many lenders he can draw on. Brokers are obliged to disclose this information. Avoid brokers who work strictly for one company – or even a handful of companies. Instead, opt for a broker who has access to the whole of the market, so that you increase your chances of getting the best deal.

Book III

Building Up Savings and Investments

Understanding how your adviser is paid

Mortgage brokers are paid by fees or commission. The broker must disclose to you which applies: If you are happy with paying a fee or for your broker to receive commission from the lender whose mortgage he recommends, there is little between the two. Much debate goes on about which form of payment makes for the most independent broker, but the most important thing is that you are happy with the method of payment – that's what matters.

If your broker receives commission, you pay nothing for the advice. Your mortgage provider will pay several hundred pounds to the broker for arranging the sale. Critics of commission argue that such brokers aren't truly independent, but a good, reputable broker has a lot to lose by recommending mortgages simply on the back of the commission he receives.

If you pay a fee, you should expect to pay anything up to 1 per cent of the mortgage amount – £700 on a £70,000 loan, for example. If you can't afford this, use a broker who receives commission but make sure you do your research carefully when choosing him in the first place to ensure he is reputable and independent.

Under rules introduced in October 2004, a mortgage lender must be authorised by the Financial Services Authority (FSA), the City watchdog. This should reassure borrowers that he has passed certain standards of training and that you can take any dispute you have with him to the Ombudsman. Check that your broker is authorised by visiting the FSA's Web site at www.fsa.gov.uk or calling its consumer helpline on 0845 606 1234.

Going online

The Internet provides a wealth of information on mortgages. Even if you don't actually apply for your mortgage online, it won't hurt to research the various deals available before contacting a lender or broker. That way, you'll know whether you are getting a good deal or not.

Researching online

Several Web sites (see the following list) provide free calculators that enable you to work out how much you can borrow and what your monthly repayments will be. This is only a general guide – there is no guarantee a lender will let you borrow the cash – but it's a great place to start.

Many brokers also have best buy tables on their Web sitesso you can see the best available deals at a glance. When you are ready to sign on the dotted line on your mortgage application form, it's worth double-checking these tables to ensure you are getting the best deal.

Here are some of the best sites, all from independent brokers:

- ✔ Charcol: www.charcolonline.co.uk
- ✔ Chase De Vere Mortgage Management: www.cdvmm.com
- ✔ London & Country: www.lcplc.co.uk
- ✔ Savills Private Finance: www.spf.co.uk

You can also find a local independent mortgage broker through the IFA Promotion website: www.impartial.co.uk.

It's also worth taking a look at www.moneysupermarket.com, which enables you to compare more than 7,000 mortgages. After supplying some basic information about how much you want to borrow and what you can afford to repay, you will get a list of suitable deals.

The Internet is a great way of saving money. By doing your own research using brokers' Web sites and applying online – if you feel confident enough – you increase your chances of getting the best deal, as well as saving on a broker's fee because you don't have a face-to-face consultation. Brokers often have access to exclusive deals not available direct, so even if a standard mortgage is involved, a broker may still be best. If a non standard mortgage is required, perhaps because you have an adverse credit record or an unusual property, a broker can really come into his own.

Applying for a mortgage online

An increasing number of homebuyers are applying for mortgages via the Internet. If you are confident that you have found the right deal and don't need advice, fill in an application form on screen and submit it to the lender. This is faster than filling out a paper application form and posting it because your application is processed as soon as it is received. If you apply by post, it has to be opened when someone is available so if you are applying at a busy time of year, it could take much longer.

Not long after you submit your application electronically, the lender emails you confirming that your application is being processed. Some lenders waive their application fee if you apply online so you could also save yourself several hundred pounds.

Filling in a mortgage application form online is not for everyone, particularly if you are a first-time buyer and don't understand the mortgage process. Forms can be complicated and many homebuyers prefer to be guided through them by a lender or broker.

Book III

Building Up Savings and Investments

Avoiding Unnecessary Costs

If you don't understand all the terms and conditions of your mortgage, it could end up costing you more than you thought it would. In the following sections, we run through where you might get caught out.

Watching out for MIG

If you don't have a deposit, or much of one, many lenders will insist on some guarantee that you won't default on your mortgage repayments, leaving them having to pursue you for the balance – which could lead to the sale of your home to cover the costs. This is why some lenders charge a mortgage indemnity guarantee (MIG) if you borrow more than 90 per cent of the purchase price. The level at which lenders charge MIG varies: Some charge it on loans greater than 80 per cent, others 95 per cent. MIG is insurance, paid for by you even though it protects the lender. It's a one-off fee worked out as a percentage of your mortgage and usually costs a few thousand pounds.

Try to avoid paying MIG. Generate as big a deposit as possible by asking relatives to chip in or simply use a lender that doesn't charge MIG – there are plenty who don't.

Escaping early redemption penalties

Most mortgage deals (other than SVR loans) carry redemption penalties if you remortgage during the offer period. If you take out a two-year fixed-rate deal, for example, the only way the lender can offer those terms is if you stick with it for at least two years. If you switch your mortgage sooner, the lender loses out. The lender imposes a penalty to dissuade you from doing this and to cover its losses if you switch regardless. The penalty is a percentage of the interest on the loan – usually around six months' interest. Most lenders charge redemption penalties during offer periods on fixed or discounted deals, although not all do.

Never take out a mortgage with an *extended redemption penalty*, or *overhang*. The rate on offer will undoubtedly be more attractive than loans without overhangs, but this is because you will be stuck on a higher, uncompetitive rate for what can seem like forever. For example, a lender might offer a market-leading two-year discount, but the payback is you are tied to that mortgage for not two but maybe five years, or longer. Although you no longer benefit from a cheap deal because you are on your lender's SVR once the offer ends, remortgaging could cost you thousands of pounds in interest. To make matters worse, these lenders often have the highest SVRs. Any of the earlier savings you made tend to be lost because you pay higher interest for years after the offer has ended.

There are plenty of loans available with no tie-ins or lock-ins after the offer period, and some lenders don't impose a penalty at any time. Such deals are cheaper in the long run. Don't be dazzled by the headline rate: Look beyond it and think longer term.

Sidestepping compulsory insurance

Some lenders force you to buy their buildings insurance when you take out a mortgage. Even though some lenders offer competitive insurance, don't assume this is the case. Usually this insurance tends to be a rip-off and should be avoided at all costs. Certain forms of insurance are unavoidable, including buildings insurance (see Chapter 3 in Book I for more on this), but you are entitled to shop around in order to get the best deal.

Some lenders, particularly building societies, offer two mortgage rates: a really cheap deal and a pricier one. The catch with the cheap deal is that you have to take out the lender's buildings insurance (and in some cases contents cover as well). The higher rate comes with no such restrictions. In the long term you are better off opting for the higher rate and shopping around for cover; this enables you to find cheaper insurance and to change insurer when your premium is up for renewal (not so easy if cover is linked to your mortgage).

Some lenders don't have compulsory insurance but make it as easy as possible for you to take out their cover. Often, the mortgage application form includes a box you can tick if you want buildings cover alongside a reminder that it is compulsory to have such insurance. Lenders count on the fact that you will be stressed by the whole home buying process so will welcome one less thing to worry about. Some lenders charge you a fee – around £25 – if you don't take out their buildings cover. Even if you have to pay, it is nearly always worth doing so as you are likely to find more competitively priced insurance elsewhere.

Book III

Building Up Savings and Investments

Chapter 4

Making the Most of Tax-Free Savings and Investments

In This Chapter

▶ Figuring out whether ISAs are the answer

▶ Saving with National Savings

▶ Looking at venture capital trusts

▶ Betting on premium bonds

*O*ne of the easiest ways of making your money work harder for you is to ensure that your interest and returns are free of tax. The Chancellor of the Exchequer demands that you pay income tax on your earnings, including your profits from shares, managed funds, and savings accounts. But you can get round this – completely legitimately – by opting for a certain number of tax-free products, of which individual savings accounts (ISAs) are the most popular type.

Saving tax should be seen as an added bonus, not the be-all and end-all of investing. Don't choose products that don't suit your risk profile or goals, simply for the tax breaks.

Tax-free investments are useful if you pay tax, particularly if you are a higher-rate taxpayer as you have the most to gain (because you pay 40 per cent tax compared to the basic-rate taxpayer's 22 per cent). But if you don't pay tax, there is no advantage in opting for tax-free investments, apart from the fact that you won't be automatically taxed and have to claim the money back.

Opting for an Individual Savings Account

The easiest way to save tax free is via an *Individual Savings Account (ISA)*. An ISA is a tax-free wrapper, which enables you to invest in a wide range of products from cash to government bonds to stocks and shares (also known as equities). ISAs replaced *tax-exempt special savings accounts (Tessas)* and *personal equity plans (Peps)* in April 1999.

ISAs are available from a range of sources, including banks, building societies, supermarkets, National Savings, investment firms, insurers, stockbrokers, and financial advisers. Not all offer the full range, so shop around until you find the best deal for your needs.

ISAs are a good way of regular saving because the minimum investment amounts tend to be fairly small – as low as £10 or even £5 in some cases. And you don't even have to declare them on your tax return because you don't pay any tax on your ISA profits, giving you one less thing to worry about.

Contributing to ISAs

During the 2007-08 tax year, you can invest up to £7,000 in a maxi ISA or up to £3,000 in a mini cash ISA and £4,000 in a mini insurance/stocks and share ISA. If you opt for a maxi ISA, you can invest your full allowance totally in equities or split it among cash, stocks, and shares (as with mini ISAs). This can present a problem, as all elements in a maxi ISA must be run by the same manager. Not all fund managers offer all these elements, so you may have to shop around for one that does. And even if they do, they may not be specialists in each field and offer the best return in each.

If you opt for mini ISAs, shop around for the best provider in each field, which should result in better returns for you.

Saving on friendly terms

One way of not paying tax on your savings is to opt for a friendly society savings account (these are not related to ISAs). Friendly societies, which often have strange-sounding names, are mutual societies, like building societies, run on behalf of members. They also offer investments in the same way as life insurance companies.

You can invest up to a maximum of £25 a month (£300 a year) or a lump sum of £270 a year tax free with a friendly society. You are only allowed to open one plan. These generally have a term, such as ten years, and the penalties for encashing your policy early can be heavy.

You may also decide that you are limited to investing such a small amount that it really isn't worth your while. You should also be aware that some of these accounts invest your cash in the stock market so there is an element of risk involved. Research the account carefully before committing your cash.

The new ISA regime from 2008

The ISA rules have been given a new lease of life by the Treasury, which in many respects is good news for investors. For a start, there's now a pledge from the government that the ISA system will remain in place indefinitely and that the annual limit will not drop below £7,000 – doing away with the speculation that has hung over ISAs for years.

From April 2008, the following changes will come into force:

✔ It will be possible to move old PEPs into an ISA wrapper, so the administrative distinction between PEPs and ISAs will gradually disappear.

✔ The distinction between mini and maxi ISAs will be removed; instead, savers will be able to take out an ISA of up to £7,200 (in the 2008-09 tax year), of which up to £3,600 may be in a cash account.

✔ Money held in cash ISAs will be able to be transferred into stocks and shares ISA investments within the wrapper – at the moment you can't switch a cash ISA into a stockmarket ISA.

✔ Young people with a child trust fund will be able to keep their investment tax free when it matures on their 18th birthday, by rolling it over into an ISA to keep on growing.

The investment limits apply regardless of any withdrawals you make. So if you invest $7,000 this tax year, and then withdraw $500, you can't invest another $500 before the end of the tax year to top your allowance back up to $7,000. Unused allowance can't be carried forward either, so plan ahead and use it before the end of the tax year – or you lose it forever.

Understanding minis and maxis

Until April 2008, there are two types of ISA: *mini* and *maxi*. You can open up to two mini ISAs or one maxi ISA in any one tax year. It is against the rules to open a mini and a maxi ISA in the same tax year, or to open two minis of the same type – for example, two separate cash ISAs.

The main thing to remember is that you aren't allowed to invest in both a mini and a maxi in the same tax year. HMRC is very strict on this: Break this rule and you will be forced to close the second one you opened even if the second ISA performed much better than the first one – you don't get to choose which one to keep. Plus, you lose the tax breaks on any interest you earned.

The whole system will be much simpler when the distinction between the two types is removed in 2008. After that, you'll simply open an ISA for a particular tax year, with the option of holding up to a certain amount of cash in it.

Deciding on your ISA investments

What can you hold in an ISA? Here's a breakdown:

- ✔ **Cash:** This is invested in deposit-based accounts, such as bank and building society accounts. You can also include National Savings under this (see 'Cashing in' later in this chapter for more details).

- ✔ **Stocks and shares:** As well as shares, unit and investment trusts, and open-ended investment companies (Oeics), you can also invest in government bonds or gilts, and corporate bonds. Investment bonds offered by life assurance companies can also be held in a stocks and shares ISA.

You can't have more than one mini of the same type in a single tax year: You can't save into two mini cash ISAs in one tax year, for example.

Cashing in

Cash ISAs are the most popular type of ISA because they are low risk and require small amounts of money to get started. They also don't require you to commit your funds for any length of time (as long as you don't opt for one with a fixed rate), so they're handy in the short term. You can have either a mini cash ISA or a cash component in your maxi ISA. A mini cash ISA doesn't have any management charges. Cash ISAs operate in a similar way to a savings account in that your money is at no risk whatsoever. The big difference from the average savings account though is that returns are tax-free, so you earn more interest on your investment.

A range of providers, such as banks, building societies, and even supermarkets, offer cash ISAs. Indeed, supermarkets often come near the top of the 'best buy' tables with their mini cash ISAs, so don't be a snob and feel you have to plump for a traditional provider.

You can open a cash ISA with as little as £10 although some ISA providers may have a higher minimum opening balance of anything from £50 to £250. Some providers insist you deposit your full allowance – £3,000 in 2007-08 – as a lump sum when you open your account.

As with standard savings accounts, you can opt for a variable-rate cash ISA (where the rate of interest goes up and down in line with the Bank of England base rate) or you can choose a fixed-rate ISA, which remains at the same rate for a set period of time. Watch out for restrictions on withdrawals from fixed-rate ISAs, as you may not be allowed to get hold of your money ahead of the maturity date.

You must be at least 16 years old to open a mini cash ISA.

Changing Tessa to Toisa

If you owned a Tessa (tax-exempt special savings account), you probably now own a Toisa (Tessa-only ISA). From 6 April 1999, Tessas were gradually phased out and replaced by mini cash ISAs. I say gradually because Tessas, unlike mini cash ISAs, had five-year investment terms during which you couldn't get your hands on your money. The last of the Tessas matured in April 2004.

Sensible investors converted maturing Tessas into Toisas so that they didn't lose the tax-free status of their invested cash. But once you've got your Toisa, you should continue to monitor it on a regular basis – just as you would a mini cash ISA. Many providers offer Toisas, so there is plenty of choice out there and no need to plump for low rates.

If the rate of interest on your Toisa starts to appear uncompetitive, you can switch your cash to another Toisa (although make sure you do this according to the rulebook or you could lose your tax-free allowance: See 'Transferring your ISA' later in this chapter for more details on this).

Shopping around for a mini cash ISA is relatively straightforward as these products are extremely simple to compare. Log onto comparison websites such as www.moneyextra.com, www.moneyfacts.co.uk, or www.moneysupermarket.com for the best deals. If you don't have access to the Internet, check out the best buy tables in the national press.

Stocking up on equities

If you can afford to tie your money up for the medium to long term (anything from five years upwards), you might want to consider stocks and shares ISAs. Over time, these tend to produce better returns than cash, along with a greater degree of risk. You must be at least 18 years old to open a stocks and shares ISA.

With a stocks and shares ISA your capital is at risk – unlike with a cash ISA – so don't invest money you can't afford to lose or that you need in the short term.

Most people hold managed funds in their ISAs. But you don't have to limit your choice to just one fund per year. By buying through a fund supermarket(see the sidebar 'Saving money down the supermarket' for more details), you can hold a selection of funds within a single ISA wrapper, thereby spreading your risk much more widely. Most ISA funds require a payment of at least £1000, so you couldn't buy more than seven with a single year's £7000 ISA allowance.

Book III

Building Up Savings and Investments

Drip feeding produces the best results

If you have a choice between investing a lump sum or a regular monthly amount into an equity ISA, it is often better to opt for the latter. By staggering your contributions throughout the tax year, you minimise the risk of buying at the top of the market, only to see it crash immediately afterwards, leaving you sitting on significant losses.

The danger of piling in with a lump sum is that you buy at the wrong time, whereas if you drip feed your money in over the year, there is no chance of doing this. You are hedging your bets: Some months your money will buy more shares or units in the fund than at other times, but you take the rough with the smooth.

If you don't want to make your own choice, most supermarkets put together a selection of 'pre-packaged' ISAs, each holding a handful of top funds and designed for investors looking for, say, growth, or income, or wanting to invest in a particular part of the world such as the UK, Europe or emerging markets.

Stocks and shares ISAs are not quite as attractive from a tax-planning perspective as they used to be. The tax credit on dividends was withdrawn in April 2004 so whereas a basic-rate taxpayer with an ISA would have received a 10 per cent tax credit (32.5 per cent for higher-rate taxpayers), this is no longer the case.

All other income and all capital gains are still free of tax, making ISAs a more tax-efficient option for investments designed to produce capital growth rather than a good income stream.

There is no penalty for making withdrawals from a stock and shares ISA as there is no fixed period or maturity date: You can cash in all or part of your account whenever you wish.

You can invest a monthly amount – usually around £50 – although you can also invest a lump sum if you wish. It is worth spreading your payments over the year in order to minimise risk (see sidebar: 'Drip feeding produces the best results').

You have to pay an initial charge when you deposit money in an equity ISA, which can be as high as 5 per cent of the sum you are investing. There is also an annual management fee, which varies between fund managers from 0.5 to 2 per cent of the total amount invested. But there are ways of saving on this initial cost: See the nearby sidebar 'Saving money down the supermarket' for more details.

Saving money down the supermarket

If you apply for a stocks and shares ISA direct from the fund manager, it's highly likely that you will have to pay an initial charge of 5 per cent of the sum you are investing (as well as only being able to choose from the funds of that manager). But you can pay much less (and sometimes nothing at all) if you shop around. This sounds the wrong way round, as applying direct usually means you get a discount. But in the era of fund supermarkets, this isn't the case.

You can get a hefty discount on the initial fee if you apply for your ISA via a fund supermarket on the Internet. These enable you to choose your ISA from a range of hundreds of funds. You can also mix and match unit trusts from different

providers within a single ISA. Thus you can increase your exposure to a wider range of investments and reduce your risk.

There are lots of fund supermarkets to choose from. The first and best established with access to over 1000 funds from 55 investment companies is investment house Fidelity's FundsNetwork (www.fundsnetwork.co.uk). Other supermarkets selling to the general public (some only deal with professional intermediaries such as IFAs) include brokers Interactive Investor (www.iii.co.uk) and Hargreaves Lansdown (www.h-l.co.uk). Some brokers will charge you a fee for this service, so read the small print before committing yourself.

You don't have to invest in the same ISA each year: In fact, if you want to build a balanced portfolio (which should be your goal), you can spread your risk by investing in different assets. Then, if something happens to a particular stock market or sector, you can take comfort from the fact that you don't have all your money invested there.

As stocks and shares ISAs are more complicated than cash ISAs, you may wish to seek advice before taking the plunge. Consult an independent financial adviser who will be able to help you choose the best investment for your needs. For details of IFAs in your area, contact IFA Promotion on 0800 085 3250 or go to www.unbiased.co.uk.

The Financial Services Authority has a comparative table on its website (www.fsa.gov.uk/tables), enabling you to compare charges and other basic information on unit trust ISAs (see Chapter 5 in this Book for more on unit trusts). You are asked to input details such as whether you are investing for income or growth, how much you've got to invest, how long you want to invest for, and the amount of risk you are willing to take on.

Selecting your own ISA

If you are fairly experienced when it comes to investing and want more of a say on where your ISA money is invested, you could opt for a *self-select ISA*. This enables you to pick and mix the investments within your ISA wrapper.

Self-select ISAs are widely available from stockbrokers and discount brokers but look carefully both at what is on offer (not all offer a full range of investments) and at the costs involved.

Within a self-select ISA you may be able to hold not only funds but also individual UK and international stocks and shares, investment trusts, gilts, bonds, exchange traded funds and REITs. The responsibility for picking and monitoring your investments rests entirely with you, so if you don't have the time or expertise it's probably safer to stick to funds.

The main thing to watch with a self-select ISA is the charges. As well as the normal dealing charges for buying and selling investments, you will be charged a fee for the ISA wrapper, which may be a one-off annual fee or a monthly charge. It may be a flat rate or a percentage of your portfolio – for example, Barclays Stockbrokers charges 0.25% of the portfolio, capped at £60, while Fidelity Share Network charges £5 a month and SelfTrade a competitive £25 per year. Other charges, such as transfer fees, dividend reinvestment fees and in particular inactivity fees, can also catch you out so do be clear exactly what costs are involved.

Transferring your ISA

You don't have to put up with a poorly performing ISA. Review the rate of interest (if it's cash) or performance (insurance or stocks and shares) annually to see whether your ISA is still competitive.

If you decide to switch your ISA, whatever you do, don't withdraw the cash from your current provider and then try to deposit it in a new ISA. Even if your intention is to transfer it straightaway to a new ISA, you lose your ISA allowance if you handle it this way. And when you open the new ISA, it will count as this year's allowance so you effectively lose out. What's more, if you've already used up this year's allowance, you will be in breach of the rules and have to close the second one.

Transfers are very simple if your money is invested within a fund supermarket, as you just fill in a form and the supermarket does the rest. It's quick – your money should only be out of the market overnight – and very cheap.

When making a transfer from an ISA invested directly with a manager, you must get your new ISA provider to handle it on your behalf so you don't see the money at all. Ask your new provider for a transfer form, complete this, and return it. The new provider will then contact your existing ISA provider and arrange the transfer. You will be notified when this is completed: It can take up to a month, so be patient.

Handled this way, the transfer doesn't affect your ISA allowance for the current year, which you can invest as normal.

Choosing National Savings Certificates

If you want security and tax-free returns, consider National Savings and Investments (NS&I) products, which are backed by the Treasury and available from your local post office. Rates used to be pretty unexciting, but they have become more competitive in recent years. You can find out more details by calling 0845 964 5000 or logging onto www.nationalsavings.co.uk.

National Savings Certificates are available for two- or five-year terms and the rate of interest is fixed for the term. You can invest a lump sum of between £100 and £15,000 in each issue.

When National Savings decides to change the rate of interest on the certificate, it brings out another issue with the new fixed rate. Your existing rate is guaranteed, but you can invest up to £15,000 in the new issue as well if you wish.

All returns are free from Income and Capital Gains Tax. But if you withdraw cash before the end of the two- or five-year term, you will be penalised. If you cash in your investment within the first year, for example, you won't receive any interest at all.

If you want to reduce the risk of inflation on your investment, you can buy an index-linked savings certificate, which is inflation proofed for three or five years. These pay a fixed percentage above the annual rate of inflation (also known as the retail price index).

Exploring Venture Capital Trusts

Another way of earning generous tax breaks on your investments is via a *venture capital trust (VCT)*. A VCT is an investment company quoted on the London stock exchange that invests in young, growth-orientated British companies with a potential for high returns over the medium to long term.

VCTs invest in a range of unquoted and AIM (Alternative Investment Market) companies (which are also expected to deliver rapid growth), with a team of professional managers selecting a portfolio of stocks. This enables you to invest in companies which by their very nature are more risky than those quoted on the London Stock Exchange, but which have the potential for faster growth and higher returns. Investing in a VCT gets you exposure to the sort of stocks that most private equity investors wouldn't achieve by any other means. Plus, you spread your risk because you are investing in a selection of such companies – not just one or two.

You can invest up to £200,000 in a VCT in the 2007-08 tax year – much higher than your annual ISA allowance. In return you get:

- ✔ Up-front tax relief of up to 30 per cent, as long as you have enough income tax payable to absorb that relief
- ✔ No CGT payable on profits when you sell your VCT shares
- ✔ Dividends also free of tax

In effect, this means that if you are a higher-rate taxpayer and invest the full £200,000 limit in a VCT, you will find that the effective cost to you is £140,000.

To qualify for the full income tax relief, you must leave your money invested for at least three years. If you sell your VCT shares during this time, the up-front income tax relief will be withdrawn. You will have to repay the lower of the tax you originally saved or 30 per cent of the sale proceeds.

While you may be attracted by the generous tax breaks, you should be wary of investing in any product purely for this reason. You must ensure that the underlying investments are right for you and shop around carefully, as the difference between the performance of the best VCTs and the worst is significant.

It is also worth bearing in mind that:

- ✔ VCTs are riskier than investing in the main equity markets, so be certain about what you are getting yourself into and make sure it fits in with your overall investment portfolio. A VCT shouldn't be the mainstay of your portfolio (you shouldn't have all your funds committed to it); instead, it's a useful addition to a well-diversified portfolio.
- ✔ Your money is effectively tied up for at least three years so don't invest cash that you will need to get your hands on during this time. If you withdraw your money early, you miss out on the valuable tax breaks that may have attracted you to this investment in the first instance.
- ✔ You may have to wait much longer than three years to make a profit, so you should only invest money that you don't need in the long term if you want a chance of making a decent return on your investment.
- ✔ VCT shares are not always easy to sell when you finally get round to doing so because trading isn't active. It may take a while to find a buyer and therefore get your hands on your cash.

VCTs vary greatly in terms of what they invest in and choosing the right one can be a complicated task, involving much more work than researching a unit or investment trust. You should always seek help from a financial adviser.

Betting on Premium Bonds

Premium bonds don't actually pay interest but give out prizes – you might land £1 million! Going for a big holding – the maximum is £30,000 – means you have loads of chances of winning each month so, statistically, you should get enough prizes each year to make your stake worthwhile.

At the moment, the prize fund is calculated at 3 per cent of the total in the bonds. So if you have £30,000, you should earn an average 3 per cent of that sum per year – £900. But as that sum is tax-free, a higher rate tax-payer would otherwise have to earn £1,500 gross to get £900 in their bank account. The equivalent gross interest rate would be 5 per cent. For basic-rate payers, the 3 per cent tax-free return turns into 3.75 per cent gross. This percentage tends to go up and down with interest rates.

Book III

Building Up Savings and Investments

Chapter 5

Delving Into Collective Investments

*I*f you're new to investing or don't have much cash to spare, opting for a collective fund or pooled investment rather than buying stocks and shares directly is the easiest – and safest – way of gaining exposure to the market. Pooled investments, such as unit and investment trusts, enable you to spread your risk by gaining exposure to 50 or more companies for as little as £50.

With several types of collective funds to choose from, and many more sectors and countries to invest in, selecting the most suitable investments can be tricky. To make matters worse, investors are often tempted by funds that have done well in the past or are flavour of the month – usually because they have a good track record. But neither reason is a sound basis for choosing an investment.

This chapter explains what collective funds are available and helps you decide what products suit you and your risk profile.

Pooling Your Investments

The greater the proportion of shares in your investment portfolio, the higher your potential return – as long as you invest for the long term, say ten years or more. Shares expose you to increased risk but by investing via a *pooled* or *collective* investment – a ready-made portfolio of shares in a particular group of companies, a sector, or a country – you can spread your risk. Collective funds enable you to reduce the damage if one of your investments suffers a downturn, while at the same time you can keep your costs low.

If you are happy to manage your own money, you can build up a portfolio of individual shares or bonds in different companies and across different sectors. But building up a portfolio in this way can be very expensive. Unless you have a serious amount of cash, you won't be able to spread your exposure beyond one or two companies at most. It can also be difficult to gain exposure to companies outside the UK, which is important for a truly diversified portfolio. Managing your own investment portfolio can be very painstaking and time consuming as you have to keep an eye on your investments and be prepared to make important decisions such as when you buy or sell your holdings. With a managed fund, you pay a professional fund manager to take care of this for you. (Chapter 6 in this Book talks about buying shares directly.)

Looking at the advantages of pooled investments

Pooling your investments has several advantages:

- ✔ **Reduced risk:** Your money is spread across tens of companies, rather than one or two.

- ✔ **Cheaper costs:** It is cheaper to buy and sell collective funds than it is to buy and sell individual shares. By pooling your resources with lots of other investors, you can buy in bulk. If you invest in lots of individual shares, on the other hand, costs can be prohibitive.

- ✔ **Professional management:** A full-time professional manager looks after your money. Funds managers are well regulated, so if the fund manager breaches the rules, leading to you suffering financial loss, you get compensation.

- ✔ **Reduced paperwork:** Owning lots of shares directly involves plenty of administration whenever you buy and sell your holdings. With a pooled investment, your fund manager takes care of this and you don't have to make investment decisions yourself either.

Losing out by pooling

You must weigh the advantages of a pooled investment against the disadvantages:

- ✔ **Paying for a fund manager**: If you invest in shares directly, you simply pay the share price when you buy them and a commission to a broker. There is usually commission to pay when you sell and you may have to pay a small fee to a stockbroker to have an account with him. But with a managed fund you pay an initial (or exit) charge and an annual management fee, which is taken direct from the fund. These tend to be far higher.

- ✔ **Lack of choice**: The fund manager makes the investment decisions, which you may not always agree with. Before you invest in a fund, ensure it matches your investment priorities.

- ✔ **No owner's rights**: If you hold shares directly, you often get shareholder perks, such as discounts on the company's products. You also have the option of attending the annual general meeting and voting on important matters, such as mergers. If you invest in a collective fund, you don't get any of the rights connected with the individual investments in a fund.

Jumping into Different Pools

There are several different types of pooled funds available, which invest in similar areas, although there are subtle differences in their structure – these are unit and investment trusts and open-ended investment companies (Oeics). Table 5-1 shows the variety of investment focuses available when choosing one of these funds, which we explain in more detail in the following sections.

Book III

Building Up Savings and Investments

Table 5-1	Focus of Unit and Investment Trusts and Oeics
Fund	*Investment Focus*
UK all companies	UK company shares. Aims to produce income and growth
UK growth	UK companies expected to produce capital gains rather than income (thus dividends will be low but the emphasis is on the share price rising in the long term)
UK equity income	Shares that produce high dividends

(continued)

Table 5-1 *(continued)*

Fund	Investment Focus
Index/tracker funds	Follows movement of a stock market index
UK gilt/fixed interest	Gilts, corporate bonds, preference shares (offering fixed dividend payments so appeal to people looking for regular income)
Convertibles	Convertible corporate bonds (pay a regular income and can be converted into ordinary shares at redemption)
Balanced	Mixture of shares and fixed interest (such as bonds)
International	Invests in shares from a wide range of markets around the world
Smaller companies	Chooses smaller, and thus riskier, companies over those with a larger market capitalisation
Countries	European countries, the US, emerging markets or the Far East
Fund of funds*	Other unit trusts
Specialist	A single sector, such as technology or healthcare

*Not Oeics or investment trusts

Understanding Unit Trusts

Unit trusts are the most straightforward type of pooled investment. A unit trust enables investors to buy units of equal value in a fund run by a professional manager. Because you are pooling your money with other investors', you get exposure to a broad range of shares – far broader than if you bought shares directly in various companies. Thus a unit trust enables you to reduce your investment risk.

The *trust* in the name refers to the fact that these assets are held by an independent authorised firm, known as a *trustee*, that oversees the running of the fund. The trustee provides comprehensive investor protection.

Most UK funds are authorised by the Financial Services Authority (FSA) and covered by the Financial Services Compensation Scheme. Some funds are authorised elsewhere in the European Union however: Check that a fund is authorised before you invest in it and where that regulator is based.

Managing with caution or aggression?

Understanding the fund manager's investment style is important to ensuring you know what you are investing in. If the manager is said to have an *aggressive* style, it doesn't mean that he is argumentative and strong-willed but instead refers to the fact that he is aiming for superior returns by investing in a small number of companies he feels will do well.

Risk is much higher with an aggressive style than a *cautious managed* fund, where the manager aims for more modest returns, opting for a greater number of underlying investments so risks are lower. This is the type of fund you need if you want to sleep at night.

Unit trusts are *open-ended*, which means the fund gets bigger as more people invest and smaller as people withdraw their cash. There is no limit to the size of the trust. Units move up and down in value, depending on how well the fund manager invests this money in bulk in cash, bonds, and equities.

You can invest on a regular monthly basis or a lump sum and you can buy or sell your investment through a fund manager on any working day. The daily price of your units reflects the value of the shares, bonds, and/or cash the fund is invested in. There are no lock-in periods, so you can sell your holding whenever you wish, but you should aim to leave your money invested for the medium to long term – at least five years.

Examining one big difference between unit trusts and OEICs

In the UK, more and more funds are, strictly speaking, defined as *open-ended investment companies (OEICs)* but almost everyone still calls them unit trusts. Technical differences exist between unit trusts and OEICs, but most of them only interest lawyers. The exception is how you see prices quoted.

Unit trusts have two prices – one around 5 per cent higher than the other. The higher price, or *offer price,* is the one you pay when you buy. If you sell, you receive the lower price, or *bid price.* The gap between the two, known as the *bid-offer spread,* goes to the fund management company, which uses some of the cash to pay the broker or other seller.

OEICs have only one price whether you're buying or selling, a setup called *single pricing.* Does that sound like you're free of the bid-offer spread? If only. Although OEICs have only one price, brokers can load the price by around

Book III

Building Up Savings and Investments

5 per cent when you buy, so you're back to where you were with unit trusts. Some OEICs in fund listings have far lower charges. They're available to anyone with a minimum of £250,000 to £500,000. And that's probably not you.

Note that holders of OEICs also receive half-yearly reports in a different format. Instead of getting a thin leaflet just detailing one unit trust, OEIC investors get a fat book listing all the various funds offered by the management company. In law, what you've bought into is a subfund of the OEIC. The one advantage is that you can see details of how the manager is coping with other assets.

Selecting the best unit trust for you

To select the right unit trust for your needs, you need to follow this step-by-step guide:

1. **Work out your asset allocation strategy.**

   You need to calculate how much you can afford to put into the different investment types. It ultimately depends on how much you have, how much you are willing to risk, and how long an investment period you have.

2. **Decide on the proportion of your cash that you want in collective investments.**

   Once you have worked out your long-term asset allocation moves, you don't have to carry them out all at once. This may be a good time to buy shares or bonds through a collective investment. But if it is not, then there is nothing wrong holding your money back for a period. A good idea is put this cash in a bank or building society accountyou keep apart from your other savings.

3. **Select your investment objective.**

   For example, is your objective income, long-term capital growth, or a mix of the two?

4. **Refine your options by working through unit trust sector listings, where you'll see all funds with similar investment patterns, such as corporate bonds, North America, or Europe excluding the UK.**

   All trusts are classified in sectors so that you can see funds pursuing roughly similar investment objectives. The sectors change from time to time, but there are currently around 30. An unwieldy number, yes. So the unit trust statisticians break down the list into two main divisions: income and growth. And those two divisions are further subdivided. On top of that, there are a few that are 'half-way houses', a mix of income and growth. Sometimes this mix comes from one set of shares which are chosen to be midway between going gung-ho for growth and working all out for income. Other times, unit trust firms set up 'managed funds' where they mix'n'match income and growth funds either from their own range or from other management groups.

5. **Ensure that the fund you choose will accept your level of savings.**

    Some trusts, for example, are aimed at large investors and broker firms with six-figure sums.

Working out charges

When you invest in a unit trust, you usually pay an initial charge – a percentage of the amount you are investing. It can be as much as 5 per cent of the value of your investment. There is no charge to pay when you sell your holding, so it costs more to buy units than it does to sell them. The difference between the price you pay (the *offer*) and what you get when you sell (the *bid*) is referred to as a *spread*.

The spread is typically 5 to 6 per cent in most unit trusts, so if you invest £1,000 in units with a bid–offer spread of 5 per cent, the value of your investment is immediately reduced to £950.

To avoid paying an initial charge – or to pay a much reduced one – buy your fund through a discount broker or fund supermarket operated over the Internet. See Chapter 4 in this part for more on these.

Some unit trusts don't have an initial charge; instead, they have an exit charge when you withdraw your cash. As well as an initial charge (or exit fee), you must also pay an annual management fee, which is deducted from the fund. The charge varies between investment houses but expect to pay in the region of 1.5 per cent.

Charges can eat into the performance of your fund, so make sure you know exactly what you have to pay and that you aren't being charged over the odds before committing your money.

Book III

Building Up
Savings
and
Investments

Comparing active versus passive fund managers

Active fund managers buy and sell shares and other assets hoping that they'll perform at least better than average and preferably hit the big time. Most funds are actively managed.

Passive fund managers don't care. The reason is that they're usually comput-ers, not people, without too much in the way of sentimental feeling. They buy all the constituents of an index in the right proportions (or occasionally come up with sampling methods to ensure that a fund doesn't have to cope with hundreds of tiny company shares).

The result of passive fund management (this is another name for the tracker fund concept as no one has to do anything to select the shares as they are automatically chosen) is that what you get is what you see. If the fund tracks the Footsie (the FTSE 100 share index of the UK's biggest stock-market-quoted firms), then your fund will go up and down each day along with the index. You'll get an income calculated as the average yield on the basket of shares your fund follows, less the annual management charge. You'll also know what level of risk you're taking.

Most passive funds in the UK track either the Footsie or the wider All Share Index. But you can buy passive funds that follow markets in other countries; that buy into sectors worldwide, such as technology or pharmaceuticals; or that only invest in an index of ethically and environmentally approved com-panies. A growing area of passive investment is to buy the replication of an index through Exchange Traded Funds. Exchange Traded Funds are traded via stockbrokers just as if they were real shares. They're big in America but largely confined to professionals so far in the UK.

Active versus passive is the big fund management debate. Both sides can come up with good (and sometimes bad) arguments:

- ✔ Active managers say that they can add value because they can sift out the wheat from the chaff.

- ✔ Passive managers say that they don't have to second-guess the future.

- ✔ Active managers say that they have a wider range of investments, including smaller companies with a great future.

- ✔ Passive managers say that most of these small-company bets fail. And even when they do well, they have little effect on the overall fund because holdings are miniscule.

- ✔ Active managers say that they offer strategies that vary with market conditions.

- ✔ Passive managers say that the market as a whole automatically adjusts to different conditions.

- ✔ Active managers say that passive funds end up with too many shares that have peaked. The trick is to look for shares that are growing fast enough to knock on an index's door.

✔ Passive managers say that a lot of active managers just buy big index stocks but charge up to five times extra for the privilege – a practice called *closet indexing* in the investment trade.

✔ Active managers say that passive funds often fail to track their chosen index properly.

✔ Passive managers say that they win on costs. They reckon that active managers have to do about 1.5 per cent better a year than the index – a tough call year on year.

✔ Active managers say that they can spread their investments more efficiently. They don't have to buy and sell whenever firms go in and out of an index. They can talk to companies and sometimes influence the stock market. But, they say, passive fund managers must buy stocks they have no control over and at whatever price the market dictates.

✔ Passive managers say that although they'll never top a table, they'll never be below halfway for long either. They say that active funds which beat them one year probably won't do so the next. Due to costs and other factors, a good index fund should always end up around 38th to 42nd place in a group of 100 funds over a typical year. Performing this way consistently is better than rocket performance one year and rubbish performance the next.

Active and passive fans will continue to swap insults and statistics to prove their cases. Don't get caught up in their ego trips. Instead, go for a core and satellite strategy. Put the bulk of your money in low-cost index funds and leave it there. This is your core. Invest the rest in selected managed funds that don't closet-index, such as smaller-company trusts, or go for specialist areas overseas.

Going with a fund of funds

Most unit trust investors start off with a UK fund, often a tracker. Then they add to it with more UK-based trusts, and then they venture overseas. But as they build up their portfolio, they have to make decisions. They have to choose the best in each sector that they select and then monitor their holdings.

The do-it-yourself approach has two big failings. Massive costs are involved every time an investor switches from one fund to another. And there's capital gains tax on profits.

The alternative is to hand over money to a fund of funds manager, who invests in other funds but in such a way that minimises switching costs and has no capital gains tax worries within the fund.

Book III

Building Up Savings and Investments

Do funds of funds beat a buy and hold strategy? The jury's out. But the fund managers must be specially gifted to overcome the drag of two sets of charges. There are annual fees on the fund of funds and yearly charges on the underlying funds. If you pick a manager badly, you'll end up paying more for less investment performance.

So far, no one has come up with a fund of funds of funds!

Checking out investment supermarkets

Buying a unit trust directly from a fund management firm is a waste of money. You'll be charged the full up-front charge, including the 3 per cent paid to brokers, which is supposedly their reward for providing you with individualised advice. But you won't get this advice unless you're a really big customer.

If you know what you want by filtering down the 1,600 or so trusts to a short list and then studying the information on each via online sources, then you can buy your trust and get all or nearly all of the commission back into your bank account via an Internet investment supermarket.

Here, you select your fund, decide whether you want it as an Individual Savings Account (ISA), and pay for it with a credit card. The supermarket site should have links to the funds you're interested in. Easy.

The best-known investment supermarkets are www.iii.co.uk, www.fidelity.co.uk, www.egg.com, www.virginmoney.com, and www.fundsdirect.co.uk. A number of stockbroker sites also offer similar facilities, sometimes via a branded link to one of the main sites.

Investment supermarkets are like Sainsbury or Tesco. They don't stock absolutely everything, instead concentrating on a pile-it-high, sell-it-cheap philosophy. If you need specialist funds from smaller providers, you may not find them on the fund supermarket shelves. But unlike the high street, these supermarkets have a strict no-refunds policy.

Understanding What Investment Trusts Are

Investment trusts share a lot of similarities with unit trusts. They give professional management in return for an annual fee, and investors get a portfolio of shares. These trusts are intended for longer-term investment, and choices range from global growth to specialist areas, such as Latin America, Thailand, and start-up companies.

But differences between investment trusts and unit trusts exist, too. The most important for typical investors are the low charges associated with investment trusts. Alliance Investment Trust, one of the biggest and oldest established funds, levies around 0.25 per cent a year in fees. That's one-sixth of the 1.5 per cent level from unit trusts that have a similar worldwide investment remit. Many other investment trusts keep their costs below 0.5 per cent. Over five to ten or more years, those savings mount up to a useful sum, with the gap growing in the investment trust's favour the more the market rises.

The Americans call unit trusts *open-ended* (or *mutual*) funds, which makes sense because the amount a unit trust manager has to invest depends on day-to-day purchases and sales of the fund. But investment trusts are different, and likewise the Americans call investment trusts *closed-end funds*. The reason? An investment trust is effectively a stock-market-listed company with shares and a fixed amount of money on its balance sheet. But instead of using its capital to buy assets (such as factories or shops) and to fund research (like GlaxoSmithKline does) or to buy the latest fashions (like Marks & Spencer does), the managers use the trust's capital to buy shares in other companies.

When you buy a Marks & Spencer share, the company itself doesn't get the money. The money ultimately (and indirectly) goes to the shareholder selling. Likewise, if investors decide to sell Glaxo, the firm itself doesn't shut down part of its research or manufacturing network. The company can look at the longer term, past the day-to-day concerns of individual shareholders.

Investment trusts are the same. Buying and selling moves the price of the trust share on the stock market. But it doesn't affect the underlying assets that are used to buy investments in other companies. So investment trusts can look to the long term. This fact may explain why so many investment trusts have been around for decades.

Book III

Building Up Savings and Investments

Examining the discount

Quoted companies never have a stock market value that's exactly in line with the value of their underlying assets:

- Some sell at a premium, where the total share value (or *market capitalisation*) is greater than the underlying assets. A typical example is a chemical research company where the market is valuing the hope of a future breakthrough over the worth of its assets (probably not much).

- Some sell at a discount. Property companies, for example, usually have a stock market value below what all the individual properties may fetch if sold. This discount is a safety barrier or breathing space in case things go wrong.

Premiums go up and discounts tend to disappear when markets are optimistic. The same happens with investment trusts. Their market capitalisation is usually below their break-up worth (known as the *net asset value,* or *NAV*), although there are occasional premiums.

The discount tends to magnify market movements. When the underlying portfolio goes up in value, demand for the shares tends to shrink the discount, so holders benefit twice. In a bear market, discounts widen as the portfolio drops, giving investors a double hit.

Should you worry? Not nearly as much as unit trust sellers and some commission-crazed independent financial advisers (IFAs) suggest. Over time, discounts tend to stabilise. Investment trusts can adjust their own discount with share buybacks. So you can ride out the ups and downs in discounts.

The discount has some advantages. If you pay 90p for a share with an NAV of 100p, you receive the dividend income on 100p worth of assets, an 11 per cent boost.

Knowing what gearing means

Because they are stockmarket-quoted companies just like Barclays Bank or Vodafone, investment trusts can behave in ways that differentiate them from other forms of collective investment.

For example, they can borrow money either through a bond issue or directly from the bank, a process called *gearing.* Trusts take loans because they believe that the stock market return will be greater than the interest costs. The loan enables them to get greater stock market exposure to the benefit of shareholders. In this way, trusts are rather like a cyclist who uses gears to go faster in good conditions (such as on the flat with the wind behind).

But as any cyclist knows, high gears are a pain going up steep hills. It's the same with trusts. Funds that gear up and then face a falling market lose out twice because they have to keep paying the interest to the bank or bondholder.

Investment trusts publish their gearing levels. Many limit gearing to modest amounts, such as 10 per cent or under. A few try more sophisticated deals, such as borrowing in one currency and buying assets quoted in another. Here, the managers are betting on getting the foreign exchange dealing right as well.

Gearing is a risk but can be a reward when market conditions are right. Buy investment trusts with above-average gearing compared with similar funds if you think markets are going to rise. Don't worry that you've spotted something that the market as a whole has ignored (thus thinking that you're wrong).

Trading in many investment trusts is sporadic and inefficient, leading to opportunities wised-up investors can grab.

Starting with the Global Growth sector

Most investors start out with the Global Growth sector, which is all many people ever invest in or need. Others use Global Growth as a core portfolio and then buy more specialist funds.

The sector is worth almost £15 billion including some 12 trusts with assets over £250 million. Among the biggest are Foreign & Colonial, Witan, Alliance, Scottish Investment Trust, and Scottish Mortgage.

The Global Growth sector is defined as trusts whose objective is to produce a total return to shareholders from capital and some dividend income. The trusts have less than 80 per cent of their assets in any one geographical area, with at least 20 per cent in UK-registered companies. They can also hold cash and fixed-interest securities.

These non-specialist trusts are suitable for beginners, and they usually form the basis of long-term savings plans for children. They can also be useful for others, however, because the format can provide a widely diversified core for any widespread portfolio. Because many London-quoted companies are really international giants, don't be taken in by the proportion invested in the UK.

Global Growth also gives an opportunity for you to spread into newer investment areas that would otherwise be difficult for private investors to research and buy. These areas can be anything from Singapore to Switzerland to start-up companies but without the constraints a more specialised portfolio may have.

 Note that a number of super-selective trusts exist. Pubs, tea plantations, alternative energy, gold mines, property, and traded endowment policies are just a few examples. Most of these trusts are so specialised that they're one-offs. They exist in a sector all by themselves without any comparisons.

Making Sense of With-Profits Investment Bonds

You can gain access to pooled investments via insurance products. A *with-profits* bond allows you to invest in the with-profits fund of an insurance company via an investment bond. The fund invests in a range of shares, gilts, and property so you get exposure to a broad spread of investments.

You get a share in the return of the insurer's with-profits fund via a *reversionary* or *annual* bonus, which is added to your fund and can't be taken away, provided you keep the policy going until its term. When the policy matures, you may get a *terminal* bonus, the size of which depends on the performance of the fund. It is not guaranteed.

To minimise fluctuating returns in bonuses each year, the insurer *smoothes* the payments. As a result, you don't see sharp variations in returns from year to year, in line with stock market movements, because part of your bonus is held back in the good years so you still get a payment in years when performance is poor. When markets are performing strongly, with-profits funds don't look that attractive as you could be making better returns elsewhere. But in bear markets, when everyone else is suffering, they come into their own because you should still see some bonuses.

With-profits funds have fallen out of favour in recent years. As the stock market has been in the doldrums, with-profits bonds have also fallen in value. Bonuses have been poor and show no signs of recovering anytime soon. However, policyholders are trapped in their funds because insurers are imposing a surrender penalty on investors who try to cash in ahead of the maturity date. This is known as a *market value reduction (MVR)* and is meant to stop policyholders cashing in their policies to the detriment of those left behind in the fund. The MVR can be as high as 20 per cent of the value of your investment.

In light of this, some advisers have stopped recommending with-profits bonds to investors. But others still recommend them to clients looking for some security but who want a higher income than they can get from cash. However, if you are thinking of investing in with-profits, check the insurer's financial strength very carefully before investing. You should take into account the level of its reserves and the nature of its assets.

For more information on with-profits funds or other insurance-based products, contact the Association of British Insurers (ABI) on 020 7600 3333 or go to www.abi.org.uk.

Buying Corporate Bond Funds

A corporate bond is an IOU from a company. In buying a corporate bond, you are, in effect, lending the company money. In return, you get a set rate of interest and the return of your initial investment after a specified number of years. Chapter 6 has more details on buying individual bonds.

Guarantees come at a price

If you want your capital to be secure, but still get exposure to shares, you can opt for an equity fund with a guarantee or element of protection. These are fixed-term investments with returns linked to the performance of an index. Investors like these funds because it is usually guaranteed that you will get your capital back at the end of the term, as long as certain conditions are met. You also get some of the upside of the market. But this is key: Returns are restricted to a percentage of the growth of the index during this period, say 60 per cent of the performance of the FTSE 100. If the market falls, you still get your capital back. But if it rockets, you lose out because you are limited to just 60 per cent of the growth.

If you are that worried about losing money on the stock market, steer clear completely, rather than opting for one of these half-hearted measures.

Investing directly in corporate bonds can be high risk, particularly if you opt for high-yield bonds. But you can minimise risk by pooling your investment via a corporate bond fund. A professional manager will invest your money, along with that of thousands of other investors, across a range of companies, reducing your investment risk and maximising your potential returns.

Not all bonds are safe investments. Generally speaking, the higher the return you are promised, the riskier the company issuing it and the more likelihood there is that it could go bust and you end up losing your money. The capital value of bonds can go down because they are traded – bought and sold. They may be lower risk than shares but there is still an element of risk.

Book III

Building Up Savings and Investments

Choosing Exchange Traded Funds

An *exchange traded fund (ETF)* is structured in a similar way to an open-ended investment company but offers you exposure to an entire index, such as the FTSE 100, or to a market sector, such as European technology, in just one share – in the same way as a unit trust. But unlike unit trusts, ETFs trade in the same way as normal shares and are quoted on the stock exchange. These funds are open-ended, so the size of the fund can fluctuate according to how many people are invested. The share price reflects the value of the investments in the fund: Shares don't trade at a premium or a discount.

Most ETFs pay you dividends while your money is invested. When you sell up, you could make a capital gain or loss, depending on how your investment has performed. ETF shares have a bid-offer spread, so there is a difference between the buying and the selling price, although this tends to be very small – just 0.1 or 0.2 per cent for an ETF tracking the FTSE 100, for example.

You pay an annual management charge of around 0.5 per cent or less, which is deducted from the fund, as well as a commission to the stockbroker when you buy and sell. You do not, however, pay stamp duty on purchases – as is the case with other shares.

ETF shares are bought and sold through stockbrokers or private client investment managers. These professionals can also provide you with advice, although you have to pay for it. See Chapter 6 for more details on choosing a stockbroker.

The Worth of Performance Tables

One of the most controversial issues in fund management is past performance and whether it has any relationship to the future. Academics have said that you have as much chance of picking a future winning fund by selecting the best from the past as you have of winning at roulette by looking at where the balls ended up earlier.

The Financial Services Authority (FSA) has said that the past has no serious predictive value. At one time, the FSA wanted to ban past performance figures because the FSA said they just confuse investors. But the fund management industry put up a spirited defence of the practice (without which it would have to rewrite all its adverts), and its view has prevailed.

Whether your collective is an investment trust, OEIC, or insurance bond, performance tables are available for you to scrutinise. The tables are subdivided into sectors, such as UK bonds or Pacific equities excluding Japan. The idea of sector tables is to compare apples with apples, not oranges or pears.

Keep in mind, though, that comparisons don't always work that smoothly. Some funds are mobile. They move their asset mix over time and change sectors, usually to make the collective look better.

And sometimes the sector boundaries or even the name is altered, making it tough to follow a fund over the years. An even bigger problem occurs when funds merge. Usually, the fund with the better record continues, and the other is air-brushed out of history.

When examining performance tables, which are subdivided into sectors, keep in mind that coming in fifth in a sector of 200 is a real achievement, but coming in fifth in a sector of 10 is just average.

The ideal collective isn't one that's currently topping the table. Too many fund managers have succeeded in heading the league one day and propping it up the next. Instead, look for consistency over the years. The fund that generally beats 60 or 70 per cent of its competitors on a regular basis is the one to aim for. If past performance shows anything, it's that managers who are consistently ahead of the majority provide better value for investors than those with flash-in-the-pan genius.

Tables that show cumulative figures

The best known tables come from Standard and Poor's, Morningstar, and Lipper. You can access them online or via specialist investment magazines. Going online is easier because most sites let you sort funds according to your criteria, usually over a set time period.

These tables assume that you start off with a set amount (usually £1,000) and reinvest any dividends received after a basic tax deduction. Then they show what you'd have after six months, one year, two years, three years, five years, seven years, and ten years.

Most unit trust and insurance fund tables are on an *offer to bid* basis, meaning they deduct the up-front charge to give a true idea of the total return to a real investor. But some tables are *bid to bid*, meaning they only show how effective the fund managers have been and ignore the hit investors take from charges. Investment trust tables are less accurate because they fail to take purchase and sale charges into account, although the best will still be best.

Performance tables showing the cumulative result of investing a set sum over a set period, such as £1,000 over five years with net income reinvested, give no idea of consistency. The good or bad performance may have been due to one great or one atrocious patch nearly five years ago. Going down to the three- or one-year tables may show the fund manager in a different light altogether. A fund may show that it doubled over ten years. But scratch that a bit, and you'll see that it tripled during its first year and then lost money ever since! The reason may be due to a change of manager, a change of style from risky to cautious or vice versa, or, most likely, a change of market conditions. Some fund managers work best in fast-rising markets; others shine when stock markets are less alluring.

So if you want to judge consistency, you may want to scrutinise a different type of table – one using discrete figures (see the following section for the scoop).

Book III

Building Up Savings and Investments

Tables that use discrete figures

Besides examining tables that show cumulative figures, you can examine tables that use discrete figures. They show every single year for the past five or ten years, so you see the results for a number of 12-month periods taken individually. If your table were dated June 2004, for example, you'd have the 12 months from June 1, 2003, to May 31, 2004, as well as the year from June 1, 2002, to May 31, 2003, and so on.

Discrete figures let you judge consistency and when the out- or under-performance occurred. A fund with a ten-year cumulative performance that was superb eight, nine, and ten years ago and then reverted to average would still look good over ten years. But the discrete figures would show this up, and you could look at its average performance since then.

Out of the ten best US collective funds in 1990, five years later, only two funds were still in the best 10 per cent on a one-year discrete basis. Three were in the worst 10 per cent of all funds, and four others were below halfway. Fast-forward another ten years, and the funds were scattered all over the table. Only one was still a real winner, a second had fared well, but many of the rest were also-rans. There's nothing special about the US. The same exercise in any other country would come up with similar findings.

Discrete period tables are a powerful past performance tool that most marketing departments would rather you didn't see. As a result, discrete tables are usually less available and more difficult to find online or in publications. The easiest place to find them is in *Money Management* magazine, a monthly publication available at newsagents. It's read by both serious investors and the packaged investment trade. Over longer periods, the tortoise beats the hare.

Ways to Separate the Good Managers from the Bad

To divide the wheat from the chaff – the good fund managers from the bad – you need to ask lots of questions. If you don't get straight answers, move on to another fund.

Here are some pointers to test the fund management company and its managers:

✔ What's the fund's purpose? Is it all-out growth irrespective of risk, total caution, or something between the two?

✔ How will the company's fund managers work to fulfill the fund's purpose in practice? Look at the present holdings to see how they fit. Is the portfolio a ragbag, or does it have coherence?

✔ How frequently does the manager buy and sell? If the manager of a collective investment is forever buying and selling, costs will drag down performance. The practice may also show that the manager has no idea what to do, so the fund lurches here and there. But if there's very little activity, what are you paying for?

✔ What markets will the funds work best in, and what's the strategy for a change of market conditions? Fund management companies are great at giving you a best-situation scenario. You want to know what will happen if the worst occurs.

✔ Who's in charge? Is it a named individual, and, if so, who's the backup?

✔ What happens if the manager quits? How easy is it to get rid of a poorly performing manager? Or is there an anonymous team of managers?

✔ Does the fund management company impose on individual managers a central philosophy or even central lists of shares to buy? Or does it let the managers think and act for themselves?

✔ If the fund is new (and most marketing tends to be around new funds), then what is the purpose? What new thinking does it bring to the party that previous funds do not?

✔ What is the history and track record of the lead fund manager? Experience is important. Don't get confused by statements such as 'Managers have 40 years of experience in markets.' Some funds may have ten managers; that's an average of just four years each! Or the average may hide that there's one experienced fund manager with 20 or 30 years in the business and a team of college leavers.

Taking Ethics into Consideration

'Ethics? That's a county to the east of London!'

That's an old City joke and probably not one of the brightest. But all jokes have some element of truth, and this one says that the mainstream neither invests nor even cares about selecting investments with a green or ethical tinge.

But many private investors and members of a growing number of pension funds want to feel that their money is backing firms they approve of. Demand has grown rapidly – from a choice of only a handful of funds for many years, by January 2007 almost 90 green and ethical investment funds were open to private investors in the UK, according to the ethical investment research organisation EIRIS. The value of UK ethical retail funds in December 2005 stood at £6.1 billion, and the figures for 2006 were expected to be in the region of £7 billion; still, though, ethical funds amount to only between 1 and 2 per cent of the total value of UK retail funds.

Ethical investors want to avoid investing in companies involved in tobacco, armaments, hardwood logging, animal experimentation, nuclear power, gambling, and pornography, or in organisations that support repressive regimes or that manufacture goods using sweatshops in less-developed countries. Equally, ethical investment (often called *socially responsible investment,* or *SRI*) is buying into firms involved in positives, including alternative renewable energy, such as wind farms, and recycling and waste management. SRI also includes buying into firms at the forefront of good employment practice and those providing high-quality services or goods that clearly benefit the wider community.

Shades of green: Ethical unit trusts

SRI enthusiasts with a large investment pot can go to a specialist stockbroker for a bespoke portfolio. For the rest of us, a specialist ethical or environmental unit trust is the only serious route. These funds come in two shades of green.

Dark green funds work on an exclusion basis. Stocks of companies involved in any of the forbidden activities are dubbed *sin stocks.* They won't appear in the SRI trust portfolio, which cuts out about half the stock market. If a company moves into a sin stock zone, then the fund sells the shares.

Even dark green funds have a threshold. If a sin activity accounts for a very small proportion of a company's sales – say tobacco in a big supermarket group – then the fund managers or their ethical advisers look for positives to balance off the banned activity. (Investment supermarkets are covered earlier in this chapter, if you're wondering what they are.) Some dark green funds invite unit holders to take part in meetings that debate where the fund is going. Also note that negatives change over time. Twenty years ago, alcohol sales were a definite no-no. Now, there's more tolerance to alcohol. Likewise, attitudes to global warming and deforestation have toughened.

Light green funds take a different line. Their fund managers say that dark green funds exclude too much and too many sectors of the business world. So although they cut out the worst of the sin stocks, they're willing to look at the least reprehensible company in each sector. Searching for firms that are trying hard to upgrade their SRI credentials is known as investing in the *best in class.*

Fund managers of both shades engage with companies by telling directors how they could improve. For example, fund managers of light green funds don't sell if a company strays into sin. Instead, these managers try to use their voting power as shareholders (they, and not the actual investors who put up the cash, hold the voting rights in a collective) to change matters for the better.

Balancing act: The pros and cons of ethical investing

Some investors are passionate about SRI. They should skip this section. Others believe that a sin stock portfolio of tobacco, armaments, and pornography publishers works best. They should skip this section as well. You can read what you like into past performance statistics, depending on the period you select and the funds you look at, so it's really a matter of balancing the pros and cons of ethical investing:

- ✔ **Pro:** Stocks screened out come from dinosaur old-economy industries, such as mining, tobacco, chemicals, and armaments, where growth is more limited and government controls are stricter.

- ✔ **Con:** Fund managers can't perform their job if they're limited by non-investment criteria.

- ✔ **Pro:** SRI-approved stocks tend to be young, dynamic firms that benefit from the general move away from dirty industries toward a cleaner future.

- ✔ **Con:** SRI companies may be less profit-conscious because they're too concerned with their employees or the neighbourhood they work in.

- ✔ **Pro:** Companies that show the management abilities to move to a more sustainable way of doing business are probably brighter and less stick-in-the-mud than elsewhere.

- ✔ **Con:** SRI concentrates too much on volatile smaller companies.

Book III

Building Up Savings and Investments

The Worth of Fund Manager Fees

The collective fund industry would rather not focus on costs. Instead, it'd prefer to concentrate on benefits. But you can't separate the two. Whatever gains professional management may bring, you may lose them, and then some more, if you pay too much in fees.

The costs of buying into a fund aren't too much of a problem. They're not far different from those involved with purchasing individual shares. You generally aren't charged an exit fee from a unit trust or an insurance fund, so think of the initial charge as a round trip in-and-out fee. Many independent financial advisers rebate part of the upfront fee. Frequent traders are harder hit by entry costs.

Annual fees are where you're hit hard. These fees are often shown at 1.5 per cent, but the counting doesn't stop there. Fund fees attract *VAT* (Value Added Tax), making the real figure nearer to 1.75 per cent. Add on some compounding, and, in rough terms, a fund held for ten years would give its managers around 20 per cent of your money. Over five years that equates to about 9 per cent.

To show value, the fund manager must add more than 20 per cent to a ten-year investment and around 10 per cent to a five-year holding for the holder to break even. Managers who can consistently deliver good results with the costs handicap can congratulate themselves.

Investment Clubs: Do-It-Yourself Fund Management

This section gives you the best of two worlds – fund management *and* fun management. You can do both, getting the advantage of diversification while adding to your personal amusement level, through an *investment club,* where a group (usually not larger than 20) gets together at set intervals to pool part of their financial resources as well as share their ideas in a social environment. Several thousand investment clubs operate in the UK.

The concept can bring together friends, families, neighbours, work colleagues, and other like-minded people. All you need for membership is a mutual desire to increase your understanding of the stock market and improve your personal investing ability. Decisions are (or should be!) made democratically by members at meetings, which are normally monthly.

A minimal amount of legality is involved in setting up an investment club. The easiest source for this framework and all the other things you need is Proshare, an organisation working for wider share ownership and the UK's only dedicated promoter of services for investment clubs. Virtually all investment clubs are set up using the materials and templates provided by ProShare. Getting the basic ProShare information is simple. Log on to its `www.proshare.org` Web site.

The *ProShare Investment Club Manual*, details on the Web site, is a useful guide to setting up and running an investment club. It's based on the experiences of clubs on both sides of the Atlantic. The manual also tells you how to ensure that no one runs off with the funds. (No such incidents have yet been reported, but there's always a first time!)

All you need to begin a club is one or two friends who share your enthusiasm and are happy to recruit a couple of friends each. Even if only a handful of people are at the first meeting, you may find that numbers grow quickly, and as the idea captures people's imaginations, you'll probably find that you'll soon have plenty of members.

Here are a few additional tips and titbits about investment clubs:

✔ Gaining recruits is far easier when markets are rising. And where you meet is important. An easy-to-find location in a pub seems to work best, but some clubs use village halls or move around members' homes.

✔ Better and more sensible investment decisions tend to be made collectively. The research work involved in investigating companies can also be shared between members, as can the cost of information.

✔ Experienced investors often find that an investment club is a good way to get ideas for their own private portfolios, and in time new investors will often use the knowledge they gain through an investment club to begin an individual portfolio of their own.

Chapter 6

Scrutinising Shares and Bonds

*A*lthough share trading has been around for centuries, technology has changed it beyond recognition. It has sped up the process of buying and selling stocks, as well as reducing the cost. Hence, share trading is now far more accessible, enabling even those who aren't fabulously wealthy to dabble with direct ownership of several companies.

While share dealing has become more accessible, it's not for everyone. Stock market investing is a volatile business as your capital is at risk, so it's not for those who can't afford to lose money. It's vital to put enough cash aside to cover emergencies, and build up a spread of bonds and low-risk investments, along with a stake in a collective investment or two (see Chapter 5 for more on these), before you even contemplate buying shares in a company directly.

Despite the risk and cost of trading shares, the stock market is the place to be in the long term if you want to generate superior investment returns. This chapter shows you how – without losing your shirt in the process.

Investing Basics

More than 12 million people in the UK own *shares* – also known as *equities* – directly in a company. As a shareholder you own part of the company in which you're invested. Your investment buys you a direct share in the company's assets and future profits. If the company performs well, you may receive a slice of the profits in the form of a *dividend*, paid out twice a year. You may also make a profit if your shares increase in value while you hold them: You realise this profit (or loss) when you sell up. The *share price* refers to the value of your investment. (See 'Looking forward to returns' later in this chapter for more on this.)

The vast majority of shareholders are not sophisticated, wealthy people: Many of them fell into share ownership by accident by receiving a handful of windfall (free) shares when their building society demutualised and became a bank. Others snapped up shares in former public utilities, such as BT and British Gas, when they were privatised.

The price of a share in a company rises or falls until it arrives at a price at which one person is prepared to buy and another is prepared to sell. When demand is high, share prices rise. When demand is low, share prices fall. Demand increases when a company has performed well or is rumoured to be the target of a takeover by another company (which could be good for business and hence more profits).

It's vital that you plan to leave your money invested for several years to maximize your gains. As individual shares tend to be more volatile than collective funds, you need time to ride out the ups and downs of the market and make good any losses.

What to Consider When Buying Individual Shares

You need to know this fact up front: You can buy great shares that slump and equities in crummy companies that go up. In other words, stock markets are fickle creatures that have no permanent rules.

When you play or watch a game of football, you know that there are two halves and that each, ignoring injury time, should last for 45 minutes. You know what the object of the game is, and at the end, each team has a result, win, draw, or lose.

But stock markets are different. In particular, there are no fixed timeframes and no clear goals. Shares go on until a company ceases to exist. This could be tomorrow or in a hundred years' time. Quality will carry the day eventually, but no one knows when that *eventually* will be or even whether the company will change directions for the better or worse in the meantime.

What you have to do is look at the big-picture items, such as the economy or interest rates, that have the power to push the great to mediocrity (or worse) or the very average to a nice little earner. And you have to keep in mind that markets swing very easily between feast and famine.

Know the psychological impact of the economy

How do you feel when you get out of bed in the morning? Do you feel (Mondays not counted) confident of your job or your pension; that you can make ends meet; that you can cope with the credit card bills; and that the mortgage is not overwhelming?

Or do you worry about your job; fear for your pension payments; fret about being able to afford a holiday this year; know your credit card is ruining you; and have no idea how you're going to pay the mortgage this month?

The likelihood, of course, is that you're somewhere between the euphoria of the first description and the misery of the second. But wherever you are on the scale of being happy or sad about your money prospects, the reason is likely because of the economy. People who prosper in good times have problems when the economy turns sour, even though they continue to work as hard and budget in the same way.

REMEMBER

Markets are driven by investor psychology. When most people are happy, they have the confidence to buy shares, so shares go up in value.

Know the power of interest rates

The most important single factor in the modern economy is the interest rate. In the UK, the base rate (which sets the tone for all other interest rates) is fixed at noon on the first Thursday of each month by the Bank of England. This base rate dictates the interest level at which banks and very large companies can borrow money. In turn, it gives the cue to banks, building societies, and loan companies in calculating the interest levels they charge to consumers for credit in stores, homebuyers for mortgages, and smaller firms for the finance their businesses need. Everyone else pays more than the base rate, of course.

Interest rates also set the tone for share prices because

- ✔ **Most companies borrow.** Finance directors calculate that borrowing is fine if that cash can be used to produce a greater return than the interest bill. Suppose, for example, that a company borrows £1m at 5 per cent per year. So the company will pay £50,000 in interest. It uses the money to buy a machine or open a new outlet that produces £70,000 per year in profits. The company is now £20,000 per year better off. If interest rates fall to 3 per cent, the cost of the bank loan falls to £30,000, so now the company gets £40,000 per year in profits. But what if interest rates rise to 10 per cent? The company is now spending £100,000 per year on the money borrowed, which produces £70,000. So it's losing money at the rate of £30,000 per year. Higher interest rates mean higher costs of borrowing. If you pay more to borrow the same amount of money, your profits will drop – vice versa if interest rates fall.

  Companies that borrow the most in relation to their size benefit the most from falling interest rates. This is called *gearing up*.

- ✔ **Most individuals borrow to buy pricey consumer goods.** Companies have to sell products or services either directly to consumers or to other concerns who provide items for stores and services that deal with the ultimate consumer. When interest rates fall, consumers have more money in their pockets (called *disposable income* by economists) because they don't need to spend as much on mortgages and credit card loan costs. If rates rise, shoppers have less scope to buy goods. So higher interest rates dissuade people from borrowing, so fewer goods are sold and companies make lower profits. This is all bad for shares.

- ✔ **Company payouts look better when interest rates fall.** Say that you bought a share for £1 that (ignoring tax) pays 5p a year in dividends. At the time you bought, a cash account paid 5 per cent, or 5p, for every £1. Now say that interest rates drop to 4 per cent. The dividend stays at 5 per cent, but the cash account rate falls to 4 per cent. Share dividends are now more attractive, so investors will buy the shares themselves, pushing up the price.

- ✔ **Falling interest rates mean the next time a company needs money, it won't have to pay the bank so much.** Therefore, it will be able to carry out its expansion, making the firm bigger and more valuable.

That said, interest rates are a blunt instrument, and they hit companies in different ways.

Here's a list of sectors that are bludgeoned the most by rising rates and that get top benefits from falling rates:

- **House builders.** They're usually big borrowers in comparison to their size. What they build is nearly always sold to consumers who need loans.

- **Retailers.** When rates rise, their customers have less cash because they're paying more for mortgages. Consumers are less likely to use credit cards. Most big purchases are nonessential and can be put off. But for how long? The new three-piece suite can nearly always wait; the new generation videocam is far from necessary; and the replacement for the clapped-out fridge can be put on hold for longer.

- **Fund managers and life insurance companies.** Firms that make their living out of the stock market hate rising interest rates, which scare people off of equities. Customers put new money into savings accounts, so the fees these people get from investing other people's money fall.

- **Exporters.** Higher interest rates can often push up the value of your currency on foreign exchange markets. This is bad for exporters who get less when their foreign earnings are turned back into their home currency.

- **Banks.** Surprisingly perhaps, banks do badly when interest rates go up. They do charge more for loans, but not as many people want to borrow. Worse, banks can't hit customers with as big a gap (technically known as the *margin*) between what they give to savers and the amount they charge to borrowers.

And here are some stock market areas that should do better than average when rates are rising:

- **Food retailers.** We have to eat! In tough times, we still need a few shopping-therapy style treats, and these are more likely to be a bottle of wine or a box of chocolates than new clothes or the latest electronic goodies.

- **Discount shops.** Stores where nothing costs more than £1 or where you can buy a complete outfit with change from £50 are obvious winners in hard times.

- **Companies with cash**. Not all companies borrow. Some have big balances at the bank, so they profit if rates rise.

Book III

Building Up Savings and Investments

✔ **Tobacco companies and breweries.** People tend to smoke and drink more when they're miserable, whatever the health effects.

✔ **Importers.** Higher rates can mean a stronger currency so importers can buy their goods overseas with a smaller amount of their home currency.

Selecting Your Shares

The advantage of buying shares directly – rather than via a collective investment vehicle – is that you can tailor your investment strategy to your own needs. With a fund, the manager makes the investment decisions for you and, while this relieves some of the pressure, she could make choices that are at odds with your risk profile.

Deciding on growth or income

Choosing the right shares for you depends on your situation and attitude to risk. First you must decide what you want from your shares. There are two different types of shares, suiting different types of investor:

✔ **Growth** stocks are for investors looking for significant capital gains – a good return on their initial investment – and substantial income in the long term, rather than short term. These companies may have excellent growth prospects but low *dividend yields* because demand for shares in the company has already pushed the price to a high level relative to the dividend payout. These companies may hold onto any profits to finance future growth rather than pay out to investors.

✔ Other stocks offer high immediate **income** with big dividends, which suits investors in or near retirement. These are likely to be companies which are less impressive than growth stocks and likely to provide more steady returns. If you invest in such stocks it doesn't mean that you aren't interested in capital growth – you want this as well as income – but it isn't your priority.

Many investors aim for a mix of growth and income, and it should be possible to tailor a share portfolio to achieve such objectives. If you are wary about doing this yourself, find a stockbroker or independent financial adviser (IFA) to advise you. (See 'Choosing a broker' later in this chapter, contact IFA Promotion on 0800 085 3250, or go to www.unbiased.co.uk for details of three IFAs in your area.)

Spreading your risk

The more speculative your investments, the greater the potential reward. But you will also be taking on a lot more risk in order to try and achieve this. Weigh up whether you are happy with this before investing and do your research carefully so you know exactly how much risk you are taking on.

Although buying shares directly is usually more risky than investing in collective funds, it doesn't have to be. Be sure you *diversify* by buying shares in lots of different companies and various sectors of the market rather than stick all your cash in the shares of a single company. By diversifying, you significantly minimise your risk. If one stock performs badly, you can hope to be making gains elsewhere so it won't be a disaster.

One way of reducing risk is to buy shares in *blue-chip companies*. These are large-cap stocks, listed on the FTSE 100 (in other words, the biggest 100 companies in the UK). Large, well-established companies such as these should maintain their value over the longer term although you are likely to see steady returns rather than impressive ones (and don't forget they can fall in value as well, no matter how big or well-established the company is).

Picking more exotic investments

The real reason why many investors buy shares directly is to gain exposure to smaller companies that they can't access via a collective fund.

Be aware that the following investments are high risk and can be volatile.

If you buy direct, you can invest in:

- ✔ Shares traded on *AIM*, the Alternative Investment Market. This is a global market for smaller companies who are growing but do not wish to have a full stock exchange listing just yet. AIM is run by the London Stock Exchange (LSE) but places fewer restrictions on the type of company that can be listed than does the FTSE 100.

- ✔ Companies traded on *OFEX* (Off Exchange). These are the newest and most inexperienced of UK companies. OFEX is a quarter of the size of AIM, with 200 companies listed so there isn't much share trading. It is good for experienced and more adventurous investors with good stock-picking skills. Unlike AIM, OFEX isn't run by the LSE.

Book III

Building Up Savings and Investments

✔ *Derivatives*, which include futures, options, warrants, and convertible bonds. They enable investors to speculate and hedge their bets, but are really only for experienced investors – not novices. Derivatives are traded on the London International Financial Futures Exchange (Liffe). Go to www.liffe.co.uk for more details.

Choosing a Broker

The only way you can deal in shares is via a specialist stockbroker, a high-street bank or building society, or an online trading service (go to www.find.co.uk for a list of online brokers). The cost and type of service on offer differ widely so choose a broker carefully.

To ensure that costs don't eat into your profits, shop around for the cheapest fees. There is plenty of competition and prices are far lower than in the past, mainly down to the growth of trading over the Internet. Many online brokers charge a flat fee of around £10 for a trade, for example. Remember: The higher the commission and fees a broker charges, the higher the profits you have to make to cover these costs. Make sure the charges are explained to you in advance: If you don't understand anything, ask. (See 'Looking forward to returns' later in this chapter.)

For a free list of stockbrokers and information about the services they offer, contact the Association of Private Client Investment Managers and Stockbrokers (APCIMS) on 020 7247 7080 or go to www.apcims.co.uk. Or try the London Stock Exchange on 020 7797 1000 and www.londonstockexchange.com.

Knowing you're protected

All APCIMS members are truly independent and aren't tied to any one company. APCIMS members are fully regulated by the Financial Services Authority (FSA). Non-UK APCIMS members are regulated by the relevant authority in their own country. Members are subjected to demanding tests of their financial resources and are obliged to meet rigorous standards in terms of operating procedures and management controls. Only those registered as being 'fit and proper' are authorised to give investment advice.

As long as the firm you use is regulated by the FSA, you get access to the Financial Services Compensation Scheme (FSCS). This guarantees to cover losses of up to £48,000 if the advice you received was misleading or the adviser was negligent, and as a result you've lost money that the firm can't repay. (You can't claim compensation if you simply lose money on your investments, otherwise the scheme would be inundated!) Many UK APCIMS members also have their own insurance, which protects clients against theft, fraud, and professional negligence.

Deciding what service you need

You can choose from three types of services: discretionary, advisory, or execution only. The type you choose depends on your level of knowledge, confidence, and skill as an investor. Cost is also a factor: If you opt for anything other than execution only, you end up paying for the stockbroker's skill. The different types of service on offer are explained in more detail in the following sections.

Discretionary services

If you opt for a *discretionary service*, also known as a *portfolio management service*, you give an investment manager authority to buy and sell shares on your behalf, without seeking your approval first. It's a bit like being invested in a unit trust where the manager doesn't consult you every time she makes an investment decision. The only difference is that rather than pool your risk with thousands of investors you are the only one.

The advantage of a discretionary service is speed: Your manager can act straight away, without having to track you down first to ask your opinion. This could make the difference between a tidy profit and more average returns.

When a manager makes a transaction on your behalf, she issues you with a contract note. Your manager should also send you detailed reports on a regular basis so you can keep track of what she is up to.

If you are worried about giving somebody total free rein over your investments, you can impose some conditions in the initial contract you draw up with your broker. You could specify that your manager can't sell stocks in your portfolio, or prevent her from investing in certain companies if you'd prefer not to. You can also set limits on the maximum she can invest in a single stock.

Too many conditions and you might as well not have a discretionary service at all. It's important to find a balance that you feel comfortable with yet gives your manager enough freedom to do her job properly.

Advisory services

As the name suggests, your broker advises you on what you should buy or sell, based on your risk profile and investment objectives. She doesn't take any action on your behalf without asking first. This is the best type of service for a novice or first-time investor.

You don't have to follow your investment manager's advice or recommendations but seeing as you are paying for it, you'd be daft not to pay some attention.

Some advisory services allow you to run your own portfolio of shares and make your own investment decisions, but you also have an adviser you can contact when you need information on a particular share. You can call them and ask whether you should buy or sell. If you have some experience of investing, this may be more useful to you than a more comprehensive service: Work out what suits you best.

Execution-only services

The cheapest way of buying and selling shares is via an *execution-only service*. This service works exactly as its name suggests: When you want to buy or sell a share, you contact your broker and instruct her to execute your order. The broker offers no advice and does not manage your portfolio at all.

You're charged dealing costs, which are usually 1 to 1.75 per cent of the value of each deal, or around $10-15 per deal.

You can access execution-only services over the telephone or Internet, but it's worth remembering that a growing number of traditional brokers also now offer this service in response to increasing demand. You should shop around for the cheapest price, as you require an extremely basic, straightforward service – there is little added value. What you get is access to the stock market.

Even if you don't buy and sell shares online, it's worth checking out the Internet, particularly if you are trading execution-only, because there are thousands of free pages of research notes and information about stocks. These can be useful in helping you make your investment decisions.

If you opt for discretionary or advisory services, assessing the risk of particular shares is the responsibility of your investment manager – after all, that is what you pay her for. But if you opt for execution only, you will have to assess your own level of risk and decide whether a particular share fits in with that – or not. Any mistakes are down to you.

Considerations with discretionary and advisory services

Discretionary and advisory services rely on at least some face-to-face contact between you and a stockbroker and the broker's need to find out exactly what you want out of your investment strategy. So you may need to do some shopping around to find a stockbroker who's right for you. Areas to look at include

- ✔ **Size of portfolio.** Make sure that your personal wealth is well within the broker's parameters. If the broker wants a minimum £25,000, then having £25,001 isn't much help because you could easily fall below the line if markets turn against you. Ask what happens if your fortune shrinks either through bad decisions or because you choose to spend some of your money.

- ✔ **Level of service.** Consider the experience of your contact or account executive, as well as whether e-mail alerts and regular newsletters or other forms of stock recommendation will be sent out. Find out whether the broker offers a portfolio based on unit trusts, investment trusts, or exchange traded funds.

- ✔ **Costs.** This shouldn't be your first consideration, but it's essential all the same. Excessive costs can wipe out gains from a clever investment strategy. Very excessive costs can turn good decisions into instant losses.

- ✔ **Protection from churning.** Unscrupulous brokers try to earn more from your investments by over-frequent buying and selling. You could agree to a limit on their trading activity.

Considerations with execution-only services

Investors who want to make up their own minds don't need advice, but they do need a broker to carry out the transaction. Most dealing is on the Internet.

The advantages of online dealing are obvious: being able to buy and sell anytime, from anywhere; seeing how your portfolio is performing in real time; and getting up-to-date prices, charts, and news. But drawbacks exist too. The obvious one is backup if your computer or Internet connection fails. Some online brokers have a telephone alternative. In addition, security can be a worry, although most sites are now encrypted to a high degree. In fact, very few instances of online frauds and security lapses have occurred. That said, you may still want to check out the nearby sidebar about online security.

Of greater concern should be your need to use one broker for all your transactions. This isn't a legal necessity, but the way online brokers operate and charge makes it difficult to have more than one broker. Many online brokers offer terms that make it cheaper to stick with one organisation. You'll have to set up a bank account if you do anything more than occasional dealing. And it's very difficult to set up portfolios that reflect your trading at another broker.

Online charges are low because very little paperwork is involved. You won't normally receive certificates because your portfolio will be in a nominee account with Crest (the London Stock Exchange centralised settlement system) so the broker can instantly buy or sell on your behalf. Most online brokers insist on a nominee account and an associated bank account so that cash for purchases can move out without fuss and you have a receptacle for money you generate on a sale.

Most online brokers hold your money in an account in *their* name, so the company you're investing in doesn't know that you're a shareholder. You may lose your rights to shareholder material, such as annual reports (but you can usually find these online at the company's Web sites), to voting privileges, and to shareholder perks. If these points are important, your broker may offer you an individual nominee account, but it could cost more.

Additional considerations

If you're considering an execution-only service, here are some additional points to consider:

- ✔ **Computer compatibility.** Not all stockbroker sites support Mac- or Linux-based machines. Some sites don't work that well on Netscape or other non-Microsoft Internet connections.

- ✔ **Trading range.** All brokers cover mainstream UK shares. But if you fancy the tiny UK companies on OFEX, traded options, or overseas shares, then your choice may be more limited.

- ✔ **How many extras you get.** Look for easy-to-use EPIC code finders (these are the letters used by professionals – for example, Abbey National is ANL), a good stock history facility, easy access to company statements and stock exchange filings, research reports, and analyst ratings. Are these things free?

- ✔ **How much money you need to open a trading account.** Some brokers are only interested in the very wealthy and will demand you deposit big sums. But all will want something to cover your trades otherwise they cannot deal for you. The days when a 'gentleman' would be allowed to run up big bills are over, except maybe for the most blue-blooded brokers and their wealthiest clients.

✔ **Extra charges.** These charges may be for statements of dividends and capital gains (or losses) so you can file your annual tax return more easily. There may also be a fee for sending proceeds of sales to another account.

✔ **Whether the broker is set up to offer another service channel.** Does the broker offer phone or post service if the Internet breaks down or if you want to deal occasionally on an obscure overseas market?

✔ **Whether the service is in real time.** Is your decision acted on at once, or does it depend on e-mail? It matters if you're a frequent trader.

✔ **What interest, if any, the broker pays on your cash balances.** You will have cash balances with your broker either because you have deposited cash ahead of purchases or because you have cash from a sale of shares or bonds. Either way, many brokers offer you interest while the money is under their roof. But don't expect too much. Often it is a derisory 0.5 per cent or less.

✔ **Whether there's a fill or kill facility.** With this kind of arrangement, you set a maximum price for a purchase and a minimum acceptable price for a sale. If the broker can't fulfill your instructions, the deal is automatically terminated.

Most brokers have a sampler service, meaning you can try out the site on a dry-run basis. You may find that you're willing to sacrifice some services and pay more for a broker that offers a site that's easy to navigate. Once you click Go, you've dealt, so don't make mistakes.

Buying and Selling Shares

Once you've decided to buy or sell a share, you call your broker and instruct her to carry out the transaction on your behalf. You can do this over the telephone or Internet.

As well as telling your broker how many shares you want to buy or sell in a particular company, you also state the price you are willing to accept (if you are selling) or pay (if you are buying). If this price is not available in the current market, your broker waits until it is reached.

Proving your identity

The transfer of the proceeds of criminal activity into the financial system – known as *money laundering* – is big business and the Financial Services Authority, the City watchdog, is working hard to stamp it out. Criminals try to hide the origins of their cash by using a false name and address to set up a bank or building society account, and to buy or sell shares, amongst other things.

To crack down on this, you will be asked to provide proof of identification when trading in shares. When you sign up with a stockbroker, you will be asked for proof of your name and address by a recent utility bill or council tax bill. To prove your name, you will usually be asked for your passport, driving licence, or a tax notification from HMRC. Because a passport or driving licence usually has a photograph, it is not easy to forge them.

If you are applying to buy or sell shares via the post or Internet, rather than face to face from a broker, you should send certified copies of your passport or driving licence, rather than posting the originals – as they could get lost. Certified copies are photocopies which a person of professional standing – a solicitor, bank manager, accountant, independent financial adviser, teacher, or doctor – has stated to be genuine copies of the originals. He or she should have seen the original and should write on the copy 'I hereby certify this to be a true copy of the original'. She should then write her name, address, and profession on each copy and sign and date it.

Once your broker has concluded the deal, you receive a contract note with details of the transaction. This includes the share price that you bought or sold at and the cost of the transaction.

What happens next depends on whether you are buying or selling shares:

- ✔ If you're buying, you've got three days to pay the necessary money to your broker so that she can complete the deal.
- ✔ If you're selling, you must ensure your broker has access to your share certificate(s) so that she can hand these over to the buyer's broker and receive the cash you are due within three days.

Holding Your Shares

Once you've bought your shares, you can hold them in one of three ways. The method you choose depends on how frequently you trade, how much you want to retain formal legal rights in the companies you've invested in, the choice of services on offer by your broker or bank, and the cost.

The three choices are:

- ✔ **Paper:** If you hold share certificates, you receive dividends, annual reports, and all other communications directly from the company. When you sell, you must send your certificate to the stockbroker or bank who undertakes the transaction. Check how much your broker charges you for holding your shares as certificates because dealing charges may be higher for such transactions than a nominee account or CREST, the electronic system.

- ✔ **Nominee account:** Your shares are registered in a nominee company's name, rather than yours. This is set up by your broker or bank to administer the holdings and transfer of shares for lots of investors. It cuts down on paperwork and the administration involved in owning shares in lots of companies. You remain the beneficial owner of the shares although your name doesn't appear on the company shares register and dividends are paid to the nominee company, which pays them to you. Important documents are sent to the nominee company rather than you, such as the Annual Report and Interim Statement: You will have to make arrangements to receive these. For further information on the regulatory aspects of nominee accounts and the rules they must abide by, contact the Financial Services Authority, the City watchdog, on 020 7066 1000 or go to www.fsa.gov.uk.

- ✔ **Personal membership of CREST:** CREST is the electronic system devised by the London Stock Exchange. Being a personal member is more straightforward than having a nominee account as it allows you to retain legal ownership of your shares. You also benefit from the CREST settlement system, which is faster than paper transactions. Your broker or bank still carries out the necessary settlement and transfer arrangements on your behalf. You receive all reports and statements direct from the companies you have invested in, but can't shelter your investment for tax purposes in an ISA through this route. For more details, contact CRESTCo on 020 7849 0000 or go to www.crestco.co.uk.

Book III

Building Up Savings and Investments

If you stay in paper rather than embracing technology and moving to CREST, the commission for dealing in trades is higher. Personal membership of CREST costs £10 a year but not all brokers or banks pass this onto investors. Clarify whether you will be charged for this, as well as any other costs, before signing up with a broker.

Looking Forward to Returns

Owning shares, or equities, is an excellent way of building up investments for the future. They produce superior returns to cash or bonds over the long term. As a shareholder, you are entitled to a share of any profits the company you are invested in makes.

Equities produce two types of return:

- ✔ **Capital growth:** When you sell your shares, you will hopefully realise a substantial profit, although there is a risk that this may actually be a loss, depending on market conditions.

- ✔ **Income:** Shares pay out dividends if the company performs well. When the company doesn't perform well, dividends will fall or may not be paid at all. There are no guarantees.

Compounding your investment by reinvesting your dividends will enable the value of your portfolio to grow more quickly.

Generating dividends

As well as the increase in value of shares over time, you may also receive an income in the form of dividends. This is the company's profits or *earnings* that shareholders receive as a thank-you for investing in the business. Dividends are usually stated as an amount in pence per share.

Dividends are usually paid every six months so you get an *interim* dividend and the *final* dividend each year. If you are a registered shareholder, you'll get a cheque for your dividend or it is paid directly into your bank account, if you request this. This is usually easier as it saves it going missing (see the sidebar 'Tracking down unclaimed dividends').

You also get a voucher showing details of your holding, the dividend per share and the tax that has been deducted and paid to HMRC. You need to hang onto this voucher to prove the tax you've paid and to work out how much more you need to pay if you're a higher-rate taxpayer (see 'Paying duty' later in this chapter for more details).

Tracking down unclaimed dividends

If you move house and forget to notify your stock-broker or the company in which you own shares, you may miss out on some dividends because your new address isn't on the share register. If this has happened to you, you can contact the Unclaimed Assets Register to find your missing dividends. Write to 6th floor, Cardinal Place, 80 Victoria Street, London SW1E 5JL, tel 0870 241 1713, or go to www.uar.co.uk.

To avoid dividend cheques going missing in the first place, arrange to have them paid by direct transfer to your bank account. Not only is this safer, it saves the hassle of having to pay a cheque into your account and then waiting for it to clear, which can take several working days.

If you hold *preference shares* you get a fixed rate of dividend paid in bi-annual instalments. You get preference over *ordinary* shareholders – hence the name – so when the company is short of cash, you are more likely to get a dividend than ordinary shareholders. Preference shares provide more security than ordinary shares.

If the company you have invested in goes bankrupt, preference shareholders also have more rights than ordinary shareholders.

Understanding charges

Although transaction costs are higher if you invest in shares directly rather than through a unit or investment trust, competition among brokers and from online share dealing services has dramatically reduced the cost. It's a competitive marketplace so shop around for the best deal.

There are various types of charge you need to budget for:

- ✔ **Commission:** Brokers charge commission when you buy or sell shares. It is usually a percentage of the amount you are investing or receiving or it may be a flat fee.

- ✔ **Fixed fees:** Brokers offering investment management services often recoup their costs via an ongoing annual administration fee. Even if you don't make any transactions during the year, you still have to pay this fee. Some brokers charge higher commission on each trade they advise you on, rather than a fixed annual fee.

- ✔ **Commission plus fees:** Some firms have a tariff that combines both charges.

Don't let charges be your only, or even main, consideration when choosing a broker (unless you are opting for an execution-only service). Otherwise, they should be considered to be important but only as part of the overall picture. Remember, you often get what you pay for.

Paying duty

On top of brokers' charges and dealing costs, you must also pay stamp duty to the Government on all share purchases. This is 0.5 per cent of the value of each purchase, with a minimum payment of £5, and is rounded up to the nearest £5. So if you are buying £1,000 worth of shares, you will have to pay stamp duty to the Government of £5.

Book III

Building Up Savings and Investments

Working out employee share ownership

Part of the reason for the growth in share ownership is the introduction of employee share ownership plans: These enable you to own shares in the company you work for. There are plenty of tax advantages available, with some schemes allowing you to buy shares at greatly reduced rates.

The Save As You Earn (SAYE) or Sharesave scheme enables you to save between £5 and £250 a month (which is deducted from your salary) with your employer for three, five, or seven years in order to buy shares in the company at the end of this period. The price is set at the start of the scheme and can be as much as 20 per cent off the market price at the time.

Alternatively, there are profit-sharing schemes, enabling your employer to give you shares free

of tax and National Insurance contributions. You aren't able to receive shares to the value of more than £3,000. Your employer sets up a trust in which you must keep your shares for at least two years. If you leave them in there for at least three years, you can retain or dispose of them without paying any income tax or National Insurance.

The other way of owning shares in your employer is via a company share option plan. This offers the option to buy a set number of shares at a stated price and at least three years in the future.

For more details on these schemes, see Chapter 4 in Book II, or go to www.hmrc.gov.uk/shareschemes.

You don't always have to pay stamp duty: For example, it isn't charged if you are buying shares in Germany, Luxembourg, the Netherlands, or Sweden. You also don't pay it if you are selling your shares.

Capital gains tax (CGT) is payable on any profit you make when selling your shares. But everyone has an annual allowance of $8,200 (for the 2004–05 tax year), so you only pay CGT on any profit above your allowance. In the unlikely event that your profit exceeds this, stagger the sale of your shares over more than one year (so you can take advantage of more than one annual allowance), or transfer shares to your spouse to enjoy double the allowance.

You also pay income tax on dividends. All dividends carry a *tax credit* of 10 per cent, which means this much tax is deducted before you receive your payment. You may have to pay further tax, depending on what sort of taxpayer you are:

- ✔ **Non-taxpayers:** Don't have to pay any more tax but can't claim back the 10 per cent they've paid either.

- ✔ **Basic-rate taxpayers:** There is no more tax to pay.

- ✔ **Higher-rate taxpayers**: You must pay a total of 32.5 per cent tax on dividend income. As you are taxed 10 per cent at source, the remaining 22.5 per cent must be paid via your tax return. Go to www.hmrc.gov.uk for more details.

Keeping Track of Your Shares

Knowledge is power and this is particularly true when it comes to deciding when to buy and sell your shares. If you are inexperienced, you should pay a stockbroker or investment manager to provide advice, while more experienced investors can get away with an execution-only service.

Whether you pay for advice or not, you should do your own research into the market. This will enable you to evaluate your broker's advice (if you get it) and decide whether it's right for you, or simply make the right decisions if you're choosing your own shares.

The first place to start your research is a national newspaper. The *Financial Times* is still the bible on share price information, as it's dedicated to business and investment. In addition, all of the broadsheets and most of the tabloids have business and City pages, with plenty of rumours, share prices, company information, and tips. There are also plenty of investment magazines and papers: These provide more in-depth coverage but won't carry the latest share prices as a daily newspaper can. Try *Investors Chronicle*, *Money Observer*, *Moneywise*, or *Bloomberg Money* for plenty of information on shares. You could also listen to Radio 4's *Money Box* programme.

The Internet is the most useful resource for private investors. There are several sites specialising in private investment and personal finance matters, such as Interactive Investor (www.iii.co.uk), Hemscott (www.hemscott.net), Motley Fool (www.motleyfool.co.uk), and Digital Look (www.digitallook.com). There are also several news services available with the latest information that might affect your share price: Bloomberg (www.bloomberg.co.uk), Citywire (www.citywire.co.uk), and Reuters (www.reuters.co.uk).

Book III

Building Up Savings and Investments

All listed companies must issue an Annual Report and accounts. As a shareholder, you are legally entitled to receive a copy, unless you hold your shares through a nominee company. You can arrange with your nominee account holder to get you a copy.

Getting to Grips with Bonds

If you are looking for income rather than growth, but want a better return than you can get from cash, you may want to consider government or corporate bonds. These can be bought from a stockbroker, bank, or the Bank of England.

Understanding how bonds work

A *bond* is a form of debt issued by a government or company. Bonds are a bit like IOUs: As a bond purchaser, you lend an amount of money to the government or company for a set period of time. In return, you are guaranteed a fixed income, known as the *coupon*, payable twice a year. When the bond matures, you should get your initial investment – your *capital* – back, though this isn't guaranteed as bonds aren't free of risk. You may get back more than your original capital or less.

Bonds return little in the way of capital growth so they are best suited for investors looking for income rather than high returns. They are ideal for the retired, although younger investors shouldn't write them off as they are less volatile than shares and provide more protection (bondholders are higher in the pecking order than shareholders if a company goes bust). It is worth including bonds in a balanced investment portfolio.

The amount you invest in government or corporate bonds depends on your attitude to risk. As a general guide, most experts suggest you use your age to determine the proportion of bonds in your portfolio. For example, if you're 30 years old, around 30 per cent of your portfolio should be in bonds.

Although bonds are issued for a specified period of time, you don't have to keep the bond until maturity. In fact, most investors buy and sell them ahead of the maturity date, trading them like shares. So while they have a fixed price when they are issued, this can fluctuate up and down according to demand from investors.

Bonds are issued in bundles of £100. So if a company agrees to pay you a set income of £10 per year, the yield is 10 per cent. If you trade the bond in the open market and sell it for £110, the income is still £10 per year but the yield has dropped to approximately 9 per cent. But if demand for the bond is low, so the price falls to £90, the yield rises to approximately 11 per cent.

Demand for bonds, and therefore the price they fetch, is influenced by the yield and rate of return investors can earn elsewhere. If interest rates are high, for example, savings accounts pay more and bonds become less attractive.

Companies issue different types of bonds. These include:

- **Debenture stocks:** secured against specific company assets.

- **Unsecured loan stocks:** pay higher yields than debenture stocks but aren't secured against the company's assets.

- **Convertible bonds:** give holders the right to swap them for shares in a company at a set price or before a specified date.

You can pool your risk when it comes to corporate bonds. Investment companies offer *bond funds* that invest in a series of individual company bonds. Expect to pay an annual management fee for a professional manager to run the fund. There are several types of bond fund available, specialising in investment-grade, high-yield, and overseas bonds. Some also specialise in emerging market bonds. (See Chapter 5 in this Book for more details on these types of investment.)

'Do I need bonds?'

You need bonds if you think they will outperform equities and other investments, such as property or cash. But you also need them if

- ✔ You're a cautious investor who wouldn't be happy with share price ups and downs.

- ✔ You have a defined aim for your money, such as you must pay education fees on fixed dates or you want to give a set sum to a child on graduation or reaching a certain age.

- ✔ You have investment funds for your retirement years, and you're within five to ten years of stopping work. Some plans allow you to move gradually into bonds from shares. This arrangement helps prevent your pension from being hit by a sudden fall in share values.

- ✔ You have retired and need certainty of income from your savings.

'Tell me the big differences between bonds and shares'

Companies that need to raise cash can issue equities – or *shares* as they're better known. They can also issue bonds (called *corporate bonds* to differentiate them from those put out by governments) and get the same amount. So what's the difference?

- ✔ Shares are permanent. Once issued, they carry on until the company ceases to exist, either because it goes bust, is absorbed by another company, or buys in its own shares to cancel them. Equally, investors have no time limit on their equity holdings (except for a few specialised investment trusts).

- ✔ Bonds usually (although a handful of exceptions exist) have a fixed life, which is shown on the paperwork you get. You know when they'll stop paying you a regular amount and give back the original cash instead.

Book III

Building Up Savings and Investments

- ✔ Shares pay dividends, which can go down as well as up. Sometimes dividend payments are missed altogether. The rate of dividend depends on the profits of the company and what it needs to do with the cash it generates.

- ✔ Bonds pay interest (known as the *coupon* because old bond certificates used to contain small squares that holders had to cut out every six months to claim the payment). This interest is fixed whether the company is doing well or not. Bond interest must be paid before any share dividends are issued.

- ✔ Shares give holders a say in the company proportional to their holding. Shareholders are the legal owners of the company, and they get to attend an annual general meeting where they can quiz the board.

- ✔ Bondholders, in most circumstances, have no ownership or annual meeting voting rights. Bondholders are only active when the bond issuer (company or government) is in financial trouble.

- ✔ Share prices can be very volatile.

- ✔ Bond prices vary less from day to day.

- ✔ Shareholders have to worry about how well the company is doing. Share prices depend on profits.

- ✔ Bondholders have to worry more about credit risk – the chance that a company will do so badly that it'll default on loan repayment or on an interest payment.

What Makes Bond Prices Go Up and Down

Put your £1,000 savings in the bank, and your money stays at £1,000. What you generally don't know, though, is how much interest you'll get. Most bank accounts have variable rates. Put the same money into a gilt or other bond, and your £1,000 could be worth more or less the next day. But you'll know how much interest you'll get. With a bond, your interest is fixed, but your capital value is variable.

Like everything else in stock markets, bond prices are driven by supply and demand. When people want to buy, the price rises. And vice versa.

Working out why people want to buy or sell shares is complicated. So many factors hit the average company that it's a real juggling act to get them all in the air and then make some sense out of them when they land. But bonds are simpler. Investors look at three main factors:

- ✔ Interest rates in the economy
- ✔ Credit risks or the chances of the bond issuer defaulting on obligations
- ✔ The remaining life of the bond

The interest rate gamble

Investors buy bonds to provide interest payments. Purchasing bonds is only worthwhile if the rate of interest is better than the rate you're likely to get from a bank or building society over the life of the bond.

It has to be better because buying a bond costs money in stockbroker fees, and the danger always exists that the bond will fall from the level you bought at or, if it's not from a stable government or company, that the issuer will go bust or have financial troubles. And even if you're happy about who you're lending your money to, the longer a bond has to run, the greater the chance that interest rates will change or something unforeseen will happen.

Bonds offer fixed interest and a fixed repayment of the nominal capital on a future date. But although they are a lower-risk investment, they aren't risk-free. Bonds are a balance between their capital value and the interest rate. When interest rates fall, bond prices go up. When interest rates rise, bond values fall. This scenario is like a seesaw, where both ends can't rise or fall at the same time.

When interest rates fall

Suppose that interest rates are 10 per cent and you buy a bond offering a 10 per cent coupon for £100. You get £5 twice a year, or £10 in all.

Now suppose that interest rates fall to 5 per cent. Bond values go up when interest rates fall, so the value of your bond to new investors would be twice as much, or £200. They'd continue to get the same £10 per year interest, but it would only work out at £2.50 every six months, or £5 a year, for each £100 they spent on the bond. You're getting twice the amount of interest compared with a new investor.

Now you have a choice. You can continue to enjoy your larger fixed-interest cheque every six months, getting more than you'd get as a new bond pur-chaser. Or you can cash in on your good luck. A new investor would pay £200 for your bond and get the fixed £10 per year. You can collect a £100 profit to reinvest elsewhere.

Book III

Building Up Savings and Investments

When interest rates rise

Suppose that rates rise from the 10 per cent at which you bought the bond to 20 per cent. No one would pay £100 for your bond because they could invest that money to earn £20 per year. So because the interest rate has doubled, your bond is only worth half as much. You have the tough choice of taking a loss on the capital value or accepting that you'll get far less interest than a new investor.

Interest rates often go up because the inflation index that measures rising prices increases. When you have high interest rates and high inflation, the paper value of your bond goes down. You're given a double hit:

✔ Interest levels rise so the capital value falls on the seesaw principle.

✔ The real value of each fixed payment and the final redemption amount also drops in purchasing terms because each currency unit (such as the pound, dollar, or euro) buys less at the shops.

The way around the interest rate gamble

Rising prices are bad news for bonds. The £100 they pay back for each £100 shown on the certificate isn't worth as much as when the bond was issued. A 5 per cent inflation rate halves the real value of money every 14 years.

And how do governments react to inflation? They try to control it with rising interest rates, also really bad news for bondholders.

Still, there's a way around this problem for investors who fear that rising prices will wreck their bond calculations. It's called the *index-linked gilt*. It's like an ordinary gilt because it pays income every six months and has a set future date for repayment – anything from a year or two to more than a quarter of a century. But that's where the similarity stops because each half-yearly coupon and the final repayment are linked to inflation using the government's retail prices index (RPI) as a measure.

Here's a simplified example (meaning it ignores compounding and the eight-month delay between the RPI figure's publication and its effect on your money): You put £10,000 into an index-linked gilt with a 10-year life with a 2.5 per cent pay on day one. Your first year's interest works out at £250 before tax. After the 10 years of 7 per cent annual inflation, prices have doubled. Your final dividend will be £500 per year, and you'll get back £20,000.

Sounds like magic, so what's the catch? You start off with a far lower interest rate than on a conventional bond, so it could take years of rising prices to catch up. And if price rises drop to nothing or go in reverse, you'll lose out.

The UK government is changing the RPI measurement to a consumer prices index of the type used in Europe. This ignores housing and mortgages and so should result in a lower headline figure. But the RPI will continue to be calculated for many years to come and RPI-linked government bonds will carry on using the RPI for calculations.

The credit rating conundrum

If only life for bond purchasers was as simple as second-guessing where interest rates and prices are due to go over the life of the bond. But, alas, life for bond purchasers isn't that simple. And that's why armies of highly paid analysts look over each bond with superpower spreadsheets.

Besides interest rates in the economy, a big factor for bond investors is whether the bond issuer will pay out the money on time or even at all. Bonds are issued by all sorts of organisations from the US Treasury to biotech or dotcom companies with a 1 in 20 chance of making it.

A bond is only as good as its issuer. There are no guarantees you can call on. In the past, bonds issued by big nations such as Germany, Russia, and Argentina all failed. They became worth as much as wallpaper, except for a few attractive-looking certificates sold to collectors who framed and displayed them. (I [Tony] have a Russian bond certificate from 1916, which I bought for £1. The frame cost a lot more.)

Alphabet soup: Looking at credit rating codes

You can get some help with working out which bonds have a higher credit rating. Agencies such as Standard & Poor's, Moody's, and Fitch look at each bond issuer and the terms being offered, and then the agencies come up with a risk rating code.

The code isn't difficult to decipher. You just follow the alphabet. The highest level is AAA (or triple A), followed by AA, A, BAA, BA, BBB, BB, B, with plenty more points all the way down to D. Plus and minus signs are used as well, showing whether a bond has been upgraded recently and is now less risky or whether it has been downgraded into a higher peril situation. Each rating agency has its own little quirks, but the higher the letter in the alphabet and the more letters used, the lower the risk is.

Triple A means a minimal risk. The US and UK governments and the biggest and best-financed companies pick up AAA. All the A grades are good, and some of the Bs are acceptable as well. Lots of bond investors draw the line at BBB, which, they say, is the lowest level of investment-grade bonds.

How low can you go?

At the top end of the quality scale, credit ratings are only for the ultra nervous. The gap between AAA and AA or A isn't really that crucial for most bond buyers. But anything below BBB is speculative. Investors have to pay more attention to junk bond ratings as the risk of loss is real. So how low can you go?

✔ BB is probably still fine, but there are long-term fears over the issuing company or government. The company is more likely to be a bit late with the cash rather than not pay out at all.

✔ B should be okay as well, but if the economy or the business turns down, you may face problems. There are no guarantees, but you should get your payments. You can expect to get around 3 per cent per year extra on these bonds compared with AAA.

✔ CCC, CC, C is for caution. There's a current problem in the business or country issuing these bonds. An improvement on what you see now needs to occur before you can rest easier. You can expect around 4 to 7 per cent extra per year on these bonds.

✔ DDD, DD, D is for distress, disaster, and default. Default is the bond dealer's shorthand for anything going wrong. The bond issuer is already in severe trouble, has missed out on payments, and may be heading toward an early death. D-style bonds are only worthwhile buying if you're prepared to take a big gamble. You should aim for at least 10 to 15 per cent per year more here to make up for the ultra risky rating.

All the rest of them, many bond investors say, are undependable rubbish. With C grades, you run a reasonable risk of problems, and with D grades or ungraded bonds, you're gambling. You may miss a payment or two, or you may never see your money back on the redemption date. But note that bond experts don't call these bonds rubbish. Instead, they call them junk bonds (or, more politely, *high yield* bonds).

The higher the rating, the lower the interest rate. Investors want something extra to make up for the dangers of a poor credit rating but are willing to give up interest for the security of a top rating, such as triple-A or AAB. The rating looks at how long the bond has to pay out. A government or company may be good for a year or two, but will it still be paying out in 20 or 30 years' time? Risk ratings are regularly revised by agencies. What starts out at AAA can fall to junk levels while rubbish can rehabilitate itself and move up the scale.

Junk bonds: Where there's muck, there's brass (maybe!)

Why invest in junk bonds when the rating agencies say they're below investment grade? The obvious answer is the risk/reward equation. Junk bond investors hope to spot bonds that are due for an upward re-rating, that should push prices up.

Issuers of junk bonds pay higher interest rates to make up for the risk. And you can often buy the bonds at far below their face value. You pay, say, £30 for a £100 face-value bond from a company that may or may not live long enough to repay investors as it should. If the company survives, you've made £70 plus bigger interest payments all the way along the line. If it fails completely, you've lost your £30, but if you've had a few years of above-average payments along the way, then your loss doesn't look so bad. It might even work out that you've received your £30 back and more.

One junk bond may be a recipe for disaster. But put together a diversified collection in your portfolio, and there's a good chance that some winners will more than make up for the losers.

Look at the following example portfolio to see how a diversified collection can sometimes work out in your favour. Assume that all the bonds have five years left to run and that you've invested £1,000 face value in each. The examples ignore tax and compounding of reinvested income.

- ✔ Bond A is bought at £60 for each £100 (£600). It pays 8 per cent nominal and survives intact. After five years, you have interest totalling £400 (£80 × 5) plus a £400 profit (£1,000 that you get less the £600 you paid). *You make £800 in all.*

- ✔ Bond B is bought at £25 for each £100 (£250). It pays 4 per cent nominal and lasts for three years before going bust. You collect £120 in interest but lose your £250 capital. *You lose £130 overall.*

- ✔ Bond C costs £50 for each £100 (£500). It pays 6 per cent nominal. But the issuer gets into trouble and never pays you a penny. The bondholders form a committee and force the firm into early repayment of the bonds at £75. You receive £750. *You make £250.*

- ✔ Bond D costs £70 for each £100 (£700). It pays 5 per cent nominal. The credit agencies decide to take the bond issuer off the junk list because it has new management, and the agencies put it on the quality list. The 5 per cent is about right for the market, so the price shoots up to £95. You sell and take a profit. *You make £175.*

- ✔ Bond E costs £10 for each £100 (£100). It pays nothing and goes bust within weeks. *You lose £100.*

Some winners, some losers. But here the gains more than outweigh the losses.

Credit ratings apply to bonds from countries as well as companies. Countries can go bust or have problems repaying interest or debts. But some countries, such as former parts of the Soviet Union or nations in Africa, are young and don't have much of a credit record, so they get low marks. But Russia has climbed out of junk status to BBB, just enough to ensure investment grade funds will accept it. Always remember bond buyers are naturally cautious. If they weren't, they'd be buying something racier.

Book III

Building Up Savings and Investments

'What is this? No date is listed for repayment!'

Some UK government bonds don't have a date for repayment. That's because the government never has to pay them back – ever! These bonds have wonderful names, such as *Consols* or *Treasury After '61*, but the best known is *War Loan,* which was raised to help pay for the costs of the First World War.

If you buy these types of bonds, you should get the same return forever. Their prices go up and down according to interest rates at the time.

But although the UK government guarantees your interest, it makes no promises to repay your bond in the future. However, if interest rates fall so low that the government is paying out more than it has to, then it might repay the bond. The small print says it can.

War Loan was a disastrous investment for the patriots who bought to help out the inter-war government. But the big interest rate falls of the 1990s made big money for those bold enough to take a plunge. Some investors tripled their money.

Working Out Government Bonds

Governments issue bonds to help fund their spending. Bonds issued by the British government are known as *gilts* and are listed on the London Stock Exchange. They are safer than corporate bonds because it is highly unlikely that the government will go bust or default on the loan. The British government has never failed to make interest payments on gilts or to pay back investors' capital at maturity.

Because gilts are rated more highly than bonds issued by companies, they also produce lower returns. Some gilts pay high rates of interest with a low capital return; others pay low interest but you get a higher capital return. The type you opt for will depend on whether your priority is income or growth.

There are two ways to deal in gilts:

✔ You can buy them by auction direct from the Debt Management Office when they are newly issued. There are no dealing charges but you must invest a minimum of £1,000. Go to www.dmo.gov.uk for details and application forms.

✔ You can buy or sell gilts via a stockbroker or bank. There is no minimum investment but there are dealing charges, so it's uneconomic to spend less than, say, £1,000.

Using Computershare's service tends to work out cheaper than buying or selling through a stockbroker or bank. Complete the relevant form, available on the website (www.computershare.com/uk/investor/gilts), and send it with the appropriate payment to Computershare Investor Services, PO Box 82, The Pavilions, Bridgwater Road, Bristol, BS99 7NH.

There is no limit to the amount you can invest in gilts. Returns are normally paid gross of tax but tax is still payable on them. Higher-rate taxpayers must do this via their self-assessment tax return, while basic-rate taxpayers can ask for returns to be paid after tax has been deducted. Capital gains are tax free.

The several different types of gilts are described in more detail in the following sections.

Conventional gilts

The simplest and most common form of government bond is the *conventional gilt*. Conventional gilts mature on a specific date, on which you get the final coupon payment and return of your capital. They can be short (under five years), medium (five to 15 years), or long (over 15 years).

Conventional gilts are denoted by their coupon rate and maturity – for example, 5 per cent Treasury Stock 2005. The coupon rate usually reflects the market interest rate at the time of the first issue of the gilt, so there is a wide range of coupon levels available in the market at any one time.

The coupon indicates the cash payment per £100 that the holder will receive per year. So if you have £1,000 of bonds at 5 per cent Treasury Stock 2005, you will get two coupon payments of £25 each (5 per cent of £1,000 is £50, divided into two payments of £25 each) paid six months apart.

Book III

Building Up Savings and Investments

Double-dated conventional gilts

Double-dated conventional gilts have a band of maturity dates. For example, the first maturity date may be three years and the final maturity date five years. The government can choose to redeem these gilts on any day between these maturity dates, subject to three months' notice. When the coupon is higher than the prevailing market rate, it is in the government's interest to redeem on the first maturity date and refinance the gilt at the prevailing rate. Double-dated gilts are fairly rare but may work out to be a good investment if you can find them.

Index-linked gilts

Index-linked gilts account for around a quarter of the government's gilt portfolio. Coupon payments and your capital investment are adjusted in line with the UK Retail Price Index (RPI), which means inflation is taken into account, unlike conventional gilts.

Undated gilts

Eight undated gilts are still in issue – the oldest remaining gilts in the government's portfolio. Some date back as far as the nineteenth century. The redemption of these bonds is at the government's discretion but they have low coupons (because of their age) so there is little incentive for the government to redeem them.

Gilt strips

Strips are Separately Traded and Registered Interest and Principal Securities. By *stripping* a gilt, you break it down to its individual cash flows – for example, a three-year gilt has seven individual cash flows: six coupon payments and the payment of the original capital – and then trade the coupons and repayment of capital as zero-coupon bonds (a bond that pays no interest and matures at face value; investors get a return because the bond is sold at a big discount). Strips are very flexible and can be used to design an income flow tailored to your needs. Gilts can also be reconstituted from all of the individual strips, but not all gilts are strippable.

Chapter 7

Investing in Bricks and Mortar

· ·

· ·

*B*uy to let has been the fastest growing investment class in the UK over recent years. From virtually nonexistent in the mid-1990s, it has grown, along with prices for houses and flats, to more than rival many collective investment schemes. And if you believe some of the media, buy to let is the most talked about subject at dinner parties, other than the prices of people's own property. After all, who wants to discuss their sagging shares when they can boast of their burgeoning buy to let portfolios?

This chapter gives you the need-to-know basics about investing in a buy to let property – the pros and cons as well as the mortgage, location, tenant, and tax issues. In addition, this chapter introduces you to the idea of investing in commercial property, in case you want to go that route.

The Pros and Cons of Buying Property to Rent

Buying to let involves buying a second (or third or fourth or sometimes even more) property in addition to the one you live in yourself. You rent this extra home to a tenant, and if all goes well, you earn rent once a month and see your initial capital investment rise as well. You gain an income and increase your wealth at the same time.

The popularity of buy to let has grown because

- Investors are fed up with shares that don't deliver.
- Investors want an investment with a solid feel.
- Investors are looking for an investment they can get involved in.
- Investors don't want to be tied to expensive fund managers who fail to deliver.
- The whole idea appeals to many people who want to operate their own spare-time business.
- Mobile people need somewhere to live but don't want to buy a property that they may have to quit at short notice.
- Property prices in some areas have soared out of reach of first-time buyers. Because they must live somewhere, they rent.
- Interest rates for borrowers have become attractive, especially because lenders now see this activity as mainstream and no longer charge a huge interest rate premium for buy to let loans.
- Estate agents have set up units to deal with rented property.
- It's far easier now to borrow in order to purchase a property to rent even if you still owe money on your original residence.

Buy to let is not guaranteed. You may find yourself without a tenant, and you may lose money on the property because prices can fall as well as rise.

Some other potential drawbacks exist as well:

- You can't get your money out in a hurry. Selling a property may take a year or longer, especially if house price rises stall or go into reverse.
- You need to be hands on, even if you employ an agent to deal with tenants.
- Getting a portfolio of properties is very expensive. Most buy to letters just have one property, so there's no diversification.
- You can unbalance a financial strategy by putting too many of your investment eggs into one buy to let basket.

A move into buy to let is far bigger than any move into equities, bonds, or cash. You can't change your mind in a few months' time. You may also have to do all the work yourself, including checking and cleaning the property between tenants.

Before considering affordability or whether buy to let is the right type of investment for your needs, use the negative points of buy to let as a checklist to see whether the idea even appeals to you.

The Affordability Issue

Very few buy to let investors can afford to pay cash for their property purchase even though in some, admittedly not too desirable, locations, flats and houses can still cost under £20,000. And even if you could afford to pay cash, you should never tie up so much of your capital in a property that it leaves you without an emergency fund or the ability to buy into other investment assets if you think the time is right. So most buy to let investors borrow the money.

The price you see or even agree to is not the property's real price. You have to pay for stamp duty (in most cases on properties starting from £125,000, although for certain rundown areas on properties starting at £150,000), legal costs, possibly a mortgage arrangement fee, a survey, and if you're letting a furnished property, an allowance for everything from curtains and chairs to cookers and cutlery. These extra expenses typically soak up at least £5,000 and represent money you can't recoup. You may also find that borrowing to fund these extra start-up costs is difficult.

Before you can think about borrowing, you need to start with how much you can put down as a deposit and how much will be soaked up by other costs. And until you know what price range you can afford, you can't go out to look at potential investment properties.

Book III

Building Up Savings and Investments

The Buy to Let Mortgage

Lenders will want to look at the colour of your deposit. There are no 100 per cent buy to let loans (and if there were, the interest rates would be prohibitive).

How much can you borrow?

Banks and building societies calculate a figure called *Loan To Value (LTV)*, which is the largest proportion of the property price that they'll lend you – the rest comes from you as a deposit. The maximum LTV generally varies from 75 per cent to 90 per cent. Because you fund the balance, you need cash of between 15 per cent to 30 per cent of the property value.

If you have £20,000 to put up as a deposit, the least generous lender with a 75 per cent LTV would add £60,000, so you could buy a property costing £80,000. The lender with the highest LTV 90 per cent) would convert your £20,000 into a loan of £180,000, so you could look at properties costing £200,000, or more than twice as much as the meanest lender's offering.

A higher LTV gets you a bigger property bang for your deposit bucks. But larger deposits often mean lower interest rates.

How much will you actually get?

Your deposit and the LTV set a maximum. But you may not get that amount.

When you apply for a loan to buy a roof over your own head, the lender looks at the property itself to check its condition, the proportion of its value that you want to borrow, and most importantly your ability to repay the debt from your earnings. A typical formula is 3.5 to 4 times the main earner's salary (or only earner if that person has no partner) plus one time the second earner's or 2.5 to 3 times their joint earnings.

Because many buy to letters already have a mortgage banging hard against the limits of their earnings, buy to let lenders use a totally different way of judging how much they offer you because they see this as a business proposition property.

Instead of looking at how much you earn, buy to let lenders judge how much the property will earn for you. Most banks and building societies are now involved in this market, although some specialise in buy to let loans. *Moneyfacts* magazine is a good first source of information on who is lending and their basic terms.

The simplest formula is where you tell the lender how much rent you expect each month. Suppose that the amount is £500 per month, or £6,000 per year. The lender then calculates how big a loan that monthly or annual amount would back.

Suppose that interest rates stood at 6 per cent. Then your £6,000 per year would, on pure mathematics, pay back enough each month to back a £100,000 loan – irrespective of your personal income. But no lender is stupid enough to go for that amount. Although interest rates have been falling for a decade or more, there's no guarantee that they'll continue to do so over the 10- to 25-year life span of a typical buy to let mortgage.

On top of that are nasty things called *voids*, which are months where you have no tenant and hence no income, or where your tenant has disappeared while owing more than the tenancy deposit. And to cap it all, there are other, unexpected, costs of ownership, such as repairs and maintenance.

Lenders insist that the rent more than covers the mortgage so you don't run on empty if something goes wrong. Typically, the rent will have to be anything from 1.3 times to 1.6 times the monthly outlay, a number called the *cover*.

A high mortgage cover sounds mean, but it's not. It protects you and gives you a cushion against the unexpected.

Buying to let is a business proposition. So there will be risks along the way.

Items to consider about the mortgage

Before you contact a mortgage company or mortgage broker for a buy to let loan, take a look at the following points. They'll save you time and stop dodgy mortgage firms trying to pull the wool over your eyes.

- ✔ **Fixed versus variable.** A fixed rate is where every payment for a set period is identical. Variable rates go up and down with interest costs in the economy at large. The fixed rate gives you security of payment for a period but sometimes at the cost of inflexibility and slightly higher interest rates. You can often set a fixed rate to match a tenancy agreement. Doing so is a good idea because raising a rent for a sitting tenant can be difficult.

- ✔ **Fees.** Some mortgages are fee-free, so you have nothing to pay initially. But this setup may be offset by higher costs later on. Otherwise, expect to pay anything from £250 to £1,500 (usually around £500-£600) as a fixed fee, or between 0.5 per cent and 1.5 per cent of the loan.

- ✔ **Minimum amount.** Few lenders lend on properties worth less than £30,000. If you want a portfolio of low-price dwellings, you must find a specialist lender, likely to be more expensive, or fund your purchases either from cash or by re-mortgaging your home.

- ✔ **Maximum loans** Many lenders are happy to lend on more than one property provided that you can come up with a deposit and finance the loan through the rent. Generally, lenders put a ceiling on the number of properties so that you can't have more than five or ten, and some lenders also limit the total lending on your portfolio at anything from £250,000 to £2.5 million.

Buy to let is considered to be a commercial activity. Buy to let loans aren't covered by either present or proposed Financial Services Authority rules, which offer safeguards against misleading sales techniques to mortgage customers who are buying their own home.

The Property Yield: A Comparison Tool

Buy to let is not a magic way to make money. You need to compare its attractions against other asset classes, such as cash, bonds, or shares.

The easiest way is to look at the *gross yield*, what you get in rent before you spend on financing a loan or calculating the lost interest on cash you've tied up in the property.

For an example, take a £100,000 property rented at £500 per month. That's a £6,000 total for the year, so the yield should be 6 per cent.

But hold on. You may be spending on property management, and you always run the risk of voids. It's far better to estimate the rent on ten months per year. Now in this example, the annual rent falls to £5,000 and so the yield drops to 5 per cent.

The yield on property goes up and down with the property value after you've bought. If a property price doubles, your yield halves. And if the value goes down by half, your yield doubles. So far, this arrangement is like a bond. But property has one big difference. When prices rise, you may be able to increase the rent over time. And if the value falls, you may have to cut your rental expectations back to ensure that you find a tenant. High property prices make renting more attractive or, often, the only way to find a home for cash-strapped people.

Serious buy to letters go in for several properties. If you can't afford the deposits all at once, buy one property, hope it goes up in value, re-mortgage it to free up the capital for a new deposit, and keep repeating this exercise. But don't forget that the more properties you have, the greater your exposure to losses if prices fall or interest rates rise.

Location, Location, Location

Why is a two-bedroom flat in Belgravia some 20 times more expensive than a similarly sized flat in Barnsley, Bolton, or Blackburn? The answer is in the property dealer's mantra of location, location, location. People pay not just for what they get but for where they get it.

Much may depend on what type of tenants you'll feel happiest with. You can provide fairly basic accommodation to students, up-market premises to top managers from abroad on short-term UK contracts, or somewhere in between.

There's no substitute for walking around an area, sizing up the amenities, looking at estate agents, and viewing properties. You can sometimes get a discount by buying *off plan*, buying from a developer who's selling units in a new or refurbished property before the building is completed (and sometimes before it's even started).

Buying off plan can be buying blind. Don't do so just because there's an advertised incentive.

Matching tenants to the property's location

Here's how to match your preferred group with the right property type:

- ✔ **Students.** They want low-cost premises near their college or university. You may be competing with subsidised halls of residence. Expect a fair amount of cosmetic damage, supply low-cost furniture (preferably from secondhand shops), and factor in long vacations, in which case you may have no tenants. You may also have costs involved in installing fire and other safety regulations, both to satisfy the educational body and the local council.

- ✔ **Employed young people.** These are the ideal target for many landlords. Look at areas where parking is easy and that have good employment opportunities. This group prefers to be near city centres and not stuck on a distant estate.

- ✔ **Families with young children.** Go for properties with gardens near schools. Public transport and access to shops can be important.

- ✔ **Professional high earners.** They want upscale properties and will pay for them. Many of these people will come to you through company deals, such as a firm renting your property for a long period and then installing members of its staff who need a roof.

Buying a house rather than a flat may involve costs in keeping gardens tidy, especially in void periods. You won't be popular with neighbours if you let gardens run wild. In some cases, local authorities can oblige you to keep the place in good order.

Book III

Building Up Savings and Investments

Considering properties in poor condition

Investment properties are cheap, but the term is generally a euphemism for houses and flats in poor condition. They can be profitable, however, provided that you pay for a full survey and then factor in the costs of bringing the property to a habitable condition. The period of repairs will bring in no rent but will involve outlays.

Here are a few additional, important points to keep in mind:

- ✔ You may have difficulty getting a mortgage until the repairs are carried out.

- ✔ Some investment properties are in rundown areas where you'll find it hard to attract tenants, as well as miss out on future property price rises.

- ✔ Some unscrupulous firms have been advertising a scam with *managed investment properties*. Here's how the scam works: You buy a number of low-cost dwellings for £100,000 or £150,000. The properties may be worth £15,000 each on the open market, but you end up paying £30,000 a time. The extra goes, according to these firms, to bringing the properties up to a minimum standard, including central heating and new wiring, so they can be let to housing associations. Sounds good, doesn't it? The scam is that there are no housing associations prepared to buy and the firms themselves carry out no repairs, leaving you with rubbish properties. Meanwhile the firms disappear with much of your cash.

How to Attract Tenants

Your buy to let is worthless without tenants. You also must be sure that the tenants are the type of people you want. The easiest way to find them is to hand the whole job over to a firm of estate agents who'll manage your property, find tenants, interview them, and take security deposits. The firm does these tasks in return for, typically, 15 per cent of the gross rent each month. Some agents specialise in finding companies that will engage in a long-term contract.

The estate agent's cut can be the difference between profit and loss. Successful buy to let investors need more than financial skills. You're managing a business, so if you hand management duties over to a third party, you need an agent you can trust on a long-term basis.

If you don't want to hire an estate agent to find tenants for you, consider using the suggestions in this section.

Advertise for them

Take a close look at the for-rent pages in your local newspaper. Doing so will give you some idea of how similar properties are priced. You can always go out and look at those properties or send a suitable friend if the flat or house is likely to appeal to a specific age group. You can then come up with a competitive and attractive advert.

Some people are put off if you only give a mobile phone number. Tenants are as entitled to know who they're dealing with as landlords.

Contact local employers

Big local firms and educational establishments are always looking for suitable properties for new staff to rent. Some of the companies may want to enter a long-term contract in which the company does all the work, including repairs, in return for a fixed-rent agreement.

Use word of mouth

Often, people ask proprietors of local corner shops and news agents whether they know of places to rent. This is a cost-free advertising opportunity. Libraries and some supermarkets also have free noticeboards.

Use the Internet

A number of sites list property for rent. But you should probably use this avenue as a backup, not a first method of attracting people.

If you list your property for rent on the Internet, draw up an application form for potential tenants to provide their name, current address, and work details. This form could be part of the online offering. Alternatively, get prospective tenants to e-mail you and then you can send them a form. Always probe to see whether the potential tenants have any financial problems. They should have a bank account (or pay a large up-front deposit in cash). In addition, always ask for references but always check them out thoroughly. Don't take them at face value because forging references on a computer is easy.

The Tax Issue

As far as HMRC is concerned, buy to let is a business and not an investment. You have to pay income tax on your profits from rentals, but you can deduct interest and the cost of adverts, repairs, insurance, and council tax. What's left is added to your other income.

You're allowed to make a loss. And in some circumstances, losses can be carried forward against future profits.

You need to keep records. And you must send a balance sheet to HMRC if your gross receipts exceed £15,000 in any tax year.

Many people employ an accountant (the fees can be offset against tax). But always agree on terms first.

If or when you sell, you'll be liable to capital gains tax on any profit. A capital gains tax taper exists, so the longer you keep the property, the lower the tax is proportionately. Because buy to let is a business, the taper is more attractive than in standard investments, such as equities. In some circumstances, you can deduct losses. (Yes, there will be setbacks at some time, so don't get too complacent or optimistic.)

You have to voluntarily tell HMRC that you're engaged in buy to let. The tax people won't accept excuses such as 'I was waiting for a tax form' or 'I didn't know I had to declare this'.

Commercial Property Investments

Commercial property, such as offices, factories, warehouses, and retail premises, has been a lower-risk investment with a good return. But most of the investment has been indirect, through pension funds and with-profits policies.

Commercial property ownership is generally structured so that you need a minimum £50m to £100m to be considered a player – and even more to get a really diversified portfolio. However, some commercial property investment opportunities exist for those whose fortunes lack most of the zeroes of the standard sums in this investment area, usually via a specialist collective vehicle.

What's good about commercial property?

In a nutshell, here are the benefits of investing in commercial property:

- ✔ Rental yields are up with higher-risk corporate bonds but with less likelihood of financial problems.
- ✔ Rents tend to increase; some properties have automatic increases every five years.
- ✔ Demand for top-class property remains high. Property buyers like the term 'primary' which can be used for a location or the quality of the building, although the two often go together as you tend to put up the best buildings on the most attractive sites.
- ✔ Overseas investors like the solidity of UK property.
- ✔ Property values tend to at least keep up with inflation.

What's bad about commercial property?

In a nutshell, here are the drawbacks of investing in commercial property:

- ✔ It's illiquid, so buying and selling can take ages.
- ✔ Returns are very susceptible to interest rates. A substantial increase can wreck the best forecasts.
- ✔ So-called secondary properties, the rubbish that top-class tenants avoid, can be difficult to let. If you want to imagine 'secondary property', think of run down shopping parades, decrepit factories, or office blocks that no big organisation would want to be based in.
- ✔ Types of property can go out of fashion. Buildings can become obsolescent or subject to new, and expensive, environmental regulations.

Book III

Building Up Savings and Investments

How to invest in commercial property

You may already have some exposure to commercial property through insurance-based with-profits or managed funds. Many packaged UK investments are also likely to have a percentage of property company shares in the portfolio. But if you want more, ways are available to get them other than going out and buying yourself an office block or retail development.

Property company shares

A number of property-owning companies are listed on the London Stock Exchange. Buying and selling their shares works the same as with any other quoted equity.

Some property-owning companies have enormous portfolios, but others focus on one type of property, such as office blocks or out-of-town retail parks. Bigger firms tend to concentrate on prime property, which they rent to top household-name firms. But a number of firms go for secondary properties, hoping to make more money out of cheap buildings that they rent to less-attractive tenants. Secondary property is generally more volatile.

Investors look at two factors beyond the portfolio constituents:

✔ **Dividend yield.** This is usually higher than the market average, with the highest returns coming from property firms that go for secondary properties. The normal investment rules apply. If the dividend yield is high, then the capital gains are likely to be lower for the same level of risk.

✔ **Discount.** This is the gap between the value of the property firm's underlying portfolio less borrowings and its stock market capitalisation. The stock market value should generally be lower than the worth of the buildings owned.

Property unit trusts

These are standard unit trusts offered by a small but growing number of investment groups to those wanting a specialist fund. They are a mix of direct investments in property, property shares, and cash. The minimum investment is usually £500 or £1,000. You can have your money back without notice when you want to sell.

Real estate investment trusts

The newest route into commercial property investment is through a REIT or Real Estate Investment Trust, which invests in income-producing properties, These were introduced at the beginning of 2007 and can be bought and sold on the stock market through a broker like any other investment trust.

REITs have various attractions for investors, but one of the main ones is that they are very tax efficient. As long as a REIT distributes 90 per cent of its income to shareholders, it doesn't have to pay income or capital gains tax on its portfolio – leaving more money available to invest and generate returns. If you're looking for a property investment that will pay a good flow of income and is easy to trade, then a REIT is the obvious choice – but remember, because they are traded as shares, they will be affected by stock-market movements even though the underlying investment is real estate.

Property bonds

Property bonds take a minimum £1,000 to £5,000. They're insurance based but with only enough life cover to convince HMRC of their status. So this life cover is as little as possible, usually just a nominal 1 per cent of their value. There's also a bid-offer spread of around 5 to 6 per cent. Much of it goes to the seller in commission, so don't forget to demand a rebate.

These bonds usually invest in properties rather than shares or cash. In some cases, investors may have to wait up to six months for a withdrawal because the fund must sell properties if too many people want their money back.

Property bonds have nothing to do with *holiday property bonds,* a form of timeshare where you can use a holiday accommodation in proportion to your holding. Holiday property bonds aren't intended as a serious investment.

Enterprise Property Zones

Enterprise Property Zones (or EPZs) are areas where the government is anxious to attract new commercial buildings, so it offers forms of tax relief to do the attracting.

Investors with a minimum £5,000 to £10,000 can buy into these projects and gain tax relief on their investment. Investors who borrow to raise the cash can also set off interest payments against tax.

The rental income is paid without any tax deduction, but it must be declared.

The tax relief that comes with EPZ investment sounds like a good idea. But there's no guarantee that the property will be profitable, and investors usually sign up for 25 years. That's a very long time, especially because no clear or easy exit exists. You could be left with a property lemon. This option is for serious investors with serious money and is best approached by taking serious advice from a professional property person!

Book III

Building Up Savings and Investments

Chapter 8

Making Exotic Investments

*I*f you have a nervous disposition, you may want to skip this chapter. It's all about how you can literally lose not just your shirt but everything else you own. It covers the one investment opportunity in this book from which you can end up with *minus nothing,* because not only can your investment money go down to zero, but you also can end up owing cash over and above those losses. Very financially painful!

That sounds unbelievably awful, and it can be. So why should you grit your teeth and read this chapter? Because these types of investment, which many people now call *alternatives,* are becoming more publicised. They include contracts for difference, spread bets, traded options, and covered warrants, and because of their more prominent publicity nowadays, you need to know about them if only to say no to their apparent charms.

Don't confuse these types of investment with fashioned alternative investments, such as art, wine, or vintage cars. These are the new style of alternatives – investments based on stock, commodity, and currency markets where you go nowhere near buying the shares, metals, or foreign exchange contracts on which they're based. Note, too, that some of these deals are called *derivatives* because they're derived from real financial securities.

All the financial schemes in this chapter are for experienced investors who can afford to make some losses. We reckon you should always stick to what you know. It's better to be safe than sorry, whatever the adverts for these products make out!

What fans and critics say about alternatives

Fans of alternative investments say that they're cheaper and more flexible than conventional investments. These enthusiasts claim that alternative investments are the future, often pointing to overseas countries where their use is more widespread.

Detractors say that alternative investments offer rapid, high-risk routes to financial wipeout; that you should treat them no differently than a bet on three-legged Sad Ken in the 3.30 at Epsom; and that although they give the veneer of investment sophistication, the only winners are the bookies, specialist dealers, and others who sell these schemes.

Getting into Gear for a Faster Ride

The big difference between the investments in this chapter and elsewhere in this book is *gearing*, an arrangement in which a set sum of investment money potentially works harder for you but involves greater risk.

To understand gearing, look at the difference between someone on foot and a cyclist. A pedestrian may cover 5 kilometres in an hour. But pedalling a bike, the same person may ride 10, 15, 20, or more kilometres in an hour. The difference is due to the fact that the cyclist has gears that transform the leg movement into greater distance once their physical effort goes through the mechanism to the back wheel. And the higher the gear used, the further the person will go. The energy expended may be the same as when walking or even less if the cyclist freewheels.

Logically, it'd be better if everyone cycled. However, bikes have disadvantages and higher risks. It's easier to fall off a bike than to fall down as a walker. The gears are great when the going is good on the flat or downhill, but life can get tough on steep, uphill climbs. You get hit worse by bad weather. And cycling has costs.

With financial gearing, you buy an alternative or derivative of a share, a share index, or bond for a fraction of its price. If the value of the underlying security goes the way you want, your investment moves up very rapidly in percentage terms. Get it wrong, and you can face total wipeout (or worse).

To help you understand the concept, consider a simple example of a winning alternative investment scenario:

✔ **Conventional investment:** You have £1,000, and you buy 1,000 shares in a company called ABC PLC at 100p each. The shares go to 110p. You sell and earn 10 per cent on your money, giving a £100 profit. Ignoring stamp duty, dealing costs, and the spread between bid and offer prices, you now have £1,100, a 10 per cent gain.

✔ **Alternative investment:** Instead of buying the shares, you go for a derivative where you only put down 10 per cent of the purchase price. You now have the equivalent of £10,000 worth of shares in ABC PLC for £1,000. The shares go from 100p to 110p. But instead of having 1,000 shares, which have gained 10p, you now have 10,000, so your profit is £1,000. Again ignoring costs, your £1,000 has turned into £2,000, a 100 per cent gain.

Now look at how you can lose:

✔ **Conventional investment:** Your £1,000 buys 1,000 shares in ABC PLC at 100p each. The shares fall to 90p. You sell. You have lost £100 but still have £900 left. Not good news but not a total disaster, either. You could've instead held on, hoping for an eventual uplift and taken the dividends as well.

✔ **Alternative investment:** Your £1,000 buys 10,000 shares in ABC PLC at 100p each. The shares fall to 90p. You've now lost 10,000 times 10p, or £1,000, so your investment is worthless. Most alternatives don't pay dividends, and they have time limits, so you can't hold on for the longer term looking for a rebound.

Now suppose that the shares fall to 80p. With all alternative products, you lose your money. But with some alternative products, such as spread betting, it gets worse. You not only give up your £1,000 (equal to the first 10p of the loss on each share), but you also owe the spread bet company £1,000 for the second 10p loss per share. If ABC PLC suddenly goes bust and the shares are worthless, you have to pay the whole £10,000!

Book III

Building Up Savings and Investments

Hedging Your Bets

If gearing is one side of a coin, where you increase your risk and, hopefully, your reward, then hedging is the other side of the coin. *Hedging* is just like insurance: You protect what you have by paying a premium to someone else. If all goes well, you continue to enjoy the gains from your investment. But if worse comes to the worse, the person who accepted your payment has to make good the losses. With hedging, you dampen down or eliminate your risk in return for losing part of any potential gain.

Suppose that your 10,000 shares in ABC PLC are worth £10,000, and you'll need that money in three months' time to buy a car. The easiest route would be to sell now and put the £10,000 into the bank. But you think that ABC shares will soar upward over that time, although, naturally, you can't be sure and you don't want to jeopardise your car purchase.

The solution is to hedge. A variety of ways are available to do so, but in essence they come down to two methods. One way is to exchange the hoped-for gain for a premium from another investor by agreeing that you'll sell the shares for 110p each in three months' time. You'll gain 10 per cent on the present price (which is more than the interest you'd earn in the bank), and the purchaser gets them for 110p each instead of the 130p or so that they may cost in three months' time. In this scenario, you lock in your present value and make a profit.

Another way is to pay someone a premium such as 10p a share in return for a promise that the person will buy the shares from you in three months' time at 100p. You get your 100p less 10p no matter how far the shares fall. But you structure this deal in such a way that you get the full price if the shares rise – less the 10p premium you've already paid.

Trading Traded Options

Here's the good news about options: Unlike with some of the fancy stock market structures in this chapter, with options you can't lose more than you invest. And you can make a lot of money in a short time. The bad news? Many (probably most) option trades expire worthless. But then what do you expect from a geared investment?

What is an option?

An *option* is a promise, backed by the stock market that you can buy or sell a set number of shares (nearly always in parcels of 1,000 shares) in a company at a fixed price between the start day and the expiry date. You can generally choose between a number of expiry dates and a number of strike prices. A *strike price* is the value the shares have to hit before your option has any value. Remember that while this promise comes from the market, it does, of course, need another investor (or investors) to be on the other side of the deal. The company whose shares are involved will know nothing of all this.

Options are available on all sorts of investments, including bonds, shares, and currencies. Equity options are the best known and the most likely to be chosen by private investors.

Worldwide, you can choose from thousands of options. In the UK, there are traded options on nearly all the shares in the FTSE 100 index, as well as on the index itself.

You have the right but aren't obliged to buy the shares no matter what happens, and that's what makes options more user friendly than many other derivative investments. If you don't like what's going on in your option, you can abandon it (and your option money). But if everything's going well, you can lock in your gains. You don't have to wait until the option date comes up.

Options can be traded at any time before expiry. They are worthless on expiry, so the nearer you get to that date, the less valuable they become – a process called *time value,* where you pay for hope. The amount you pay for the option is called the *premium*, and it goes up with time value.

What are call prices and put prices?

Each option series for an underlying share has two sets of prices:

- ✓ **Call prices.** These prices are for investors who think the shares will go up. They give the right but not the obligation for an investor to buy the underlying shares.

- ✓ **Put prices.** These prices are for investors who think the shares will go down. They give the right but not the obligation for an investor to sell at a pre-agreed price.

A call option example

Say that phone group BT has options that expire on a fixed date each month. You can buy up to one month ahead or for longer periods. A snapshot on one day with a stock market price of 194p per share shows that you can choose a 180p or 200p strike price. The 180p strike price is 'in the money' for call option purchasers because the underlying shares are more valuable. The 200p strike price is 'out of the money' and has no immediate value because it's higher than the current stock market price.

If you want to buy the call option at 180p expiring in one month's time, it costs 17.25p per share. So if the share price between now and then tops 197.25p, you have a profit.

If you think the price will go up even further, you will do better buying the 200p strike price series. Here, a one-month call option costs 5.5p. If BT tops 205.5p over the next month, you win. If not, your loss can't be greater than 5.5p a share.

Investors who want to take a chance on BT over longer periods pay more for their options – around 2p for an extra month.

A put option example

If you hold the shares and want to put a floor under the price, then take out a put option. Doing so gives you the right but not the obligation to sell so you receive a set price. With the BT example, guaranteeing a right to sell in around a month at 200p costs 11p a share.

Have a look at some possibilities:

- ✔ The BT price falls to 150p. You win! You collect 200p for each share less the 11p premium. So you get 189p.
- ✔ The BT price stays unchanged at 194p. You lose. You get 200p for each share less the 11p premium. So you end up with 189p.
- ✔ The BT price soars to 250p. Your right to sell is worthless. You lose 11p per share, but some investors think this worthwhile to buy insurance-style protection. The share price might have gone the other way.

Always study how traded option premiums move for a wide number of underlying shares before dipping your toe in this particular water. Options that have expiry dates each month rather than every three months are more heavily traded and tend to have lower dealing charges. Many strategies exist, but all involve either gearing up your investment or hedging your risk.

Strategies involving selling shares you don't own can bring limitless losses.

What is option volatility?

Winning on traded options requires having a good feel for the direction of a particular share. Will it go up or down? But you also need to know about *volatility*, the amount the shares jump around. High-volatility shares have unstable prices. The more volatile a share is, the greater the chance of the option making money but the higher the cost of the option. It's like motor insurance. The 20-year-old with the Ferrari pays a lot more for cover than the 60-year-old with a Ford Fiesta because the younger person is more likely to claim.

You never own the shares or other securities with traded options and other forms of derivative trading. So you have no shareholder rights. You don't get dividends either.

Taking a Gamble with Spread Betting

Died in the wool gamblers used to bet on which of two moths would hit the light bulb first and frazzle. But long gone are the days of just betting on winners in horse or dog races or football matches or moths. Nowadays, there are bets on the total number of runs scored in a cricket match or points total at rugby. Both of these bets are irrespective of which side scored them. You can take a punt on when the first goal will be scored in a soccer match or the number of players sent off for foul play in a month. You can take bets on house price moves. And you can bet on shares, bonds, currencies, stock market indexes, and other financial matters.

If there are numbers, there can be a spread bet. Whether the numbers are total points scored in a rugby match or a share price, all spread betting works in the same basic way:

1. **The bookmakers try to second-guess the most likely result.**

   Perhaps it's a total of 50 points in a rugby match or a probable price of 50p for a share in a week's time.

2. **The bookmakers create a spread either side.**

   In this case, it could be 47–53, which is called the *quote*.

3. **The punters must decide to be either long or short of the spread.**

   If they go *long,* they think that the match will be more high-scoring or the share price will be higher than the bookmakers' quotes. If they go *short,* they're thinking of a low-scoring game or a poor share price.

4. **The punters bet so much per point or penny.**

   There might be a £10 minimum.

5. **When the match is over or the share bet reaches its expiry date, the punters look at the result.**

In this example, assume £10 a point bet:

- ✔ Say that the result is 60. Those who were long win. They multiply their stake by the points over 53 to calculate their gain. So they collect £70. Those who were short lose. The bookmaker starts counting at 47, so they have to pay £130.

- ✔ Say that the result is 40. Those who shorted the bet receive £70, and those who went long lose £130.

- ✔ Say that the result is 50. All bets are lost, and all participants owe the bookmaker £30.

Book III

Building Up Savings and Investments

Spread betters on financial instruments can lose limitless amounts. They may have to put up margin money each day to cover losses if they want the bet to continue to the expiry date. But punters can take profits or cut losses whenever they want. They can also re-set limits one way or the other. Spread betting is leveraged, so there can be big gains and big losses without putting up money to buy the underlying investment.

Worried that the value of your home will drop or that your dream property will soar in price well out of reach? By taking out a spread bet on the Halifax House Price Index, you can protect yourself. If you worry that property values will soar, take a spread bet on the index rising. And if you think that prices are about to plummet, take a bet on the index falling. Of course, the Halifax index is an average across the country and won't exactly replicate what's happening to the prices that concern you. And know that if you get it wrong, it could cost you more than your shirt!

Getting Contracts for Difference – for a Different Kind of Deal

Contracts for difference, or *CFDs* as they're known to stock market insiders, are a low-cost route for frequent share buyers who want a deal with, well, a difference. Instead of buying a share and holding it, the CFD investor comes to a deal with a CFD provider (usually a specialist broker) that at the end of the contract, one side or the other will pay the difference between the opening price of the contract and the closing price. Some 20 per cent of all UK equity deals are now through CFDs.

You can trade CFDs on most large UK companies, share price indexes, and many foreign companies. You can take a position in a price fall as well as hope for a rising price. And because all you're paying is the difference, you get the advantage of leverage.

At the start of the contract, you may only have to put up a small proportion of the contract value. This amount is often around 10 to 20 per cent, depending on how volatile the share is. So expect a lower percentage for a dull utility share and a higher amount for a technology stock. But because your losses could eventually exceed this margin money, brokers often insist that you deposit a minimum £10,000 before trading.

How CFDs work

Suppose that you decide shares in ABC PLC look cheap at 100p and expect them to rise over the next week. You want £10,000 worth. Instead of paying dealing charges of around 1.5 per cent, plus stamp duty, plus the cost of the underlying stock, which would add up to £10,200, you go to a CFD broker. Here, you put up 10 per cent (ABC is a big company that's not volatile), and you 'borrow' the other £9,000 from the CFD provider in return for interest at a pre-set but variable level.

For a week, this arrangement might cost £10. You'll probably pay 0.25 per cent commission on the whole £10,000 in costs (£25). There's no stamp duty.

A week later, ABC shares can be sold for 120p, putting the value of your holding up to £12,000. You receive a £2,000 profit less £30 selling commission (that's 0.25 per cent of £12,000). Subtracting this amount plus your interest and buying costs gives a total profit of £1,935. (Note, though, that if ABC shares had gone down to 80p, your bill would've been £2,000 plus all the £65 costs.)

You can also profit if you correctly guess that a share price or an index will fall in value. This scenario is called *short trading*. Suppose that you think ABC PLC is going to fall in value. If you're right, you gain. If you're wrong, you lose. It's simply the preceding example turned on its head!

Book III

Building Up Savings and Investments

The benefits and drawbacks of CFDs

Here are some plus points and drawbacks of CFDs:

- ✔ You can go long (expect the price to rise) or short (expect it to fall).
- ✔ You have a wide range of shares and indexes to choose from.
- ✔ Commissions are low.
- ✔ You leverage your stake – bigger profits but bigger losses.
- ✔ There is no stamp duty.
- ✔ You are gambling so you can forget capital gains tax or offsetting losses against capital gains elsewhere
- ✔ You can hold CFDs for very short periods.
- ✔ They are a bad value for long-term investors.
- ✔ You receive dividend payments where applicable.

✔ Investors who go short must pay the dividend to the broker.

✔ Not all brokers allow you to place a *stop loss*, a device that automatically closes a losing position to prevent even more of your cash from bleeding away.

✔ A few brokers allow free trading.

✔ If you buy CFDs, the Financial Services Authority will consider you to be a professional and experienced investor, even if you aren't. So you can say goodbye to a large slice of your consumer protection.

Don't ignore the commission and other costs, even if they sound small. CFDs are intended for short-term trading. But frequent traders face huge costs. If you have a £10,000 deposit and trade on 10 times leverage (that's playing with £100,000), each buy and sell round trip will cost you 0.5 per cent of the amount you're playing with at most brokers. That's £500. If you trade just once a week for a year at this level, you end up paying your broker an amazing £26,000 plus interest (say £6,000). You've got to be really good to make money after all of this.

Understanding Warrants

Warrants have been around for years, at least in their traditional form. They often came with investment trust launches as a free gift for the original investors (this sort is rare now because investment trust launches are few and far between). The traditional warrant gives the right but not the obligation to buy a set number of shares in the underlying trust (sometimes in other sorts of quoted concerns) for a fixed sum during a set period each year for a number of years.

A typical launch deal might be to offer one warrant for every five shares bought at the original 100p. A £1,000 investor would get 200 warrants. These warrants then give the option to buy the underlying shares for 100p no matter what the price each September for seven years. After seven years, the warrants expire worthless.

But warrant investors in this particular trust aren't limited to trading in September. While the warrants have value, they can be bought or sold at any time on the stock market. They're a long-term gamble on the price rising.

How about an example? Say that the warrant you received as part of an investment trust flotation allows you to buy the actual shares for 100p in any July for the next five years. The underlying shares are worth 200p at the moment, but you want out. So another investor buys the warrant for 110p.

The 10p extra is compensation for the hope value. Four years later, the shares stand at 400p. The warrant holder converts into shares. The bill is 100p, plus the 110p for the warrant, plus the interest cost of holding the warrant (there are no dividends), but the final reward is 400p. Not bad! But note that if the trust shares had slumped to 50p and stayed there, the 100p-a-time warrant money would've been wasted. Disaster!

Note that *covered warrants* are the latest in the menagerie of high-risk, high-reward geared derivative products, which allow you to bet equally on falling as well as rising prices. The good news is that a warrant investor (whether of traditional or the new covered versions, which can be created on any major company or share price index) can't lose more than his or her original investment no matter how bad the forecast turns out to be.

Note too that warrant producers have also come up with *certificates*, which are just as artificial and let investors go short as well as long. But unlike the other exotic creations in this chapter, they aren't geared so you can't gain or lose more than you would with conventional shares. What you buy is what you get.

So what's the point?

- ✔ Low cost
- ✔ No stamp duty
- ✔ Can be created for a sector, such as banks or pharmaceuticals
- ✔ No annual management fees

Book III

Building Up Savings and Investments

Book IV
Retiring Wealthy

'Talk about wealthy retired
– that's a <u>stretch</u> walking frame.'

In this Book . . .

Retiring wealthy with a decent pot of money sounds great, doesn't it? This Book helps you devise a personal long-term strategy to build your nest-egg. If you don't fancy working until you're 103, or scrimping and saving your way through retirement, this Book shows you the way forward.

Here are the contents of Book IV at a glance:

Chapter 1

Planning for a Wealthy Retirement

· ·

· ·

*A*t some point, you've probably daydreamed about what retirement may hold for you. In your mind's eye, retirement may give you an opportunity to live it up, splash the cash and follow your dreams, or maybe your ambitions are more modest – quality time spent indulging a favourite hobby perhaps.

In this chapter, we explain how you can turn these daydreams into concrete goals.

Once you have a set of clear, costed goals you can start making the necessary personal and financial moves to guarantee you achieve them.

Making Some Vital Decisions about Retirement

How you save for retirement depends on four factors:

✔ What age you plan to retire

✔ How much cash you need in retirement

✔ When you start saving

✔ What you can afford to save

Plucking numbers out of the air is futile: Each of these factors needs examining in detail. Only then will you discover whether your lofty aims are unreasonable given the limitations of your wallet and the time you have left. You may have to revise your expectations or start saving a lot more than you are doing.

Planning your retirement age

The first step is to decide when you're going to retire. If you're in your twenties you may feel this is ridiculous: How on earth can you possibly predict how you will feel about working in 40 years or so? Or it may be one of the easiest questions in the world to answer if you have long had no intention of working past the age of 50. Whichever type of person you are, thinking about the age you plan to give up work is crucial because it has an impact on your retirement planning – how much you need to save and where you invest it.

Here's some great news. We're all living a lot longer. Life expectancy has shot up in the past couple of decades. If you're a woman born in 1980 you can expect to live until your early nineties. Government boffins reckon that the news on life expectancy is going to get better, with the average woman born today expected to live until they are nearly 100 years old!

This means if you retire in your mid 60s and enjoy just average health you're going to need enough money to live on for at least 20 to 30 years.

Retiring at 50 or indeed anytime before the official state retirement age of 65 for men and 60 for women (until 2020, when it becomes 65 for both) is an impossible dream for the majority. Realistically, you'll probably have to work until your seventies because you simply can't save enough to retire before then. Retiring at 50 requires a huge pension pot, supplemented with additional investments. If you are in a well-paid job and start saving a significant percentage of your salary from your early twenties, it might just be possible. Otherwise, it won't be. Doing the sums could make you appreciate that your dream is unrealistic. Either you invest more cash to make it possible or get used to the fact that you'll have to stay in the rat race for longer.

Calculating how much income you need to live (and play)

It's not easy trying to work out what you will need to live on some 20 or 30 years in the future, particularly as price levels will be very different by the time you retire. But it's worth establishing a ballpark figure. Think in terms of today's prices and make a rough estimate of day-to-day expenses (see Table 1-1).

Your outgoings should fall in retirement. For one thing, your mortgage will probably be paid off so you can live rent-free. You don't need to buy smart suits to wear to the office; pay train and bus fares for your daily commute; or fork out a fiver for lunch at an over-priced sandwich shop either.

Don't underestimate your financial needs. Certain outgoings cease but you have more free time on your hands. Filling this costs money: You may want to travel several months of the year, take up golf, dine at fancy restaurants twice a month, or spoil the grandchildren. A retirement spent watching television all day is no fun: Plan carefully so that you've got enough cash to enjoy yourself.

Table 1-1 Everyday Outgoings in Retirement	
Expense	*Yearly Cost*
Gas/electricity/water	£..........
Telephone/mobile	£..........
Council tax	£..........
Television licence	£..........
Satellite TV	£..........
Travel: bus/train	£..........
Buildings and contents insurance	£........
Pet costs: food/insurance/vet	£..........
Running a car: insurance/petrol/road tax/breakdown cover	£..........
Dentist/optician	£........
Private medical insurance	£........
Food	£..........
Clothing	£..........
Dining out/cinema/theatre/concerts	£........
Other	£..........
TOTAL OUTGOINGS	£..........

After you work out the cost of everyday essentials, start dreaming. Make a list of what you'd like to do and the cost. Your list might look something like the one in Table 1-2.

Book IV

Retiring Wealthy

Table 1-2	Retirement Wish List
Expense	*Yearly Cost*
Three holidays a year at £1,000 each	£3,000
Three weekend breaks a year	£900
Dinner out once a week (for two)	£5,200
Day trips with grandchildren	£600
Golf membership	£5,000
TOTAL OUTGOINGS	£14,700

Working out your current position

Add together the total outgoings from Table 1-1 and your own version of Table 1-2: This is the yearly income you need in retirement. The next step is to work out what you are actually likely to retire on, taking into account your current saving levels. If there's a shortfall between what you're saving and what you need – which is more than likely – you can start planning to bridge this gap.

If you plan ahead, you should be able to rely on several sources of income in retirement:

- ✔ The basic state pension
- ✔ The state second pension (S2P)
- ✔ A private pension (occupational, personal, or stakeholder plan)
- ✔ Other investments, such as individual savings accounts (ISAs) and property

To get a rough idea of how much of an income you will get in retirement based on your current pension contributions, use the pension calculator on the Trades Union Congress (TUC) Web site (www.worksmart.org.uk). Be prepared to be horrified by what you discover, but try not be too disheartened – you may have time to rectify the situation.

The size of your pension also depends on annuity rates at the time you transform your private pot into a yearly income for the rest of your life. Three-quarters of your pension pot must be used to purchase an annuity by the age of 75. See Chapter 5 in this Book for the low-down on annuities.

Starting saving

The earlier you save for retirement, the better. Investing early gives your money longer to grow, which means you can opt for riskier investments, such as stocks and shares, which have historically produced higher returns in the long run. You will also end up investing more over the years than if you start your pension in your forties.

It's not worth having sleepless nights over your lack of pension. Save what you can afford to, when you can do so. Stakeholder pensions (see Chapter 3 in this Book) are ideal because they require a minimum investment of no more than £20 a time. Then, when you can afford to invest more, make sure you increase your contributions.

 If your employer offers an occupational scheme, it contributes to your pension: If so, join immediately. You may not have to make a contribution but you still benefit from money going towards your pension. See Chapter 2 in this Book for more on occupational pensions.

Reviewing your plan

Review your pension planning on a regular basis – yearly at least. Pension providers are required by law to send you an annual statement detailing how much you have contributed, your fund's value, and a forecast of how much you could get on retirement. This is not a guaranteed amount but should give a good indication as to whether you need to put more cash aside for retirement.

 If a fund isn't performing well, consider shifting your money elsewhere. If you leave your cash in badly performing investments for many years, you'll end up with a much lower income in retirement than you would have done if you'd ditched the dog funds. (This is not possible with final salary schemes.)

Realising Retirement Can Be Sudden

As touched on earlier in this chapter, the age at which you stop work is crucial to assessing how much money you need to live on. The earlier in life you retire the more money you need – simple.

However, predicting when you retire can be far from simple. Some people – particularly those who work in the public sector – have a pretty good idea when they will give up work. Their employer tells them way in advance that they expect them to be gone by a certain age, 60 or 65. These people can plan with certainty.

Converting your retirement pot into retirement income

When you get to retirement you have the option of buying an annuity. The concept behind an annuity is very simple. You hand over your savings to an insurance company and it pays you an income until you pop your clogs. The amount of income you get depends on how much money you hand over and the annuity rate when you purchase the annuity.

Unfortunately in recent years annuity rates have been falling because people are living longer and interest rates have been historically low. In fact, since the late 1980s annuity rates have halved to around 5% or 6%. This means that £100,000 will buy you an income of around £5,000 to £6,000. This very rough ball-park figure should give you a good idea of what sort of retirement income your savings and investment will buy you. Annuities are looked at in much greater detail in Chapter 5 in this Book.

But for others retirement may come suddenly or can be phased over many years.

The reality in UK industry is that on average workers retire in their early sixties – a few years earlier than the age at which men can claim the state pension – either through their own choice or due to redundancy or ill health.

But even if you think you have job security you should prepare for the possibility that you may stop working earlier than planned.

Since April 2006 you can continue to work for your employer and collect your workplace pension. However, the pension scheme has to give the go ahead for you to be paid a pension while staying employed. See Chapter 2 in this Book for more on workplace pensions.

In 2006 the government introduced legislation making it illegal for firms to discriminate against job applicants on the grounds of age. However, despite the law change widespread age discrimination is likely to be with us for many years to come. Check out the government's age positive Web site on www. agepositive.gov.uk for more info on the new anti-age discrimination laws, or take a look at Liz Barclay's *Small Business Employment Law For Dummies* (Wiley).

If you're offered early retirement or voluntary redundancy late in your working life you may be best taking independent financial advice as to where to invest any lump sum pay-off you receive from your employer.

Looking at What You've Got Going for You

It may seem that you have a long, long way to go to have enough cash even to cover basic retirement living expenses. But don't lose heart: You probably have lots of things going for you, such as the following.

The younger you start the better the result can be

The simple truth is that the younger you start saving and investing for your retirement the better the chance you have of building up a whopping retirement pot. Here are three ways that starting young and having time on your side can benefit your retiring wealthy strategy:

- ✔ The money you save and invest has a longer time in which to grow.
- ✔ You probably have a long working life ahead of you during which you can save and invest really hard.
- ✔ You can afford to take a few more risks with your investments because you have time to recover financially if they go wrong.

It has been estimated that every pound you save in your twenties results in the same amount of money being available to you in retirement as three pounds saved in your forties.

Don't get depressed if you didn't start young: It's never too late to start saving for your retirement. Middle age can present lots of opportunities to save and invest plenty of cash. See the next section for more details.

Your finances are turbo charged later in life

If you're not a twenty or thirty something no problem; you can still scale the retiring wealthy peak with aplomb. Think about the wealthiest people you know – are they in their twenties or thirties? (And by wealthy we mean people who have access to real assets not just designer clothes and a sports car.) Er, probably not. The people with real wonga tend to be the middle-aged. Generally, they have the largest houses, fattest savings, and biggest share dealing accounts.

Book IV

Retiring Wealthy

This is all because a bit of money magic is introduced into your finances as you reach your forties and fifties. Here's how it works.

Middle age should mean that you are at the top of your career and from an earnings perspective you've probably never had it so good.

The kids have probably flown the family nest and are striking out on their own. This is great news as it stops the little treasures draining your finances.

You may have repaid your mortgage. All that money you borrowed in your twenties or thirties to buy your home has probably now been repaid – happy days! This takes a big weight off your finances.

Increasingly people are finding that their little treasures are staying at home into their twenties or even thirties. This phenomenon has been given a name – kippers – which stands for kids in parents' pockets eroding retirement savings. Funny? Yes, but from a personal finance perspective, kippers are no laughing matter.

Since April 2006 you have been able to pay 100 per cent of your income – up to a maximum of £215,000 per year, if you have that much spare – into a personal pension. This represents a huge increase in the level of contributions that you're allowed to make into a pension scheme and frees people up to build up a big pot of pension money fast if they've got a lot of disposable income. See Chapter 3 in this Book for more on personal pensions.

You're probably richer than you think

It may not feel like it when you open your credit card statement each month but you're probably far wealthier than you imagine. Firstly, the value of your assets, shares, savings, and investments is probably far higher than you think. Ask any home insurer and they can tell you that people regularly underestimate or have no real clue as to how much their personal possessions are worth.

What's more, it's not all about what you're worth today but what your current financial circumstances mean for your future. Even if your savings and investments are dwarfed by a great big mortgage debt then no worries – as long as you can afford repayments of course – because this is a really important investment that can provide a much needed financial boost in later life. See Chapter 6 in this Book for details on how owning property can make your old age more financially secure.

Why not spend a couple of hours working out your financial worth? Assessing your wealth gives you an idea of how close, or far away, you are from being able to finance a wealthy retirement.

Taking Your Loved Ones Along for the Retirement Ride

If you have a partner or family you are unlikely to be planning a solo retirement – although it's one way of ensuring you always have custody of the remote control. You naturally want to take your partner along with you for the ride (or should that be a post-retirement luxury cruise?). If this applies to you, it's time to get your nearest and dearest in on the act. After all, it's pointless saving and investing really hard if your partner is a secret spendthrift running up huge debts. Ultimately they're going to drag your finances down to their level.

You need to sit down with your loved ones and talk about what you'd like retirement to hold. Perhaps your ideas about retirement differ. Your partner may want nothing more than to give up work while you want to work until you drop because you just love it. Whatever the scenario, you can only help the matter by talking things through.

Hopefully, you can come to an agreement over where you want to be in your golden years and how you intend to get there.

Retirement is a major life change and it can take some adjusting to. Several organisations run pre-retirement courses explaining how to best meet some of the key challenges that retirement brings such as sensible budgeting and claiming state benefits. As the big day nears you may be best going on one of these courses. Contact Life Academy (formerly the Pre-Retirement Association) on 01483 301170 or the Retirement Trust on 020 7864 9908 or www.theretirementtrust.org.uk for course details.

Of course, if you have a partner on board you have an even better chance of scooping the retiring wealthy prize. Two incomes are better than one as are two savings accounts and even two properties.

Here's an action plan for how to effectively join forces with your partner to drive for that retiring wealthy finishing post:

> ✓ **Establish when you both want to stop work.** One of you may be younger and therefore have longer to go to build up a full state pension entitlement. You should agree the dates at which you can both retire. If there is an age gap, perhaps the older person in the partnership can carry on working for a little while to build up a big enough cash pot to allow the younger person to retire earlier than would otherwise be the case.

Book IV

Retiring Wealthy

✔ **Decide between you how much you need.** You need money to take care of life's basics plus cover emergencies, not forgetting a few of life's luxuries of course. You may have very different ideas of how much money you both need in old age. See earlier in this chapter for more on what sorts of expenses your funds need to cover in later life.

✔ **Examine how much you're on course to receive.** When you've totted up your joint worth you may find you're a long way short of what you need.

✔ **Discuss if there are any high value retirement goodies you want.** This can be anything from a flashy motor to a home in the sun. If there is something really special you want to aim for, then the sooner you start working as a team the better the chance you have of reaching your combined goal.

✔ **Calculate how much you need to reach your joint goals.** In order to buy retirement income for you both to live on – normally through an annuity – you need a big pot of cash. See earlier in this chapter for more on turning a pot of cash into an income you can both live on.

✔ **Agree on what you're willing to sacrifice to reach your dreams.** It stands to reason that in order to build up a big enough cash pot to enjoy a comfortable retirement you have to save, invest, and work really hard. You can't do any of this without making sacrifices whether that is curbing your spending – perhaps going to Cornwall instead of Cancun this summer – paying a portion of your income into a pension or simply setting time aside to monitor your savings and investments.

✔ **Determine what you want to leave behind for loved ones.** If you have children it's likely you'd like them to benefit financially on your death. If that's the case you want to ensure you've enough money to take care of your combined needs in retirement and leave a tidy legacy for your children, perhaps taking out a life insurance policy to benefit them as well.

An increasing percentage of marriages end in divorce. If you take a trip to splitsville you can find your retiring wealthy plans take a battering.

If you divorce the court may well award part of your pension entitlement to your spouse. Such awards are getting more commonplace and are decided upon a case by case basis.

You and your partner may want to both visit an independent financial adviser (IFA). An IFA will be able to look at your two sets of finances and plot a course for both of you to follow to your retiring wealthy goals. However, good independent advice doesn't come cheap.

Good news for same sex couples

Same sex couples who go through a civil ceremony can enjoy the same tax and legal advantages that were once only open to married heterosexual couples. This means that same sex couples can now pass property and money to one another free of capital gains or inheritance tax. However, unmarried cohabiting different-sex couples do not benefit from the law change because the government argues that they always have the option of getting hitched.

Protecting Your Retiring Wealthy Plan: Buying Insurance

You don't need me to tell you that life doesn't always go to plan. In fact, sometimes things can all go horribly wrong. A bout of ill health or suffering an accident can damage your long-term earnings potential and with it your hopes of ever retiring wealthy.

But help is at hand. Seemingly, for every unfortunate event an insurance product is available to soften the blow. Of course, insurers are in the business of making money and try to set their premiums so that they take in more money than they end up paying out to claimants. However, this doesn't mean that insurance is a bad deal. Some people love the peace of mind that having insurance offers.

The types of insurance that you may want to consider include:

- ✔ **Income protection cover.** This pays you an income if you become unable to work due to ill health or injury.

- ✔ **Critical illness cover.** This pays a lump sum if you suffer a major health event such as cancer or a stroke.

- ✔ **Private medical insurance.** If you fall ill you should be able to receive prompt private medical attention at no cost. No NHS waiting list for you!

- ✔ **Redundancy insurance.** This does exactly what it says on the tin: Lose your job, through no fault of your own (so no taking out a policy and telling the boss where to get off!), and you should receive an income for a set period or until you get a new job.

- ✔ **Legal expenses insurance.** Suing and being sued are getting more common. Have a prang in the car or cause any sort of injury to a member of the public and it may end in court. Luckily, you can insure yourself against someone suing you successfully.

Book IV

Retiring Wealthy

Each of the insurance schemes above has its merits and drawbacks. If you like the look of any of them, you'd be best off taking independent financial advice or talking to an insurance broker.

Mortgage and loan payment protection insurance has been hitting the head-lines of late for all the wrong reasons. Consumer groups claim that insurance is overpriced and has lots of get-out clauses for the insurer so that they don't have to pay out. What's more, if you take out payment protection insurance all it does is cover your loan repayments. It doesn't for example pay you an income you can live off.

When it comes to insurance cheapest isn't necessarily best. You need to examine the policy small print for any hidden nasties. For example, some income protection products will only pay out if you're injured and are unable to do any work whatsoever while others will pay if your condition merely stops you from doing your current job. As you can imagine, it's much better to have the latter type of policy than the former.

Chapter 2

Making the Most of State and Workplace Pensions

*F*or many the word pension is an instant cure for insomnia. But stifle those yawns and put the coffee pot on. It's worth staying up for this chapter.

Your state and workplace pensions may well prove to be your biggest source of retirement income.

In this chapter we lay bare both state and workplace pensions so that you can make a better decision about the part you want them to play in your retiring wealthy plan.

Realising the Importance of Your Pension

Pensions have had a really bad press of late. It seems that whenever the word pension is used in newspapers or TV news reports it is invariably followed by the word crisis!

This idea of a pensions crisis follows widespread anger at minimal rises in the state pension, mis-selling of personal pensions, and the collapse of some workplace pension schemes.

Reading and listening to some of the doom-laden reports you'd think that the whole pension system was headed for collapse and that you'd be wise to ignore pensions altogether, perhaps investing your cash elsewhere – in property, for example.

But in reality pensions aren't headed for the knacker's yard. Although things aren't quite as rosy as they once were for UK pensions, state, workplace, and personal pensions are still set to be the chief vehicle that most people use to cross the retiring wealthy finishing line.

If you work or have worked in the past you've already built up a state pension. Your state pension won't be enough to pay for living the high life, but it can provide a more than useful backstop.

And workplace and personal pensions – as I explain below – offer unique tax breaks that can help supercharge your retiring wealthy plans.

All in all, pensions – state, workplace, and personal – provide the foundation upon which you can build your retiring wealthy project. Fail to understand pensions and what they offer and you may well be missing a trick.

Understanding the great pensions tax break

The next sentence may be a tad dull, but it's probably the most important in this Book.

When you make contributions to workplace and personal pensions something magical happens: The government gives you tax relief on your contributions. In effect this means that for basic rate taxpayers, for every 78p they pay into a pension the government matches this with 22p. From April 2008 basic rate tax will fall to 20p in the pound so basic rate taxpayers will contribute 80p per pound of their pension. Higher rate taxpayers benefit by even more. For every 60p they pay into a pension the government gives them 40p in tax relief.

How does this fact benefit a basic rate and a higher rate taxpayer, both paying into a workplace pension?

Christine is a basic rate taxpayer; her gross annual salary is £20,000. Her workplace pension scheme asks members to pay in 5 per cent of their salary. In Christine's case 5 per cent of her gross salary equals £1000 a year. Hypothetically if the 5 per cent contribution were to come from her net salary then it would only be £780.

Blossom is a higher rate taxpayer; her gross annual salary is £40,000. She is a member of the same workplace pension as Christine and pays 5 per cent of her gross salary into it, equal to £2,000 a year. The true cost to Blossom would be £1,200, although her pension would be swelled to the tune of £2,000.

In effect the government is subsiding Christine and Blossom's pensions to the tune of several hundred pounds a year. Over the long term – say 20 or 30 years – this makes a huge difference to both pension pots.

You earn a state pension when you make National Insurance (NI) contributions. If you're an employee NI is deducted from your gross income in the same way as income tax. The longer you pay National Insurance contributions the more chance you have of earning an entitlement to a full state pension. See later in this chapter for more on this.

One of the key advantages of a workplace pension is that your employer may – and often does – make a contribution to it.

Remembering the pension tax break has strings attached

Allowing pension contributions to be paid from gross rather than net income is a whopping tax break. The government wants to ensure that the money is used for the purpose of providing a retirement income rather than as just a way of dodging tax. Therefore there are strict rules imposed on pension investment such as:

- ✔ Money invested in a workplace or personal pension cannot be accessed by the saver until they have reached the age of 50. This rises to 55 in 2010.
- ✔ Most of the money saved in a pension goes to buying an annuity – an income for life – before age 75 or may be used by the workplace pension fund to buy the scheme member a guaranteed income.
- ✔ The size of a person's pension pot is capped at £1.6m. This is set to rise to £1.8m in 2010.

In short, with pension investment you trade flexibility and control for a tasty tax break.

Book IV

Retiring Wealthy

An exception to the no pension until you're at least 50 rule is made for people who take early retirement from an occupational scheme due to ill health.

Although most of the cash saved in a pension has to go towards providing retirement income, schemes allow members to take up to 25 per cent of their money as a tax-free lump sum. The scheme member is free to do with this money as they please.

Getting to Grips with the State Pension

For a large percentage of the UK population the pension provided by the state is all they have to live on in retirement. Relying on the state pension alone is a one-way ticket to a miserly old age. The current (2007-08) basic state pension for a single person is £87.30 a week. Fancy living off that? No, we thought not!

But saying that you shouldn't pin your retiring wealthy hopes on the state pension does not mean that it is irrelevant and that you should ignore it.

The state pension system can provide you with part of the retiring wealthy answer – a base from which you can plan your assault on the big wealth prize. Get to know the ins and outs of the state pension. The benefits of the state pension are as follows:

- ✔ **It provides a regular and increasing income.** The income provided by the state pension may not be a king's ransom but it's not to be sniffed at. In order to buy an annuity – an income for life – equivalent to the current state pension you'd have to have a pension pot worth between £60,000 and £70,000. What's more, the state pension is guaranteed to rise each year at least in line with prices.

- ✔ **It is tax free.** The state pension is so small that it flies under the income tax personal allowance. Of course, if you have other sources of income they may take you above the personal allowance threshold – then you start to pay tax.

- ✔ **It is free of National Insurance Contributions (NICs).** Once you're sufficiently long in the tooth to receive the state pension then you no longer have to worry about making NICs. In your autumn years the boot is on the other foot and you benefit from what's in the NIC pot rather then paying into it. After a life toiling away you may think you deserve to let others work for you.

Building up entitlement when not working

Home Responsibilities Protection (HRP) has been around since 1978 and is designed to protect the National Insurance contribution records of people caring for a child or sick or disabled person. In short HRP helps you protect your state pension.

You're entitled to HRP if you meet any of the following criteria:

✔ You get child benefit for a child under 16.

✔ You get income support because you're looking after someone.

✔ You're in receipt of Carer's Allowance or are a foster parent.

If any of the above cover you, contact your local benefits office and ask them for details of HRP. You may be automatically enrolled for HRP but double check that you have been. After all, if you don't take advantage of HRP and as result fail to build up enough National Insurance credits then you won't receive a full state pension.

One year of HRP equates to one year of full National Insurance contributions.

The state retirement age for women is set to rise to 65. However, if you're a woman born before 5 April 1950 you will be able to retire at 60. If you were born between 6 April 1950 and 5 March 1955 you come under a transitional arrangement and your retirement age will be set according to your birth date and fall somewhere between 60 and 65. Check out the government's pension service Web site at www.pensionservice.gov.uk for more on how this transitional arrangement works.

If you retire with less than 25 per cent of the qualifying years for a state pension then you won't get anything at all. People aged 80 or over can claim a non-contributory pension worth 60 per cent of the state pension.

Relying On the State Alone Is Not an Option

The full state pension, as of April 2007, is:

✔ £87.30 a week for a single person (£4,539.60 a year)

✔ £139.60 a week for a married couple (£7,259.20 a year)

Book IV

Retiring Wealthy

These benefits are uprated every April. Details of the rates are available in leaflet GL23 *Social security benefit rates*, available from your pension centre or social security office.

Over time it is widely predicted that the state pension is going to become even less generous, particularly when compared to the incomes of those in work.

The reason for this is that the state pension rises in line with prices and not average earnings. Prices traditionally rise more slowly than wages. As a result those living off a state pension have found their income falling behind that of wage earners. Today the state pension is worth less than 20 per cent of average earnings – by 2050 Age Concern predicts that it may be worth as little as 7 per cent.

The government is planning to restore the link between earnings and pensions. The price of that move will be a later state pension age. Whether or not the government sees its plans through, relying on the state pension for support is no way to retire wealthy. In fact over the next few decades it may well be a guaranteed ticket to poverty-ville! The UK has one of the least generous state pensions in Europe. In countries such as France and Sweden the state pension is worth over half average earnings. What is more, on the continent the age at which the state pension is paid is earlier and the level of pension is equal to around half national average income.

The demographic time bomb means that the UK state pension age will increase in the coming decades. The government has announced plans to raise it to 66 in 2024, 67 in 2034 and 68 in 2044. Meanwhile, the state pension age for women is due to rise from 60 to 65 between 2010 and 2020.

Working Out the Value of Your State Pension

The amount of pension you get depends on your National Insurance contribution (NIC) record during your working life. Your working life is usually calculated from the beginning of the tax year in which you are 16 years old to the one before you reach state pension age. This is taken to be 49 years for a man and 44 years for a woman born on or before 5 October 1950, rising to 49 years for women born on 6 October 1954 or later.

Postponing your retirement in return for extra cash

Some people don't want to retire at 60 or 65. They enjoy their work and want to carry on for as long as possible. The government wants to encourage people to stay at work for longer – after all if they're at work they earn more and therefore pay more tax. To this end, since April 2005 the government has paid extra state pension to people who defer claiming it people if they deferred collecting their state pension.

You build up *extra state pension* at 1 per cent of your normal weekly state pension rate for every five weeks you put off claiming, which equates to around 10.4 per cent for every year you defer your claim. So if you decided to put off claiming

the current state pension of £87.30 for one year, you would receive an extra £9 a week for life. You must defer your pension for at least five weeks under this option.

Alternatively, if you want to defer your state pension for at least a year, you can take a taxable lump sum payment, based on the amount of state pension you would have received, plus interest at 2 per cent above the Bank of England base rate.

You can find out how much you could claim by phoning the Pension Forecasting Team on 0845 3000 168.

To qualify for the full state pension, you must have paid full-rate NICs for approximately 90 per cent of your working life: These are known as *qualifying years*. Men need 44 qualifying years and women 39 to get a full state pension. From 2020, women will also need 44 years.

Don't let the size of your state pension be a surprise. You can get a free estimate of how much state pension you have earned to date from the government's pension service. Write to The Retirement Pension Forecasting Team, Room TB001, Tyneview Park, Whitley Road, Newcastle upon Tyne, NE98 1BA or call them on 0845 3000168 and ask for form BR19. Alternatively you can do it online at www.thepensionservice.gov.uk/resourcecentre/e-services/home.asp.

Women are more likely than men to suffer a state pension shortfall because they take time out of the workforce to bring up children and look after elderly relatives.

When UK citizens take up residency abroad, they automatically stop making UK National Insurance contributions. As a result, they can find when returning to the UK that they have not paid enough National Insurance to be in line for a full state pension. If you are returning after a stint living abroad it may be a good idea to get your chequebook out and repair your state pension.

Book IV

Retiring Wealthy

Repairing a state pension

If you're heading for a state pension shortfall you're allowed to fill in any gaps in your NI contributions dating back up to six years.

For example, during the 2007-08 tax year it is possible to make voluntary contributions dating all the way back to 2001-02.

Your pension forecast sets out how much state pension you have built up to date and, crucially, how much it is likely to be worth at age 65, assuming you continue to pay full National Insurance contributions.

In addition, the forecast should highlight any shortfall in National Insurance contributions and indicate how much you would need to contribute in order to make it up. The forecast letter should tell you how to actually make up the gap

in your contribution record – in short, where to send the cheque.

Of course, you may decide to let sleeping dogs lie and not repair your state pension. It costs you cash to do so and perhaps it's money you feel would be better spent paying off your mortgage or investing in shares. Bear in mind, though, that most financial experts suggest that in nearly all instances when there is a chance to do some repair work and make up missing contributions then it should be seized with both hands and then some!

After all, as mentioned earlier in this chapter, it takes an awfully large pension pot to buy an income equivalent to the state pension. HMRC will tell you exactly how much it will cost you to make up the gap.

Getting into the Second State Pension

Why have just one state pension when you can have two? As well as the basic state pension there is the very intuitively titled second state pension or S2P for short. Put simply, the S2P provides a top up to your basic state pension. In return for higher NICs you get an extra state pension. The S2P isn't as large as the basic state pension but it can provide extra retirement income.

You contribute extra NICs in order to earn entitlement to the S2P. The S2P is income related which means the size of the eventual payment depends on your level of income during your time working and how long you contributed to the S2P for.

S2P is the replacement for the State Earnings Related Pension Scheme (SERPS). They are in essence the same except that under S2P people on low and modest earnings have more of a chance to build up a better pension. Under S2P rules the system 'credits' or 'bumps up' earnings for eligible groups to a flat rate of around £13,000. In other words, if you earn under this amount, the S2P rules treat you as if you had earned £13,000.

SERPS morphed into S2P in 2002 so if you were working before that date then you are likely to receive some income from SERPS and some from S2P – unless, of course you were contracted out. There is more on this later in the chapter.

According to the Pension Advisory Service (Opas) a S2P/Serps member who has earned enough to pay the top rate of income tax since 1978 would be entitled to around £70 a week extra pension if they retired tomorrow.

But most people aren't in the fortunate position to be top rate taxpayers for nearly thirty years. In reality, most people find that when it comes time to retire their S2P is worth perhaps no more than £10 or £15 a week.

You don't have to be a member of the S2P. You can choose to *contract out*. This means your NICs contributions that would normally go to the S2P go into another pension scheme – either a workplace or a personal pension.

If you contract out using a personal or stakeholder pension, HMRC reimburses part of your NICs and these go into your private pension fund. This is invested and the idea is that you build up a replacement pension for the S2P you have given up.

The government sets the level of reimbursement that is paid into your pension scheme.

Contracting out was all the rage in the early 1990s. Millions left SERPS in the big hope that through investing their cash elsewhere they may get a better pension. However, contracting out hasn't turned into the retiring wealthy panacea many people hoped for. Some commentators say that many people who have chosen to contract out would have been better off remaining in the S2P. They argue that the S2P provides a higher income in retirement than if the NICs were paid into a personal pension which would then have to be invested and in turn buy an annuity. The advice from many money experts these days is if at all possible, stay contracted into the S2P.

If you are a member of a workplace pension scheme you may find that you're automatically contracted out of the S2P. In other words the cash that would have gone into the S2P to provide you with a top up state pension is actually going into your workplace pension scheme.

If you're self-employed then at present you can't contribute to the S2P. However, the government has said that it wants to correct this anomaly and allow the self-employed to contribute to the S2P in future.

Book IV

Retiring Wealthy

If you're self-employed you may be well advised to save and invest some extra cash to make up for the fact that you don't have any entitlement to S2P.

Getting Credit for Your Pension and Other Benefits

The pension credit replaces the minimum income guarantee and provides extra money from the state if you are 60 or over and on a low income. For tax year 2007-08, you are guaranteed to receive at least:

- ✔ £119.05 a week if you are single
- ✔ £181.70 a week between you and your partner

If you're 65 or over and have some pension savings, you will be rewarded for making this provision. You can get up to £19.05 a week if you are single or £25.26 for you and your partner. The amount is calculated at £1 a week income for every £500 or part of £500 over £6,000 that you have in savings. So if you have saved £8,000, you will get £4 a week pension credit.

The Pension Service has produced leaflet PC1L *Pension Credit, Pick it up. It's yours*, with more details on what you can claim. This is available from your local JobCentre or social security office.

As well as pension credit, there are several other benefits available:

- ✔ **Christmas bonus:** If you get a state pension or pension credit, you also get a tax-free Christmas bonus every year.

- ✔ **Cold weather payments:** If you receive pension credit, you automatically get a cold weather payment when the average temperature is 0 degrees centigrade or below for seven consecutive days.

- ✔ **Winter fuel payments:** One-off payments of up to £200, depending on circumstances. You don't have to be receiving benefits to qualify but you must be 60 or over.

- ✔ **80+ annual payment:** If you are 80 or over and entitled to a winter fuel payment, you get an extra annual sum of up to £100, depending on circumstances.

- ✔ **Council tax and housing benefit:** If you are on a low income, you can claim council tax benefit. If you are paying rent, you can also claim housing benefit. Contact the Pension Service for more information: www.thepensionservice.gov.uk.

Supplementing the State Scheme with a Private Pension

With the state pension declining in value relative to earnings during the past couple of decades, the government wants everyone to save for our own retirement via a private pension. This can be an occupational or company scheme from your employer, or a personal pension or stakeholder plan.

There are several advantages to saving for retirement via a pension, as opposed to other investments, such as property. We go through those benefits in the following sections.

Taking advantage of the tax breaks

The biggest selling point of private pensions is the generous tax relief on contributions:

✔ For **basic-rate** taxpayers (paying 22 per cent tax), every 78p you invest in your pension fund is topped up to £1 by the government (though the government's contribution will fall to 20p from April 2008 when basic rate tax is cut to 20p).

✔ For **higher-rate** taxpayers (paying 40 per cent tax), every £1 that goes into your pension pot costs you 60p.

You aren't taxed on your contributions but are taxed on your pension income. Most people tend to be on a lower rate of tax in retirement, so you may have tax relief at 40 per cent on your contributions but be taxed at 22 per cent (or 20 per cent from April 2008) when you draw your pension.

Locking away your cash

Once you have made a contribution to your pension, you won't see that money again until the age of 50 at least (and it could be much later, depending on when you retire). This ensures that you have a chance of accruing a reasonable sum of money. If, instead, you invest in equities or savings accounts, you can withdraw cash to buy a car, pay for your daughter's wedding, or go on a cruise. Without restrictions on withdrawing your pension money, you could run out of cash by the time you get to retirement age – particularly if you aren't disciplined when it comes to saving.

Book IV

Retiring Wealthy

The whole point about pensions is that they give you an income in retirement. To do that they have to be inflexible: If you want flexibility, supplement your pension with other investments that can be cashed in when the need arises.

Guaranteeing an income

A pension provides you with an income for life. By purchasing an annuity (see Chapter 5 in this Book for more on these), you get an income for as long as you live, whether that is three years or 30 years beyond retirement. There is no chance of running out of cash – an extremely comforting thought.

Being Smart by Joining the Company Scheme

When you start a new job, your employer should give you details about any pension scheme you are eligible to join. You may be invited to join the company scheme straight away or may have to work a probationary period of six months or a year before you are allowed to do so.

If you are allowed to join the company pension scheme only after you have worked there for a certain length of time, make a note in your diary of when you are eligible to join and ensure you sign up at that point, if it's in your interest to do so.

Joining the company pension has several advantages, particularly if your employer contributes money to your retirement fund. Your employer may also cover the running costs of the scheme, saving you money. There is an annual management fee, for example, to cover the cost of the manager investing your pension money. And if you have to retire early as a result of ill health, you should be able to start drawing your pension, providing you with useful income.

We discuss these major benefits in more detail in the following subsections.

Benefiting from employer contributions

If your employer offers an *occupational scheme*, he has to make a 'significant' contribution to your pension pot. From your perspective, this is getting something for nothing. It also means that you should end up with a much bigger pension pot than you would have done if only you contributed to it. Some occupational schemes require no contribution from you, while others enable you and your employer to contribute to them.

If your employer doesn't offer an occupational scheme, he may instead offer a *group personal pension scheme* (GPP). Organisations with more than five employees and no other pension provision in place are now legally obliged to offer a *stakeholder scheme*. These schemes work slightly differently from an occupational pension: The main thing to remember is that your employer doesn't have to contribute to your pension pot if he offers a GPP or stakeholder (see 'Exploring the types of workplace pensions' later in this chapter for more details on these schemes).

There's no restriction on the percentage of your salary that can be contributed to an occupational scheme (this came into force in April 2006). Instead, you're free to save as much as you like into any number of pensions (company and personal), and you'll get tax relief on contributions up to 100 per cent of your salary. The only restriction, apart from your own ability to put money away, is an upper *annual allowance* above which contributions (whether from you or your employer) will be taxed at 40 per cent. This stands at £225,000 for 2007-08.

Rather than a restrictive annual cap, there is a lifetime allowance, set at £1.6m in 2007-08 and due to rise to £1.8m by 2010. If your pension gets larger than the lifetime allowance, you'll be heavily penalised on the excess when you start to draw benefits. If you take the excess as a lump sum there will be a lifetime allowance charge of 55 per cent to pay; if you take it as a regular income the lifetime allowance charge will be 25 per cent.

You don't *have* to join your occupational scheme, and it may not be suitable for you, depending on your personal circumstances, such as your working patterns, and existing pension arrangements. If you aren't planning on staying with the company for longer than a couple of years, say, you might decide not to join the company pension: If you leave within two years your contributions are refunded to you. (See 'Changing jobs – and your pension' later in this chapter for more information.) In such a situation you may be better off taking out a personal pension that you can take with you when you move jobs.

Book IV

Retiring Wealthy

Employer contributions to pensions vary enormously. The cost of building your own pension is going up every year, and any employer contribution will help to meet this cost, so make sure you check it out. Although membership is voluntary, it is nearly always worth joining. Many employers contribute more to their employees' occupational schemes than the employees do themselves.

Some employers run schemes in which their employees don't have to make any payments at all. This can be useful if you are on a low salary and simply can't afford to contribute at this point. It is still worth joining because your employer's contributions will build up in the meantime and you can start contributing when you get a pay rise, for example. There is no point in delaying joining until you can afford to contribute as well.

Your contribution is shown on your monthly pay slip. At the end of each tax year you should receive an annual statement detailing how much has been invested in your pension, what share of the fund this has bought, and how much it is worth. It should also provide a projection of how much you stand to retire on if you continue making contributions at that amount and retire at state retirement age.

Protecting your family with life cover

Rather depressingly, this is also known as *death in service benefit*, but then that is exactly what it is. If you die at any time while you are employed by the company providing your occupational scheme, your beneficiary receives a lump sum payout. This insurance is very often expressed as a multiple of your salary; four times salary is quite common. However, the lump sum on death can be up to £1.6 million before it hits HMRC limits.

Death in service benefits can be very lucrative, but you still may want to consider taking out life insurance that pays your loved ones on your death. You should strongly consider life insurance if you have large debts such as a mortgage that your loved ones may find difficult to pay if you died suddenly.

The beneficiary is either a person nominated by you or selected by the trustees of the occupational scheme. Make sure that you nominate somebody to be your beneficiary; you usually receive a form enabling you to do this from the administrator of the scheme. But no matter whether you nominate someone or not, the trustees have the final say as to who receives the money. There are two reasons for this:

✔ The money is not technically your property on your death so is not liable for inheritance tax.

✔ The trustees can take other circumstances into account. For example, suppose you have not changed your beneficiary for 20 years. During that time you got divorced and had children with someone else, yet your ex-wife is still named as beneficiary. The trustees are likely to determine that your second family has a greater need and award them the death benefit. Also, if you have asked for something that the trustees deem unreasonable, they can veto it.

To ensure your wishes are followed, keep your nomination form up to date. If your circumstances change – and you get married or have children, for example – contact your pension administrator to complete a new nomination form.

Your beneficiaries are no longer entitled to this death benefit once you retire.

Providing pensions for surviving partners

If you die while employed your occupational scheme usually pays out a pension to your husband, wife or civil partner (and in some cases to your partner if you are not married). HMRC limits on what can be paid out as a pension are now quite generous, however most schemes still express the dependents' pension as a proportion of the member's entitlement – for example a half of what the member would have received. Again, check out exactly what the scheme offers as it can vary widely.

Money purchase schemes tend to give only a pension bought out of the fund that has built up for the member by the time they die, which could be very small if you die young.

If you die after you retire, your spouse or civil partner should still receive a pension. This is usually no more than half of your pension.

It is worth checking whether the death benefits offered by your pension, both on life cover and a pension for your spouse or civil partner, are reasonable to protect those who are left behind. If not, you should raise this with your pension administrator or consider making alternative arrangements.

Exploring the Types of Workplace Pensions

Occupational pension schemes, also known as *company schemes*, are set up by employers for the benefit of their employees to provide them with an income in retirement. Your employer and/or you invest cash in this fund, which is spread across a variety of assets such as shares and property. Over a number of years, this money builds up and forms your pension pot, which you receive as income in addition to the basic state pension when you retire.

Book IV

Retiring Wealthy

If your employer offers an occupational pension scheme, he must contribute to your pension pot on a monthly basis. In most instances you will also contribute to the scheme, but not all occupational pensions demand that you do. Your own contributions should not exceed 100 per cent of your salary, and the combined total of your own and your employer's contributions shouldn't exceed the annual allowance.

Although the contribution limits have changed, in practice many company schemes retain their old rules stipulating that no more than 15 per cent of your salary can be contributed to the company pension (though of course there's now nothing to stop you setting up separate private pensions). Your employer may contribute a set percentage of your salary, or may match your contributions each month up to a cap of, say, 5 per cent.

Some employers let you join the company pension as soon as you join the workforce, while others demand that you serve a probationary period first. Find out from your employer whether it is possible to join the scheme at a later date.

The two main types of occupational or company pension scheme are *final salary* or *money purchase*. With the former you are offered a pension as a proportion of your earnings on retirement, but because the employer takes on all the investment risk, they are becoming less common. As a result, when you start a new job you are far more likely to be invited to join a money purchase scheme. With these schemes, the contribution you make is fixed but the pension you end up with depends on how the investment fares over the years your money is invested. You can also be offered a hybrid or mixture of the two.

Your employer may offer an occupational pension but it is legally required to have a board of trustees to run the scheme: Your employer is not allowed to do this himself. However, if you work in the public sector, for the civil service or the NHS, for example, your pension is a *statutory* scheme run according to Acts of Parliament rather than trustees.

Many schemes offer an *Additional Voluntary Contribution* (AVC) option. AVCs, as the name suggests, allow you to top up the main scheme benefits with an amount of your choice. Most AVCs are run on a money purchase basis, but some final salary schemes allow you to buy 'added years' – in effect to 'buy' extra service in the scheme, which will then result in a larger pension. Alternatively, you can use any other form of individual pension, such as a stakeholder pension, a personal pension or a self invested personal pension.

The two key limits are that your cumulative annual contributions shouldn't exceed the lower of 100 per cent of your income and the annual allowance (£225,000 for 2007-08), and that your total benefits at retirement shouldn't exceed the lifetime allowance (£1.6 million for 2007-08).

Figuring Out Final Salary Schemes

Final salary pension schemes are also known as *salary-related* or *defined benefit* schemes because you are promised a certain pension income once you retire. Your pension will be based on your *final pensionable salary*. The definition of this varies between schemes: Some base it on your income in the last year before retirement; others average the last three years' income, and may include overtime and bonuses in this or not. Check the scheme details to find out which applies. Your employer (and sometimes you) makes contributions to a pension fund. The amount you receive in retirement rests on three factors:

- The **length of your pensionable service,** otherwise known as the amount of time you belong to the pension scheme as an employee of the company.

- Your **earnings just before retirement** or when you leave the scheme or final pensionable salary. Your final pensionable earnings may be an average of your earnings over the past two or three years before retirement, or years further back if your earnings dropped just before retirement.

- The scheme's **accrual rate,** which is the proportion of salary that you get for each year you worked for your employer. For example, if the scheme has an accrual rate of 60, you receive 1/60th of your final pensionable salary (see previous bullet point) for each year you worked for the company. In this example, if you worked for the company for 20 years and your pensionable salary was £25,000, your pension would be £8,333 a year (20 years multiplied by £25,000 final salary divided by an accrual rate of 60).

Final salary pensions must also be protected against inflation of up to 2.5 per cent a year or the annual increase in the Retail Price Index – whichever is lower. This starts from the date you leave the scheme up until retirement.

Traditionally, most employers offered final salary schemes so if you have been with a company for a while, you may be lucky enough to have one.

When you retire, most final salary schemes give you the option of taking part of your pension as a tax-free lump sum, though how big this lump sum can be is limited. HMRC rules limit your tax free lump sum to 25 per cent of your total pension rights. Very often your pension scheme may impose its own additional limits, such as a lump sum of 3/80ths of your final earnings for each year of service. It is worth checking this because in some cases the newer HMRC limit may be more generous than the original scheme rules, and it may be in your interests to ask the scheme to change its rules.

Mourning the demise of the final salary pension

The granddaddy of all pension schemes, the final salary plan, is a generous arrangement, which is why employers are abandoning it in droves. According to a report from the Pension Protection Fund, almost 60 per cent of final salary schemes are now closed to new members, and they could be all but extinct in as little as five years' time.

This decline is not really surprising, as final salary schemes are extremely expensive for employers who take on all the investment risk and have to fulfil the guarantee element of the scheme no matter how poorly the markets perform. If stock markets don't perform well, as was the case between 2000 and 2004, employers have to make up a large shortfall between the pensions they are obligated to provide and the low investment return they received.

As well as closing final salary schemes to new entrants, some employers have frozen them so existing members can no longer build up further pension rights.

If you're lucky enough to be offered a final salary scheme snap it up straight away – before your employer has a chance to change his mind!

If you move jobs frequently, signing on for a final salary scheme at an early employer may not be the best plan for you. If you leave the scheme before you retire, your pension benefits are based on completed service up to the point of leaving. These will be increased to take account of inflation up to your retirement age. But a salary-related pension derived from a short period of service early on in your career, when you weren't earning much money, may not grow as much as it would have done if you'd invested your cash in a good money purchase scheme. Money purchase schemes are also easier to switch from employer to employer (see 'Making the most of a money purchase scheme' later in this chapter).

Final salary schemes tend to be the best sort of pension. But if you move jobs a lot, work on short-term contracts, or have gaps in your employment, they may not be the best option for you. A good personal pension that you can take from job to job regardless may be more suitable. Seek independent advice from a pensions specialist and see the next chapter for more on these.

Of late, some final salary schemes have morphed into *career-average defined benefit schemes*. In plain English this means that instead of being based on length of service and final salary, retirement benefits are linked to length of service and the average salary of the worker throughout their time spent with the employer.

Having given final salary pensions the big up, there is a note of caution to be sounded. In the past few years, some final salary schemes have failed to pay the pensions promised when the company backing them up has gone to the wall. The government has set up the pension protection fund (PPF) to prevent this happening in future. Under the PPF, final salary schemes pay an insurance premium and in return if they go belly up the PPF pays the pensions of scheme members. However, some experts suggest the PPF is underfunded and wouldn't be able to cope if a really big final salary scheme couldn't pay its members' pensions.

Making the most of a money purchase scheme

Money purchase schemes are also referred to as *defined contribution* schemes. Generally, both you and your employer contribute to your pension plan under a *money purchase scheme*. Often the employer matches your contributions, but in other schemes the employee contributes much more than the employer or makes no contributions at all. The contributions are invested in a range of different investment funds, with most employers offering a choice of equities, bonds, property, and cash.

How much risk you're prepared to take on and your age are factors to consider when deciding where to invest your pension. You may also have personal preferences, such as wanting to invest in ethical funds, for example. Someone in their 20s or 30s, for example, can afford to take on a lot more risk by investing in company shares than someone in their 40s or 50s because the younger person has more time to make up any losses. As you get closer to retirement, it makes sense to switch your money into less risky investments, such as government bonds or cash. These produce lower returns than company shares but there is also less chance of losing your money, which is important as you come closer to relying on the income from your pension. If you incur losses at this stage, you might not have any time to make these up again before retirement.

If you can't decide where to invest your pension, or don't want the responsibility of choosing, most schemes have a *default* option. This makes the investment decisions on your behalf. Initially, your contributions will be invested in riskier investments, shifting to safer havens with lower returns as you move closer to retirement.

Book IV

Retiring Wealthy

The aim of a money purchase scheme is to build up an individual pot of money, which you then use to buy an annuity. The way an *annuity* works is that you give your pension pot to an insurance company that in return gives you a guaranteed income for the rest of your life. The amount you receive in retirement depends on several factors:

- ✔ The **amount of money paid into the scheme** by you and your employer. Generally speaking, the longer your payments are invested, the larger your pension will be when you retire.

- ✔ The **performance of the investment funds** your cash is invested in.

- ✔ The **annuity rate** when you retire. The annuity rate is calculated according to how long the provider reckons you will live in retirement: in other words, how many years you will be receiving a pension for. It may also make payments to your husband or wife if you die first. Chapter 5 in this Book has more information on annuities.

At retirement, you may be able to receive part of your pension pot as a tax-free lump sum, with the rest purchasing an annuity. If you have a large pension fund – at least £100,000 – you can defer purchasing an annuity until the age of 75 and drawdown a limited but regular income on the fund instead. Schemes are obliged to offer you the option to shop around for the best terms at retirement. This is called the *Open Market Option*. This is fairly straightforward and nearly always results in a better price for your annuity so it's worth doing this. (See Chapter 5 in this Book for more details on shopping around for annuities.)

Birth of hybrid schemes

There is a new kid on the pension block – hybrid pensions. As the name hints at, this type of pension combines some of the elements of money purchase and final salary schemes.

The most common hybrid is the *nursery scheme*. Here, you are a member of a money purchase scheme until you reach a given age, say 40, at which point you become eligible to join a final salary scheme. This type of scheme tries to offer the best of both worlds. First, if you're a young worker who stays with the company for only a short period, you benefit from the full value of your own and your employer's contributions.

But if you're an older worker, with the same company for many years, the final salary element of the hybrid pension means that you enjoy a degree of certainty. You know for a fact that at least part of your retirement income is dictated by how long your have worked with the company, your final salary, and the scheme's accrual rate – how much you get for each year's service.

The disadvantage of a money purchase scheme is that you have no idea how big a pension you are going to get. The annual projection you receive from your pension provider is just a forecast, not a guarantee. You have to make sure you put enough aside, yet you can have no idea how your investments will perform. There is an element of pot luck involved. If you aren't happy with the level of income indicated on your projection you need to think about putting more money aside, if you can afford to.

Going with a group personal pension or stakeholder scheme

An employer unable or unwilling to make the pension contributions required by occupational pension schemes may still offer a group personal pension or stakeholder scheme, which is cheaper for the employer to run.

Investing with a group

The *group personal pension (GPP)* is a type of personal pension that shares many of the characteristics of an occupational pension scheme. It is organised by your employer with a single life insurance company. Your employer chooses the company and if you sign up to the GPP, you have a personal pension with that provider. The advantage of signing up to a personal pension via a GPP is that your employer may be able to negotiate lower charges with the provider than you would have been able to on your own. Your employer may also contribute to your scheme as well, although he is not obligated to. Contribution limits are the same as for other types of pension: the lower of 100 per cent of your salary and the annual limit of £225,000.

A GPP offers no guarantee as to how large your pension will be. Your money is invested in equities, bonds, cash, and property, and you end up with a pension depending on how much you contribute, how well the investment performs, and the annuity rate when you retire. See 'Making the most of a money purchase scheme' earlier in this chapter for more on annuities.

Claiming a stake in your workplace

Some employers have replaced GPPs with stakeholder pensions because they have guaranteed low charges. Stakeholder pensions have been around only since April 2001 and most people between 0 and 75 may take one out. Employers with five or more employees are required by law to offer this type of pension if they don't have some alternative form of pension provision. Stakeholder pensions are straightforward and uncomplicated, designed to encourage those who don't contribute to a personal pension to start doing so.

Book IV

Retiring Wealthy

Stakeholder pensions have a number of advantages for you, the employee:

- ✔ **Low cost:** They have an annual management charge of a maximum of 1.5 per cent and no other fees
- ✔ **Easy access:** You can invest just £20 a month and don't have to make regular payments

Stakeholder pensions have not been the big success the government had hoped because while many employers are obliged to offer them, they aren't forced to contribute to their schemes. As a result, many don't bother. And this means there are few incentives for employees to join the scheme, resulting in plenty of *empty shells* – stakeholder pension schemes in the workplace with no members at all – across the country.

Looking at Limits on Your Pension

Although it may be tempting to try and build up the biggest pension possible to ensure a comfortable retirement, the Inland Revenue imposes an upper limit on your pension as you receive tax relief on the contributions you make to an occupational scheme. The main limit to bear in mind is the lifetime allowance. This is the overall maximum value of pension rights that HMRC is prepared to allow you to build up before you start getting hit with additional tax charges. The current lifetime limit is £1.6 million.

As a member of a money purchase scheme you receive a yearly illustration of the amount of pension you might receive when you retire. Although this is only a projection and not guaranteed – unlike with a final salary scheme – you should check that you are happy with this level of income. If you aren't you need to think about increasing your contributions – if you can afford to do so. HMRC also limits the contributions you can make to your pension, which has an effect on the size of your final payout. We talk about these limits in the following sections.

Bumping into the contribution ceiling

The more you invest in your pension now, the greater the amount you will have to retire on. But there are limits to how much can be paid into your pension every year. You are allowed to contribute up to the lower of 100 per cent of your income and the annual allowance – which is set at £225,000 for the tax year 2007-08. In addition, your employer can top up your own contributions up to a maximum of the annual allowance. If the combined value of yours and your employer's contributions exceeds the annual allowance then you will be personally liable for 40 per cent tax on the excess.

The combination of the lifetime allowance and the annual allowance means that most people can enjoy a fair amount of flexibility around their pension planning. Bear in mind that even if you don't have any income you can still contribute up to £3,600 a year to a pension. This loophole can be useful for making pension contributions in the name of a non-working spouse.

Getting tax relief

The big attraction of pensions is that you get tax relief on any payments you make, up to a set limit. The amount of tax relief you get depends on how much tax you usually pay:

✔ For a basic-rate taxpayer paying tax at 22 per cent (based on the tax year 2007-08), every time you make a payment into your pension the Government tops this up by 22 per cent. So if you invest £78 into your pension, this is topped up to £100. From April 2008 the basic rate of tax will fall to 20 per cent, so from then on your contribution will rise to £80 of every £100, and the government's contribution will drop to £20.

✔ For a higher-rate taxpayer who pays income tax at 40 per cent, every £100 that goes into your pension costs you £60 (based on the same tax year), with the government paying the other £40. Higher-rate taxpayers must claim back this additional 18 per cent of tax relief (20 per cent from April 2008) on their contributions via their tax return.

To find out how much tax relief you get, go to HMRC's Web site (www.hmrc. gov.uk).

Increasing your contributions

Review your pension on a regular basis to ensure it is on track to provide enough cash for you in retirement. Most people aren't contributing enough to ensure that they will enjoy a comfortable standard of living in retirement. With the new flexibilities introduced in April 2006, and the removal of any restrictions on mixing different types of pension together, the key question to consider is 'how much can you afford to save towards your retirement'.

As mentioned above, there are various different types of pension, which you can now use to top up your main scheme benefits.

Book IV

Retiring Wealthy

For many people an AVC scheme is the simplest, as it is available alongside your employer's scheme, and very often it will also benefit from subsidised administration costs. If you do decide that you want to plough your own furrow, then you can look at an alternative individual pension. Stakeholder pensions are perhaps the simplest, having a limited range of investment choices and just one set of charges. At the other extreme, you could set up a self invested personal pension, which gives you access to a wide range of investment funds and even direct equity investment. See Chapter 4 in this Book for more on SIPPs.

Contracting In or Out of the State Second Pension

When you join an occupational pension scheme, you may be asked whether you want to contract in or contract out of the State Second Pension (S2P) scheme.

This is the additional state pension, which you may get in retirement as well as the basic state pension. It is based on your earnings above a certain level and your National Insurance Contributions (NICs). You are entitled to S2P unless you have contracted out. For an explanation of whether you should contract in or out, read on:

✔ If you **contract in,** you pay the full amount of National Insurance Contributions (NICs). When you retire you receive the basic state pension (which is unaffected whether you contract in or out), an occupational pension, and the S2P as well.

✔ If you **contract out,** you give up some or all of the S2P and rely on your occupational pension instead. You and your employer pay lower NICs.

The shortfall between what you would pay if you contracted in and what you actually pay is the *rebate*. The rebate is supposed to compensate for the S2P you are giving up. The government pays this into your occupational scheme in the autumn following the end of the tax year. When you retire you get the basic state pension plus your occupational scheme, which should be bigger than it would have been if you'd contracted in. Most members of occupational pension schemes contract out of S2P, but whether you are better off contracting out or not depends on your personal circumstances.

In a money purchase scheme the decision about opting out or not is up to you; with final salary schemes, it is usually up to your employer to decide. If the scheme is contracted out, you have no choice in the matter. If your employer's scheme is contracted in to S2P, however, you can contract out if you wish.

Traditionally, the decision to opt in or out largely depended on your age and your attitude to risk. Younger employees tended to contract out because the feeling was that over the long term they would be better off investing in the stock market, rather than relying on the government to provide part of their pension income.

Since 2003, pension providers have been recommending that all of those contracted out of S2P contract back in, no matter what age they are. These providers believe that the rebate you receive for contracting out is too low and that returns will be better if you stay contracted into the S2P.

The rebate you get from contracting out depends on your age: The older you are, the more money is paid into your pension scheme from the National Insurance Fund.

Ask your pension administrator for advice as to whether you should be contracted in or out of the S2P. And after you make a decision, review it on an annual basis to see whether it is still the right choice for your circumstances. You can change your mind at a later date if you wish.

For an occupational scheme to be contracted out, it must meet certain conditions imposed by HMRC. For more details on these, you can obtain a copy of *Contracted-Out Pensions – Your Guide (PM7)* from Opas, the Pensions Advisory Service. Contact 0845 7313233 or check out the Opas Web site at www.thepensionservice.gov.uk.

Changing Jobs – and Your Pension

Employers pay into occupational pensions belonging only to their employees, so when you leave to work for someone else you can no longer contribute to your former employer's pension scheme and he will no longer contribute on your behalf. It may be possible to transfer your pension to your new workplace and carry on contributing to it. However, you will probably have to pay a fee for transferring and it might not be in your best interests to do so. Seek advice from a pensions specialist before making your decision. You may have to pay for this advice. The best way of finding a good independent adviser is through personal recommendation; if you don't have one, contact IFA Promotion (IFAP) on 0800 085 3250 or www.unbiased.co.uk, for details of IFAs in your area.

Book IV

Retiring Wealthy

When you change jobs, your employer should give you an up-to-date statement of the value of your pension, known as the *transfer value*. This cash lump sum can be paid on your behalf into another occupational, stakeholder, or personal pension plan. The one you choose will depend on your circumstances: If you are moving to another job and there is an occupational pension available, this is the best bet. Otherwise, check out a stakeholder or personal pension (the next chapter has more information on these).

If you were in a money purchase scheme this transfer value reflects the value of your fund, but if you were in a final salary scheme it reflects the value of the fixed benefits provided under the scheme. This is often 1/60th or 1/80th of the pensionable salary you were earning at the time you left the company. If you had a final salary scheme with your old employer and your new employer is offering only a money purchase scheme, it may not be worth transferring. This is because you give up the promise of a fixed level of pension income. Instead, your pension will depend on how well the invested money grows.

The transfer value doesn't take into account discretionary benefits that the scheme or your employer may choose to give you but is not obliged to provide. These could include discretionary increases to your pension once you retire, for example. If you transfer your pension to your new employer or a personal pension scheme, you may lose these benefits. Consider carefully what you could lose out on if you transfer your pension.

You may find that you aren't allowed to transfer your pension to another provider. If this is the case, you will be told what pension benefits your money entitles you to. Or you can leave the amount you have in your present scheme and start a new one with your new employer.

If you have worked for your employer for less than two years, you will normally receive back your contributions but not your employer's, less the tax relief you benefited from on those contributions. You are not obliged to put this cash into another pension (indeed, the limits on the amount you can invest in any one tax year may prevent you doing so) but it is worth bearing in mind that you have lost some pension provision. For example, if you worked for your ex-employer for 18 months and have your contributions returned when you leave that employment, you will be 18 months behind on your pension planning.

Chapter 3

Picking Through Personal Pensions

*P*ersonal pensions – also called private pensions – can help you make the most of the whopping tax breaks available to you in saving for retirement. What's more, the rules governing personal pensions changed in April 2006, making them even more flexible.

Personal pensions are also portable – you can take them with you from job to job. You can even pay into one when you're out of work or self employed.

In this chapter, we take a long hard look at personal pensions so that you can decide what role they should play in your retiring wealthy plan.

Understanding What Personal Pensions Have to Offer

A personal pension is a scheme that you set up yourself rather than through an employer. You choose the provider – from literally hundreds – and have the option if things go badly to move your money to another provider.

The big idea of a personal pension is that the money invested grows sufficiently to enable you buy a large annuity – income for life – to tide you over in old age.

Millions of people have a personal pension and you can see why they are so popular when you consider what they offer:

- ✔ **Flexibility**. If you move job your pension moves with you. With a personal pension you get to choose where your money is invested, while under a company scheme the decision is made for you.

- ✔ **Choice**. Hundreds of pension providers exist – insurers, banks, investment houses, even supermarkets have got in on the act. You can scan the market and go for a provider that offers the pensions nirvana of low charges, high performance, and oodles of investment choice.

- ✔ **Tax-free lump sum**. You can take 25 per cent of your pension pot as a tax-free lump sum. Some people invest in a personal pension purely to scoop this tasty tax break.

You can choose to have some of your National Insurance Contributions (NICs) rebated by the government and paid into your personal pension. This process is called *contracting out*. By contracting out you lose entitlement to the state second pension (S2P), but the gamble is that the NICs invested in your personal pension will perform well enough to provide you with a larger income in retirement.

A growing consensus exists that most people would be better off remaining contracted into the S2P rather than having NICs rebated into a personal pension. Many experts argue that the government rebate is too small and as a result it won't grow sufficiently within a personal pension to make up for the loss of S2P entitlement.

The Personal Pension Tax Break

By far the biggest thing that personal – as well as workplace – pensions have going for them is generous tax relief on contributions. This tax relief works as follows:

- ✔ **Basic rate taxpayer** – every 78p you invest is topped up to £1 by the government.

- ✔ **Higher rate taxpayer** – every 60p you invest in your pension is topped up to £1 by the government.

A great plus point for some pension savers is that their contributions – provided they earn enough – may receive tax relief at a rate of 40 per cent, but when it comes time to receive retirement income from their pension they may only be earning enough to be taxed at the basic rate, currently 22 per cent.

Figuring Out Personal Pension Performance

Whether your personal pension will grow sufficiently large to provide the basis of a wealthy retirement depends on four factors:

- **How much you pay in over the years.** It's an investment truism that the more you pay in the more you should get out and this is never truer than with pensions. Contribution levels used to be tightly controlled, but now you can contribute up to 100 per cent of your income, up to a maximum of £215,000 in any tax year, into a personal pension. You can read more about contribution levels later in the chapter.

- **When you start making contributions.** The younger the age at which you start a personal pension, the longer the money has to grow. It has been estimated that every £1 you pay into a pension in your 20s is worth £3 that you pay in during your early fifties.

- **Level of charges.** Your pension provider levies a charge for managing your pension. It may also levy charges if you stop contributing or want to transfer your pension pot to another provider. Think about it: Every pound you pay in charges is a pound that can be invested to help provide you with a wealthy retirement. Charges on personal pensions have been falling of late, but some investors who opened plans in the 1980s and 1990s are saddled with high charges.

- **Annuity rate.** Personal pension rules used to dictate that by the age of 75 you had to use 75 per cent of your fund to buy an annuity – an income for life. That's no longer the case (it is now possible to buy an Alternatively Secured Pension or ASP – see 'Working out annuities', later in this chapter), but for most people an annuity will still be the obvious choice. In recent years annuity rates have fallen, which means that it has cost people more to secure a decent retirement income. If annuity rates fall further you may have to save more in your pension to enable you to buy an income which will allow you to enjoy the finer things in life in old age.

At retirement your pension provider offers to convert your pension pot into an annuity for you – that's nice of them, isn't it? No, it's not. You're likely to find that you can get a better annuity by ignoring your pension provider's

Book IV

Retiring Wealthy

generous offer and shopping around for an annuity. Choosing the right annuity is hardly glamorous – in the way that making a killing on the stock market is – but it's one of the most crucial financial decisions you can make. See Chapter 5 in this Book for more on buying an annuity.

A major plus point with annuities is that they guarantee an income for life and not just for a set period of time. It doesn't matter if you're lucky enough to retire at 55 and live to 100, you still continue to receive an income.

Weighing Up Personal and Workplace Pensions

So what's better – company or personal pension? Which type of pension promises the quicker route to a wealthy retirement?

The answer always used to be a company pension, for the following reasons:

- ✔ **Employer contributions.** Companies offering a pension scheme to staff often make contributions, which can help boost the size of the pension pot. It's unusual for an employer to make payments into a worker's personal pension plan.

- ✔ **Employers meet the cost.** The company bears the costs of administering the pension, while with a personal pension plan it's up to the saver. And as I mentioned earlier in this chapter, every pound disappearing in charges means a smaller pension pot. With company schemes the costs of administering the scheme is borne by the sponsoring employer.

Personal pensions were seen as bit of a poor relation to company schemes. If you were self-employed or didn't have access to a company pension then you would go for a personal pension plan, but otherwise forget it.

But the pension goalposts have been moved for a number of reasons. What's been happening in the world of company and personal pensions should make you question the 'company pension is always best' theory:

- ✔ **Lower charges on personal pensions.** The introduction of stakeholder pensions with their low charging structure led to a general lowering of charges across the whole personal pension sector – although being a member of a company pension is still the low-cost option.

> ✔ **Falling away of employer commitment.** The company pension system has been going through turmoil in recent years, with many employers closing lucrative final salary schemes to new members and cutting the amount of cash they pay into their workers' pensions.
>
> ✔ **Greater flexibility.** In the past personal pension providers often levied penalties on savers who stopped making contributions. Nowadays, providers increasingly offer savers the chance to lower or stop contributions at will without penalty.

All in all, the gap between personal and company pensions has closed a little. This is due to personal pension providers pulling their socks up and employers cutting back on their commitments.

Having Your Pension Cake and Eating It

It's no longer a case of choosing a company or personal pension – you can have both!

It used to be the case that if you were paying into a personal pension and then decided to join a company scheme you had to stop contributing to your personal pension. As a result, your personal pension provider levied a penalty and the pension became *paid up* – barred from making further contributions.

Fortunately, the days of penalties and pension freezing have gone. New pension rules from April 2006 allow you to have as many different pensions as you want, all running alongside one another.

Let's see how this can work in practice. Ivan is self-employed and decides to open a personal pension. He pays into the scheme but after a few years decides to get a salaried job; in other words he becomes an employee.

Ivan's new employer offers an occupational pension scheme – a type of company pension where the employer has to make a contribution – which he decides to join.

In the past Ivan would have had to stop paying into his personal pension, but not any more. Instead Ivan pays money into his occupational scheme *and* his personal pension. This way Ivan is able to save really hard towards a wealthy retirement and make maximum use of the tax relief on pension contributions.

Book IV

Retiring Wealthy

After ten years being an employee, Ivan decides to return to self employment. His occupational scheme won't allow Ivan to contribute once he has left the firm's employ. However, this doesn't bother Ivan, as he puts the money he would have paid into the occupational pension into his personal plan.

When Ivan eventually decides to retire, he has the income from his occupational scheme and his personal pension to rely on. And because Ivan was able to contribute into his personal pension over many years – rather than stopping when he was a member of a company scheme and then starting again – he has been able to build up a bigger pension pot.

One big advantage for Ivan of having both personal and workplace pensions is that he has reduced his risk. If one of his pensions underperforms then the other may ride to the rescue by performing well.

Some people with personal pensions may find that they still face penalties and having their pension paid up if they stop contributing. Best check with your pension provider what the rules of your scheme are.

Choosing the Best Scheme for You

You hope to contribute to your pension for many years to come, so picking the right scheme is vital. Your choice may make the difference between retiring on a decent income or on a much poorer one. You may be able to switch providers if you aren't happy with your plan's performance, but this may cost you (unless you have a stakeholder plan).

If you opt for a group personal pension or stakeholder provided by your employer, she chooses the provider, you don't have a say; but if you take out a personal pension yourself, you choose.

Even if your employer offers a pension scheme, you may decide to do your own thing with a personal pension. Your employer's occupational scheme may not be suitable for you if you're pretty certain you'll move jobs in less than two years or you're on a short-term contract so don't qualify to join. If your employer doesn't offer an occupational scheme and doesn't contribute to a stakeholder or group personal pension on your behalf, a personal pension might be a better way of supplementing the basic state pension in retirement.

Compare pension plans by asking providers for their *key features document*, which includes a breakdown of charges and how these affect your pension. It also offers a projection of what you should receive in retirement so you can decide which plan is more likely to perform better. Providers must offer prospective policyholders their key features document.

Bear in mind the pension provider's reputation and past results. While these are no guarantee of future performance, a fund that has performed consistently well over the years is likely to be a better option than one that has done consistently badly. And make sure you pay attention to the penalties for changing schemes, in case you find yourself having to do this.

Searching for sources

You can buy a personal pension from an insurance company, high-street bank, other big financial institution or retailer, such as a supermarket. The easiest way of finding information about the range of pensions available is to log onto the Internet, where you will be able to do a search on various providers' Web sites to check the details of each pension scheme.

Some employers offer a personal pension scheme through the workplace: either a stakeholder scheme or group personal pension (GPP). Your employer chooses the provider and deducts your contributions from your pay packet, but otherwise these operate in the same way as a personal pension. Chapter 2 in this Book deals with company pensions in more detail but it is worth reiterating the benefits of a personal pension via this source:

- ✔ Your employer may contribute to your pension (although it is not obliged to do so). If it does, your fund will build up more quickly and you'll retire on a bigger pension.

- ✔ Charges for running the scheme are usually paid by your employer. Even if it doesn't foot the bill, it should be able to use its purchasing power to negotiate lower charges.

- ✔ Pensions advice should be available. With scores of employees signed up to a GPP or employer-designated stakeholder scheme, your employer may ask a financial adviser to visit the workplace and talk you through what's on offer. If you take out a personal pension yourself and require advice, you'll have to pay for it (see 'Seeking advice' later in this chapter).

However, there are downsides to a personal pension through the workplace if you quit your job or are made redundant:

- ✔ If your employer was making contributions to your GPP or stakeholder, it is likely to stop doing so. However, you can continue contributing to your scheme yourself and should consider increasing your contributions to cover the shortfall left by the cessation of your employer's contributions.

- ✔ You may have to foot the bill for belonging to a fund after you leave the company. Charges vary according to the pension provider but you may have to pay an annual fee. You may have to increase your contributions accordingly to ensure the same amount of cash goes into your fund each month.

Book IV

Retiring Wealthy

Seeking advice

You can buy a pension two ways: direct from the provider or via an intermediary, usually an independent financial adviser (IFA). If you know what you want, buying direct from the provider cuts costs as you don't have to pay for advice and may be able to negotiate lower charges.

However, if you aren't sure, you should seek impartial advice. Any old IFA won't do, however: You need one who specialises in pensions. You may have a perfectly good adviser you use most of the time, but you need someone who knows this specialist subject inside out.

You may have to pay a fee for this advice or your adviser will receive commission from the pension provider you end up signing up with. If you are paying a fee, you will be told at the initial consultation how much the advice will cost. With commission, you should also be told how much your adviser is earning for recommending a particular product.

You may prefer to use a fee-based IFA to ensure that she is completely independent and supplying the best advice for you – rather than recommending a product because it pays the most commission.

If you can't afford financial advice, at least shop around for the best pension for you. Ask the provider if you don't understand the key features document and compare several deals to ensure you find the best one. It is also worth looking at the Department of Work and Pensions Web site at www.dwp.gov.uk, as this has plenty of advice to bear in mind when making your decision.

To find an IFA specialising in pensions, contact IFA Promotion at www.unbiased.co.uk.

Deciding where to invest

Choosing the pension itself is just the beginning: Many providers also let you choose where your money is invested. However, not all providers offer this choice, so if it's important to you, shop around for a provider who gives you this freedom.

When deciding where to invest your fund, bear in mind your attitude to risk and your planned retirement age: The younger you are, the more risk you can afford to take on. But make sure that you will be able to sleep at night because if you are of a nervous disposition, plunging your life savings into high-risk hedge funds is not a good idea.

In the long run, equities produce better returns than less risky investments such as bonds and cash, so if you have some years to go before retirement, you can afford to opt for stocks and shares.

The main investment choices available are:

- **Stock market funds,** such as UK, American, or European equities. You could even opt for emerging markets or the Far East, if you're feeling more adventurous. You also have the choice of actively managed funds or *index trackers*, which simply follow the performance of a stock market index, such as the FTSE 100. These are less risky than actively managed funds and tend to produce lower returns. With some funds, you can also choose ethical investments.

- **Managed funds,** which can be less risky than stock market funds because they invest in a spread of assets – including shares, property, and fixed interest – via a balanced portfolio. Over the longer term they may not grow as well as stock market funds, however. (See Chapter 5 in Book III for more.)

- **Property funds,** investing in shares of property companies or commercial property. These can be extremely risky, depending on the number of properties you are exposed to and market conditions.

- **Fixed interest funds,** such as bonds and government securities, also called gilts. These are suitable for more conservative investors or those nearing retirement, as they are considered less risky than stocks and shares.

- **Cash,** which is not much riskier than a building society or bank account. Your money is guaranteed but you won't generate much in the way of returns, so avoid unless you are just about to retire.

If you haven't the first clue about where to invest your pension, you can leave it to the experts. This is known as a *default* arrangement. Your money is allocated to a range of investments on your behalf and you're told where your cash is invested. All stakeholder schemes must have a default arrangement.

The default arrangement may not be the best place for your money because it doesn't take into account your particular circumstances. Look out for providers offering a *lifestyle* option instead: This is when your money is invested according to your age and risk profile, so as you move closer to retirement your money is automatically moved to lower-risk investments, such as bonds and cash, where there is less volatility (and potentially lower returns). This means you have less chance of experiencing significant losses as you near retirement and need to get your cash. Lifestyling often happens even if you initially chose where your money was invested, with the fund automatically switching to less risky investments as you near retirement.

Book IV

Retiring Wealthy

If your scheme provider offers a lifestyle option, check out how flexible it is. You should be able to choose your retirement age and have the funds moved to safer investments to accommodate that.

Making Contributions

You must contribute the same amount to your pension on the same day every month – unless you have a stakeholder plan. With a stakeholder pension, the minimum investment is no more than £20 and you can make contributions as large or small as you like as often as you like.

Contributions are usually made via direct debit or standing order from your account to your pension provider's account and are made net of tax. You can also pay by debit card or cheque. If you are contributing to an employer-designated stakeholder scheme or GPP, your contributions are made from net salary.

Mostly, you will make all the contributions to your fund, but in some instances your employer may also contribute. This usually happens where the employer would have made contributions to an occupational scheme if you'd joined but is prepared to pay into your personal pension instead.

If your employer offers an occupational scheme, think carefully before deciding not to join it. You may not be able to join at a later date and your employer might not make the same contributions into your personal pension. It is nearly always in your interests to join an occupational pension if there's one on offer (see Chapter 2 in this Book for more on these).

Limits to pension contributions

Up until recently a limit was imposed on pension saving. This limit was an ultra-complex formula based on age. The good news is that this complex system was swept away in April 2006 and replaced with something a lot easier for savers – and money experts – to get their heads around.

You may now contribute up to 100 per cent of your annual income into a pension, up to a maximum of £215,000. In addition, non-taxpayers are able to contribute up to £3,600 a year into a pension scheme.

You are also able to contribute to any number of pensions at the same time.

However, the total value of all your pensions must not exceed £1.5m, rising to £1.8m in 2010. You are allowed to save over this threshold, but if you do the tax system becomes punishing rather than generous, so it's best to keep below the lifetime limit.

One solution worth considering is to join the occupational scheme (so you receive your employer's contributions) but instead of contributing to the plan yourself, continue to pay into your personal pension. This gives you the best of both worlds.

Stopping contributions

At some stage you may stop contributing to your pension. This could be down to joining a company with an attractive occupational scheme that you've decided to join. Or you may be short of a bob or two and decide to skip your contributions.

If you have a stakeholder plan, nothing happens if you miss a payment: The fund manager continues to deduct the annual fee (no more than 1 per cent) and your money is still invested. You can contribute again whenever you want or make no further contributions before retirement.

If your personal pension isn't a stakeholder scheme, it isn't so easy. The pension may become *paid up* once you miss three months' worth of contributions so you can't make any more contributions. Charges are deducted as normal, if this is the case, and the fund continues to grow (because it is invested in the stock market) until you are ready to draw your pension. Some schemes enable you to start paying into the pension again at a later date but your provider may charge a fee for this. However, it may be worth paying the fee as it's likely to be cheaper than starting a policy from scratch.

If you stop contributing to your plan, even for just a couple of years, you are likely to retire on a smaller pension than you would otherwise have done. Missing contributions for several years could leave you with a significant shortfall, which you never have a chance to make up. Think carefully before you stop contributions.

Transferring to another fund

If your circumstances change – for example, you join a company with an excellent workplace scheme – you may decide to transfer your existing pension to the new scheme. See Chapter 5 for more on how to transfer your pension.

Think twice before transferring your personal pension into an occupational scheme (unless it's a stakeholder) as you may be heavily penalised for doing so. It might be in your interests to leave the money where it is and simply allow the pension to become paid up, while you join your employer's scheme and start contributing to it from scratch.

If you have a stakeholder pension, you can transfer it at will, without charge. So you can move the cash you've saved into your employer's scheme or another stakeholder or personal pension, without penalty. This is one of the main benefits of such schemes.

Understanding the Effects of Charges

You may have noticed the words 'charges' cropping up a lot in this chapter. That is because the level of charges has a huge effect on your pension.

Pensions tend to be held for longer than other investments and savings – usually twenty or thirty years. As a result, even small differences in charges – say a quarter or a half per cent a year – can make a huge difference to the ultimate size of your pension pot.

The dramatic effects that charges can have are demonstrated in the following example.

Twin sisters, Imogen and Samantha, each open a personal pension at the same time but with different providers. Imogen's provider charges her 1 per cent per year to manage her pension fund. Samantha's provider charges her 1.5 per cent a year to manage her pension fund. The sisters both pay £100 a month into their pension funds for 35 years. Both pension funds grow at 7 per cent a year for the full 35 years.

When Imogen came to retire, her pension fund was worth £138,000 and over the 35 years she paid £34,000 in charges.

However, paying just 0.5 per cent more each year than Imogen in charges meant that Samantha's pension at the end of 35 years was worth £124,000 as she paid £48,000 in charges.

The message is keep an eagle eye on charges to make sure your pension provider isn't taking too big a slice of your retirement wealth.

Securing low charges is important, but it's not the be all and end all. You should also consider past performance, choice of investments on offer, and whether you can stop or vary contribution before choosing your pension.

The personal pensions market is very competitive and as a result charges have been falling in most of the industry during recent years. However, some horror pensions are still being sold that have very steep charges and penalties. Not too long ago I came across a pension which levied an annual charge of 2.5 per cent – two and half times the maximum allowed charges under a stakeholder pension.

The different types of charges you should keep a watchful eye on include:

- ✔ **Initial charge** – the fee for setting up the pension plan.
- ✔ **Annual charge** – the ongoing management fee.
- ✔ **Transaction charge** – a small, incremental charge levied for new investment by your fund.
- ✔ **Transfer charge** – the fee for transferring your money out of one pension and into another.

Don't just look at one charge in isolation, look at the whole package. One pension may have low annual charges but hefty penalties for transferring out. Another pension may have slightly higher annual charges but impose no charges for transfer out. The latter may be the best choice, because if the pension underperforms it is easier for you to cut your losses and take your money elsewhere.

Stakeholder pensions have some of the lowest charges in the pensions universe and you can stop contributing at anytime without fear that the fund will become *paid up*.

Staking Your Future on a Stakeholder Pension

Stakeholder pensions are a low-cost, easy to understand, flexible personal pension with no hidden costs. Stakeholder pensions offer the same tax benefits as a standard personal pension but with the added appeal of low charges and flexibility.

Stakeholder pensions are designed to be simple, easy to understand products encouraging low- to middle-income people to save more for their retirement. Generally, stakeholder pension funds tend to be a safety-first long-term investment.

For a pension to be called a stakeholder, it must conform to the following rules:

- ✔ The annual management charge is capped at 1.5 per cent a year and there are no other fees. (The charges cap is 1 per cent if the stakeholder was opened before April 2005.)
- ✔ You can invest as little as £20 a month and can stop and then restart contributions at any time.

Book IV

Retiring Wealthy

A strong case exists for investing in a stakeholder pension rather than a standard pension as the charges are lower. However, you may consider going for a standard pension if the charges are just a little over 1 per cent and the fund offers a wide range of investments for you to choose from.

Although stakeholders haven't caught the public imagination, they have had a marked impact on the rest of the personal pensions universe. Standard, non-stakeholder, personal pensions have often cut their charges to compete with stakeholder schemes; this can only be good for investors.

Even if you are a non-earner you can pay into a stakeholder pension. Some wealthy parents and grandparents have opened and paid into stakeholders in the name of their children or grandchildren with the idea of giving their long-term pension saving a kick-start.

The cost of your pension isn't the be-all and end-all – performance is more important – but the charges eat into your investment returns. Avoid paying more than is absolutely necessary. However, don't pick the cheapest stakeholder plan just for the sake of it: It may have particularly low charges because it invests in tracker funds, which simply follow a stock market index and are unlikely to produce the best returns. Check to see exactly what you are investing in before taking the plunge. You can compare the charges imposed by pension providers on the Financial Services Authority's Web site (www.fsa.gov.uk).

Chapter 4

Taking Control with a Sipp

*P*ensions are supposed to be impenetrable products. You hand over your cash each month and a huge hulking insurance company invests it on your behalf. You have very little say in where your money goes and just hope that everything will be well and you will have a tidy pile of cash to live off in retirement. In short, the one word you don't associate with personal pensions is control.

But Self Invested Personal Pensions (Sipps) are all about control. You get all the tax breaks of a standard pension but *you* make the investment decisions.

In this chapter, we explore Sipps, what they are, and what role they can play in your retiring wealthy plan.

Introducing Self Invested Personal Pensions (Sipps)

Think of a Sipp as a shopping trolley, in which you hold lots of different investments. You get tax relief on your contributions, like a personal or workplace pension. Tax relief is not to be sniffed at; it can give your pension fund an enormous boost.

If you're a basic rate taxpayer for every 78p you pay in your pension fund the government adds another 22p. From April 2008, the basic rate of tax falls to 20p in the pound, so you have to contribute 80p and the government will top it up to £1. If you're a higher rate taxpayer for every 60p you pay in, the government adds another 22p initially and then you can claim a further 18p through your tax return. In addition, all income and growth on investments held in a Sipp is tax free.

You can contribute to a Sipp even if you're not earning an income. You can pay in at least £2,808 per year, which with basic rate tax relief is boosted to £3,600. This means that children, retired people, and non-working carers can contribute to a Sipp.

Using a Sipp as your pension plan offers several advantages:

- ✔ **More control**: You make the investment decisions rather than some highly paid pension fund manager. Whether or not you retire rich or not is down to you. What you say goes and that can be very empowering.

- ✔ **More choice**: Sipps allow you to pick from lots of different investments allowing you to build up a diversified investment base while taking advantage of the tax relief available on pensions.

- ✔ **More fun**: Building your pension pot can become a bit of a hobby. Weighing up different types of investment and deciding what funds to commit requires research, time, and know-how. Sipps are a good way of expanding your personal finance knowledge – which you can also do by reading this book, of course!

The Sipps revolution that never happened

Exciting is not normally a word you associate with pensions. But for a few months in 2005 pensions got just a little bit, well, exciting. The reason? The government announced that from April 2006 it planned to allow people to hold residential property and collectables, such as fine wine and classic cars, in their Sipp. It took potential buy-to-let investors and collectable enthusiasts about a nano-second to see the pound signs floating in front of their eyes. They were looking at the delicious prospect of getting

tax relief on their investments just as long as they held them in a Sipp. The press reported that thousands of investors were poised to open a Sipp to take advantage of the fab tax breaks.

Facing the prospect of giving away lots of money in tax relief, the government got spooked and in late 2005 effectively reversed its decision to allow people to use their Sipps to invest in buy-to-let and collectables.

But inevitably Sipps also have a downside. These are the sort of problems you need to consider:

- **Making the wrong choices:** You may not have huge faith in pension fund managers, but who is to say you'll do any better – in fact you may do a lot worse. In fact your understandable desire to get things right may cloud your judgement resulting in you putting your money into investments that are too risky or too safe. Can you really be dispassionate and think clearly when your retirement wealth is on the line?

- **Being time consuming:** You may set out on a Sipp full of enthusiasm but do you have the time to keep at it year in year out? You need to track your investments to see how they are doing, whereas with a standard personal pension you leave the fund manager to get on with his or her job. Pension saving is not a fad, it is a long-term commitment.

- **Carrying high charges:** Bizarrely, Sipps can sometimes be as expensive as a standard personal pension. The Sipp providers argue that fees are high due to 'administration costs'. But you may find it odd that you're being asked to shell out when it's you making all the tricky choices, such as where to invest. The good news though is that the Sipps market is becoming more competitive and charges are falling fast.

Sipps are generally a higher risk option than a standard personal pension run by an insurance company. Personal pension funds are huge business – some are worth many billions of pounds – so are managed by professionals to achieve growth without putting financial security at risk.

Sipps are not to be entered into lightly, they can be costly and if things go wrong you have no one to blame but yourself. You may want to seek financial advice from a qualified professional before starting a Sipp.

You are allowed to invest in property through your Sipp. You can invest directly in commercial property or through a property investment fund. These funds pool investor cash to buy up property. Borrowing up to 50 per cent of the value of your Sipp to fund a commercial property purchase is allowed; so, if your Sipp has £100,000 in it you can borrow £50,000. Just remember, if you borrow and are unable to keep up with repayments the commercial property may be repossessed by your lender.

If you own shares in a non-stock market listed business or one listed on OFFEX – which simply means *off exchange*, a sort of baby stock market for fledgling firms – then you can put these into your Sipp too.

This can be very handy as any dividend that you receive slots into your Sipp tax free and what's more if you sell your shares you'll do so free from capital gains tax (CGT).

Moving out of the Sipps fast lane

In all the excitement about the freedom offered by Sipps it can be easy to forget the fact that it's just another personal pension and still subject to strict rules on access to funds.

Sipp investors can't access their pension fund until they are at least age 50, rising to 55 in 2010.

They can only take 25 per cent of their fund in cash at retirement. The remaining money usually goes towards buying a retirement income – called an annuity.

Annuity rates have been falling for the past decade, so are becoming less popular. They are also an ultra-safe investment, which maybe a bit hard for someone who has been managing their own Sipp to deal with. Using cash from a Sipp to buy an annuity has been likened to being made to sell a Ferrari and buy a Morris Minor! Check out Chapter 5 in this Book for more on how annuities work.

Looking at Sipp Investments

Sipps allow you to divide your pension pot into many different types of investment. These investments range from the quite risky (single company shares) to the ultra safe (government gilts).

Most but not all the traditional Sipp investments involve the stock market in some way. Your choices are as follows:

- ✔ **Collective investment schemes:** These pool investor cash to buy a range of shares and sometimes other investments such as bonds. Qualifying collective investments include unit trusts (also called OEICS), investment trusts, and with-profit funds.

- ✔ **Single company equities:** You can invest in any share on any stock market throughout the world through a Sipp. See Chapter 6 in Part III for more on picking shares.

- ✔ **UK government gilts:** You lend the government cash and in return it promises to pay back the loan plus a regular rate of interest, which is usually fixed at the outset but can be linked to the level of inflation.

- ✔ **Corporate bonds:** Essentially, these work the same as gilts only they tend to have a shorter lifespan and are a little riskier as companies are more likely than the UK government to go bust.

✔ **Shares futures and options:** Put simply this is the right to buy or sell a quantity of shares at a specific date in the future. Futures are high risk and very specialist.

✔ **Permanent interest bearing shares (PIBS):** These are shares issued by building societies which normally pay a fixed rate of interest. Pibs are a safe but very little known investment. All in all, the corduroy jacket of investing – not very sexy!

✔ **Cash deposit accounts:** These need little introduction, being a standard savings account in which your money earns interest and the capital is safe. The nitty gritty of savings accounts is explored in Chapter 2 in Book III.

✔ **Traded endowment policies:** These are second-hand endowment policies that are yet to mature bought through a traded endowment broker. The investment is indirectly related to the stock market because at least part of the underlying performance of the endowment will be reliant on share price growth.

✔ **Commercial property:** Some Sipps allow you to hold commercial property such as offices, warehouses, and retail outlets. A Sipp can also invest indirectly in property through a property unit trust. An attractive alternative to property unit trusts is the Real Estate Investment Trust (REIT). This is a tax efficient trust investing in real estate; investors simply hold shares bought and sold on the stock market. The way a REIT is structured means that both income and capital gains are truly tax-free if they are held within a Sipp. In contrast, income earned in a commercial property unit trust is paid net of basic rate tax, and this cannot be reclaimed within a pension. See Chapter 7 in Book III for more on investing directly and indirectly in commercial property.

The investments to consider for your Sipp depend on your age, approach to risk, and the size of your fund. If you don't have a lot of money in your Sipp, or you are near your planned retirement date, you're best going for safer investments, such as collective ones. On the other hand, if you have a large fund or are quite young you can afford to take some risks. See the section 'Building a Balanced Sipp Portfolio' later in this chapter for more on high-, medium-, and low-risk Sipp investments.

Some Sipp providers offer you a wider range of investment choice than others. The Sipp provider tries to strike a balance between breadth of choice and the need to keep down its administration costs.

Any investments held in a Sipp aren't strictly yours. Everything is legally owned by the Sipp pension fund, overseen by a scheme trust. The Sipp provider acts as the trustee.

Book IV

Retiring Wealthy

Keeping Your Sipp in the Family

Family members, friends, and even business partners can have what is called a *linked Sipp*. They all have their very own ring-fenced Sipp pension pot with the same provider but have the ability to pass on the cash they have invested to the other linked Sipp members when they die.

The inheritance tax (IHT) implications of a linked Sipp are yet to be finalised – the Treasury is still umming and ahhing over this one. But if the money held in the linked Sipp goes to the other Sipp members free of IHT, it may prove to be a real boon for those with large estates looking to minimise any eventual IHT bill.

In the 2007-08 tax year, IHT at 40 per cent is charged on estates worth in excess of £300,000. However, transfers between spouses, and to exempt beneficiaries such as charities, are free of IHT. See Chapter 4 in Book V for more on IHT.

Choosing the Right Sipp Provider

You need a Sipp provider to oversee your investments. Insurance companies offer Sipps as do some large Independent Financial Advice firms.

Your Sipp can eventually be worth a lot of money, so you have the right to demand the best. Only consider Sipp providers that offer you the following:

✔ The ability to make new investments by phone, post, and online.

✔ Lots of free information such as regular updates on how your Sipp is doing and analysts' reports.

✔ As varied a range of investments as possible.

✔ Access to independent financial advice if you need it.

There are three areas you need to bear in mind when choosing a Sipp provider:

✔ The level of service on offer.

✔ The level of charges.

✔ The range of investments.

There are lots of providers out there each claiming to be the best. It maybe best to see an independent financial adviser (IFA) who'll look at the whole market and recommend the one that's right for you.

Provider services

The Sipp provider will offer either an advisory or execution only service.

- ✔ **Advisory service:** Under this arrangement you will receive advice on which investments to put into your Sipp. But the final decision on whether to act on the advice offered is up to you.

- ✔ **Execution only:** You call all the shots from start to finish, and your Sipp provider follows your instructions to the letter.

From time to time the Sipp provider will send you a statement detailing how your Sipp investments are performing – usually once a year.

Keep your Sipps statement safe; you will need it if you fill in your tax self-assessment form.

Sipp charges

Sipp charges break down into two different types:

- ✔ **Upfront charges:** This is an initial setting up fee, often several hundred pounds.

- ✔ **Ongoing charges:** The provider may levy an annual charge for managing the fund as well as a transaction fee for each new investment made.

For example, if you buy shares to put in a Sipp the provider will charge either a flat fee or a percentage of the money being invested.

High annual charges can eat into the performance of your Sipp investments.

Some providers offer what are called 'free Sipps' but nothing in life, apart from fresh air, is free. The providers of 'free Sipps' may not levy an upfront charge, but this is on the proviso that you invest some of your Sipp money in a fund that they run. These funds come with guess what? Charges!

Range of investments

Not all providers will offer access to the full universe of Sipp qualifying investments. They may for example only be able to offer access to shares in the UK's largest companies, leaving out all the medium and small companies.

Changing Sipp provider

There really are only a couple of reasons to transfer any sort of pension, including a Sipp, between providers and they are the following:

✔ **The new provider charges less**: It may cost you cash to move so make sure that the provider you're switching to is offering enough of a financial incentive in the way of lower charges to make this worthwhile.

✔ **The new provider offers more choice**: Not all providers may offer the range of investments that you require. Diversity is very important to building a successful SIPP.

If you transfer your pension to another provider you may find that you have to pay a penalty.

The greater the range of investments on offer, the more flexibility you have. Flexibility is a good thing as it makes it easier for you to diversify your investments.

Building a Balanced Sipp Portfolio

You should look to build a Sipp which includes low-, medium-, and even some high-risk investments. The idea is that if all goes wrong with your high-risk investments then the safe low-risk investments give you a good fall-back position. If you have all your money in high-risk investments and they go wrong you can conceivably lose everything.

Table 4-1 categorises Sipp investments by degree of risk.

Table 4-1	How Risky Is Your Sipp?
Low risk	
Deposit savings	
UK government gilts	
Permanent interest-bearing shares (PIBS)	
Medium risk	
Gold bullion	

Medium risk	
Bonds and other fixed interest securities	
Collective investment funds such as unit and investment trusts	
Traded endowment policies	
Commercial property	
High risk	
Individual company shares	
Share futures and options	
Private company and Offex shares	

Your pension is likely to be vital to your retiring wealthy plans, so don't take too many risks with your choice of investment. The closer you are to retirement the less investment risk you should take.

Some share investments are obviously riskier than other. Shares in a multinational such as Tesco or BP are less likely to nosedive than say shares in an Internet company.

 When deciding which types of investment you should put into your Sipp, look at the investments you already hold. If you have lots of cash in savings deposit accounts you can probably afford to introduce a little risk into your Sipp by buying shares.

To Sipp or Not to Sipp

Sipps aren't for everyone. They are expensive and require a good deal of financial knowledge to manage effectively. You have to be confident that you know what you are doing and are up to the job.

Also Sipps involve a lot of work. Ask yourself whether you have the time to keep an eye on how your investments are performing.

Sipp charges can be high, so it may not be worth you opening one if you don't have a large amount of cash to invest or are on a low wage. If you don't have much cash then you may be best going for a low-cost personal pension called a *stakeholder*. See Chapter 3 in this part for more on this type of scheme.

If you have any doubts about your ability to manage your Sipp you may be best sticking to a personal or workplace pension, particularly if your employer makes a contribution.

You can open a Sipp even if you're contributing to a company pension scheme as well. Having more than one pension on the go gives you greater investment diversity.

Chapter 5

Working with Your Pension

*I*n this chapter, we show you how to work with your pensions – state, workplace, and personal – so that they produce the most bangs for your buck.

Take a peek at the pension management tactics outlined in this chapter and you'll have an A1 chance of being able to kick off your shoes and enjoy a wealthy retirement.

Deciding When to Retire

When you retire isn't totally your decision: The state retirement age is 65 for men and 60 for women. This is when you receive the basic state pension and most people can't afford to retire before this because they need to live off this pension. The state retirement age is gradually being raised for women from 2010 so that by 2020, women will also officially retire at 65. The amount of basic state pension you receive depends on the amount of National Insurance contributions made during your working life (see Chapter 2 in this Book for more on this).

You don't *have* to retire at state retirement age. You may not want to or be able to if you haven't saved much for retirement. The government is keen for you to work longer, if this is feasible, and is offering incentives, such as a higher state pension, if you do so.

The government is also raising the age at which you can take your private pension (if you have one). Under current rules, you must be between the ages of 50 and 75, although your particular scheme may have its own rules preventing you from retiring at 50. From 2010, the minimum age at which you can draw your private pension will be 55.

Those people with an early normal retirement date, such as professional foot-ballers, will still be allowed to retire and draw their pension before the age of 55. But there will be a 2.5 per cent discount off the lifetime allowance for each year they don't work before the age of 55. (The lifetime allowance is the maxi-mum amount of pension savings that can benefit from tax relief; it is set at £1.6m for 2007-08, rising to £1.8m by 2010.)

The longer you work and put off claiming your pension, the better. Avoid retir-ing in your 50s if you can help it as you will get a much smaller pension than if you pack in your job at 70. Table 5-1 shows the difference delaying your pen-sion by a few years can make. The figures in the table assume an index-linked, single annuity for a male non-smoker bought using a £100,000 pension pot. Payments are monthly in advance. You will have to pay tax on these.

Table 5-1	Monthly Pension Payments at Different Ages
Age	*Monthly Income*
50	£251
55	£289
60	£333
65	£392
70	£474
74	£568

Source: Financial Services Authority

If you have several pensions, you could draw one or two in your 50s or 60s and leave the others invested until later on to maximise your income.

Taking early retirement

Early retirement is beyond the means of most of us, as we won't have a big enough pension pot to enable us to give up working before 65. You can't claim the state pension until this age (60 for women until 2020) – even if you're no longer working. You may also have to carry on making National Insurance Contributions (NICs) if you retire early, to ensure you get the full basic state pension.

If you suffer a disability so can't work, you may be able to take early retirement if you belong to an occupational scheme (see Chapter 2 in this Book).

One of the questions you must consider before giving up work is whether you have enough cash to see you through a long retirement. If you've got enough savings and investments to tide you over, you may not have to draw your pension until state retirement age anyway. But if you haven't got a comfortable income to rely on, you will struggle and it won't be much fun at all.

You can take up to 25 per cent of your pension pot as a tax-free cash lump sum from the age of 50, using the remainder of your fund by the time you are 75 to buy an annuity or take out an Alternatively Secured Pension.

If you retire early, you'll receive a smaller pension than you would have done if you'd worked up until normal retirement age (65 for men, 60 for women, 65 for women from 2020) because you'll have invested less money and it won't have had as long to grow. Check whether early retirement is feasible before taking the plunge: The Trades Union Congress (TUC) Web site (www.worksmart.org.uk) has a calculator that works out how big a retirement income your pension pot will purchase.

Retiring at the usual age

Most people retire at the official state retirement age of 65 (60 for women until 2020 when it rises to 65). Private pension savings are usually made with this target in mind, and you can draw the basic state pension and state second pension at this age as long as you have made enough NICs to qualify.

Working past retirement age

You may want to continue working past the official state retirement age but it's not always straightforward. New legislation means your employer can't automatically chuck you onto the scrapheap once you reach 65, but whether

Book IV

Retiring Wealthy

you can stay on depends on whether you are still competent to do your job. If you aren't, your employer doesn't have to continue employing you.

You can receive your pension and carry on working if you wish, although normally you can't work for an employer and receive your pension from that employer's scheme. But you could work for another employer or go self-employed in order to get over this hurdle.

Delaying Your State Pension

The government is now paying people to take their state pension at a later date, which is called deferral. In return for agreeing to forgo receipt of the state pension you will receive either of the following:

- ✔ The amount you deferred as a taxable lump sum payment.
- ✔ A higher income from your state pension when you do eventually collect it.

The size of the payment you receive for not taking your state pension depends on the length of time that you have been making National Insurance contributions. If you have saved enough to earn a full basic state pension you can expect to receive top whack for deferral. If, on the other hand, you have a patchy NIC record – not enough to earn a full basic state pension – it follows the deferral payment will be lower too.

If you build up enough NICs to qualify for a full basic state pension, you don't have to make any more after retirement age, saving you up to 11 per cent of your salary. However, you need to pay income tax on your earnings and if you haven't paid enough NICs, it might be a good opportunity to top them up (see Chapter 2 for details).

Doing the state pension deferral sums

If you defer taking the full basic state pension – currently £87.30 per week for a single person in the 2007-08 tax year – you may choose either of the following payments (depending on how long you defer for):

- ✔ A taxable lump sum equivalent to your state pension for the amount of time you have decided to delay claiming the state pension (which must be for at least 12 months) plus interest set at 2 per cent above the Bank of England base rate

> ✔ A higher level of pension income when eventually you do decide to collect your state pension. You earn state pension at an extra 1 per cent for every five weeks you put off claiming (equivalent to about 10.4 per cent for every year you defer)

If you want to gain extra pension income you have to defer for at least five weeks, but if you want to scoop the lump sum you must defer for 12 months. You are free to defer taking your state pension for as long as you want – a five year limit used to exist but this has now been removed.

But face facts, the government would not be offering this if it didn't make financial sense for it to do so.

The government employs a whole army of actuaries. The jolly job of a government actuary is to calculate how long the population is likely to live. These stats are used to set the maximum deferral payment. The law of averages suggests that sufficient numbers of people die before collecting their deferred state pension to make it worth the government's while.

By choosing to defer you are in effect gambling that you will be one of the lucky ones to make it through to collect your enhanced state pension or get time to spend your lump sum payment.

The lump sum for delaying taking the state pension is only payable after you start to collect your pension. So delay taking the state pension until age 70 and you will only receive your payout at age 70, not at the time you decide to delay.

Asking the key question: Can you afford to defer?

Regardless of all this grim reaper talk, the bottom line with deferral is that you have to be able to afford to do without your state pension. It makes no sense to live on out-of-date own brand spaghetti hoops for five years just so you can collect a higher state pension.

In truth, to be able to defer your state pension you have to be able to carry on working past retirement age. Otherwise, you need enough money tucked away to support yourself. Hopefully if you follow the tips in this book you'll be able to build a big enough cash pile to allow you the option of deferral.

Women generally live five years more than men. It may be morbid, but this gender longevity gap should play a part in your deferral decision. Odds are higher that you live long enough to collect your deferred state pension if you're a woman than if you're a man.

Book IV

Retiring Wealthy

Be sure you can afford to do without your state pension before going for the deferral option. You do not want to leave yourself short today in a bid to collect a higher pension tomorrow.

Investing a Lump Sum at Retirement

Retirement often coincides with the receipt of a cash lump sum. This lump sum can take different forms, including:

- ✔ A payment from your employer for taking early retirement.
- ✔ A tax-free lump sum taken when you collect your pension.

This retirement cash lump sum can be worth a lot of money and what you do with it can have major implications for how comfortable or uncomfortable your old age is.

If you want to know if your occupational pension scheme offers a lump sum, check out the members' handbook. For more on the ins and outs of occupational pensions see Chapter 2 in this Book.

You can spend your lump sum on whatever you please – fast cars, luxury holidays, even miniature golf, the choice is yours – or invest it in order to produce an income or with the idea of it growing into a larger cash pile later in life.

Most people, to be honest, choose to spend a bit and save a bit of any lump sum they receive.

As far as personal pensions go you can take up to 25 per cent of your pension pot as a tax-free lump sum; in most circumstances the rest of this cash is used to buy an annuity – an income for life – by age 75. This lump sum can't be any larger than 25 per cent of the lifetime limit on a pension fund – £1.6m in 2007, rising to £1.8m in 2010.

There are advantages to investing your lump sum, such as:

- ✔ **Higher growth.** Money invested in a pension tends to grow rather slowly. You can take your lump sum and invest it somewhere where there is a better chance of higher returns, for example the stock market.
- ✔ **Tax efficiency.** Income from an annuity is taxable but income from some other types of investment – such as cash ISAs – is not. Therefore, it may be a smart tax ploy to plough as much of your pension pot as possible into an investment which produces tax-free income.

Be careful of sinking a substantial part of your lump sum into risky investments such as company shares. After all, stock markets have a habit of going down as well as up. The golden rule is only ever invest in medium- and high-risk investments if you can afford to lose your cash.

Just because you're allowed to take *up to* 25 per cent of your pension as a lump sum doesn't mean you *should* do it. You may be best taking nothing at all or just 5 or 10 per cent of your pension as a lump sum and leaving the rest to buy an annuity. See later in this chapter for more on buying an annuity.

Getting It Right: Buying an Annuity

An *annuity* is a guaranteed income for life. Until April 2006, you had to buy an annuity with, at least three-quarters of your pension pot by the age of 75 at the latest. However, the rules have changed; it's no longer obligatory to buy an annuity (see later in this chapter), though for most people the guarantee of a regular income, no matter how long they live, is preferable to an ASP.

You give an insurance company your pension pot and – *shazzamm!* – it converts the cash into an annuity for you to live off.

Buying an annuity is one of the most important financial decisions you can make. But many people spend next to no time deciding which annuity to buy. This laziness – for want of a better word – makes some pension providers very happy, because it means they can get away with a great big confidence trick.

The con works like this. When you decide you want to retire and collect your pension, your pension provider – invariably an insurance company – tells you how much money you have in your pension pot. More often than not they offer to magically convert this pension pot into an annuity, saving you the hassle of shopping around. But you can nearly always get a higher annuity by exercising what is called the *open market option.* This simply means you have the right to take your pension pot and shop around for an annuity.

Hundreds of companies offer annuities and the amount of income they offer can vary wildly, sometimes by up to 20 per cent. If you look on the bright side you may spend 30 years or so retired, so get your choice of annuity wrong and you can be missing out on tens of thousands of pounds.

Once you've signed up to an annuity that's it, you can't switch from one provider to another. One way around this problem is to buy a limited period annuity rather than a lifetime annuity. This type of annuity allows you to buy an annuity to provide income for a limited period of time, say five years, allowing you to shop around for a better deal on a lifetime annuity later on.

Shopping around for an annuity can be a long job if you do it alone. An independent financial adviser can help you find the right one for you. You can also check out the annuity bureau Web site www.annuity-bureau.co.uk which collates all the available annuity rates on offer.

Understanding annuity calculations

Your retirement income depends on the size of your pension pot and the annuity rate offered by the insurance company. Simple enough you may think, but the complexity kicks in when you look at how the annuity rate is calculated.

Annuity rates are calculated on a case-by-case basis as the insurance company's aim is that your pension pot runs out at the same time as you die. If you outlive the insurance company's predictions then it loses out as it continues to pay an annuity income. On the flip side, if you die before your pension pot runs out the insurance company makes money (although there are some annuities which allow you to sign over your annuity on death, see later in this chapter for more).

The insurance company makes some assumptions as to your mortality and how long the annuity income is therefore likely to have to be paid based on the following criteria:

✔ **Age.** The older you are when you buy an annuity the better the rate you're offered. This is because the insurance company calculates that it needs to pay an income for fewer years.

✔ **Gender.** Women live on average 5.2 years longer then men. This is great in all other respects apart from the fact that this means they get a lower annuity rate. Recently there were moves by EU commissioners to equalise the annuity rates of men and women, but this has come to nothing so far.

✔ **Lifestyle.** If you're a smoker or a heavy drinker then the insurance company figures you won't live as long, therefore it pays a higher annuity rate.

✔ **Health.** If you have health problems such as heart disease or a degenerative condition you can get an impaired life annuity. The annuity on offer is far more generous than for someone who is in rude health.

The annuity income you can expect in retirement is based on a prediction of how long you're likely to live.

To illustrate how annuity rates work in practice, take the example of Mark and Philippa. Both have a pension pot of £100,000 and are looking to buy annuities on their 65th birthdays.

Mark as a man is likely to live five years fewer than Philippa therefore he stands to get a higher annuity rate. However, while Mark survives on tofu and runs marathons, Philippa is a lifelong smoker with a heart condition. Therefore the insurer cuts Philippa's life expectancy by three years. Mark still gets a higher annuity rate as he is predicted to die two years earlier than Philippa.

Some insurance companies specialise in annuities for impaired life and smokers. Best go see an independent financial adviser for more on choosing one of these annuities.

Interest rates have a major influence on annuity rates. This is because insurance companies invest the money they receive from people buying annuities. Insurers invest this money in low-risk investments such as government bonds, known as gilts, which are very sensitive to interest rate moves. If interest rates decrease the return on investment also falls and this means the insurance company is less able to afford to offer high annuity rates.

Choosing a level or rising annuity

Whether you go for a level or rising annuity can have a major impact on your financial position in retirement. The differences between these types of annuities are as follows:

- ✔ A level annuity is fixed for life so you get the same amount until you die.

- ✔ A rising annuity starts off lower then a level annuity but increases each year to keep pace with inflation or by a pre-set percentage.

To illustrate the differences between these two types of annuity let's look at Mark and Philippa again.

Mark uses his £100,000 pension pot to buy a level annuity. The insurance company offers him an annuity rate of 7 per cent. Mark's income for his annuity is £7,000 a year. He's very happy with this for a few years, but then he notices that his income is buying him less in the shops because prices are rising but his income isn't.

Philippa on the other hand uses her £100,000 pension pot to buy a rising annuity. Philippa was in line for a slightly lower annuity than Mark anyway, because of their respective life expectancy calculations. However, this difference is exacerbated because Philippa wants to buy the guarantee that her income will rise to keep pace with inflation each year. At first Philippa earns far less than Mark but over time her income increases at least in line with prices and ultimately overtakes his.

Level annuities offer jam today and you can budget easily as you know exactly what is coming in. Rising annuities, on the other hand, offer the security that if you enjoy a long life then your income should increase in line with prices or by a set percentage.

If you buy a level annuity and inflation takes off you may find that the buying power of your income shrinks alarmingly.

You can buy an investment-linked annuity. Your pension pot is invested in a range of different low- to medium-risk investments and your income rises or falls in line with their performance. However, investment-linked annuities should be approached with caution as there is the potential for big falls (as well as rises) in income.

You have the option of buying a *limited period annuity*. This product provides an income for five years. At the end of the five year term you can either buy an annuity to last your whole life or another limited period annuity.

Figuring out when to buy an annuity

It used to be the case that like night follows day retirement would prompt the purchase of an annuity. However, times have changed and many people hold out to the last possible moment before buying a lifetime annuity.Delaying buying an annuity can have the following advantages:

- ✔ **Higher income.** The longer you leave it the higher the income you should get because the insurance company calculates that you're likely to draw an income for less time.

- ✔ **Investment performance.** By delaying buying an annuity you give your pension pot more time to grow. When eventually it's time for you to take the plunge then you may find you have a larger pot enabling you to buy a bigger annuity. An alternative to this strategy is to buy an investment-linked annuity, see earlier in this chapter for more.

The 'longer you leave it the higher income you should get' theory doesn't always stand up. If interest rates fall sharply while you're delaying buying an annuity the insurance company reduces the annuity rates it pays to reflect the fact that the return it gets from investing the money you use to buy an annuity has fallen.

You should only consider delay buying an annuity if you have enough money coming in from other sources to live off. The delay option should only be considered under the following scenarios:

✔ You continue to work and earn beyond age 65, in other words you haven't fully retired yet.

✔ You have substantial savings and investments you can live off without need to use your pension to buy an annuity.

You must also choose when to receive your annuity payments. The state pension is paid weekly but most people receive their private pension monthly. Alternatively, you can have your pension paid quarterly, half-yearly, or yearly. You can be paid in advance or arrears. If you opt for the former, payments start immediately; the latter starts after the first month, quarter, six months, and so on. The longer the delay before receiving your payment, the greater your income – a deferred pension is bigger than one paid in advance. Table 5-2 shows annual payment amounts for a retiree with a £100,000 pension pot.

Table 5-2	Receiving Annuity Payments in Advance or Arrears	
Income Paid	*Male Aged 65*	*Female Aged 65*
Monthly in arrears (level)	£7,263pa (£605 pcm)	£6,806pa (£567 pcm)
Monthly in advance (level)	£7,228pa (602pcm)	£6,774pa (£564 pcm)
Monthly in arrears (RPI)	£4,767pa £397pcm)	£4,298pa £398pcm)
Monthly in advance (RPI)	£4,744pa (£395pcm)	£4,279 (£357pcm)

Source: The Annuity Bureau

Retiring gradually

If you have a large pension pot (at least £250,000) and don't want to purchase an annuity just yet – because rates are poor or because you're cutting back on work gradually so only need a small income – you can opt for *phased retirement*. Your pension fund is divided into segments and each one treated almost as if it were a separate pension. You can take up to a quarter of each segment as a tax-free lump sum, purchasing an annuity with the remainder.

The advantage of phased retirement is that you don't have to draw all your segments at the same time, although they must all be encashed by the age of 75. You could purchase an annuity with one segment and leave the remaining segments invested in the stock market until annuity rates (hopefully) improve.

There is no guarantee that annuity rates will improve while you are phasing retirement. They could fall instead, leaving you in a worse position than you would have been in if you'd taken your pension in the normal way instead of staying invested in the stock market.

You must convert enough segments to purchase an annuity. Some insurance companies have a minimum purchase price, so if one of your segments doesn't provide enough cash, you may have to encash several at the same time.

The benefit of phased retirement is that if you die before encashing all your segments, your spouse or other beneficiaries inherit those you haven't yet turned into an annuity. No tax is payable, as long as your funds came from a personal pension. If they come from an occupational scheme, your spouse may receive a lump sum equal to 25 per cent of the fund, with the remainder used to buy an annuity. As for the funds already placed in your phased retirement plan, your beneficiaries may receive income from these.

As of April 2006 you can simply cash in a pension fund worth up to £15,000 at retirement, rather than having to buy an annuity with it. You can take 25 per cent as a tax-free lump sum while the remainder of the fund is taxed as earned income. Therefore if you're a basic rate taxpayer you pay 22 per cent but if you're a higher rate taxpayer you're taxed at 40 per cent.

Making sure your annuity survives you

Under a *single-life annuity* when you die your annuity dies with you.

This isn't much good if you're married. You may, therefore, consider buying a joint-life annuity. Under a joint life annuity when you die part or all your income passes to your spouse. Of course, in order to pay for this, you have to accept that your annuity rate will be lower than it would have been if you'd purchased a single-life annuity.

The greater the proportion of your annuity income that passes to your spouse the more it is going to cost you.

From April 2006 there is a way to pass on your pension fund even after you've used it to buy an annuity. Under a value-protected annuity, if you die before age 75, what's left in your pension fund goes to your named beneficiary, usually a spouse. However, there is a one-off tax charge of 35 per cent levied on the residue of the fund. A value protection annuity is only available up to the age of 75.

Checking out income drawdown

You don't have to buy an annuity at the same time as you take your lump sum: until the age of 75 you can opt for *income drawdown* instead, which provides increased flexibility and control. This enables you to draw a certain amount of income from your pension while your fund is still invested in the usual way.

HMRC imposes a minimum and maximum limit on what you can take, which is reassessed every five years, but the amount you take can be varied from year to year. The maximum income you can draw down is 120 per cent of the amount you would receive from a single-life non-increasing annuity with no guarantee. The minimum you can draw down is nothing.

Ultimately, when you do buy an annuity, not only should your pension fund be the same or higher than it was when you started the drawdown process but it should buy you a bigger annuity because you're older.

Sometimes you'll find income drawdown referred to by pension industry insiders as an *unsecured income*.

Here's an example of how income drawdown can work.

Herdeep has a pension pot worth £500,000. If at age 65 he were to buy an annuity his insurance company would pay him 6 per cent, equivalent to £30,000.

However, Herdeep decides to go for income drawdown and receives an income equivalent to 6 per cent of his total pension for the next ten years. At age 75 Herdeep buys an annuity. His pension pot has been eroded a fraction to provide him with an income but is still worth £480,000. Now because he is a lot older and only likely to live a few more years his annuity rate has risen sharply to 8 per cent, equivalent to a whopping £38,400 a year.

If you want to draw an income from your pension fund then your pension provider levies a charge. These charges can be high so best be 100 per cent sure that it's worth it.

Income drawdown comes with a major health warning. If your pension fund falls in value – as can happen due to say a stock market crash – then there won't be any investment growth from which to draw an income. Therefore, any income you draw will come direct from the capital value of the fund. A few years of investment underperformance combined with income drawdown can see your pension fund fall in value alarmingly.

Income drawdown is a bit of a gamble and for this reason most money experts reckon that unless your pension fund is worth more than a cool £250,000 you shouldn't consider it.

You don't have to wait until age 65 to start income drawdown – you can do it from age 50 if you want.

Review your decision as to when to buy an annuity at least once a year.

Opting for an Alternatively Secured Pension

April 2006 saw the introduction of an alternative to annuities, in the shape of Alternatively Secured Pensions or ASPs. Effectively, ASPs are a form of income drawdown – instead of buying an annuity at the age of 75, you leave your pension savings invested and draw an income from the fund.

The amount of income you can take out is limited. The minimum is 65 per cent of the single-lifetime annuity (for someone of the same sex as you and aged 75) that your fund would buy, calculated from a table produced by the Government Actuaries Department; the maximum is 90 per cent, but this level must be recalculated every year to make sure you are not eating into your fund.

It's not an all or nothing situation, so you can if you wish buy an annuity with part of your pension pot and draw down from the remainder. You can also change your mind, stop your ASP and buy an annuity at a later date.

ASPs sound attractive because you may get a better income from your investments if they are doing well. But they are riskier too, because a stock-market crash could decimate your fund. There's also a risk that you could simply run out of money if you live long enough.

When ASPs first came in, in April 2006, many people hoped they might be a means of passing on the contents of their pension pot to their children, with or without inheritance tax. To close that loophole, the government has introduced strict rules on where your fund can go. Most importantly, though, it can be used to buy an annuity or ASP for your spouse (or dependent children), or to provide income drawdown for them if they are under 75.

Making the Most of Lots of Little Pensions

It's likely you have more than one pension fund, and you may in fact have lots of small pensions. What to do with these little critters?

You have the following options:

- ✔ Transfer all into one pension.
- ✔ Cash them in.
- ✔ Leave them where they are.

Taking the pension transfer option

The attractions of pension transfer are plain to see. You put all your pensions under one roof, at a stroke easing your administrative burden. What's more, if you're in luck, your one super-charged pension may perform well.

However, often pension providers levy a charge for transferring funds. Some providers even charge you for transferring funds *into* a pension. Sometimes working with your pension can be a bit like living life as a pelican – everywhere you look you're confronted with a bill!

Cashing in your pensions

If you're a member of an occupational scheme for less than two years you're allowed a refund of your contributions – although not your employers' contributions – but the fund is taxed at a rate of 35 per cent.

Leaving your pensions alone

This may well be the best option. By leaving your pension schemes intact you avoid having to pay transfer charges and you benefit from investment diversity.

Book IV

Retiring Wealthy

Most money experts agree that it's usually a bad idea to transfer from a company pension into a personal pension scheme. Often company pension schemes come with the guarantee that you receive a percentage of final salary for each year of service. What's more, some schemes even guarantee your spouse a pension on your death. Under a personal pension the size of your pension pot relies on investment performance – there are no guarantees. For the low-down on the different types of workplace pensions see Chapter 2 in this Book.

Executing a pension transfer

Pension providers used to impose all sorts of penalties on investors for transferring their pension fund out. Put simply, they figured that if they made it difficult and expensive for people to transfer their pension they wouldn't bother. However, thankfully, those days are disappearing fast and it is now relatively easy and inexpensive to transfer a pension.

But just because it's getting easier to transfer a pension doesn't mean necessarily that you should do it.

You may choose pension transfer under the following circumstances:

✔ Your current pension is underperforming and you think you're better off if the money is invested elsewhere.

✔ Your current pension is small and you feel for ease of administration it would be worthwhile transferring it into a larger pension fund that you already hold.

✔ You have spotted a top-drawer pension offering the panacea of investment choice and rock-bottom charges.

The older your pension plan, the more likely the provider is to charge a hefty fee for transfer out. Always check with your pension provider how much it costs to transfer your pension.

Some with-profits pensions levy a *market value adjuster* (MVA) on the funds of investors looking to transfer out. The insurance industry, which runs with-profits funds, tries to deny it but MVAs are nothing more than a pension penalty with a fancy name. Unfortunately it's hard to avoid exposure to this charge as most with-profits funds reserve the right to impose an MVA at any time.

Stakeholder pensions – a type of low-cost personal pension – as a rule don't charge their savers for transferring funds out. Stakeholder pensions are the easiest and cheapest type of pension to own. See Chapter 3 in this Book for the low-down on stakeholders.

If you decide that a pension transfer is the way to go simply follow the easy procedure below:

- ✔ Ask the provider of your pension for an estimate of how much your pension is worth if you transferred it out – this is called the transfer value. Pay particular attention to any penalties.

- ✔ Inform the providers or scheme administrator of the pension you'd like to transfer into. They should send you some forms to get the pension transfer ball rolling.

- ✔ The scheme you're transferring into should now contact the scheme you're leaving and between them they will sort out the transfer.

If you're transferring a pile of cash from one personal pension into another then it should be a cinch for the schemes to come to an agreement over the transfer value. But if you're transferring into or out of a final salary pension scheme – where benefits relate to final salary and number of years' service – then actuaries of the accepting and crediting scheme may have a job reaching agreement as to the right level of transfer value.

Dangers of Unlocking Your Pension

If you've ever watched daytime TV – and let's face it we've all watched an episode of *Trisha* at some low point in our lives – you've probably seen an advert from a firm offering to unlock your pension.

Unlocking a pension is advertising speak for taking pension benefits before you retire. If you're over 50 you may be able to draw benefits from your pension. However, according to no less an important body than the Financial Services Authority (FSA), the City regulator, it is rarely in your long-term interests to unlock a pension. Now the FSA, in my experience, is a rather staid safe organisation that doesn't like saying boo to a goose, so for it to say something is rarely in your long-term interests you know it's got to be a bad idea – in fact a monumentally bad idea.

Here are some reasons why, when you see those pensions unlocking adverts, you should simply switch over:

- ✔ If you draw pension benefits early you will have less – much less – to live on in retirement.

- ✔ If you're in money trouble then by unlocking your pension you may automatically bar yourself from state benefits.

Book IV

Retiring Wealthy

- ✔ By drawing your pension you may lose in death-in-service benefits.

- ✔ Drawing your pension early may result in penalties being levied by your pension provider, further depleting your money pile.

- ✔ Daytime TV, which features the adverts, isn't good for your soul (I just threw that one in).

- ✔ And if that isn't all bad enough, firms offering to unlock your pension will no doubt charge you a great big fee for the privilege!

Check out the Financial Services Authority Web site for more on the dangers of pension unlocking – www.fsa.gov.uk. And if you're having money problems then you should go see your local Citizens Advice Bureau. Check out your phone book for the nearest branch or the CAB Web site on www.nacab.org.uk.

Keeping an eye on the creep of pension credit

Back in 2003 the government introduced pension credit. The idea was to boost the incomes of Britain's poorest pensioners – great, you may think. Pension credit is a means-tested benefit which takes into account retirement income, including that from savings. It guarantees everyone aged 60 and over an income of at least £119.05 a week, or £181.70 a week for couples (in the 2007-08 tax year).

However, the government soon realised that people who had built up a small pension pot felt a bit miffed. After all they had made sacrifices during their working life to put money aside only for the government to come along and boost the incomes of those who hadn't put anything away.

The government therefore added a 'reward' element for those who had saved for their retirement, up to £19.05 per week for single people or £25.26 for couples (2007-08).

Therefore we have an income element of pension credit – available to pensioners with very few means – and the savings element of pension credit – available to people with small pension pots. In practice this means that there's a spectrum of income and savings levels under which you may be eligible for pension credit. So someone aged 65 or over with a relatively high weekly income of, say, £150 but savings of less than £14,000 or so would be likely to qualify, as would someone else with a weekly income of only £90 but savings of £43,000.

The government has said that it intends to raise these two credits in line with earnings for the next few years at least. This means that over time more and more pensioners are going to be able to claim pension credit. The government anticipates that by 2050 two thirds of pensioners may be able to claim either the income or savings element of pension credit.

But some suggest this is a disincentive for people to save – they will either choose not to bother and rely on the income element or see the reward for saving as too small.

Your pension and retiring abroad

Lots of us – me included – fancy spending a large chunk of our golden years in sunnier climes. But before selling your home in Luton to take up residence in Lisbon or trading Tamworth for Torremelinos, you need to give some thought to what you're going to live on when you get there, in other words, your retirement wealth pot.

If you leave the UK permanently (in tax parlance this is called *becoming non-resident*), you are no longer liable to pay tax on any overseas income, but you'll have to pay tax on this in your new country of residence. But income earned in the UK may be taxed in the UK and in your new country – two tax hits, ouch! Yet don't despair, if your new country of residence has what's called a *double taxation agreement* with the UK then you'll only have to pay one lot of tax on your income deriving from the UK – now that *is* a relief! Countries that have such agreements include: Australia, France, Ireland, New Zealand, South Africa, Spain, and the US.

If you receive a pension from the UK civil service or armed forces then that is taxed in the UK.

It's always worth bearing in mind that most western countries have higher taxes than the UK – you knew there was a reason why you put up with the awful weather!

The position with the UK state pension is even more complex. If you retire to an EU country the government will increase your pension every year, normally in line with UK inflation. However, if you retire outside the EU you may find that your state pension payments do not increase every year. This probably doesn't make much of a difference over one or two years but over 10, 15, or 20 you find your UK state pension buying you less and less.

For more details on your pension rights when retired abroad call the HMRC centre for non-residents on 0845 0700 040.

Assessing Pension Alternatives

Lots of people don't like pensions and you can kind of understand why. Pensions are not very flexible – you normally can't get your money out until you're at least 50. What's more pensions with their promise of a steady income a long time into the future are hardly the stuff of seat-of-the-pants excitement.

Yet in one way pensions are risky. You can die before being able to cash in your pension. Think about it: You contribute for years and years only to get run over by a bus on the morning of your retirement from work – how very annoying!

If you simply can't abide pensions then you want to cast your eye over the alternative tactics you can deploy to reach your retiring wealthy goal:

✔ Instead of saving in a pension invest in property. This can offer the twin benefits of capital growth and investment income. See Chapter 6 in this Book for how to buy-to-let your way to a wealthy retirement.

Book IV

Retiring Wealthy

✔ Make sure you use your full tax-free savings allowances. You're allowed to save up to £7,200 a year in a Maxi Individual Savings Account (ISA) tax-free. Over many years you can build up a tidy nest egg by using ISAs. What's more, you're free to spend any money in an ISA as you want and don't have to use any of it to buy an annuity. See Chapter 4 in Book III for more on tax-free savings.

If you're a UK taxpayer then you're building up entitlement to the UK state pension. Even if you hate pensions with a passion you shouldn't ignore your state pension – it can provide a useful base income in retirement. See Chapter 2 in this Book for more on the basic state pension.

Chapter 6

Using Property for Retirement

*I*n this chapter, we show you how you can turn your bricks and mortar into pounds in your retirement pot.

In addition, we outline how you can push down your mortgage debt, freeing you up to concentrate your financial firepower on bringing off your big retiring wealthy plan.

Cashing In Your Property

There are three main ways to use your own home to increase your retirement wealth pot:

✔ **Sell up and move somewhere cheaper.** The option of selling your home and buying somewhere cheaper can make a lot of sense, particularly if you own a family home and your children have now left and struck out on their own. Downsizing, as it's called, can help you free up cash and perhaps relocate somewhere that you really want to spend your autumn years.

✔ **Sell up and buy-to-let.** For many this is ideal scenarioville. You sell your main home, buy somewhere cheaper, and with a portion of your profit buy a place to let out. The income you receive from your buy-to-let helps see you through retirement and you have the option of selling the buy-to-let at any time.

✔ **Equity release.** In effect you sign over a portion of your home to a bank or building society and in return receive either a lump sum or an income in return. Equity release is explored in much greater detail later in this chapter.

Exploding the 'property is better than pension' myth

You may have heard lots of people say that their property is their pension. What do they mean by this?

Well, they are trusting that the increased value of their property can be converted into a big enough income or lump sum to see them through their autumn years. Looking at what's happened in recent years – property prices booming while pension values have suffered due to stock market performance – you can see why choosing property over pension saving has become so de rigueur.

Case closed then, just go for property? Err, no! Pensions have an ace up their sleeve – you get tax relief on contributions.

If you're a basic rate taxpayer, for every 78p you pay into a pension the government through tax relief will top it up to £1 (the basic rate of tax is to be cut to 20p from April 2008, so basic rate taxpayers have to contribute 80p of every £1 from then on). Higher rate taxpayers get an even better deal – for every 60p they pay into a pension the government tops it up to £1. In effect the government – yes the government! – is giving you free money. And there's more: If you're a member of a workplace pension you may well find that your employer makes additional contributions into your pension – again, this is free money!

However, not all is rosy in the pension garden. You have to tie up your money for a long time and 75 per cent of the fund usually goes towards buying an annuity, an income for life.

On the down side for property, tax relief no longer applies to mortgage interest and over the long term a mortgage can cost you a lot of money in interest payments. For example, a £200,000 interest-only mortgage at a 5 per cent rate of interest will actually cost you £250,000 over 25 years and that all comes from after tax salary. Next time you hear someone boast about how much their property has increased in value, ask them if they've factored in mortgage interest payments – I bet you they haven't even thought of this huge expense!

Having said all that, I wouldn't be foolish enough to do down property as an investment. Some friends of mine have made an absolute killing in recent years and their retiring wealthy prospects have been given a stellar boost. The key is to have a balance of property, pensions, and other investments. Primarily, enjoy your property for what it is – a home – and if needs be use any increased value to boost your retirement pot.

In June 2007 home information packs (HIPs) – also called sellers' packs – were introduced. This means that when you put your home on the market you have to make available to would-be purchasers an information pack containing, among other things, a report on how energy efficient the property is, as well as local searches. You can also include a survey (known as a home condition report), but in the face of pressure from the anti-HIP lobby, the government has decided that this is not mandatory. It's arguable whether HIPs without the key document – the survey – will add much benefit for buyers, and they are likely to cost sellers between £600 and £1000.

Downsizing

If you have paid off your mortgage and have a lot of cash tied up in your home, you can increase your income by selling up and buying a smaller property with the profits. The surplus cash can be used to bolster your income by investing in low-risk products such as gilts or corporate bonds or be put into a savings account paying a high rate of interest.

Apart from generating extra income, there are several reasons why you might downsize:

- ✔ You simply don't need such a big property once your children have flown the nest.

- ✔ A smaller property is more manageable when it comes to cleaning, heating, and maintenance as you get older.

- ✔ You may become less mobile as you get older and not be able to negotiate lots of stairs.

- ✔ You reduce your estate's inheritance tax (IHT) liability. Under current rules, everything you leave over £300,000 (including property in the 2007-08 tax year) is taxed at 40 per cent after you die. If you downsize before death, and spend the proceeds, there will be less to leave your family in your will. Thus the IHT liability may be greatly reduced, although you may prefer to ensure your family get a decent inheritance instead. See Chapter 4 in Book V for more on IHT planning.

Don't downsize before you need to. You could be a long time retired and moving into a cramped one-bedroom bungalow with your spouse at the age of 65 could be a recipe for disaster. Think carefully about when it is practical to sell up.

Book IV

Retiring Wealthy

Understanding Equity Release

Equity release gives older homeowners the opportunity to turn some of the value of their home into cold hard cash. For most people the path to equity release goes like this.

They buy a home with a mortgage, as they work they pay off this mortgage and the value of the property rises. The difference between the mortgage and the value of the home is called the property's equity. Many homeowners get to retirement or beyond cash poor but asset rich – they don't have a huge amount of cash tucked away but they do have the equity in their homes.

For some years now banks and building societies have been offering to free up this equity. Banks and building societies pay homeowners either a lump sum, a guaranteed regular income, or a combination of both; in return when the homeowner dies or sells up the bank or building society gets a slice of the property's value. Equity release is a lucrative business – for banks and building societies – and the number of older homeowners choosing this option has mushroomed in recent years (along with house prices throughout the UK).

The big idea behind equity release is that you bring in some extra retirement cash and get to stay put in the family home – this is what appeals to so many homeowners.

Different types of equity release explained

The idea behind equity release is pretty straightforward, but that doesn't stop banks and building societies complicating matters.

Over the years the straight equity release where you signed over a portion of your home in return for a cash pile has evolved into several different variants on a theme, each with their own advantages and disadvantages to be considered (see Table 6-1).

Table 6-1	Different Types of Equity Release Schemes	
Type of plan	*Advantages*	*Disadvantages*
Rolled-up interest loans		
You take out a loan against the value of your home but do not pay off any interest or	The loan doesn't have to be repaid until you sell your home. If you choose you're able to stay in your	If the loan runs for a very long time you may end up owing more than your home is worth. This can be

Type of plan	Advantages	Disadvantages
capital until the property is sold.	home until you die, with the loan being repaid when the property is sold on your death. Under this type of equity release interest rates are usually fixed. This means that the amount you owe won't be affected by changes in rates throughout the wider economy.	a real problem if subsequently you simply have no choice but to sell up – perhaps you become infirm and have to move into a residential nursing home or simply can no onger cope with stairs lin the property.

Interest-only arrangements

A bank or building society lends you money against the value of your home. You then make monthly interest payments but don't have to repay any of the capital.	The fact that you keep paying off the interest means that when you come to sell you only have to pay off the value of the loan. If in the interim the value of your house has risen you're able to pocket all or most of this profit. Likewise, if you leave your home to someone, they are able to pocket whatever's left after the loan has been repaid.	Interest rates may vary, which means that the monthly interest charge may go up or down. Interest charges can be quite hefty. In order to cope with meeting the interest payments, you have to have sufficient regular income in place.

Home income plans

You take out a mortgage on your home and buy an annuity with the money raised. Mortgage interest payments are deducted from the annuity income. When you die the property is sold and the equity release provider gets back the money they lent you at the outset. Any cash left over goes into your estate.	The annuity provides you with a regular income for life and that is not to be sniffed at. If you live to a ripe old age you and your estate can end up winning on the deal. First up, live a long time and you can enjoy years' worth of income. Secondly, because you pay interest as you go along – from the annuity income – then on death the home income plan provider only gets the	Home income plans have fallen out of fashion in recent years. They are very much the bell-bottomed flares of the equity release world. This is all due to a combination of falling annuity rates and super-boring complex tax relief changes. Put simply, the amount of income on offer through these plans has shrunk massively

(continued)

Table 6-1 (continued)

Type of plan	Advantages	Disadvantages
	capital value of the mortgage. Hopefully in the interim property values have gone up sharply and the beneficiaries of your estate benefit from what's left over.	and subsequently so has their popularity.
Home reversion		
You sell your home in part or outright to a property investment company, but you remain living there as a tenant for the rest of your life, rent-free. If you and your partner sign up to the scheme, you both have the right to live in the property until death. On death the property is sold and the home reversion provider receives a share of the proceeds, in proportion to how much of the property you have signed over. Home reversion providers offer the options of a cash lump sum, an annuity, or a combination of the two.	You get to remain in the property and don't have to pay any interest, because you're not actually borrowing money, instead you're selling your property. Some schemes offer the option for you to choose to sell a proportion of your property when you need extra cash, for example start off selling 25 per cent at retirement, then a further 25 per cent every few years to give your finances a shot in the arm.	If you sign over your entire home then any future increase in value is scooped by the home reversion provider rather than by you or your relatives. You're in effect turning yourself from a property owner into a tenant. Some people consider this a step to far.

In the past few years equity release in most of its forms – the home income plan format excluded – has really taken off. Almost inevitability, there have been growing concerns that consumers can be mis-sold equity release. To head this potential problem off at the pass, where there is a mortgage involved equity release is now regulated by the City watchdog the Financial Services Authority (FSA). As for home reversion schemes, which have no mortgage element, the government has agreed that these too should be regulated by the FSA, though this has not yet happened. The regulator will watch firms involved in equity release to ensure that they treat customers fairly and that their advertising isn't misleading.

If you fancy going for equity release, remember there are costs involved. You have to pay solicitors' fees and administration fees charged by the company arranging the scheme. Costs can vary markedly between providers. Some equity release providers charge hefty administration fees, so best avoid these.

Even if you sign over all your property through equity release you're still responsible for all repairs and building maintenance costs. You also have to pay council tax, electricity, gas, and insurance bills. Equity release is a big step – only do it if you're sure it's right for you.

Qualifying for equity release

All because you fancy the idea of equity release doesn't mean that providers will fall over themselves to dole out the cash to you. There are some hoops you have to jump through to get your hands on the money:

- ✔ **You need to own your home outright.** Most providers insist you've paid off your mortgage before they consider you for equity release. A few providers consider a property with a small mortgage on it just as long as the mortgage is paid off as part of the loan.

- ✔ **You have to be old enough.** Most providers insist that you're at least 60 or 65 years old before they consider you. This isn't because they're striking back against ageism – not a bit of it – the provider is making the cold, calculated analysis that the older you are the sooner you die and they get their hands on your property.

- ✔ **Your property has to be right for the provider.** Some companies don't consider certain types of property, such as flats, ex-local authority, or leasehold property. In addition, the property can't be a wreck. In short, it has to be in a reasonable state of repair.

Some providers are very strict about the type of property and person they consider for equity release. Other providers, though, are a little more free and easy in whom they consider, perhaps allowing people in their late fifties for equity release.

You may well find that the valuation the equity release provider puts on your home is below what an estate agent may advise you to put it on the market at. This is because, generally, property does not fetch the full asking price. Property market experts reckon that sellers can expect to receive between 92 per cent and 96 per cent of the asking price.

Book IV

Retiring Wealthy

Treading carefully with equity release

Just because you can release equity, doesn't mean you should!

Lots of good reasons exist for being ultra-cautious when it comes to equity release, either through a scheme or by selling up and buying somewhere less expensive.

We have heard some people say that they have no worries about their retirement because they will simply sell their home – but when it comes to biting the bullet it may not be so clear cut.

For most people the family home is a special place with memories, not just a pile of bricks and mortar. What's more, releasing equity from your home isn't straightforward – you can't sell up a brick at a time. The firms offering equity release are in it for the profit and want their pound of flesh.

They have done the sums and the offer they make factors in a healthy profit. You either have to fund their profit when you sell up or your estate does on your death.

As for selling up and moving somewhere cheaper, again it's easier said than done. Uprooting yourself in late life can invigorate you, but it can also lead to isolation and in some cases depression.

If you make plans early, save hard and invest wisely, then there is no reason for you to have to sell your own home just to provide life's basics or a few luxuries in retirement.

Many independent financial advisers we have spoken to view equity release – in all its forms – as an option of last rather than first resort.

Equity release is not to be taken lightly. You should always take independent financial advice if you're considering equity release. A good adviser will assess the equity release provider's offer and see if it suits you. They can also suggest alternative strategies that you may not have even thought of, which can mean you don't have to start signing over your home to provide retirement income or a much needed injection of cash.

Pushing Down on Your Mortgage

Your mortgage is likely to be your biggest outgoing. Therefore, it stands to reason that if you work to reduce your mortgage debt you can divert more cash to savings and investments to bring off your big retiring wealthy plan. We look in detail at mortgages and how to select the best one for you in Chapter 3 of Book III. Remember, however, the value of overpaying as far as your retirement plans are concerned. Financial experts reckon that one of the smartest financial plays you can make is to pay off your mortgage early. Remember, the quicker you repay your mortgage the less interest you end up paying. For example, on a £70,000 mortgage just overpaying by £4.20 a day on your mortgage can wipe nearly ten years off the mortgage term. Just think about it, £4.20 a day – less than the price of a packet of cigarettes – and you can enjoy being shot of your mortgage 10 years sooner!

In the early years of a standard repayment mortgage a large portion of your monthly repayments goes to meet interest charges.

When you overpay on your mortgage your lender may ask if you'd like the money to go towards reducing monthly repayments or the mortgage term. The choice is really six of one or half a dozen of the other, but most people prefer the latter option, opting to slash time from their mortgage debt.

Swapping Lenders to Save a Packet

The lengths some people go to save money amazes me – cutting out coupons for two pence off a can of beans or driving miles out their way to fill up at the cheapest petrol station.

We suppose they are living their life by the maxim: 'Look after the pennies and the pounds will look after themselves.' However, they would do a lot, lot better by moving their mortgage between providers every few years. Most financial experts agree that banks' SVRs are a very bad deal. Far better offers exist, but these are only available if you switch providers. Remember, 1 per cent interest on a £100,000 mortgage is equivalent to £60 in monthly repayments. You can literally save thousands by steering clear of SVRs.

It's never been easier to switch and this is how you do it:

1. **Apply over the phone to the lender.**
2. **Send proof of income (usually a P60 and your last three monthly payslips).**

3. **Fork out for the mortgage company's valuation of the property.**

4. **Get your solicitor to dot the I's and cross the T's.**

From start to finish the whole process shouldn't take any longer than four to six weeks. What's more, some lenders offer free valuation and legal fees to tempt you to switch your mortgage to them.

Mortgage companies charge 'mortgage administration exit fees' for switching, and these have gone up in recent times – expect to pay anything from £200 to £500 to leave your existing mortgage, but do check that you are not being charged any more than was stated in the original contract. If this is the case you can reclaim the difference. If you switch to a good mortgage you may be able to make the exit fees back in reduced repayments within a year.

As soon as your present mortgage deal comes to an end look to move elsewhere, otherwise the lender shifts you on to an uncompetitive SVR or worse! If you really don't want the hassle, still tell your current lender that you're looking to move. They may well offer to reduce your interest rate to keep your custom – if you don't ask, you don't get!

Book V

Protecting Your Wealth for the Next Generation

'As you know your late father was a great boxing enthusiast and one of the will's conditions includes a little contest between you all.'

In this Book . . .

Planning and writing your own will doesn't have to be a nightmare of expense and confusion. You'll find lots of great advice in this Book, which explains the process from minimising the stress of first-time probate, to using knowledge of UK inheritance tax law to keep down your family's bill down.

Here are the contents of Book V at a glance:

Chapter 1

Working Out Why to Write a Will

*Y*our will is your big chance to make sure that your loved ones are looked after once you've gone. Through a properly drawn up will you can pass on your property to whoever you choose – with certain provisos. Even if you're not rich, your will can have a huge impact, even if you just leave an item to bring a smile to someone's face or jog a happy memory. Get your will right and you can ease the pain of your parting and help people to move on.

Recognising the Advantages of Putting Your Estate in Order

A particular life event can prompt you to start thinking about planning for the inevitable. Alternatively, you may just have a general feeling that it's time to stop putting off writing down your big plan.

Oddly, people spend days choosing everyday items such as cars, kitchens, or just the right colour scheme for the downstairs loo, but won't spend a few hours – and that's all it has to take – drawing up a will and getting their bits and pieces into tax-saving shape to save their loved ones a mountain of heartache.

Debts don't die with you!

When coming up with a figure for how much you're worth, don't forget to subtract any debts you have. Most people have some form of debt, often in the form of a mortgage. Your *creditors* (those you owe money to) have to be paid before any beneficiaries (those you want to give money to). Some people's debts outweigh their assets. If you find that you're in this position, consider taking out a life insurance policy to ensure that your nearest and dearest at least get something on your death.

Working out your debts and assets can be a lot more complex than simply sitting down and creating two columns on a sheet of paper. You may need to have your assets independently valued. As for debts, check out whether penalties exist if you were to die and the debt repaid early.

Whether you're in your twenties and have just got your foot on the property ladder, or you're an octogenarian with a gaggle of grandchildren around you, making a will and tax planning have huge benefits. The benefits include:

- ✔ A will allows you to set out clearly who should get what from your *estate* (everything you own at the time of your death, from your home to your teapot).

- ✔ A will empowers you to appoint special people to deal with your estate and look after your loved ones when you've gone.

- ✔ A will enables you to give your property away in a tax-efficient way.

- ✔ Tax planning while alive can reduce inheritance tax when you die.

If your estate is worth more than £300,000 (2007-08 tax year) when you die, HMRC may impose an inheritance tax (IHT) charge (no, we don't know what the 'H' stands for either). Turn to Chapter 4 in this Book for ways around paying too much IHT.

If you do decide to make a will and have a spouse, ex-spouse, children, or other people who depend on you for their upkeep, you are required to look after them through your will. Failure to provide for these people could lead to your will being challenged in the courts. Chapter 2 in this Book has more.

The Circle of Life: Events to Prompt You into Will-Writing

Life is eventful, and would be pretty dull if it wasn't. Many life-changing events prompt people into making a will, including the following:

- **Getting married.** When you get married or divorced this automatically impacts how your estate – all your property, money, and belongings – is distributed after your death. If you die without a will your spouse will inherit every penny – up to a set level. But you may not want your spouse to get absolutely everything, however lovey-dovey you are. For example, you may have an elderly parent or children from a previous marriage whom you want to support in the event of your death. Alternatively, you may want your spouse to be better provided for. The simple truth is, if you want to ensure that your wishes are followed, make a will.

- **Getting divorced.** If your marriage comes to an end and you die without a will, your ex-spouse usually has no right to any part of your estate. If you want your ex-spouse to get anything when you die, make a will and name them as a beneficiary.

- **Having children.** Dying without a will, or just leaving your money to your spouse, means that your little ones – or not-so-little ones – may go without. Your estate may be large enough to attract the interest of HMRC – who impose iinheritance tax at a whopping 40 per cent. Early transfers of property between parent and child reduce any eventual tax bill. For more details on how to sidestep inheritance tax, check out Chapter 4 in this Book.

You can also use your will to give gifts to your grandchildren so that they inherit a family heirloom – or even a fat wad of cash.

> Children younger than 18 can't inherit. The answer is to put what you would like them to have into trust. You can instruct the people running the trust to hand over the asset, such as shares or property, to the child when they reach a specific age. Chapter 5 covers using trusts to help your children.

- **Owning property.** You don't need me to tell you that buying your first home is a very expensive undertaking. Overnight, your financial affairs become many times more complex both for you and for whoever eventually sorts out your estate. A will can help make dealing with your home far easier and you might be able to do something with your home to benefit others. With house prices having more than doubled in the past six years, more people than ever own enough for their estates to incur inheritance tax (IHT). If your estate is worth more than £300,000 (2007-08), there's a good chance that the taxman cometh – but you can avoid passing part of your inheritance on to him if you're clever with your will and financial planning. Go to Chapter 4 in this Book for more info.

- **Hitting the jackpot.** Wealth apparently doesn't bring automatic happiness, but wouldn't it be nice to check that theory out? A sudden injection of readies into your life through a bumper work bonus, prize win, or inheritance means that you can do more with your estate and, on the flip side, that the tax authorities may be able to get their claws in. Make a will to ensure your new-found wealth goes where you want it to go – assuming you don't blow it all in a weekend.

✔ **Counting crows' feet.** Becoming aware of your own mortality can either creep up on you or hit you all of a sudden. The death of someone close, experiencing serious illness, or reaching a major birthday can put everything into perspective. Realising you're not invulnerable and that the world will carry on when you're gone can prompt you into making a will.

✔ **Working on the edge.** People in high-risk occupations such as deep-sea divers, security specialists, and members of the armed services are wise to make a will. You're the best person to know whether your work is high-risk or not; an insurance company will tell you if you're unsure.

✔ **Feeling compassionate.** A family member or friend may fall on hard times. Naturally you'd like to help. You can help by breaking into your savings, selling shares, or even your home. Alternatively, you can make a will naming them as a beneficiary; if you're a fair bit older than the person then there is a good chance they will benefit. You can also name a favourite charity in your will.

If you don't make a will you can't choose an executor to deal with your estate when you die. The burden of dealing with HMRC, creditors, and distributing your estate is likely to fall on your very nearest and dearest. If you want a particular person or group of people to tie up all the loose ends once you've gone, make a will and name executors.

Some people can make a claim from your estate if you don't leave them enough in your will. Individuals who can claim include your spouse, any children, anyone treated as a child of the deceased, a former spouse who has not remarried, a person being maintained by you (such as an infirm relative), or anyone you have been cohabiting with for two years prior to death. If any of these people make a claim, the courts decide whether they should get some or all of your estate.

If you die leaving money or an asset to someone who is bankrupt their creditors may grab it. If you want to gift an asset to someone who is in financial difficulties, think about putting it into a trust. See Chapter 5 in this Book for more on using trusts to help your loved ones.

Making a Will with Your Spouse

You share your life together so why not your will? For the sake of simplicity, and as long as you have similar goals and objectives, you can join forces with your spouse, partner, or same-sex partner and make your wills together.

Book V

Protecting
Your
Wealth for
the Next
Generation

There are three ways that you can do this:

- ✔ **Joint will.** This is a single document stating the wishes of two people. Joint wills are rare and can be very complex.

- ✔ **Mirror wills.** This is when two wills are made in identical terms, although these can be revoked at any time by the people making the will. These are the most common form of will written by a couple.

- ✔ **Mutual wills.** These are very similar to mirror wills, but each party agrees that the wills cannot be revoked at any time. Mutual wills can have complications and are therefore not common.

If you think that joining forces with someone close through a joint, mirror, or mutual will is a good idea, see a solicitor for advice.

Considering Who Can't Make a Will

If you are aged 18 or over and are in possession of all your mental faculties, you should be free to make your own will or sign one drawn up by a solicitor on your behalf. Here we cover those who are not allowed by law to make a will.

Checking the grey matter: Being of sound mind

Picture those will-reading scenes in period dramas – the sombre oak-panelled solicitor's office with a gaggle of relatives hanging on every word – and remember the will's opening gambit: 'I, Lord Farquar Dalrymple Bazelgette, *being of sound mind hereby leave . . .*'

But what does the phrase *being of sound mind* actually mean?

In simple terms, it is a declaration that the person making the will enjoys a sufficiently robust mental state to fully understand what they are doing through their will. The sound mind hurdle is designed to protect the person making the will – a vulnerable person can have undue pressure put on them by a dishonest person or avaricious relative.

Solicitors are duty-bound to turn away people who are clearly not of sound mind who wish to make a will. However, anyone can make their own will, but if the court decides that they were clearly not of sound mind when they drew it up, then it can be considered to carry no legal weight after their death. In such circumstances the law of intestacy (see 'Understanding the Consequences of Dying without a Will' later in this chapter) is invoked or a previous will may apply.

A person is deemed *not* to be of sound mind if they are an in-patient of a psychiatric hospital or have been declared criminally insane.

However, grey areas exist. Some wills may not be accepted by the courts. Possible problem areas include:

- ✔ People with degenerative brain conditions such as senile dementia, Alzheimer's disease, Creutzfeldt-Jakob Disease (CJD), or late-stage brain tumours.
- ✔ Wills drawn up for people with severe learning disabilities.

Seek the advice of your GP if you think that the will of a friend or relative, or even your own will, might be challenged on the grounds of mental capacity. This action can lead to the will being overturned in the courts. A GP can give a medical opinion on whether the prospective will-maker is of sound mind. However, a medical opinion isn't a get-out-of-jail-free card, as a court is able to disregard it if they wish and overturn the will anyway.

If you fail to jump the sound mind hurdle, then your previous will stands. If there is no previous will, then the estate is distributed according to the rules of intestacy, which are explained later in this chapter.

Unusual circumstances where the will is still valid

If someone suffers from one of the following conditions, their will is still valid:

- ✔ **Being illiterate.** Not being able to read or write isn't a bar to making a will. The law allows illiterates to dictate their will to a solicitor and then make their mark – usually a cross – at the bottom of the document.
- ✔ **Having a physical disability.** If someone has been paralysed and is unable to sign, they may still make a will. Likewise, blind people may make a will. The law allows blind people to appoint a person to sign their will on their behalf, but the signing must take place in their presence after the will is read to them and they have understood it.

✔ **Being eccentric.** You have probably heard of cases where a person spends their last years looking after a beloved pet, then leaves their fortune to fund its upkeep. If there are no near relatives, such a bequest should be fine. However, if there are close relatives they can challenge the will claiming they and not the pet should be provided for. The key point of their challenge is unlikely to be made on the grounds that the person making the will was mentally incapable, instead it will be made on the grounds that the relatives relied on the deceased for support.

✔ **Being terminally ill.** People diagnosed with a terminal illness no doubt suffer a great deal of stress and anxiety, but this fraught mental state does not bar them from making a will. After all, the person making the will doesn't have to be of sound body – just of sound mind.

✔ **Suffering from certain mental illnesses.** People suffering from a bout of a depressive illness or even schizophrenia, for which they are receiving medication, should be fine to make a will provided that the will is made during a lucid interval. Consult your GP for advice.

✔ **Being in prison.** Prisoners are allowed to make a will, unless sent to a secure psychiatric hospital by a court of law.

Minor inconvenience: Being too young to make a will

Your 18th birthday means that you are allowed – at long last – to legally drink in a pub. The birthday also marks the day when you can make a valid will. (But don't celebrate both at the same time.)

People in the armed services under the age of 18 and on active service are allowed to make a will. In the army and air force 'on active service' is defined as either being in combat or on duty somewhere where there is terrorist activity. Taking part in a military exercise doesn't count as being on active service. Sailors under 18 have to be at sea to be allowed to make a will.

There is no upper-age limit for making a will, just as long as the person is clearly of *sound mind*.

In legal circles a man who makes a will is referred to as a *testator*. The female version of a will-maker is a *testratrix* – which sounds vaguely kinky to me!

The estate of a child who dies, including any assets held in trust, usually passes to the surviving parents under intestacy rules, which are explained below.

Understanding the Consequences of Dying without a Will

Sorry to bring the tone down – this part is about death and taxes, after all – but think about the situation if you were to die next week, tomorrow, or even right now! What state would your financial affairs be in? Most people would answer: A bit of a mess.

More than half the UK population dies without making a will, and an even higher percentage make no tax-saving plans during their lifetimes. The tax collector loves these people because they leave their estates wide open for a tax grab. However, the family left behind is probably less pleased at the lack of forward planning.

What's more, the tax collector doesn't hang around, but, in most cases, demands IHT before the deceased's assets can be sold. As a result, the deceased's nearest and dearest sometimes need to borrow money to pay the tax. Just a small planning step like buying a life insurance policy to cover any IHT bill can save loved ones a great deal of hassle and heartache at what is likely to be a very difficult time.

If you die having made a will, you're deemed to have died *testate*. To die without making a will is to die *intestate*. If you die intestate, your estate is distributed under the *law of intestacy*.

The law of intestacy is a serious business and there is no way around it for your family other than for them to unearth a valid will of yours and trump it. However, the law of intestacy is certainly not an ass: It places your nearest and dearest in a clear pecking order and distributes the goods to them accordingly.

You might find that the law of intestacy does a great job for you and your estate, and you don't need to make a will at all. Take a look at how your property will be divided up and see for yourself. Remember, though, if intestacy doesn't work for you then you need to make a will outlining your wishes.

The spouse gets it all (well, nearly!)

Your husband or wife is in pole position to benefit from your estate under intestacy. If you don't have any children or any other surviving relatives, then it's simple: Your spouse gets every penny – minus any administration costs. If you have a partner but are unmarried, they won't see a penny under intestacy.

See 'Modern Life: Intestacy Isn't Geared Up for It!' later in the chapter for more details.

The order of priority in divvying up the estate goes like this:

1. **Your spouse**

2. **Your children**

3. **Your parents**

4. **Your brothers and sisters**

5. **Your half-brothers and half-sisters**

6. **Your grandparents**

7. **Your uncles and aunts (your parents' siblings)**

8. **Your uncles and aunts (your parents' half-siblings)**

9. **The government**

Where any of the relatives above die before you, their *issue* – this is legal speak for children or other descendants – automatically take their place in the order of priority. For example, if your adult child is dead, your grandchildren will inherit.

If you have children, then see below. If you die without children but your parents are still living, then your spouse gets:

✔ All your personal items, often called *chattels*

✔ The next £200,000 of the estate

✔ Half of the remainder of the estate

The other half of the residue goes to your parents. If your parents are dead, then your brothers and sisters inherit half the estate residue in equal shares, and so on down the line of priority.

As long as you own your home together – known as *joint tenancy* – then your spouse automatically inherits your share of the property. Legal eagles call this situation one of *beneficial joint tenants*.

But if the deceased spouse owned the property outright on a *sole tenancy* basis, then the home goes into the mix and is distributed according to the order of priority above.

If your estate is worth less than £200,000, and you die intestate, your spouse gets everything.

A kingdom for a spouse

Your spouse gets the lion's share of your estate if you die intestate. You can try and disinherit a spouse through a will, but that would leave it open to a likely successful legal challenge. In order to inherit, your spouse must 'survive you' – that is, live – for 28 days after your death.

Under the laws of intestacy, if your spouse dies within 28 days of your demise, your estate will be treated as if there was no spouse in the first place and passes on down the order of priority (see earlier in this chapter).

Don't forget that any gifts between spouses are free of inheritance tax (unless one spouse lives outside the UK).

Letting the kids in on the act

If your spouse is still living and you have children, then your estate is divided up as follows:

- ✔ Your spouse inherits all your personal items (*chattels*) and the first £125,000 of the estate. Your spouse also gets half of the remainder of the estate after the £125,000 has been deducted.

- ✔ Your children get the other half of the residue of the estate in equal shares and when your spouse dies they inherit the other half.

Living it up with life interest

From the half of the estate residue that your surviving spouse inherits, he or she receives a *life interest*. Their share is invested to produce an income, a maximum of 6 per cent a year, while at the same time keeping the capital intact.

The job of investing any money used to create a life interest for a spouse falls on the person administrating the deceased's estate (often called the *administrator* or *personal representative*). The administrator can employ a suitable professional such as an independent financial adviser to help choose the right investments. The administrator is likely to be your surviving spouse.

Here's an example: The case of husband and wife, Mark and Pauline, and grown-up son, Graham.

What is a child?

Easy, I hear you shout, a child is a little person who on arrival takes over your entire life. But for the purposes of intestacy the actual definition of what constitutes a child is a lot more complex.

A child can inherit if they fall into any of the following categories:

✔ They are from a current or former marriage

✔ They have been legally adopted

✔ They were born out of marriage

✔ They were conceived but not yet born at the time of the father's death

✔ They were conceived by artificial insemination or surrogacy

However, stepchildren are not blood relatives and cannot inherit under intestacy.

When Mark dies he is worth £400,000 after taxes, debts, and funeral expenses are paid. But Mark failed to make a will – boo, hiss! As a result his personal items (chattels) worth £25,000 and the first £125,000 of his estate go straight to Pauline. £250,000 is now left in Mark's estate. Of this £250,000, Graham inherits half (£125,000) immediately. The other half (£125,000) goes to Pauline on a life-interest basis.

Pauline's £125,000 is invested and used to produce a maximum income of 6 per cent a year – equivalent to £7,500 for Pauline – but the capital is left untouched. When Pauline dies ten years later, the £125,000 passes to Graham, who is free to spend it as he wishes!

Over the years, inflation will erode the value of the £125,000 that passed to Pauline on a life-interest basis. When Graham gets his hands on the £125,000 on Pauline's death it will buy a lot less than it would've done ten years earlier.

If your spouse dies before you and then you die, your estate goes to any surviving children. The children can get their hands on their inheritance when they are 18 or marry, whichever is soonest.

No spouse, no children – if, if, and more ifs

You may notice a lot of ifs in this part of the chapter. Intestacy is full of ifs and if there is no spouse or children to leave your estate to, the ifs start multiplying.

Pride and prejudice

Britain is recognised around the world as a liberal society. But same-sex couples still face prejudice. Gay rights groups report numerous cases of relatives of the deceased excluding same-sex partners from benefiting from the estate, keeping small items of sentimental value, or even from attending their loved one's funeral. Sadly, when money is at stake, niceties and common decency can fly out of the window. Even if your relatives are comfortable with your lifestyle, making a will that clearly outlines how your partner should be treated is a sensible step. It also helps to become civil partners, ensuring legal recognition for your relationship.

If you die without any living children or a spouse, then the order of priority in dividing up the estate is as follows:

1. **Your parents**

2. **Your brothers and sisters**

3. **Your nieces and nephews**

4. **Your half-brothers and half-sisters**

5. **Your half-nephews and half-nieces (or their issue)**

6. **Your grandparents**

7. **Your uncles and aunts (your parents' siblings)**

8. **Your uncles and aunts (your parents' half-siblings)**

If no relatives survive, the Crown – in other words, the Government – takes your estate, and spends it very wisely no doubt!

The Crown can claim your cash because it is deemed *ultimus haeres* – no, not the name of a hirsute wrestler. The phrase roughly translates into 'last or remaining relative'. Bet you never knew you were related to royalty!

Under intestacy rules, the spouse has to survive the deceased by 28 days to inherit their share of the estate.

Modern Life: Intestacy Isn't Geared Up for It!

The law of intestacy has developed over a long period of time and to some extent is a bit of a relic. There has been the odd nod made to modern living, such as including children born out of wedlock, but not nearly enough for many people's liking. The following are just some 'modern life' circumstances to bear in mind if you haven't made a will yet:

- ✔ **Divorce.** A divorced person has no right to any part of the estate of a former spouse who has died following the granting of the decree absolute (that is, when the divorce is formally recognised by law). However, they can make a claim through the courts.

- ✔ **Separation.** If a Magistrates' Court Order rules that you're separated from your spouse, then your spouse still retains the right to inherit under intestacy. But if a separation order is granted as part of divorce proceedings, then your spouse loses his or her right to inherit.

- ✔ **Cohabitation.** If you're living with someone at the time of your death, that person doesn't get a bean through intestacy. However, a cohabiting partner can apply to a court to receive an income from the deceased's estate. Normally, they must have lived with the deceased for two years to stand a chance of receiving a penny.

- ✔ **Same-sex couples.** Under the government's recent Civil Partnership Bill, same-sex couples in the UK who have gone through a civil ceremony enjoy recognition under intestacy.

  Unmarried heterosexual couples are barred from benefiting under any Civil Partnership legislation, as the government argues that they are always free to marry.

The order that your nearest and dearest inherit under intestacy is dictated by a sub-section of the Administration of Estates Act 1925 – no wonder it's not in tune with the way we live today!

There is something far worse than dying without a will and that is dying with one that's badly written. By badly written, we don't mean that the grammar's askew, although using proper English is important. The language used in a will needs to be precise and unambiguous: Avoid words like 'around', 'approximately', and 'about'. Be very specific about what you want people to inherit and who you're leaving stuff to, otherwise family and friends may end up squabbling over who gets what. It makes sense to use a lawyer to draft the document, as he or she will steer clear of ambiguous terms.

Ashes to ashes

You can use a letter attached to your will to indicate what you would like to happen to your remains. Just make sure that your loved ones and executors know that the letter exists, so that they read it soon after your death and before the funeral. If you made any pre-paid funeral arrangements, make the details of this clear in the letter. This will save your loved ones a packet!

Looking at the Different Rules in Scotland

The laws governing intestacy discussed so far apply to England and Wales only (the differences in Northern Ireland are infinitesimal). There are key differences in the laws governing intestacy in Scotland. If you are resident in Scotland, you need to take note.

Whichever set of intestacy laws apply to you depends on where you live, rather than where you die.

The spouse does get it all!

Under Scottish law your spouse or surviving civil partner has *prior rights* to your estate. Prior rights mean that after debts and liabilities have been covered, he or she has first call on your assets when you're dead.

The level of prior rights is often large enough for the spouse to end up with the entire estate. Only after the prior rights are satisfied do children get their share. If the value of the estate is larger than the prior rights, then the spouse has extra *legal rights* in the remaining estate.

The level of prior rights is set every five to seven years. At assessment time, the amount of prior rights normally goes up to keep pace with inflation. The current levels date back to the last update in 2005.

The spouse has prior rights on three distinct property areas:

- ✔ **Home.** The surviving spouse will inherit the family home. If this is a farmhouse, or part of a shop, or where the house is worth more than £300,000, the survivor inherits up to a value of £300,000. (However, even if the family home is worth more than £300,000, the administrators or the court will almost certainly allow the spouse to remain in the home.)

- ✔ **Furnishings.** The spouse has the right to furniture and furnishings – known as *plenishings* – up to a value of £24,000.

  Plenishings is a Scottish legal phrase to describe goods as diverse as linen, glass, books, pictures, televisions, washing-machines, and other items of household use.

- ✔ **Moveable assets.** If the deceased spouse left children or grandchildren, the remaining spouse takes the first £42,000 of the remaining estate. If there are no children or grandchildren, then the spouse can claim the first £75,000 of the estate.

Prior rights are a first claim on the estate. But once they have been settled, the spouse or civil partner (along with any children) is entitled to legal rights out of the remaining *moveable estate*. In Scottish law, moveable property includes such things as money, shares, cars, furniture, and jewellery. The surviving spouse is entitled to one third of the moveable estate if the deceased left children or grandchildren, or to one half of it if there were no children.

Even where you leave a valid will, in Scotland your surviving spouse or child can claim *legal rights* to your estate as an alternative. The surviving spouse is entitled to claim one-half of all moveable assets if there are no children, and one-third if there are children. However, by exercising any legal rights they forgo rights granted to them under the will. For example, if a woman leaves her husband £2,000, then the widower has the choice of either accepting the £2,000 or taking one-third or one-half of the estate (the proportion depends on whether there are any children).

Letting the kids get a look in

Children are collectively entitled to one third of the deceased's moveable estate if there is a surviving spouse or civil partner, and one half if there is none. Each child has an equal claim.

If a child – say a daughter – dies before the parent, then when the parent dies, the daughter's share of the parent's estate is shared equally between any offspring she has produced – the grandchildren.

For example, say that after a widow has been given her prior rights and her share of the residual estate on the death of her husband, £100,000 is left. The couple had a son and a daughter; the son died before his father, but not before having produced two grandchildren. The couple's daughter will inherit £50,000, while the remaining £50,000 will be split equally between the son's two children (the couple's grandchildren).

Under the intestacy laws of Scotland, Northern Ireland, England, and Wales, your grandchild only has a right to a part of your estate if their parent – your son or daughter – dies before you. If you want your grandchildren to inherit anything, make a will.

Other rights on intestacy

After any prior rights and legal rights have been claimed, the remainder of the estate – both real estate (*heritable assets*) and moveable assets – is passed on in the following order. Any surviving relative in a higher group takes precedence, so lower groups only inherit if there are no living members of a higher group on the list.

Planning to die intestate

What, draw up a document to say I don't want to draw up a will? Surely some misprint. This may seem like a strange idea, but bear with me. Drawing up a very simple document stating that you wish the law governing intestacy to deal with your estate is a wise move. Otherwise, family members may spend time hunting for a non-existent will. By making it plain you never made a will, you will save them time and the heartache of rooting through your possessions.

---

1. **Living children and the descendants of dead children take the whole**

2. **Brothers and sisters (or their descendants) and the parents of the deceased get half each**

3. **Brothers and sisters take the whole**

4. **Either or both parents take the whole**

5. **Surviving spouse or civil partner takes the whole**

6. **Aunts and uncles take the whole**

7. **Grandparents take the whole**

8. **Brothers and sisters of any grandparents take the whole.**

If you die intestate in Scotland with no relatives, the government scoops the lot.

These rules apply subject to three general principles:

- There is no preference for males or for age.

- If a relative who would have inherited the estate but has already died leaves children, those children are entitled to their parent's share between them.

- Full parents or siblings have preference over step-parents or half-brothers/sisters.

 You can leave your estate to be dealt with under the law of intestacy while making provision for your loved ones through a life insurance policy. Under this scenario, intestacy takes care of the basics. However, there is a drawback: The proceeds of any life insurance policy are included in your estate for inheritance tax purposes.

Chapter 2

Deciding Who Gets What

. . . .

In This Chapter

▶ Assessing who gets what

▶ Looking at gifting to your family

▶ Avoiding gift failure

▶ Owning property and the impact on your will

▶ Looking at property trusts

. . . .

*I*t's pointless knowing your executor from your testator or your credit from debit if you don't match up what you own to the right people.

We're not just talking about a beneficiary getting slightly miffed that you didn't leave them that nice bone china dinner service they always admired. Make an error dishing out the dosh, and your loved ones can end up slugging it out over your property. Your will may even be declared invalid. And watch out for the tax collector taking a whopping bite out of your estate.

Relax! In this chapter we show you how to make sure that your bequest fits your beneficiaries like a glove.

Who You Have to Include in Your Will

You can leave your estate to whomever you choose, but if you exclude your closest family they can apply to the courts to have your will changed or over-turned. The Provision for Family and Dependants Act 1975 sets out that, wherever possible, your dependants should get enough to live on. So if you plan to leave everything to charity, unless you have the backing of your near-est and dearest, forget it!

Disputing your will in England and Wales

There are six groups of people who can apply to the courts for provision from your estate if you leave any of them out of your will:

- ✔ Your spouse
- ✔ Your children (including adopted children; see Chapter 1 for what legally constitutes a child)
- ✔ Any person being maintained by you prior to your death, such as an infirm close relation
- ✔ A former spouse who has not remarried
- ✔ A partner who cohabited with you for a minimum of two years prior to your death
- ✔ A person who, though not your child, was treated as a child by you or your family, a stepchild for example

The court doesn't give equal weight to all of the people in these categories. If you don't leave enough for your spouse and children it's a racing certainty that the court will order that your estate be re-jigged with the aim of providing for them. But your spouse and children are very likely to be considered by the court to be more important than, say, a former spouse. Therefore, you don't have to share out your loot equally to head off any possible legal challenge.

Disputing your will in Scotland

Under the 1964 Succession (Scotland) Act (revised in 1999), in Scotland your surviving spouse or child can claim *legal rights* to your estate if you have not provided for them sufficiently in your will. The surviving spouse is entitled to claim one-half of all moveable assets (cash, jewellery, cars, and so on) if there are no children and one-third if there are children. However, by exercising any legal rights the surviving spouse or child forgo whatever has been granted to them in the will. For example, if a man leaves his wife £10,000, the widow has the choice of either accepting the £10,000 or taking one-half of the estate if there are no children or one-third if there are.

If the spouse claims their legal rights, the remainder of the estate is distributed by the executors as closely as possible to the terms of the will.

Book V

Protecting
Your
Wealth for
the Next
Generation

Sticking to the letter

You have the option of outlining some of your bequests in a letter attached to your will. Using a letter in this way keeps the will itself from being bogged down in a monotonous litany of who gets what. After all, does everyone present at the reading of your will have to hear who gets the cutlery?

The letter has the same legal weight as the will document itself.

Still, keep what happens to the really big stuff – your home, savings accounts, and highly personal items – in your will as they are probably of most concern to your loved ones. Just don't forget to refer to the letter in your will and make sure your executors have a copy of it.

Assessing What Everyone Should Have

If your goal is to look after your immediate family first and foremost, you need to consider what significant life challenges they may face when you have gone. Taking a 'what if' approach to your loved ones' finances will help you assess what you need to leave them in your will.

If you make a gift to someone in your will and subsequently sell it or dispose of it some other way, your unlucky beneficiary has no claim on it. This principle is known as *ademption* and your disappointed beneficiary won't be happy about it!

Taking care of your spouse

You probably have a pretty good idea of the financial situation of your spouse. However, it's still a good idea to discuss what they might need from your will. At the very least they are likely to want your share of the family home. You may want to leave them the whole kit and caboodle, which may be very appropriate if you have young children.

There are two ways to leave money to your spouse (or any other beneficiary) – through a lump sum or the setting up of a regular income.

> ✔ Leaving a **lump sum** (*capital*) gives your spouse immediate access to ready cash at a time when they need it most. You can leave a lump sum by naming your spouse as the beneficiary of a life insurance policy or you can leave them the contents of your savings accounts. Alternatively,

you can simply state in your will that a percentage of your estate should pass to your spouse.

✔ Leaving a **regular income** (*life interest*) for your spouse provides them with major reassurance. No matter what life now throws at your partner, the income you set up will provide a helping hand. You can set up a regular payment by simply leaving them an income-yielding investment such as a bond, or a fund that invests in a basket of company shares, or arrange for them to benefit from your pension. Alternatively, you can set some assets aside in trust (see Chapter 5 in this Book).

Many people, provided they have assets large enough, choose to leave a lump sum *and* arrange for an income to be paid.

If you divorce your spouse, any gifts you leave them in your will are automatically cancelled. Under such a scenario the gifts given to a spouse go into the estate residue, which in turn may end up being distributed under intestacy. All in all, divorce can throw will plans into chaos, and if you take a trip to Splitsville you should seriously consider making a new will.

Providing for your children

Children cost buckets of cash. They need feeding, clothing, and boy do they need entertaining! But apart from the day-to-day expense of bringing up your little treasures, you may also consider what extra cash they will need while growing up. Here are some likely areas of expenditure on them that you may want to consider including in your will:

✔ **Schooling.** Although the State provides free primary and secondary education to all, there are extra costs associated with schooling such as uniform, textbooks, home tuition, and after-school activities and trips. If you choose to have your child educated in a public school the costs can run into thousands, or even tens of thousands, of pounds per year.

✔ **Going to university.** This is a big area of concern as the cost of further education has rocketed and the old student grant – when the State paid people to drink, sorry, study – is no more. The average student now leaves university with an average debt of more than £12,000.

✔ **Buying a first home.** With house prices so high, clambering onto the property ladder is harder than ever. You may decide you would like to leave something in your will to help your child achieve their property ownership dream.

✔ **Getting married.** Seeing your child walk up the aisle is a red-letter day in any parent's life. It's no surprise, therefore, that people leave money in their will just in case they are no longer around to help with the often huge expense of the wedding day.

Book V

Protecting
Your
Wealth for
the Next
Generation

On one condition . . .

Sometimes gifts made to children through a will come with conditions. For example, a gift of cash can be made under the condition that it will be used for a wedding or university fees. However, conditions that are too restrictive and smack of the deceased trying to play God can be set aside by the court. What's more, the condition has to be enforceable. Who, for example, would be able to monitor if the three adult children of one Edith S of Walsall really didn't spend the £50,000 she left them on 'slow horses and fast women' as she specifically asked them not to. If you do add conditions to a gift, you should say what should happen if those conditions are not met.

It may not be possible for you to set aside enough in your will to cover all eventualities. What's more, you may feel that there are certain things it would be good for them to provide off their own bat such as a deposit on a first home or further education.

If you want a child to use a gift for a specific purpose, such as paying university fees or funding a deposit on their first home, you may want to make the gift *conditional*. See the nearby sidebar for more on tacking conditions onto a gift.

If you make a gift in your will to a child, then the executor has to hold onto it in trust until the child turns 18. A child cannot inherit until he or she turns 18. This can be a bit of an administrative pain for the executor or trustee you appoint through your will, and there is always the possibility that the executor dies without their financial affairs being in order. The gift can conceivably be lost. The simplest way of dealing with this problem is to state in your will that if you die before the child has reached adulthood the gift should go to the child's parents with the proviso that they should hand it over to the child when the child becomes an adult.

Gifting to your grandchildren

For many, leaving something for the grandchildren to give them a head start in life is a big motivation for making a will. You must include your grandchildren in your will if you wish them to inherit, as they have no legal right to your money. If you leave your grandchildren out of your will they can't appeal to the courts for redress unless you were *maintaining* them (looking after them financially). Even through intestacy – the law that governs what happens when you die without a will – your grandchildren come way down the pecking order of beneficiaries, only inheriting if their parents are dead. There are a couple of other things you need to bear in mind when deciding how much or how little to give the grandchildren, as follows:

- ✔ **The amount you are leaving to their parents.** If you plan to leave a hefty inheritance to your children, you can, hopefully, rely on them to use it in the best interests of your grandchildren. In such circumstances you may wish to just leave a small sum to be paid when they reach a particular age or to help them buy a home or study. Make these terms clear when writing your will.

- ✔ **The age of your grandchildren.** If your grandchildren are grown up, then you probably have a good idea of what would benefit them in your will. However, if your grandchildren are minors, then they can't inherit property or cash directly, and you will have to leave the money in trust for them to access at a particular point in the future. See Chapter 5 in this Book for more details on trusts.

You can keep things simple by allowing your grandchildren to have access to the bequest on their 18th, 21st, or 25th birthdays and they can then decide for themselves what to do with it.

When you put money in trust for your grandchild it is the trustees' job to invest the money until it's time for the beneficiary to inherit in their own right. Trustees are duty bound to invest the money prudently. Don't forget that your executors can double up as trustees.

Seeing your parents right

You may believe that your parents gave you everything. Hopefully they were responsible for giving you a good start in life, teaching you a moral framework to take out into the world and, when you were in trouble, who did you turn to? Although the natural scheme of things says that you outlive your parents, you may still want to include them in your will.

Born under the pound sign

A will allows you to leave something to someone not yet born. This tactic is often used by aspiring grandparents. The big advantage is that when the beneficiary is born you don't need to change the will. However, it is advisable to name someone else who should inherit just in case at the time of your death the unborn child still hasn't come along.

It may not be as easy to gauge the financial position of your parents as easily as you can your spouse's. Your parents may not feel comfortable talking about money with you. However, you can probably come up with a good guess as to what they are worth. Some factors to consider include:

- ✔ **Do they own their own home?** If your parents have lived in their house for a long time, the value has probably vastly increased, and the mortgage may be paid off. In this case, you don't need to worry about leaving your parents without a roof over their heads.

- ✔ **Are they employed?** If your parents are still working, they are still earning. Hopefully, they have paid off the mortgage and the children have flown the nest. This time in a person's life, when they are still working but have reduced their responsibilities, is often a golden age for building up a pot of money. In short, they may not need your bequest.

- ✔ **Are they still married?** If your parents are no longer together, one parent may be poorer than the other. Bear in mind that women make up a disproportionately high percentage of the elderly poor. Your mother may have taken time off to bring you and your siblings up. As a result, she may not have paid enough National Insurance contributions to be entitled to a full state pension. You might consider leaving more to your mother than your father, but explain to them in person or in a letter why you have done this.

If you leave money or property to an elderly relative and they end up needing local authority nursing home care, your bequest may be lost. In England and Wales the local authority (such as the town or city council) can force residents of their care homes to sell some of their assets to pay for the cost of care.

If your beneficiary's estate is over the threshold for inheritance tax (£300,000 until April 2008), he may not welcome an addition to his tax liability!

Including everyone: The catch-all approach

What about showing your feelings for that gaggle of not-so-near family?

You may only know them a little and may not be sure of their financial needs, but you might want to show that blood does indeed run thicker than water and leave them a little token. A good way to do this is to specify in your will a gift to more than one person, or group of people. For example, you may decide to leave £5,000 to be divided equally between all your surviving nieces and nephews.

Thanking those who carry out your wishes

There are a host of people who you can name in your will whose job is to ensure your wishes are carried out and your loved ones taken care of. The roles of these people are explored in Chapter 3 in this book, but you might wish to consider what to leave each one as a token of thanks.

✔ Executors – The executers of your will make sure your estate is distributed according to your wishes. Executors also deal with HMRC and any creditors. It would be a nice gesture to leave them some small token for all their hard work.

✔ Trustees – These people administer and distribute any assets you choose to put in trust. In some cases trustees may have to look after money or property for many years.

Being a trustee is a highly responsible and sometimes technical job and you may choose to leave them something in your will as a thank you. However, if the trustee is a professional (such as a solicitor or accountant), then their financial reward comes from the fees they charge. Often the same people act as both executors and trustees.

✔ Guardians – A guardian is the person you appoint to look after your children when you are gone. It is essential that you decide with them how much they will need from your estate to bring up your children. Leave money in trust for the child, instructing the trustees to use the money to help the guardians meet the cost of bringing up the child.

Even after you gift your home, cash, shares, items of furniture, and jewellery there may still be quite a bit left over. Instead of going into the minutiae of every golf club, handbag, and watch, you can simply use your will to gift someone the rest of your estate. What is left after all taxes and debts are paid and all specific items of property are doled out is referred to as your *residuary estate* or *estate residue*.

Solicitors refer to a gift of land as a *devise* and everything else as a *legacy*.

Gift Failure and How to Prevent It

A gift failing doesn't mean it hasn't pleased the recipient (not like those glow-in-the-dark socks you gave your father last Christmas). Instead, *gift failure* means that something has gone wrong to prevent the gift ending up in the hands of the intended beneficiary.

Gifts can fail for a number of reasons, for example:

Book V

Protecting
Your
Wealth for
the Next
Generation

- ✔ The beneficiary has died before you

- ✔ The beneficiary or their spouse has acted as witness to the will and thereby lost any right to inherit

- ✔ The gift fails as a result of divorce (see 'Taking care of your spouse' earlier in this chapter)

- ✔ The details of the beneficiary or gift were incomplete or incorrect

- ✔ The charity you wanted to leave a gift to has ceased to exist

If the gift was left to your child, and your child dies, the gift passes to their child (your grandchild). In other cases, a failed gift becomes part of the *residuary estate*. The residuary estate is what is left after all the beneficiaries have been paid. You may want to leave the residue of your estate to someone through your will otherwise what's left is distributed under *intestacy* (see Chapter 1 in this Book for a rundown of how this works).

The estate residue is often worth a lot of money. Think carefully about whom you want to leave your estate residue to. Most people leave the residue of their estate to the main beneficiary of their will, usually a spouse.

You can take some simple steps to stop your gifts from failing. For starters, be thorough about describing the gifts and whom you're leaving the gifts to. And whatever you do, don't get a beneficiary or the spouse of a beneficiary to witness your will signature because they then cannot inherit.

If a beneficiary dies before you, change your will and name a replacement beneficiary. Better still, name an alternative beneficiary in the original will. Naming an alternative beneficiary is a good way of ensuring that a particular asset of yours finds its way to a specific branch of your family. This measure also means you don't have to worry about changing your will every time one of your named beneficiaries dies.

Don't just limit naming alternatives to your beneficiaries. Take the time to consider naming alternative executors, guardians, and trustees. All three groups have a huge role to play in securing your loved ones' future after you've gone (see Chapter 3 in this Book for more).

You can incorporate a *survivorship clause* into your will, naming an alternative beneficiary for your bequest if the first beneficiary doesn't survive for a set period of time after your death (usually 28 days).

Abatement: Spreading it thin

If there isn't enough money left in your estate to cover all your bequests, then it is up to your executor to apply the rules of *abatement* and reduce how much is paid to your beneficiaries. For example, if your bequests tot up to £300,000 but there is only £200,000 in the estate, then your beneficiaries will only pick up two-thirds of what you bequeathed them. This abatement process can play havoc with your best-laid plans. The only way to avoid this unforeseen event happening is to be thorough about estimating your total worth and realistic about how much you actually have to leave. In some cases, the beneficiaries are left with nothing because the deceased died with debts large enough to swallow up the whole estate.

Playing the Philanthropist

After you have taken care of your nearest and dearest, you may want to leave something to charity. Hundreds of millions of pounds are left to charity each year and without this money many charities would struggle to exist.

Generally, all gifts made to charity through your will are free of inheritance tax.

Like companies, charities can fold or amalgamate with one another. If the charity you leave money to in your will ceases to exist your gift will fail. To avoid this failure, you can grant your executor the power to choose an alternative charity if needs be. That way the executor can make sure that the money finds its way to a similar charity to the one you chose originally. Add a clause to your will specifying this detail.

Specify the full name and address of the charity in your will, otherwise the gift may fail. For example, it is not enough to write 'I leave £5,000 for the prevention of heart disease'. Specify precisely which charity the cash is destined for: The British Heart Foundation, for example (with the full address of their main office).

It is a good idea to note the charity's registration number, which you can find on their Web site or stationery.

Gifting to Cut the Tax Bill

When deciding who gets what from your estate, bear in mind that you can give presents of cash or possessions while you are still alive. Giving gifts throughout your life – not through your will – not only makes you the generous one of the family, but also reduces your estate and any eventual inheritance tax liability. However, the tax authorities won't allow you to get away with simply giving away everything to your loved ones in your twilight years. In fact, any major gift of property or cash is still considered part of your estate for the purposes of calculating inheritance tax for seven years after it is made.

Gifts you can make that are exempt of inheritance tax include:

✔ Gifts between spouses (as long as they both reside in the UK).

✔ Wedding gifts of £5,000 for each child, £2,500 for each grandchild, and £1,000 for anyone else.

✔ Gifts made to charities, some museums, and political parties.

✔ Small gifts of up to £250 in a single tax year to any number of individuals, just as long as an individual receiving a small gift doesn't also receive the £3,000 large gift too.

✔ Large gifts of up to a total of £3,000 in a single tax year. Any unused large gift exemption can be carried forward to the following tax year. If you haven't used your large gift exemption this tax year, you can give double (£6,000) next year.

If you have taken full advantage of your gift exemptions, this may give you pause for thought when you consider who gets what in your will. After all, you may already have taken care of a child through a series of large gifts made over many years or a favourite niece through a £1,000 gift on her wedding day.

Disinheriting your not-so-loved ones

Disinheriting someone means to reject someone as your heir – it all sounds very dramatic! In effect, you disinherit someone by removing him or her from a will in which they were originally named as a beneficiary. However, there's no two ways about it, if you want to disinherit your nearest – although perhaps not dearest – relations, you probably won't be allowed to do so. The law takes a simple view: Your family are entitled to their piece of the pie.

If you really want to disinherit someone it is best to indicate in a letter addressed to the executors and the court explaining why you have taken such a drastic step. It will then be up to the court whether to overturn your decision.

You can specify in your will that gifts are made *free-of-tax*. This means that any inheritance tax due on your estate is to be paid out of the residual estate. Leaving gifts free-of-tax means that the executors don't have to decide what to sell from the estate in order to meet any tax bill, they simply take it out of the residual estate. Non-residuary estate gifts are deemed to be free-of-tax unless the will indicates to the contrary.

You can make any amount of gifts from *income* (that is, not from your capital) for the upkeep of loved ones. As soon as you make gifts from income they disappear from your estate as far as HMRC is concerned.

Understanding How Ownership Affects Your Bequest

You own your home so you can do what you want with it in your will, right? Wrong!

In this section I look at how different types of ownership affect who can and can't inherit your home when you're gone.

Sole tenancy

Ah, this is the easy one! You are the sole tenant, which means you personally own the house 100 per cent (not forgetting the mortgage lender, of course). But this situation doesn't mean you can leave your home to whomever you choose, not a bit of it!

If you choose not to leave your home to your spouse or children, they can ask the courts to overturn your bequest. Under the Inheritance (Provision for Family and Dependants) Act 1975, the court is likely to overturn your decision and allow them to inherit.

No direct equivalent to the Inheritance (Provision for Family and Dependents) Act 1975 exists in Scotland. Nevertheless, in Scotland, the spouse and children of the deceased are allowed to claim *temporary ailment* and *continuing ailment* from the estate (*ailment* is legal mumbo-jumbo for maintenance).

Good deeds

A *deed* of title is the legal evidence of property ownership. If you have a mortgage, your lender may be holding onto your deeds but it's a good idea to retain a copy of them.

Keeping a copy of your deed of title with your will and a list of any debts, such as a mortgage secured on the property, makes life easier for the executors of your will.

If you sign over your deed of title to someone else the title becomes *defective* for several years at least. Most banks or building societies won't make a loan secured on the property while its title is defective. The lenders are protecting

themselves just in case the courts rule that the signing over of the deed of title should be set aside.

Since 2003, the Land Registry has *dematerialised*. No, this doesn't mean it's vanished into the space-time continuum, Doctor Who style, it simply means the Registry no longer issues Land Certificates (the name for a deed of title) or Charge Certificates (which show the boundaries of a property and give details of covenants affecting it). Instead, the Land Registry relies on its computer records to keep track of who owns what.

The Act may have been passed a long time ago but the idea behind it is still sound – it's designed to stop people that rely on you being left destitute or homeless as a result of the terms of your will.

As for live-in lovers, the executors or the court can still deem that they should be able to stay in your home after your death, if only for a short time while they find somewhere else to live. The court will make any such decision based on how much the person making the request to remain depended for financial support on the deceased.

If you live alone, are unmarried, and don't have children, as sole tenant you can leave your house to whomever you want.

With complex wills or a complicated estate it can take well over a year for the executor to sort everything out.

Beneficial joint tenancy

Beneficial joint tenancy means that you own the home jointly with someone else, usually a spouse or partner. When you die your share of the property automatically passes to the person who owns it with you. The surviving joint tenant becomes a sole tenant and they can dispose of the home as they wish.

Intestacy and beneficial joint tenancy

If you die without a valid will you die *intestate*. If you die intestate, strict laws governing the distribution of your estate kick in. The laws of intestacy are explained in full in Chapter 1 in this Book. What happens when your home is held in beneficial joint tenancy and you die intestate? When two laws collide you only get one winner. In this case, the laws governing tenancy overrule those of intestacy.

If you die intestate, your share of the home passes to the other joint tenant and is not included in the rest of your estate that is subsequently dished out according to the laws of intestacy. This situation shouldn't matter a jot if your joint tenant is a close relative or spouse, the same person who would benefit under intestacy rules.

Joint tenancy is a painless way of leaving your home. Because joint tenancy rules take precedence, it means that you don't even have to include your home in your will. Having said that, it never hurts to make your wishes crystal clear and state that the beneficial joint tenant is to inherit. A good form of words to use is:

> *For the avoidance of doubt I give all my share and interest in the property known as (name of property) to (name of beneficial joint tenant).*

The surviving joint tenant has the legal authority to decide who can remain living in the house. If your spouse is the joint tenant and remarries, the new apple of his or her eye may become the new joint tenant. If your spouse dies, the person they have remarried takes possession of the home and can force your children to leave (if they're feeling really nasty). Such situations are more common than you may think!

The right of the surviving joint tenant is considered by law to be more important than any rights you grant a beneficiary in a will.

Joint tenancy arrangements don't offer protection for your children if your surviving spouse remarries. You may want to change the ownership basis to tenants in common and then leave your share of the property to your children. Read more about tenants in common later in this chapter.

Tenants in common

Being *tenants in common* means that you own property with one or more people upon terms that give each of you a share in it. Under this type of ownership each tenant is free to dispose of their share of the property as they see fit through their own will. If a tenant in common dies without a valid will the law of intestacy kicks in but is only applied to their share of the property. The share of one tenant in common never passes automatically on death to the other tenant or tenants in common.

Take the case of Gita and Massoud. They buy a house together worth £300,000. Gita stumps up £200,000 to fund the purchase, while Massoud scrimps together £100,000. Unless Gita is in a particularly generous mood, she will insist that as tenants in common she has a two-thirds share, leaving Massoud with the other third. If Gita then dies, her two-thirds share will pass to either the named beneficiary in the will or, if there is no will, will be distributed under the laws of intestacy (see Chapter 1). This leaves Massoud in the position of owning the house with Gita's beneficiaries.

If you own property on a tenants in common basis, make crystal clear in a will who inherits your share. The normal options are:

✔ **Give your share to your surviving spouse.** If your spouse is the other tenant in common, on your death they become sole tenant (they own the family home outright), and can do with it what they want.

✔ **Give your share to your adult children.** If your spouse is the other tenant, your home will be owned jointly by your surviving spouse and grown-up children as tenants in common. Your spouse has the legal right to live in the property until their death.

✔ **Give your share to someone outside your family.** Some people choose to leave their share to charity, which is all very nice but if you plan to go down this route discuss it with your spouse and immediate family. Nasty surprises in wills can lead to legal challenges!

Looking at common property in Scotland

In Scotland a home can be owned as *common property*. Like tenants in common, each owner possesses a portion of the property and on death this is dealt with according to the terms of the will or intestacy. However, the title of the property may contain a *survivorship destination*. This means that the share of the first co-owner to die passes automatically to the surviving co-owner(s). It is not possible to change a survivorship destination except by re-arranging the title, which requires the consent of all the co-owner(s). The deeds must be prepared by a solicitor. A survivorship destination normally prevents an individual from leaving his or her share of the property by will to anybody other than the co-owner(s).

Freehold or leasehold?

Property is owned on a freehold or leasehold basis. *Freehold* means you own your home lock, stock, and barrel (not forgetting the spectre of the mortgage lender), while *leasehold* means that someone else owns the land your property is built on (and often the property itself) and has agreed that you can live there for a set period of time – anything up to 999 years. Whether your house is leasehold or freehold can have a major impact on its value, but it doesn't affect your rights to leave the property in your will. If you own property on a leasehold basis your beneficiary can automatically assume the remainder of the lease.

Dividing your property between your spouse and grown-up children can be a very smart tax play. Such a move can reduce the size of the taxable estate on the death of your surviving spouse, as half the house has already been passed to the adult children.

Be realistic about the relationships your loved ones enjoy – or not – with one another. If your spouse and adult children do not get on, it's not a bright idea to write your will so that they own the family home as tenants in common.

To make life simple, you can change the terms of ownership of the property from *tenants in common* to *beneficial joint tenancy* so that your property automatically passes to your spouse. All parties must agree to this change and you need to alter the title deeds to the property. Remember, you might have to get the permission of any mortgage lender involved. After divorce, couples often go the opposite route and change from joint tenants to tenants in common. However, owning a property on a tenants in common basis is far more flexible from an inheritance tax avoidance point of view. If you're considering changing the terms of ownership, consult a solicitor.

Putting Your Faith in Trusts

A trust is a legal arrangement whereby one group of people – the *trustees* – are made legally responsible for property for the benefit of another group of people called the *beneficiaries*. You can write a trust into your own will or ask a solicitor to do it for you.

By putting your home into trust you pluck it from the rest of your estate and place it in the hands of the trustees. You rely on the trustees to follow what they see as best for the beneficiaries, or you can outline what you deem to be best under the terms of the trust. A trust can come into effect after your death or even when you're alive. This section deals solely with leaving your property in a trust. See Chapter 5 in this Book for more on trusts.

Your executors can double up as trustees; after all, both jobs require similar administrative skills as well as a hearty dose of common sense. See Chapter 3 in this Book for more on choosing the right trustee.

You might put your home in trust for a variety of reasons, including:

- ✔ To ensure that the surviving spouse gets to live in the property and, on their death, an adult child or other beneficiary inherits
- ✔ To provide a regular income for a specified beneficiary from renting out the property
- ✔ To prevent a child from inheriting before they have reached a particular age.

To reduce the likely inheritance tax bill on the death of the surviving spouse (see Chapter 4 in this Book). A property can be *held* in trust either for a set period of time or until a particular event takes place, such as the death of a surviving spouse.

Putting your home into trust can make the trustees all-powerful. Under some types of trust, the trustees say what goes – not the beneficiary. Trustees have to act in the best interest of the beneficiaries but it doesn't follow that they always do what the beneficiary wants. The ins and outs of trustees are discussed in Chapter 3 in this Book.

Helping the aged

Trusts are sometimes used to sidestep laws forcing people to sell their homes to pay for care in a local authority care home. In England and Wales, people can only receive free local authority nursing home care if their assets are £20,500 or less. This rule forces many people to sell the family home in their twilight years, reducing the size of their assets. By putting your home in trust it is possible to ring-fence it from any calculations the local authority makes about the value of the assets, because the property is considered to belong to someone else.

However, the property should be worth less than your nil rate band (£300,000 in 2007-08) in order to avoid inheritance tax charges on your death.

Putting your home in trust and then hobbling down to the local nursing home the next day is bound to arouse suspicion. This action is known in legal circles as *deliberate deprivation*. Local authorities and creditors can ask the court to overturn a trust in these circumstances. It's up to the court to judge whether deliberate deprivation has taken place.

When generosity backfires

Simply giving away your home to children or relatives can increase your tax bill. If you remain living in the home you have given away via a trust, you must prove to the tax authorities that you pay the correct market rent to the new 'owners'. Since April 2005, under what's called the *pre-owned assets* rules, people who continue to live in property that they have given away will be hit with an income tax bill. What's more, under new rules introduced in April 2006 you will have to pay a tax charge on the value over the nil rate band (£300,000 in 2007-08) when the property is transferred into the trust, plus ongoing charges every ten years. Moreover, the person you signed the property over to may have to pay IHT if you die within seven years of making the gift. In short, HMRC is cracking down hard on these types of arrangements!

Check out Chapter 4 in this Book for how to protect your estate from inheritance tax pitfalls, and Chapter 5 for more on the use of trusts.

Chapter 3

Choosing the Right People to Follow Your Wishes

*N*o one is an island and everyone needs a little help sometimes. This is never truer than when it comes to sorting out your estate after you've gone. The best-laid plans in your will can fall apart unless someone reliable is willing to follow your wishes. Picking the right people to carry out the terms of your will is as important as what goes into it in the first place. Choosing people who are on the ball will make life a lot easier for your nearest and dearest.

As you prepare your will you may need to consult a solicitor or an accountant unless your affairs are very simple – and your family may have to call in a professional for help with dealing out the dosh. Knowing when to call on the help of the professionals and ensuring you're getting the right deal is vital. Remember, forewarned is forearmed.

In this chapter, we explain the roles of everyone who makes sure your wishes make it off the page and into reality.

Considering the People Who Make Your Will Work

If you want a friend or family member to act as an executor, trustee, or guardian, make sure you are 100 per cent certain that they are up to the task. You must carefully consider if you are asking too much of them.

Talk the situation over with your nearest and dearest; be honest and upfront about what you're looking for, and stress to them that it's okay to say no. You can set out what you want from these people in writing (a job description, if you like). Even buy potential executors, trustees, and guardians a copy of Julian Knight's *Wills, Probate & Inheritance Tax For Dummies* (Wiley) to read so that they know what they're letting themselves in for.

You must also make sure that you're not asking too much from any professionals – accountants and solicitors – you might employ. Yes, you pay them, but make sure that they are not advising you beyond their capabilities.

And, finally, if you decide to draw up your own will, are you asking too much of yourself? If you have complex tax and financial affairs, you might be biting off more than you can chew.

Any problems with your will are unlikely to come to light until after your death, and by then it's too late! Choose your helpers carefully.

The Big Cheese: The Executor

As the name suggests, an executor is the person whom you appoint to *execute*, or carry out, the terms of your will. The female version of executor is *executrix*, which sounds rather kinky, so for the sake of our blood pressure we stick to 'executor' in this book.

An *executor* is your representative after you die. Executors make sure all the loose ends are tied up – it's a position of considerable responsibility. In your will, your executor – a role often referred to in legal circles as *personal representative* – gets near to top billing! Executors, once they've been approved by the courts, track down all your assets and arrange for all outstanding debts and taxes to be paid. Then the executor distributes what's left of your loot according to the wishes expressed in your will.

If you did not make a valid will the court appoints a personal representative called an *administrator* for you. An administrator fulfils the same duties as an executor and, confusingly, is also sometimes referred to as the personal representative. See Chapter 6 in this Book for who can act as administrator of your estate.

Choosing an executor

When choosing an executor think organised, literate, numerate, trustworthy, good at handling money, and not afraid of a bit of hard work. As you read this, hopefully a name or two has popped into your head.

Anyone can be an executor but they have to be at least 18 years old, which is no bad thing. Would you really want Kevin the teenager sorting out your estate? In addition, they must be of *sound mind* (see Chapter 1 in this Book for the definition of being of sound mind).

Executors normally come from one of the following groups:

 ✔ **A beneficiary.** The executor can be a close family friend or member of the immediate family. This has the big plus that your friend or relative will want to do right by you when you've gone. But be wary of appointing the family black sheep as executor: Antagonism between the executor and the other beneficiaries can lead to delays and even legal challenges. Close family friends usually make good executors.

 Always ask the person you intend to name as your executor if they feel that they are capable of undertaking the job. A very complex estate – or one where the deceased has left an organisational mess – can take ages to execute from start to finish (although the estate should be distributed within a year). Overseeing that process is quite a lot to ask, even of a close friend or family member.

 ✔ **A professional adviser.** A solicitor or an accountant should have both the experience and knowledge to deal with your estate. Relatives and friends that you appoint may never have acted as an executor before but a professional has probably played the part hundreds of times before. However, professionals cost money – and sometimes lots of it. Some charge a fee while others will want a percentage of the estate.

 ✔ **A bank.** All high street banks offer an executor service. But as you can guess, they charge a pretty penny! Some high street banks levy a charge equivalent to 4 per cent of the value of the estate to act as executor.

> ✔ **The Public Trustee.** If you don't know anyone who can act as executor, you can appoint the Public Trustee to do the job. The Public Trustee is a Government body, set up under Act of Parliament, to deal with people's estates. They charge fees (the more work they do, the higher the fees), and cannot execute wills that involve them running a charitable trust or managing a business. Check out the Web site at www.guardianship.gov.uk.

If you own your own business, try to appoint as executor someone who has experience of running a business of their own.

Appointing an older executor has the attraction that they are wise and experienced but if, fingers crossed, you live to a ripe old age, they might die before you. If the executors you appoint in your will are dead, then someone else – often a close relative of yours – steps into the breach to administer your estate.

Homing in on the detail

An executor cannot be sacked, even if the beneficiaries and other executors want them out. Only a court can order an executor to step aside, and that only ever happens if they are deemed guilty of misconduct.

Too many executors spoil the estate

Being an executor can be a lot of work. No surprise, then, that it is common practice to appoint more than one. You should trust your executors completely, but being trustworthy doesn't mean that they won't make mistakes. By appointing more than one executor you ensure that a second pair of eyes sees everything that is done in the name of your estate.

Often people choose to share the burden of executing their estate between a beneficiary and a professional, such as a solicitor. In theory, this choice offers the best of both worlds – the knowledge of the professional combined with the human touch of a friend or family member. If you plan on drawing up a simple will you may be best appointing just one executor, perhaps a close relative.

But remember, having too many executors can lead to delays in administrating your estate and can push up costs. You should appoint no more than four executors.

If one of the executors *renounces* (states that he or she does not want or is unable to fulfil the duties of an executor, before they start acting as executor), the alternative or substitute named in the will automatically takes their place. If none of the executors named in the will wants the job, then the catchily named 'Non Contentious Probate Rule 20' kicks in. Under this rule, any trustee appointed in the will takes over executor duties. If the trustee refuses, then it's left up to the beneficiaries to distribute the estate. If your executor (or trustee or guardian) refuses to act, they automatically forgo any payment you set aside for them as a thank you in your will.

Your executor can claim their expenses from your estate, such as photocopying costs, buying stamps, and stationery. In addition, many people choose to leave their executor a small gift in their will, a thank you for all their hard work. Of course, if your executor is a substantial beneficiary or a professional receiving a fee, you may well think that they have already had enough of your loot.

A Matter of Faith: Trustees

Trustees run any trusts set up by your will. A *trust* is a legal device whereby a trustee is legally responsible for looking after property for a beneficiary. Property isn't just bricks and mortar – it means any type of asset, such as cash or shares. A trustee can also be a beneficiary. If you don't plan to set up a trust in your will, you won't need to name trustees. You have our full permission to skip this section!

Trusts are most commonly used to leave property to a minor (someone under 18). Trusts are explained in much greater detail in Chapter 5 in this Book.

Being a trustee can be a long drawn-out process. If, for example, the minor you left property to is only a few months' old when you die, then the trustees have to look after the property for them for the best part of 18 years. In cases where a trust is set up to provide an income for the whole of the life of a beneficiary (for example, a trust set up to provide for a spouse who keeps going strong for years and years), it can end up running for decades. Often with long-running trusts the trustees retire and are replaced by someone happy to step into the void. The replacement or retirement of a trustee may require the permission of the trustees, the courts, or the trust beneficiaries.

Trustees are usually family friends, solicitors, or siblings. Choose a trustee who has all the qualities of an executor but who is also prepared to be in it for the long haul. You can use the same people as executors *and* trustees.

Trustees can be relieved of their duties by the beneficiaries, provided they are all in agreement. Furthermore, if one of your trustees refuses to act, or dies, existing trustees have the power to appoint a replacement.

Any trustee you appoint has a duty to treat all of your beneficiaries fairly. Trustees are obliged to

- Act unanimously if there is more than one trustee.
- Ensure 'reasonable care' is taken of the assets in the trust; for example, a house in trust should be properly insured.
- Not make a profit from the trust. Nor are trustees allowed to charge for their services, unless the charges are specified in the will. Trustees, like executors, can claim their expenses, though.
- Be prepared to provide accounts if beneficiaries of the trust ask.

Protecting Your Children: Guardians

Guardians are people you appoint to look after your children in the event of your death. Your surviving spouse automatically assumes sole guardianship of your children. But you need to think of someone else to appoint as guardian if your spouse dies before you or in the nightmare scenario that you and your spouse die together.

You may have close relatives – grandparents or a brother or sister – willing to look after your children when you're gone. The courts may grant your close relatives guardianship without a hitch, but you can make their case more watertight if you name them as guardians in a will.

You can name more than one guardian or set of guardians. This provision is very useful if you want one set of relatives to look after your children during their early years and someone else to take over as they become teenagers, perhaps someone younger. You can also appoint a separate guardian for each of your children. If, for example, one child is close to one set of grandparents, while another child favours the other grandparents, you can split them up.

Eighteen is the cut-off point for a child needing a guardian, as they are considered an adult instead.

Key questions to consider when choosing a guardian include:

✔ Do they have experience of bringing up children?

✔ Do they share your world view, values, and religious beliefs?

✔ Are they able to take on the responsibility of caring for your child emotionally, financially, and physically?

✔ Does your child like the person, and feel comfortable with them?

✔ Do they live close by? If the potential guardian lives far away it may prove a real wrench for your child to up sticks, leave friends and move, particularly at such an upsetting time.

✔ Does the person you are considering have lots of children? Would your child get lost in the crowd or relish new siblings to play with?

If you have someone in mind to act as guardian, have a talk with them about everything you'd want them to do for your child. Tell them what you want but give them a way of refusing without any hard feelings. Being a guardian is a huge task!

Keep a letter with your will setting out how you want your child to be raised. The letter should give your guardians an idea of your hopes and aspirations for your child, rather than a prescriptive list of do's and don'ts.

Not every parent is able to appoint a guardian. In order to appoint a guardian upon death, a parent must have had *parental responsibility* for the child. Ironically, not all parents have this responsibility. If, for example, the biological father has been absent from the child for years they may not have parental responsibility.

Parental responsibility means that you have a legal duty to care for the child. You can apply to the courts for parental responsibility. Sometimes a survivor in a same-sex partnership applies for this so that the child of their deceased partner can live with them. In all cases, the court decides who has parental responsibility based on the best interests of the child.

Divorce and guardians

A mother and father are joint guardians for as long as they live together. On the death of one parent, the surviving parent becomes the sole guardian. On the death of the surviving parent, the guardian is the person(s) appointed by the surviving parent. The same is true for adopted children. That's a nice easy scenario.

The complexities kick in when the parents divorce. If the parent granted custody – through a residence order – dies, then the guardian appointed by that parent takes joint responsibility for the child with the surviving parent. If the surviving parent and the appointed guardian can't agree who should look after the child, then one party has to apply for a fresh residence order. The court decides who gets custody.

You may be vehemently opposed to your child ever living with the other parent (your ex-partner), even after your death. If you feel this way, you can explain your case in a letter kept with your will. However, it's rare for a willing biological parent to be denied the right to joint guardianship, except in cases where chronic alcoholism, drug abuse, or a history of violence is proven. Where it all gets horribly complex is when children from current and previous relationships all live under one roof as a family unit. Following the death of one parent in this type of household, several different guardians – each one most relevant to the individual child – can be appointed by the courts. At this stage it may be up to social services to step in and sort out the mess. Talk to the parties concerned and see where everyone goes from there.

No-guardian situations

If no guardian is appointed for a child, or the person appointed under a will is unable or refuses to act as guardian, the child is in effect split in two. Rest assured this isn't some wisdom-of-Solomon style ploy to get a willing guardian to step forward. The *estate of the child* – the child's property – is looked after by the Public Guardian and Trustee, while the person of the child is taken in by social services and is placed with close relatives where possible or, failing that, a foster parent. Any surviving relatives have to apply to the courts for guardianship of the child.

Appointing a guardian without using a will

It's best to make a will to make your wishes concerning your estate and your children absolutely clear. However, parents can appoint a guardian without making a will. You must draw up an *Appointment of Guardian* form, which you can write yourself. Give the full names of your children, the chosen guardian(s), and sign and date the form. But be warned that like the guardianship wishes expressed in a will, the court can overrule the parental choice of guardian. What's more, the forms cannot be used to leave property to the guardian to pay for the upkeep of the child: You can only do that through a will.

You can avoid this situation happening by naming an alternative guardian in your will just in case your first choice is unable to look after your child.

Money, money, money isn't child's play

If you're a parent you probably won't need reminding that children cost money, and lots of it – they have to be schooled, fed, clothed, and entertained. Letting the guardian(s) you appoint pay for all this from their own pocket isn't fair. You need to leave the guardian enough money in your will to cover the cost of bringing up your children.

You can use a trust to set money aside for your guardian either through property or from the proceeds of a life insurance policy. The trustee can monitor what is being spent on the child. Even if you trust the appointed guardian completely – and you should do if they are to look after your little treasures – it is not a good move to name him or her as sole trustee or executor. See Chapter 5 in this Book for more on this.

As a general rule, the older your children are, the less money you will have to leave behind for their upkeep, as your guardians will be looking after them for a shorter amount of time. Be open! Discuss with the guardians what they need to look after your children. If your child has a disability, your guardian probably needs more money to provide proper care. A smart move is for you all to take independent financial advice.

The Eyes Have It: Witnesses

A will in England and Wales has to be witnessed by two people, who sign their names next to the name of the *testator* (the person writing the will) at the end of the document. Witnesses do not have to read the contents of your will and dot every 'i' or cross every 't'; but they must be present when you sign your will and put their mark to that effect in your presence and the presence of each other. These two people are witnessing the signing of the will and not the drawing up of the will document. Members of the armed forces on active service can write a will without having to have it witnessed.

A witness, or their spouse, is not allowed to inherit a bean from the will, so make sure you don't ask a beneficiary or their spouse to be a witness.

Witnesses in Scotland

The rules on witnessing a will in Scotland are a lot less strict than in England and Wales. Only one witness is needed and he or she doesn't have to see the testator sign. All the testator has to do is indicate to the witness that they have signed their own will. What's more, the witness can benefit from the will.

However, just to confuse these simple matters, wills in Scotland made prior to 1 August 1995 must be witnessed by two people.

As well as making sure the witnesses are not beneficiaries, bear the following in mind when choosing a witness:

✔ Blind people can't witness a will. (Those blind in just one eye can, though.)

✔ A witness must be mentally capable of understanding what is going on.

✔ Under 18's can act as witnesses, but the will can be challenged on the grounds that the minor did not understand what they were witnessing. Best not bother!

The witnesses you choose don't have to be pillars of the community – you aren't appointing them to look after your children, after all. What's more, the witnesses don't have to have the skills of an executor.

A close family friend, neighbour, or even a trusted work colleague makes a good witness. If any possibility exists that your mental health could be called into question, your doctor makes a good witness.

It's a good idea (although not legally required) for the witnesses to write their full names in capitals and addresses next to their signatures just in case the will is challenged and they need to be traced. Pick witnesses who are home-owners, as they are most likely to stay put.

A beneficiary or the spouse of a beneficiary who witnesses your will is auto-matically disinherited. The rest of the will remains valid.

Considering Getting Expert Help

Book V

Protecting
Your
Wealth for
the Next
Generation

You've lined up your executors, trustees, and witnesses. Now what? Writing your will needs an entire chapter to itself but for now you need to decide whether to write your will yourself, perhaps using a DIY will kit, or if you need to bring out the big guns and call in a professional to help.

If your estate is simple you can write your will yourself. If you feel you are in danger of reaching the limits of your knowledge it's time to contact a professional for help, even if it's just to check over your plans to date.

Many believe that the solicitor or accountant you choose to help you with your will should be an old family friend. However, in the real world few people have family solicitors or accountants and, instead, rely on personal recommendation and the Yellow Pages! But that shouldn't matter a jot as long as you approach the professional in the same way you would a plumber, electrician, or car mechanic – with healthy scepticism and unafraid to ask questions.

Many solicitors and accountants offer a free initial consultation to discuss your requirements. Go to at least two different professionals to compare the services they can offer you before choosing who to work with. Any solicitor or accountant you engage should give you a clear idea of how much they charge at the outset.

Solicitors

When it comes to writing your will or dealing with someone else's estate, the right solicitor can be very useful, even if soliciting a solicitor might be last on your list of favourite activities.

Think of a solicitor as someone you can call on when you reach the edges of your knowledge or confidence about wills and inheritance. It is up to you when you feel you have reached the limits; it can be simply how to word your will right up to including complex trusts and codicils.

Consider using a solicitor for the following situations:

✔ A solicitor can act as a trustee or an executor of your estate.

✔ The advice of a solicitor can be invaluable when you're trying to administer someone else's will, a tricky process called *probate*. (The probate process is explained in Chapter 6 in this Book.)

✔ A solicitor's office is as good a place as any to keep your will – they are used to storing many types of legal documents, such as deeds to property.

Some solicitors charge a nominal fee, about £10-£25 a year, to look after your will. The fee is often waived if you name the solicitor as an executor, as this can be quite lucrative for them.

✔ Above all else, a solicitor can stop you from making a horrible mistake in your will that can invalidate it or inadvertently disinherit someone precious.

Each professional you consult has their own area of expertise. A solicitor can advise on wills but may not be well-versed on the ins and outs of inheritance tax – you may be better off talking to an accountant. However, solicitors with expertise in estate planning are well honed in the art of writing a trust into your will. You can call the Society of Trust and Estate Practitioners (STEP) on 0207 838 4885 or visit their Web site at www.step.org. STEP's membership comprises both solicitors and accountants.

Lists of solicitors can be obtained from the Law Society of England and Wales on 0870 606 2555, Scotland on 0845 1130018, and in Northern Ireland on 028 90 231614. Alternatively, check out these Web sites for details of solicitors in your area: http://www.lawsociety.org.uk/choosingandusing/finda solicitor.law, www.lawscot.org.uk, and www.lawsoc-ni.org.

A solicitor usually charges a flat-rate fee of between £200 and £500 to draw up a will, depending on how knotty your affairs are. If you require specific legal advice on complicated issues such as trusts or administering someone else's estate, then expect to pay more.

Bargain wills ahoy! Every few years the Law Society of England and Wales runs *Make a Will Week*, when solicitors write wills for a one-off donation to charity, often less than the usual cost of making a will. Another scheme is *Will Aid*, when thousands of solicitors donate the fees they make for will work to charity during a particular month. By taking advantage of *Make a Will Week* and *Will Aid* you and a good cause can benefit at the same time.

Accountants

Accountants immerse themselves in the tax system, looking for ways to enable people to keep more of their own cash – it's not sexy but it is clever! Seeking the advice of an accountant, when you are preparing to draw up your will, can save your beneficiaries a pretty packet because they are experts in tax loopholes.

An accountant can also help with your short- and long-term estate planning:

Book V

Protecting
Your
Wealth for
the Next
Generation

✔ **Short term.** An accountant can advise you on trusts to incorporate into your will to help set in stone who gets what and when after your death.

✔ **Long term.** An accountant can advise you on how to distribute your estate to your nearest and dearest and reduce any eventual inheritance tax liability.

This book can help you understand the legal and financial basics so you are well informed to write your own will, but getting an accountant to check it over can put your mind at rest. After all, if you make a mistake it may only come to light when your beneficiary has an unexpected tax demand land on their doormat with an ominous thump.

Accountants either charge a flat fee for completing a specific task, such as setting up a trust, or charge by the hour. Charges varywidely according to region and the complexity of the work, but even small regional firms and sole traders are likely to charge £100 or £150 per hour. With hourly fees like these, it is very important to agree at the outset how much work needs to be done and at what price.

You can find an accountant through the Institute of Chartered Accountants, www.icaewfirms.co.uk, or the Association of Certified Chartered Accountants (Acca) www.acca.co.uk. If you're a business owner, check out the Government's business link Web site for tips on choosing a good accountant at www.businesslink.gov.uk.

Preparing to meet the experts

Take advantage of the free initial consultation that many solicitors and accountants offer.

Take the following information with you when consulting an accountant or solicitor:

✔ Your personal details and those of your partner

✔ Your children's details

✔ Details of any stepchildren or ex-spouse

✔ Details of your executors, trustees, and guardians

✔ The approximate value of your home and the most recent mortgage statement

Making a complaint about a professional

Both the accountancy and legal professions are self-regulating. If you want to make a complaint, you have to complain to the firm in question first – then, and only then, can you take your case to the professional body that the accountant or solicitor belongs to. Accountants can belong to several different professional organisations such as the Association of Certified Chartered Accountants and the Institute of Chartered Accountants.

Solicitors belong to the Law Society. Each organisation – representing accountants or solicitors – has its own set of procedures for dealing with complaints about members. Usual complaints revolve around poor service and/or overcharging. The relevant organisation investigates your complaint and decides whether or not you can be compensated.

If you are unhappy with the response to your complaint from the organisation representing the professional, then you are free to take court action.

✔ Life insurance policies

✔ Information about your pension arrangements

✔ A list of all your assets and debts

✔ A list of all major gifts you have made in the past seven years (these may be subject to inheritance tax. See Chapter 2 in this Book for more on gifts and their tax implications)

Before agreeing to engage the services of a particular accountant or solicitor, ask yourself the following questions:

✔ Do I feel confident about using this professional?

✔ Do I understand everything the professional told me?

✔ Did the professional fully understand what I am looking for?

✔ Am I certain how much the advice costs me?

If the answer to any of these questions is no, either ask for clarification or simply don't go there! Remember, the one thing the UK definitely isn't short of is solicitors and accountants.

Going Solo: Using a Will Kit

A will kit is a legally valid off-the-shelf pack that includes all the documents you need to complete your will yourself without using a solicitor. A will kit includes a pre-printed will form, and advice on how to fill it out.

The will form enables you to appoint executors, guardians, and trustees.

Some sections of a pre-printed will form won't be relevant to you. If you don't have young children, you don't need to appoint a guardian. Instead of leaving these sections blank, draw a line through any parts of the will form you don't fill in to make your wishes absolutely clear.

You can download pre-printed will forms and will kits from many solicitors' Web sites. Lawpack publishes DIY will kits, which are sold in Tesco, W H Smith, and Office World all for around £15. See www.lawpack.co.uk.

A will kit can't stop you from making mistakes – such as getting a beneficiary or their spouse to witness the will and thereby disinherit themselves. What's more, the advice offered in a will kit is very general and doesn't come anywhere near that of a solicitor or accountant.

A will kit saves on the hassle of drawing up will forms yourself, but can't replace professional help.

Keeping Your Will Safe

It's pointless going to the time, trouble, and expense of writing a will if you leave it lying around willy-nilly just asking to be lost.

Several options are available for safekeeping your will:

- ✔ **Your own home.** Lock away your will in a small fire-proof safe, which costs about £100 from DIY shops. This action protects your will from all sorts of dangers – including your children's sticky mitts.

- ✔ **Your solicitor.** Solicitors can keep your will under lock and key. This is a particularly good idea if you want your solicitor to act as executor of your will.

- ✔ **The bank.** This is the ultra-safe option. Your bank can keep your will in their safe for a fee of around £10–£25 per year. Just remember to tell your executors where the will is!

Before locking away your signed will, take two photocopies of it. Keep a copy for yourself to refer to whenever you want, without having to hassle your solicitor or bank. Give the second copy to your appointed executor so they know what to expect before the time comes to start administering your estate.

Your executors must have your original will, and not a photocopy, to have the legal muscle to administer your estate. Give your executors the photo-copy purely as a sneak preview – but let them know where the original signed will is kept.

Chapter 4

Dealing with Inheritance Tax

- -

In This Chapter

▶ Making sense of inheritance tax

▶ Working out your tax liability

▶ Looking at tax exemptions

▶ Telling tax avoidance from evasion

▶ Exploiting your spouse's nil-rate band

▶ Using gifts to cut tax

▶ Understanding potentially exempt transfers

▶ Protecting the family home from inheritance tax

- -

Death may be inevitable but huge tax bills don't have to be. Even if you're quite well off – lucky you – you can minimise the amount of tax your estate has to face.

But before you can make the right tax-saving moves you have to know your enemy – inheritance tax (IHT) – and what weapons you can utilise from your armoury.

If you're serious about avoiding IHT, you really need to make a will to use all your IHT-busting weapons.

In this chapter, we explain how IHT works and show you lots of different tactics you can use to sidestep IHT: It's time to get with the tax-fighting programme!

Making Sense of Inheritance Tax

Inheritance tax has been called many things over the years, some printable, some not. During the hundred-odd years IHT's been around it's been called 'estate duty' and 'capital transfer tax'.

Whatever its name, IHT has always amounted to the same thing. When you die the executors or administrators of your estate are legally bound to assess your wealth and if your estate is worth more than a particular amount of money, then it's IHT time!

IHT may seem unfair. After all, you pay taxes throughout your life. You earn money at work, you pay income tax; buy something in a shop, you pay VAT; buy a house, you pay stamp duty – tax, tax, and more tax.

However, IHT is a crucial revenue-raiser for the government to pay for hospitals, schools, and the subsidised bar in the House of Commons! So don't hide under the covers hoping that the IHT bogeyman will go away – he won't.

IHT is the looming iceberg on the horizon for your estate, and you need to plot a course to steer well clear of it. Forewarned is forearmed. Fortunately, you can employ all sorts of tactics to deny HMRC a piece of your estate.

Your executors or administrators will probably have to pay some or all of the IHT due on your estate before they can obtain grant of probate or letters of administration (see Chapter 6 in this part for more on these). HMRC get their money first!

The estate of any member of the armed forces who dies while on active service (or later from wounds received on active service) is totally exempt from IHT.

Doing the Inheritance Tax Sums

If your estate is worth more than £300,000 – in the 2007-08 tax year – when you die it may be liable to IHT. The starting point for paying IHT is called the IHT *threshold*.

IHT is charged at 40 per cent, the same as the top rate of income tax. So if your estate is worth £500,000 the tax hit could be a whopping £80,000 – ouch! (This sum works as follows: £500,000 – £300,000 IHT threshold = £200,000;

Book V

Protecting
Your
Wealth for
the Next
Generation

40 per cent of £200,000 = £80,000.) The people inheriting your estate have to find that money somehow.

The threshold for IHT is raised by the Chancellor every year. The idea of raising the threshold is to keep pace with inflation or, in another word, prices. Inflation has been relatively stable in recent years, bobbing along between 2 and 4 per cent. All very good you might think.

However, your financial worth probably rises faster than inflation. For starters, wages normally rise slightly quicker than inflation, and if you're savvy and shop around for the best savings account then it's probably paying comfortably more than inflation. What's more, share investments over the long term tend to beat inflation hands down.

Don't forget the daddy of all your assets: Your home. According to the Halifax, the average UK house price has almost doubled in the past five years to 2007. In parts of London and the south-east just an *average* home is now worth more then the IHT threshold. The number of estates that attract IHT is predicted to grow during the next ten years. One of these estates could be yours!

The message is clear: What used to be a tax for the mega-rich and toffs with a huge ancestral pile is now stalking the ordinary man or woman on the street.

Individuals who are *domiciled* in the UK – regard the UK as their permanent home and pay tax in the UK – are liable for IHT on all their worldwide assets. Yes, that includes your gîte in France!

Everyone has a *nil rate band*. This is the amount of money you can leave in your will before it becomes subject to IHT (the same as the IHT threshold). A married couple have two nil rate bands, which can be very useful indeed when IHT planning.

The tax year doesn't run like a calendar year; it runs from the 6 April in one year to 5 April the next.

We know it's boring, but try to study the Chancellor's Budget speech, which usually takes place sometime in March. The Chancellor often uses the speech to announce any increase in the IHT threshold. Alternatively, if the idea of a man in a suit droning on about 'fiscal prudence' and 'inflation targets' isn't your cup of tea, check out the HMRC Web site for the latest information on tax thresholds, www.hmrc.gov.uk.

Working Out Your Tax Liability

Your first move in the IHT avoidance programme is working out your estate's potential liability. In brief, try and arrive at a value for the following assets:

- ✔ Property, such as your main home and any holiday property
- ✔ Business interests
- ✔ Cash held in bank and building society accounts
- ✔ Stocks and shares
- ✔ Life insurance benefits
- ✔ Personal possessions, such as your car and jewellery
- ✔ Collectables, such as works of art or expensive wine

If after doing the maths your estate is worth more than the IHT threshold (£300,000), the alarm bells should start ringing – it's time to get your estate into a tax-efficient state.

As far as HMRC is concerned your estate doesn't just include all your property at your death. Your estate may include property that you gave away during the seven years prior to your death.

You only need a bit of time and application to work out what your estate is worth today. But working out what your estate may be worth in future takes a little bit of crystal ball gazing. Fortunately, you can use some likely estate growth scenarios to work out if you have to worry about IHT:

- ✔ **Savings growth.** Most safe investments – savings accounts, bonds, and the like – are reckoned to grow in value at around 5 per cent a year.

- ✔ **Share growth.** Insurance companies believe that share prices grow by between 5 and 9 per cent a year over a long period of time. Financial advisers reckon that 7 per cent a year is a good ball-park figure.

- ✔ **Property growth.** The stellar growth of the past eight or nine years has been unusual, but over the last 40 years, house prices have increased on average by more than 10 per cent per year.

It doesn't take a rocket scientist to work out that if your main assets grow by 5, 7, or 10 per cent a year while the IHT threshold increases by 3 per cent a year, then sooner or later your estate might well catch up with the IHT threshold.

Book V

Protecting
Your
Wealth for
the Next
Generation

Recognising the 'Must Plan' Scenarios

Some situations should make you ponder planning to avoid IHT, even if the value of your estate is currently below the IHT threshold. See if you fit into one of the following scenarios:

- ✔ **Age can equal wealth.** Age is supposed to make you wiser. It can also super-charge your estate. As people enter their fifties they often enjoy a golden financial era – assuming they're in good health and still working. Fifty-somethings are at the height of their career, their mortgage is probably paid off, and the children have flown the nest!

- ✔ **Marriage and children.** At first glance, marriage and children seem good things for your estate. Property that passes to your spouse on your death is free of IHT. However, this increase in wealth means that your spouse's estate can be burdened for IHT purposes when your spouse dies. If your spouse dies without taking IHT avoidance measures, then the beneficiaries – perhaps your children – could face a whopping tax bill.

If you're young, free, single, and poor IHT should be the last of your worries, unless you're set to inherit a substantial sum from a close relative!

The Cruellest Cut of All: Tax and the Family Home

Becoming a homeowner is very exciting, from the moment you move in and discover the previous occupier has taken everything to bringing up a family there. But on becoming a homeowner you have suddenly made it more likely that one day – hopefully many years off – your estate will be subject to inheritance tax.

If you don't plan properly, your estate's executors or administrators may have no option but to sell the family home – even if your nearest and dearest have their hearts set on continuing to live there. Of course, this action is a last resort, but if most of your wealth is tied up in your home then it may have to be sold. Sadly, the incidence of homes being sold to meet an IHT bill is on the increase.

Facing Up to an Inheritance Tax Bill

The second part of this chapter is chock-full of ideas on how to avoid IHT. But, hey, maybe you're simply loaded and you've got to face the IHT music. So be it! But nothing's stopping you from taking steps to ensure that any IHT bill is sorted out with the minimum of fuss and financial pain. The following sections offer some ideas to make the tax-paying job easier.

Build up a handsome estate residue

The estate residue is everything that's left after funeral expenses, prior gifts, and payments to creditors. By having a healthy estate residue you're leaving your estate's executors with the wherewithal to pay HMRC. The estate residue often makes up the majority of the estate.

Check your estate and will at least once a year so you can get a handle on whether the residue will be large enough to cover the tax bill.

Squeeze the life out of life insurance

You can take out life insurance with the aim that on death it pays out enough to cover any IHT bill.

The proceeds of the life insurance policy may be subject to IHT itself. Ironic, eh? The way around this situation is to write your policy in trust to a beneficiary (perhaps one who is also your executor) and they can use the proceeds to pay the tax bill. Head to Chapter 5 in this book for the low-down on trusts.

Below are two insurance options – it's crucial that you purchase the right insurance to meet your specific IHT needs.

- ✔ **Term insurance.** This pays out for a fixed period of time, say, until you're 65. Once the time period has expired and you turn 65, that's it, all bets are off and you're no longer insured!

- ✔ **Whole-life policy.** This pays out when you die whether it's the day after the policy is taken out, or a hundred years hence. This type of policy is particularly useful when looking to cover the total IHT bill on an estate. As a rule of thumb, whole-life insurance is more expensive than term insurance.

If you decide to buy life insurance, obtain advice from an independent financial adviser, especially if you decide to write the policy into trust. Check out www.unbiased.co.uk for a list of independent financial advisers in your local area.

Life insurers don't require grant of probate or letters of administration to pay out if the policy is not payable to the estate; all they need is a copy of the death certificate. As a result, the money can be there to meet any IHT bill in double-quick time.

A Taxing Question: Avoidance or Evasion?

Question: What's the difference between inheritance tax avoidance and evasion?

Answer: Fines and possibly a spell in prison.

Both avoidance and evasion are about making the estate seem smaller than it actually is for tax calculation purposes. In the second half of this chapter, we give you heaps of tips about how to avoid paying tax and how to pass on as much of your loot as possible to your loved ones. But we tell you about ways to *avoid* tax, not ways to *evade* it.

Avoidance is about getting the tax laws to work for the good of the estate. IHT exemptions exist for good reason and you're free to use them.

Essentially, *evasion* amounts to the non-disclosure of assets to HMRC and the illegal spiriting away of parts of the estate. These actions are underhand and if HMRC find out they crack down hard!

Any IHT evasion you commit probably won't be discovered until after your death when HMRC looks at the accounts submitted by your executors or administrators. And although you can't be punished, your estate can be. Likewise, if your executors are found to be complicit in your tax evasion or undertake their own naughty tricks, they could face fines and, in extreme cases, even be thrown in jail.

Tax: A question of morality?

We go on and on about being boxing clever to avoid IHT. However, tax avoidance has a moral dimension. Although you may not always recognise it, the State provides us with a lot during our lives – the school system may have taught you how to read this book; the National Health Service may have helped you or a loved one get over a serious ailment; and the armed forces have defended your liberty, often with their lives.

You may think that taxing an estate in excess of a quarter of a million pounds is fair enough, and why shouldn't you contribute to your country from beyond the grave through IHT? For one thing, the tax collector would be proud of you!

Simple Steps to Reduce Inheritance Tax

Fighting the tax collector to protect your hard-earned dough from inheritance tax (IHT) has a downside and an upside. The downside is that you won't be around to pull on your boxing gloves if any problems with your IHT planning come to light; it's up to others to sort out how any tax bill is paid. The upside is that you can work out if IHT is coming and you can start planning now on ways to reduce the tax liability on your estate for the ultimate benefit of your nearest and dearest.

If you're a beneficiary, executor, or administrator for someone's estate and they weren't very switched on to tax avoidance, you can use a deed of variation to claw back some cash from HMRC.

Exploiting Your Spouse's Nil-Rate Band

This book does not condone spouse exploitation, even if it's to get your hands on the TV remote control!

However, you can do a certain sort of exploitation together as a team: Exploiting each other's nil-rate IHT band.

The sums are simple: You and your spouse can both leave up to £300,000 each in 2007-08 free of IHT. Your combined nil-rate bands are worth £600,000 – that's an awful lot of money!

Book V

Protecting
Your
Wealth for
the Next
Generation

The ideal situation is to write your will leaving enough for your spouse to live off (which is IHT-free), but gifting your other assets up to the nil-rate band to a *non-exempt beneficiary* (someone who would usually have to pay tax) such as your child.

The big no-no that you're trying to avoid is the *bunching of assets*, which is when one spouse leaves the other spouse so many assets that when the second spouse dies, the estate attracts IHT.

Any money or assets that pass between spouses in life as a result of death are exempt from IHT.

Doing it the wrong way

Time for an enlightening example of bunching of assets. Here, Winston's estate is worth £400,000 while Jasmine's is worth £165,000. On his death, Winston leaves his wife Jasmine his share of the house, cash, and all his shares to a total value of £360,000. Winston leaves his son and daughter the rest between them: £20,000 each. As a result, Jasmine is now quite a wealthy woman, with total assets of £525,000. However, six years later Jasmine dies, leaving her estate to her son and daughter. But before they can collect their gifts, the son and daughter face having to pay IHT.

Due to interest earned on savings and increases in share and property prices, Jasmine's estate increased to £600,000. The mortgage on the family home was paid off, so she didn't really need the big pot of money she had been left by Winston.

Jasmine left £300,000 free of IHT (the nil-rate band), but on the rest of the estate – £300,000 – the son and daughter have to pay 40 per cent tax. The total tax bill is a whopping £120,000.

Jasmine's son and daughter are both making a start in the world and can't possibly afford to pay the IHT bill. Therefore, the executor of Jasmine's estate borrows the money to pay the IHT bill (remember the tax vampire must be fed first) and sells the family home to raise the money to pay back the debt.

Final result: HMRC scoops a cool £120,000 and the cherished family home has gone forever!

Doing it the right way

Now look at the same estate where Winston and Jasmine planned ahead a bit better and partly exploited their nil-rate bands.

On his death, Winston leaves his wife his share in the family home and a little cash, to a total value of £175,000. The rest of his estate, £225,000, is divided evenly between his son and daughter. No IHT is due because it falls well within Winston's nil-rate band (£300,000). Winston could have left less to Jasmine but he wanted to make sure that she had enough to live off; after all, he has to presume that she will outlive him for many years. Jasmine is now worth £300,000 – including the family home.

Sadly, after six years, Jasmine dies. Her estate has grown in value to £345000 (she had to use some of the interest from savings accounts to live off so the wealth growth is smaller than the previous example) and this passes to her son and daughter.

Jasmine can leave £300,000 free of IHT, but on the rest of the estate – £45,000 – the son and daughter have to pay 40 per cent tax. The total IHT bill is £18,000. This example assumes no increase to the IHT threshold, although in reality the threshold is raised every year by the Chancellor.

This tax bill is a fairly substantial hit but the executors can raise the cash from Jasmine's savings and the sale of some shares. Crucially, the son and daughter inherit the family home.

Doing even better

Even in the second example, Winston and Jasmine could have done a lot more to avoid IHT. In fact, with some extra smart moves, HMRC could have been cut out of the equation altogether – despite the fact that their combined estate was worth more than a cool half million pounds.

Throughout this chapter you'll see other ways in which Winston and Jasmine could have reduced their IHT bill further.

The key message is that exploiting two nil-rate IHT bands should be at the heart of combating IHT for a married couple.

Using Exempt Gifts to Save Tax

During your life you can make certain gifts that are exempt from IHT. Once these gifts are made, they disappear from your estate for good and become invisible to HMRC.

Gifts made for the maintenance of children or dependant relatives are also tax-free. You can make the following exempt gifts each year:

- ✔ Small gifts of up to £250 as many times as you like in any one tax year, but each gift must be to a different person. This is called the *small gifts exemption*.

- ✔ One big exempt gift of up to £3,000 a year. This is called the *annual exemption*.

You're not allowed to give the same person a small gift and a large £3,000 gift in the same tax year.

In addition, you can make the following gifts to mark a loved one's or even a friend's wedding:

- ✔ A gift of £5,000 on the wedding of a child. They could pay for the whole show with that or simply put it in the bank.

- ✔ A gift of £2,500 on the wedding of a grandchild. Should help them pay for that nice honeymoon.

- ✔ A gift of £1,000 to celebrate the wedding of other family or friends. Not a huge sum but better than a set of steak knives!

These exemptions apply no matter how many times the person gets married.

If you add the value of all these gifts together it's possible to move large amounts of money out of your estate in a relatively short period of time, and you get to see the beneficiary enjoying the gift.

As far as the tax collector is concerned gifts larger than the tax exemption levels remain in your estate for a period of seven years, although the rate at which they're taxed falls over time. But the recipient of these gifts has to foot any tax bill in the event of your death.

Count me out

If you give money to an *exempt beneficiary*, through your will for example, that money is not included in your estate when IHT is calculated.

Exempt beneficiaries include: Your spouse, parliamentary political parties, museums, housing associations, sports clubs and community associations, and even your local authority. But by far the most popular exempt beneficiaries (not including your spouse, of course) are charitable organisations.

Only a charity registered in the UK qualifies as an exempt beneficiary. If you're in any doubt whether a charity qualifies as an exempt beneficiary, check to see if they have a UK charity number.

You can set up a charitable trust to drip-feed money into your chosen good cause and reduce your IHT liability – talk to a solicitor to find out how.

Make it crystal clear in your will which charity or other exempt beneficiary you're leaving a gift to. Note the charity's official registration number, which you can find on its Web site or in its literature.

But you can't just leave thousands to Battersea Dogs Home and leave poor Granny Gertrude out in the cold. Remember, if you gift a large part of your estate to an exempt beneficiary other than your spouse, then anyone who was financially dependent upon you could have the gift overturned on the grounds that it causes them hardship.

Two gifts for the price of one

Anyone can use these tax exemptions but married couples have an advantage in that they have two sets of gift exemptions to use up. Also, because gifts between spouses are automatically exempt, married couples can give money to and fro to ensure that the exemptions are used to the maximum. This is particularly useful when one spouse is richer than the other.

Back to Winston and Jasmine to show how this works: Remember, Winston's estate is worth £400,000 while Jasmine's is worth £125,000.

Winston gives Jasmine £3,000 each year. Jasmine in turn drip feeds this money each year to their son. In addition, Winston uses his annual gift exemption to give his daughter £3,000 a year.

The son gets hitched. Winston makes a gift of £5,000 from his estate to mark the happy occasion. In addition, he gives £5,000 to Jasmine who in turn gifts the cash to her son to mark the big day.

By working together, the couple have managed to move lots of cash out of the estate. The tax inspector won't even get a sniff of this cash!

You can easily see how using exempt gifting, along with the nil-rate band, can ensure that large estates become pretty small.

Don't go overboard with exempt gifting: Make sure that you can afford it. Remember, once the gift's gone, it's gone!

Carrying an exempt gift forwards

If you don't use up your full exemption in one year, you can carry it forward to the next. This, ingeniously, is called a *carried-forward* exemption. The carried forward exemption only applies to the £3,000 annual exemption, and not to the small gifts exemption. Carried-forward exemptions are manna from heaven for hurry-up estate planning.

So if you don't make a £3,000 gift in one tax year, you can make a £6,000 gift the next. Likewise, if you only used part of your exemption in one tax year, you can use it the next. However, you're not allowed to carry forward to any subsequent year.

Gifts always use up the exemption for the tax year in which they are made before using up any exemption carried forwards from the previous tax year.

Exempt assets

HM Revenue & Customs allows special exemptions for certain types of property. These types of property can be either inherited free of IHT, at a discounted rate of IHT, or the payment of the IHT bill can be spread out over many years.

If you have any of the following assets in your estate, then you may be able to claim an IHT exemption:

✔ **Business assets.** Sole trader businesses, shares in a business partnership, land, buildings, and machinery can all attract an IHT tax break called *business property relief*.

✔ **Agricultural property.** Agricultural land, working farmhouses (not pretty piles in the Home Counties), and barns can attract IHT *agricultural property relief*.

✔ **Woodland.** You can postpone the payment of IHT on woodland until the timber on the land has been sold.

✔ **National Heritage property.** If you're lucky enough to own National Heritage property – including some listed homes but also some important works of art – this should be exempt from IHT. If you own one of these types of property, talk to an accountant to see how the exemptions work – just get your butler to fetch them!

Gifting from Everyday Income

You're allowed to gift money from your income. If you can clearly show that a gift doesn't erode your capital or savings, then it is exempt.

Gifts from income are often used to slowly drain money from an estate to reduce its size and ultimately any IHT bill. The capital isn't touched; the interest earned on the capital is siphoned off into the pockets of your nearest and dearest.

Take the case of kind Aunt Jane, a widow.

Back in 2004, Jane's estate was worth £500,000, with some £240,000 held in building society accounts paying a fixed interest income of £18,000 a year. Jane doesn't need this much to live on so she gives her niece Margaret, her only surviving relative, £500 a month or £6,000 a year. This action doesn't eat into her gift exemptions because she is paying the money from income.

By the end of the 2007-08 tax year Jane has given Margaret £24,000 this way, but in order to keep it kosher she hasn't reduced the overall value of her estate in the process.

But clever Aunt Jane has gone a stage further and utilised her gift exemption in each of the previous four years by giving Margaret a total of £12,000 (£3,000 a year). These gifts are all above board and this time legitimately drawn from her estate assets. And as the icing on the cake – forgive the pun – Jane gives Margaret a further £1,000 to mark Margaret's wedding.

By April 2008, Jane will have managed to move £37,000 into Margaret's pocket and reduced her estate from £500,000 to £487,000.

If she had done nothing, Jane's estate would be worth £524,000.

All the time, the threshold for paying IHT had been on the increase, from £263,000 in 2004-05 to £300,000 in 2007-08.

Stick to the readies when making gifts of income. If you give anything else, say a car, you must prove that it was bought out of income rather than the capital. Tricky!

When making an exempt gift to someone, give them a signed note stating clearly which exemption – small gifts, wedding, or annual exemption – you are using. Doing so will make things easier for your executors when they sort out your paperwork.

Maintaining the family – tax-free

Payments made for the *maintenance*, or upkeep, of a spouse, children, or dependent relatives automatically leave your estate for IHT purposes and don't eat into your gift exemptions. This exemption is irrespective of whether you make these payments from income or by dipping into your savings or selling assets to meet the expense.

The definition of children is very wide and includes stepchildren, illegitimate, and adopted children.

If you're divorced, any maintenance payments to your former spouse are exempt from IHT.

Money that you pay to put your children through college can even be considered maintenance. Just think – next time your little treasure asks you for that £100 that she swears is for books, you can cross it off your estate for IHT purposes.

Premiums on a life insurance policy written in trust for the benefit of someone else are considered gifts out of regular income and therefore leave your estate for IHT purposes.

Revving Up Potentially Exempt Transfers

Exempt gifts disappear from your estate as soon as the cheque is cashed or the money handed over. However, you can transfer larger assets to someone else with the *potential* that one day they'll be deemed exempt from IHT. Funnily enough, these are called *Potentially Exempt Transfers (PETs)*. Like most pets, they can be deeply rewarding but they can also bite.

With PETs, it's all about playing the waiting game. Seven years after you make the transfer it is considered outside of your estate and is exempt from IHT.

But what if you die six years and 364 days after making the PET? Well, the beneficiary of the PET is liable for IHT. However, even the tax collector understands that it's not fair to treat a PET made so long ago as one made the day before death. So the IHT liability on the asset is *tapered* – which means it tails off over time, with nothing to pay after seven years. *Taper relief* sums work as follows:

Years between transfer and death	Rate of tax reduction
0-3	No reduction
3-4	20% reduction
4-5	40% reduction
5-6	60% reduction
6-7	80% reduction
7+	100% reduction

You can't make a PET to a spouse because transfers of assets to a spouse are automatically exempt from IHT.

The pros and cons of keeping a PET

You can adopt the simple PET strategy: Gift everything above the IHT threshold to your nearest and dearest in the hope that you'll live for another seven years and, hey presto, your estate is tax-free!

This strategy is fraught with danger for three simple reasons:

- ✔ **You could die within seven years.** If you die within three years of making the gift, the asset is still considered to be in your estate and any tax due has to be paid. After three years, the amount of IHT starts to reduce.

- ✔ **The gift can owe capital gains tax.** If you sign over property that has gained in value since you bought it, you may be liable for a CGT charge. Even if the person you transfer the asset to doesn't pay a penny for it, CGT could still be due on its market value. And CGT is every bit as big a beastie as IHT – it's charged at a whopping 40 per cent.

- ✔ **Once it's gone, it's gone.** By transferring an asset you're giving up all rights to it. You can't sell this asset if you need the money, and if it's your home you can't live in it unless you pay a market rent and pay Income Tax. Think hard before going ahead with a PET; you must be absolutely sure you can do without the asset you're giving away.

Don't let these dangers scare you off using PETs. PETs can play a crucial role in IHT planning, but only after you utilise your spouse's nil-rate band, and use exempt gifts and give gifts to exempt beneficiaries. A PET may ease your tax

Book V

Protecting
Your
Wealth for
the Next
Generation

bill enormously, but just as easily – say, if you die soon after the transfer – not make a blind bit of difference!

If IHT does become payable on a PET it is usually levied on the asset's value at the time of the transfer rather than at the time of death. However, if the PET falls in value between the time of transfer and the date of death, it can be priced at the lower value for IHT purposes.

The person who has received the PET has to foot any IHT bill. However, if the recipient of the PET doesn't pay this bill within 12 months, then your executors are liable.

Avoiding the triple-tax rap

When you make a potentially exempt transfer and other gifts, it's not only inheritance tax you need to take into account. Capital gains tax (CGT) and income tax (IT) can also hit hard.

CGT occurs when an asset is sold for more than was paid for it. If you transfer a large non-cash asset to someone – a holiday home, for example – you could be hit with a CGT bill. Even if the person you transfer the asset to doesn't pay for it, CGT could still be due on its market value.

Everyone is allowed to make a certain amount of capital gain each year free of tax. In the 2007-08 tax year, you can make £9,200 before CGT is due. Couples each have their own allowance to use up.

When transferring an income-earning asset, be careful that you don't boost your beneficiary's income to such an extent that they have to pay a higher rate of income tax.

Using a trust to ease the triple-tax rap

To steer clear of the triple-tax iceberg, you can transfer an asset into a discretionary trust and claim *hold-over relief*. HMRC work out the gain on the asset – this is called the *chargeable gain* – and deduct it from your tax-free CGT allowance for the year (£9,200 in 2007-08). Whatever gain is left over is then deducted from the beneficiary's CGT allowance. Let's look at an example.

Talia wants to gift a buy-to-let property to her daughter Claire. She realises that this is a PET and that ordinarily CGT is due when she transfers the property – despite the fact that Claire isn't paying her a penny – and that if she dies within seven years, Claire faces a hefty IHT bill, too. Talia bought the property for £100,000 and it's now worth £200,000. Ker-ching!

Talia transfers the property into a discretionary trust, naming Claire (and others) as potential beneficiaries. Talia claims *hold-over relief*, which means that no CGT is paid immediately.

Instead, after Talia's annual £9,200 CGT exemption is deducted, the chargeable gain of £90,800 (£100,000 minus £9,200) is knocked off the transfer value of the property. Therefore, when Claire and the trustees come to sell, for CGT purposes the property's value is £109,200 (£200,000 minus £90,800).

In essence, Talia has just postponed the tax hit by using hold-over relief. Hold-over relief buys time.

Hold-over relief is available for assets transferred into trust. Check out Chapter 5 in this Book for more on trusts.

Don't Let the GROB Get You!

A GROB sounds like one of those papier-mâché monsters from the original Doctor Who! GROB, though, is an acronym and stands for *Gift with Reservation of Benefit* and if you fall foul of it then no amount of hiding behind the sofa can help you!

If you sign over an asset you can no longer *benefit* from it by using or enjoying it. With a house, that means you can no longer live there. If the asset is a work of art, then it can't hang in your home – otherwise it's a GROB.

A GROB means that your PET tax prize goes up in smoke regardless of whether you cross the seven-year finishing line or not.

You can bet your bottom dollar, pound, or euro that if you transfer a major asset (PET) in the years prior to your death, the tax inspector is going to examine it closely to see if you benefited from it. If you did benefit, the person you transferred the asset to could be in line for a major tax hit!

Gifts between spouses are not subject to GROB rules.

There are, however, perfectly legal ways in which you can still enjoy your asset:

Book V

Protecting
Your
Wealth for
the Next
Generation

✔ **Visitation rights.** If you give away your home to your child as a PET, naturally you're still entitled to visit them there. You can even stay with them for weekends or over Christmas, just as long as your main residence is somewhere else (perhaps that lovely Tuscan farmhouse).

✔ **Pay rent.** You can continue to use an asset as long as you pay the asset's new owner the going market rent for it. So if you give your home away to your child and continue to live there, you must pay them rent.

Don't be tempted to fiddle the rent. HMRC is watching and if they deem that a fair market rent wasn't paid, then bang goes any IHT benefits.

From April 2005, under the *pre-owned asset* rules, people continuing to live in property they have given away can be hit with an income tax bill. Take advice from a solicitor.

✔ **Your circumstances change.** If your circumstances take a turn for the worse, then you may be able to use the asset in a limited way once more without risking GROB. This situation most often applies when someone gives away their home to a relative and then falls seriously ill – they may be able to move back in without fear of GROB. If you encounter this situation, seek the advice of a solicitor.

No law exists against you giving away an asset as a PET and then continuing to use it as before. All that happens is that the clock doesn't start ticking on the PET transfer until you stop using the asset – only then does the PET start on its seven-year journey to becoming free of IHT. Bear in mind that HMRC values the asset from the date you stopped using it and committing GROB, not on the day of the transfer. Overall, no tax advantages exist in continuing to use an asset you've given away.

Strategies for Singletons

If you're single you may feel a little left out by all this talk of how great the spouse's nil-rate band is. But don't despair – you can also use lots of weapons in your fight against the tax collector.

While it's true that only married couples can pass assets between each other regardless of size without fear of waking the IHT ogre from its slumber, you can also box clever and use other tools to avoid IHT. Keep your estate below the IHT threshold by using one or more of the following:

✔ **Give lifetime gifts.** Anyone is free to use exempt gifts and PETs to reduce the size of their estate.

✔ **Generation skip.** If you inherit a sizeable sum but already have enough money to live off, you can pass on the gift to your children to prevent your estate becoming so large that it attracts a whopping tax bill. Generation skipping is explained more fully in the next section.

✔ **Give to an exempt beneficiary.** You can leave money to charity and some other institutions free of IHT.

✔ **Use trusts.** Trusts take money out of your estate for the benefit of someone else. Trusts can be a very powerful tool in avoiding IHT (see Chapter 5 in this part for more on trusts).

✔ **Have the right assets.** HMRC allows special IHT exemptions for some types of property such as business, woodland, and agriculture.

✔ **Use your own nil-rate band.** You may not have a spouse but you still have your own nil-rate band to exploit to the full.

Funeral expenses and debts are deducted from your estate before IHT is calculated.

The Generation Game: Reducing Tax by Generation Skipping

Generation skipping isn't some sort of competitive sport played by families, but instead a useful way of saving tax.

What happens under *generation skipping* is that you give up the right to a gift in favour of your children. Ask a solicitor to draw up a *deed of variation* (a document whereby the beneficiaries agree to alter the gifts made in the deceased's will) to generation skip. Usually, this act involves you giving up the rights to a gift from your parent so that your son or daughter (the grandchild of the deceased) can inherit.

A beneficiary can choose not to take a gift left to them – this is called *disclaiming*. If a gift is disclaimed, it goes to the named alternative beneficiary; if there is no alternative beneficiary, it goes into the estate residue – what's left after taxes, creditors, and beneficiaries are paid.

Generation skipping can reduce the IHT liability on the original beneficiary's estate. Take the case of Frida, Miguel, and Gloria. Frida is Miguel's mother and Gloria's grandmother.

Frida leaves her entire estate, valued at £100,000, to Miguel. Miguel is wealthy and doesn't need the money, and also fears that the sudden injection of Frida's gift will push his estate above the IHT threshold. So, through a deed of variation, he changes the destination of Frida's estate and it goes to Gloria.

A swift look at quick succession relief

Sometimes IHT is due on two estates in quick succession. For example, suppose a parent dies and leaves lots of money to their child, who pays IHT, only for the child to die shortly after. Unless the estate passes to a spouse or another exempt beneficiary, then IHT is due again. The tragic circumstances are made even worse!

However, under such circumstances the beneficiary can claim *quick succession relief*. The closer the second death is to the first, the higher the percentage of relief from IHT can be claimed.

Years between first and second death	Tax relief as a percentage
Up to 1 year	100%
1-2	80%
2-3	60%
3-4	40%
4-5	20%
More than 5 years	No relief

Quick succession relief is only available on the proportion of the estate inherited from the first death. The remainder of the second person's estate is subject to IHT as usual.

The key is that no IHT is due on the estate because the £100,000 is well below Frida's nil-rate band of £300,000 (2007-08 tax year). However, if Miguel had allowed the estate to pass to him, and increase his wealth above the IHT threshold, then when *he* dies IHT may be payable on his estate.

With generation skipping, IHT is not saved immediately, but you avoid estate bunching and hopefully future IHT.

If you consider generation skipping, ask yourself some serious questions.

- ✔ **Can I afford it?** You're giving up a valuable inheritance. You have to be 100 per cent certain that you can live without the money.

- ✔ **Can my child handle the money?** You don't want a spendthrift teenager to inherit or the money could disappear in double-quick time. Remember, even the most responsible people can go a little wild when the financial shackles are off!

- ✔ **What is my state of health?** If you're suffering from ill health you may need long-term care, which can rapidly eat into your estate. You might need that money yourself in the future.

Reducing tax on collectibles

If you ever watch the BBC's *Antiques Roadshow* you know that having a set of collectibles or items of furniture is worth a lot more than having just one.

Owning a complete set of six Chippendale chairs is worth a lot more than owning one, two, three, four, or even five of the chairs.

If you own any valuable collectibles or furniture, take this unwritten law into account when making plans to avoid IHT. It may be a smart move to break the sets up, giving some items away as a PET to a child or relative.

If you gift some of the chairs to your spouse, then HMRC could treat all the chairs as *related property*. These are special rules that allow HMRC to value an asset as a proportion of an enhanced combined value.

The tactic to share out sets of collectibles and thereby reduce their worth for tax purposes can also be used when it comes to sharing out a majority shareholding in a business. After all, 60 per cent ownership of a firm is a controlling stake and worth a lot more than three 20 per cent stakes doled out to different family members.

Protecting the Family Home . . . By Moving Out!

Making sure your family home passes to your children without an unpleasant tax bill attached is probably your number one objective! But a home is most people's biggest asset and as a result it's not easy to hide it from the tax collector.

If your estate is worth more than the nil-rate band, then you need to employ some or all of the following tactics to deal with your family home:

- ✔ **Use the nil-rate band.** Spread your assets about – make sure that your will is written so that other assets go to different beneficiaries. This uses the nil-rate band to the max and prevents bunching of assets.

- ✔ **Leave your home.** Alternatively, leave your home, or the share of your home, to someone other than your spouse in your will. You're trusting that the beneficiary will continue to allow your spouse to live there; perhaps the beneficiary – a son or daughter – could move back in. Make sure your spouse is happy with this arrangement, as they have the right to challenge the gift through the courts.

Book V

Protecting
Your
Wealth for
the Next
Generation

From one home to another

In England, Wales, and Northern Ireland, you can only receive free local authority nursing home care if you have assets of less than £21,500. This rule forces many people to sell the family home in their twilight years, reducing the size of the inheritance pot. The way to counter this enforced sale is to get the asset out of your estate – through a PET, explained earlier in this chapter, or through a trust.

By putting an asset in trust you can ring fence it from any calculations the local authority make about the size of your estate. (See Chapter 5 in this Book for more.)

However, local authorities and creditors can ask the court to set aside a trust. Putting your home in trust and then entering a nursing home soon after can lead to the court overturning the trust. This action is known in legal circles as *deliberate deprivation.*

✔ **Put the home into trust.** You can arrange that on your death the home goes into a discretionary trust (explained in Chapter 5 in this Book) for a beneficiary other than your spouse, but the trustees allow the spouse to carry on living in the property. This arrangement uses your nil-rate band and your spouse is protected. You could even name your spouse as a trustee as well as a beneficiary. Importantly, when your spouse dies, the home is not in his or her estate for IHT purposes.

✔ **Give your home away.** You can simply sign your home over to a beneficiary as a potentially exempt transfer, and if you live for a further seven years no IHT is due. However, if you continue to live in the property, you fall foul of the GROB, explained earlier in this chapter.

✔ **Downsize.** If the children have gone you may not need your big old house. Why not sell up and move to somewhere smaller? For this action to be truly effective at reducing your estate, you have to move the money you make from the sale out of your estate fairly sharpish through using your annual gift exemption (explained earlier in this chapter).

✔ **Split the home.** If you have a big home, then you could split it into two or more residences. You can rattle about in one and your family take possession of the other. PET rules still apply but you don't have a problem with GROB. If you do go down this route, remember you need planning permission for the conversion.

Your main residence is exempt from capital gains tax, so if you sell your own home, you're fine. However, if you pass on your home to someone who subsequently rents it out rather than living there, when they sell the property, the sale will be liable to CGT.

Fleeing the Country to Avoid IHT

Sounds very dramatic, doesn't it? More people than ever are now retiring abroad. Few up sticks with the sole intention of avoiding IHT; most people do it for the warmer weather and the hope of never again navigating the M25. Nevertheless, from an IHT avoidance point of view, you might find it pays to leave dear old Blighty!

If you live in the UK, IHT is levied on your *worldwide* assets, but if you live abroad, it's levied just on your *UK* assets. So if you have large assets abroad, you can move to sunnier climes later in life to protect those assets from the UK tax system!

By moving abroad permanently, you might be able to take advantage of two nil-rate bands: One in the UK on UK assets and one abroad on the foreign assets. If you have a spouse, you could exploit four nil-rate bands!

But IHT avoidance is never simple. If you've lived in the UK for at least 17 out of the 20 previous tax years, you're treated for IHT purposes as still living in the UK. As a consequence, IHT is still due on worldwide assets. If you leave the UK permanently, it's still a further three years before you escape the UK's IHT rules altogether. Bother! Nevertheless, if you move abroad you may find that the IHT bill on your estate is reduced. Seek out specialist tax advice before you go.

You're deemed to be living (the official word is *domiciled*) in the country in which you have a permanent home. You can only be domiciled in one country at a time. If you own a holiday home overseas and your main residence is in the UK, you're classed as living in the UK. However, if you sell or let out the UK residence and move permanently to the holiday home, that's classed as your main home.

IHT isn't just a British phenomenon; most major nations impose some form of tax on a deceased's estates. Make sure you don't jump from the frying pan and into the fire!

Book V

Protecting
Your
Wealth for
the Next
Generation

If you move abroad and die soon after, you could owe IHT in both countries. HMRC levies IHT on all worldwide assets, but any IHT bill arising in another country is deducted. If the UK tax bill on worldwide assets is £100,000 and the IHT bill from another country is £20,000, your estate pays £80,000 to the UK and £20,000 to the other country.

If you live abroad but want your remains to be returned to the UK when you die, consider setting money aside in your will to cover the costs.

Dropping the Temperature: Estate Freezing

Wrap up warm, we're about to take you on a tour of a frozen estate. Bring out the huskies!

Estate freezing takes place if you decide that your estate is quite large enough, thank you. In this situation, you then ensure that all nil-rate bands, (your own and that of your spouse) exempt gifts, potentially exempt transfers, and gifts out of income are fully exploited – in short, the whole kit and caboodle of IHT avoidance is deployed to prevent your estate from getting any bigger.

Think about it: You don't even have to reduce the size of your estate because over time the IHT threshold will increase – if you can just keep your estate frozen, then you will find the tax liability shrinking.

But don't go on a mad splurge – giving away all you possess in order to get one over on the tax authorities. Remember, you have to keep enough in your estate to enjoy a comfortable and hopefully long old age.

Estate freezing takes a lot of effort as you have to be 100 per cent sure that you won't need the assets you're giving up. Over the long term, the results of estate freezing can be quite dramatic.

Chapter 5

Understanding Trusts

*I*n this chapter, we examine the different types of trust. Trusts used to be like a magic potion for your estate, which makes it appear almost invisible to the tax collector. You could use trusts to reduce tax, to protect your family's long-term finances, and to ensure that your beneficiaries got the full value of the gift you leave to them.

However, much has changed with the introduction of the Finance Act 2006, which clamped down on the use of trusts for tax planning. They may still be useful, but you need to take professional advice.

Starting at the Beginning: A Quick Tour of Trusts

A trust is a legal arrangement where one group of people, the *trustees*, are made legal owners of the assets in the trust for the benefit of another group of people called the *beneficiaries*. The assets are held in trust, perhaps for a set period of time or until a particular event takes place, such as the beneficiary reaching adulthood.

Putting an asset into trust is like using one of those prize-grabbing machines in a seaside arcade. You pluck the asset out of your estate and deposit it somewhere else. The reasoning behind this action is that if an asset isn't in your estate when you die, then it can't be taxed.

Trusts have usually involved a sum of money or a property being kept by the trustees, with the income from that property, such as rent or interest, passed on to the beneficiary or beneficiaries or, in some cases, paid back into the trust.

Trusts may have their uses in the fight with the tax collector but they are only one method (with reduced powers) in a wider strategy of tax saving – they should not be considered as a complete replacement for anything else you do to save tax such as using your exempt gift allowances (see Chapter 4 in this Book) and making potentially exempt transfers.

Time for some legalese. A person setting up a trust is usually known as a *settlor* or occasionally a *grantor*. Any property put into trust is called *trust property* – easy one, that! The document setting out the terms of the trust is the *declaration of trust*, *trust deeds*, or *settlement*. The act of putting an asset into trust is called *trustor settling*. Confused yet?

As we mention many times in this book, Scotland has a different legal system to England, Wales, and Northern Ireland. However, the laws governing trusts and trustees in Scotland are almost identical to those in the rest of the UK, so we won't make distinctions here (although some of the terminology may be different).

So, putting this all together, you can use trusts for the following objectives:

✔ Protecting the family fortune over the long term

✔ Making sure that the beneficiary is looked after

✔ Avoiding tax

These objectives are explored in greater detail below and in Book V, Chapter 4.

Protecting the Family Fortune

Consider using a trust to protect the family fortune if you face one of the following scenarios:

Book V

Protecting
Your
Wealth for
the Next
Generation

✔ **The beneficiary is too young to inherit.** A beneficiary cannot take legal possession of assets until she is 18, so you can put the asset in trust until she comes of age. If you think that this legal age limit is not enough of a safeguard, then you can stipulate an older age. Just pop the asset into trust so that the beneficiary can profit from the interest on or income from the gift but is prevented from getting her hands on the asset itself. When the beneficiary finally inherits, she will be a little older and, hopefully, a little wiser.

✔ **The beneficiary is a spendthrift.** Not everyone is good with money. In fact, some of us are terrible with cash, and like to spend what we haven't got. If a loved one falls into this category you may consider putting any gift to them in trust. The asset helps them day-to-day, because the beneficiary receives income from the asset, but the asset is protected, to be passed onto someone else after a set period of time or when the beneficiary dies.

✔ **The beneficiary is bankrupt.** If your beneficiary is declared bankrupt, then her creditors can take whatever assets you leave her. However, if you put the asset into trust the worst that can happen is that the creditors get their hands on any income that the asset produces, such as interest.

✔ **The beneficiary is infirm.** Your beneficiary may need long-term residential nursing home care. Outside Scotland, the local authority can insist that people sell their assets to pay for care, which means a gift could end up being swallowed by the beneficiary's care home fees. However, if the gift is in trust the income from it helps the beneficiary and then the gift can be passed on to someone else.

The principle is the same whatever the scenario: You want the beneficiary to have some use of the asset but at the same time you want the asset protected from either an unfortunate event or the beneficiary's poor judgement.

Protecting the Family

Trusts can be used for the benefit of a vulnerable or very special beneficiary while ensuring that on the death of the beneficiary the asset passes on to someone else.

✔ **Surviving spouse.** Perhaps your spouse is retired or you simply want to ensure that an asset is used by your spouse but passes on to someone else at their death. Your spouse may be very happy with the idea of a regular income from an investment or the use of a property.

Talking it through with your spouse before going ahead and setting up a trust is essential.

✔ **Mentally or physically disabled beneficiary.** Perhaps your beneficiary has some form of mental or physical disability that requires special care. Under such circumstances a trust is ideal. The trust ensures that your beneficiary is protected from having to look after an asset or even from being hoodwinked out of it by an unscrupulous person. The regular income from the asset could help meet medical and care costs or the use of the asset may mean that such costs are not required. Chapter 4 in this Book covers looking after vulnerable family members through trusts.

✔ **Charity.** You can set up a trust to pay money to a charity, providing it with a regular income stream. The charity doesn't own the asset outright so can't sell it, but you can make a difference over the long term.

Deciding Which Assets to Put Into Trust

You can put anything you own into trust from the family home to your toothbrush. But remember: A trust is likely to cost a lot of money in solicitor's fees, so it's important to put the right property into trust with the aim of saving tax and looking after your loved ones.

Four different types of asset are usually put into trust:

✔ **Property.** This can include your main home, holiday home, investment property, or land. These types of assets make up the bulk of most people's estates.

✔ **Life insurance.** The proceeds of a life insurance policy can be considerable and can be written into trust.

✔ **Money and shares.** Cash and shares that you don't intend to use for yourself (and that you don't think you need for an emergency) can be put in a trust.

✔ **Personal property.** This covers things like antiques and personal items of high value.

Don't bother with small items of personal property. Having lots of little items in trust costs more in solicitor's fees and proves a real pain for the trustees to administer.

Always ask yourself if the asset is large enough to be worth your while setting up the trust.

Matching the Asset to the Trust Beneficiary

One of the keys to a good trust is that the gift matches the needs of the beneficiary.

Think of your trust like an empty gift box that you're going to fill to make life easier for a loved one. Decide what the objective of your trust is, then fill the box with the asset that most closely meets this need.

If the beneficiary needs an income, leave them an *income-producing asset*, such as savings accounts, rental property, shares, and investment bonds. If the beneficiary needs a wad of cash in the future, leave them a *capital-enriching asset*, such as land, business interests, art, antiques, or the family home. When sold, these assets can provide a hefty lump sum.

You can leave a capital-rich asset and ask your trustees to sell it to provide an income for a loved one. However, the sale entails costs and hassle for the trustee.

Activating a Trust Before You Die

Most people think of trusts kicking in on death. But lots of trusts are lifetime trusts, which start when the person setting them up is still walking around right as rain. In fact, you can find big advantages to having a trust active while you're alive. The advantages include:

- ✔ You can see your trust in action, and make sure it – and the trustees – are up to the job.
- ✔ You can be a trustee yourself, and so retain control over the way the trust is run.
- ✔ The earlier you remove property from your estate, the more inheritance tax (IHT) your estate may save.

Once you put an asset into trust it's no longer yours, but belongs to the beneficiary (or beneficiaries). You must be 100 per cent sure that you can do without the asset before putting it into trust.

A trust that takes effect while you're still alive is called an *inter vivos trust*.

A trust that takes effect when you're alive can be either *revocable* or *irrevocable*. Once you put an asset into an irrevocable trust, it's gone forever. You have no future claim on the asset. Under a revocable trust, you're allowed to bring the trust to an end and take back control of the asset. A revocable trust is handy if you want the trust to fulfil a short-term goal while you're alive, such as looking after an elderly relative, or paying for your child's university education. Use a revocable trust if you want the safety net of being allowed to pull your money out of a trust if your circumstances change in some way.

Revocable trusts can have a major downside, however. Assets held within most kinds of revocable trust are still considered part of your estate for IHT purposes. Under some types of irrevocable trust, though, the asset has left your estate as far as the tax authorities are concerned.

There may well be income or capital gains tax considerations for the settlor of the trust, especially if the trust is revocable, or if the settlor stands to benefit in some way.

Table 5-1 sums up the pros and cons of each type of trust.

Table 5-1	Trusts: Advantages and Disadvantages
Revocable Trust	
Advantages:	**Disadvantages:**
Short-term objectives can be easily achieved	Pretty useless as far as tax savings is concerned
You get your asset back if you need it	
Irrevocable Trust	
Advantages:	**Disadvantages:**
The asset is out of your estate and as a result there is the potential to save IHT	You better be 100 per cent sure that you can do without the asset because once it's gone, it's gone!
The beneficiary has the security that the asset is, in effect, theirs and they can plan their future accordingly (although most modern trusts allow the trustees to make amendments if necessary).	

Putting Your Trust in Solicitors

Book V

Protecting
Your
Wealth for
the Next
Generation

Trusts are complex beasts and it's a smart move to use a solicitor if you decide to have one set up.

You may only need a trust once in your life, but a solicitor will have set up hundreds of trusts during their career. Ask yourself – who is more likely to make a mistake?

If you choose to put your faith in a solicitor it doesn't mean you should sit back passively. Ask any questions you need to, and check the solicitor's trust document. A properly drawn up trust should do the following:

- ✔ **Call a trust a trust.** The trust document should clearly state that a trust is being set up. This may seem an obvious point, but it's important that everyone involved in the process, from the trustees to the courts, is aware of what they're dealing with.

- ✔ **Set out the trustees' obligations.** The trust must give the trustees a clear job to do. Typical duties and obligations include how and when to make payments from the trust, and how to manage an asset put in trust.

- ✔ **Clearly identify assets and beneficiaries.** The solicitor should make crystal clear the assets that you want to put into trust, together with the full name of the beneficiary and your relationship to them. The solicitor shouldn't leave anything to chance; ambiguity may lead the courts to decide that the trust is void.

Chapter 3 in this Book goes into finding the right solicitor.

Trusts don't come cheap

Setting up and running a trust costs money and sometimes lots of it. You need to pay for the advice of a solicitor and for them to draw up your trust deeds. The more bells and whistles attached, the costlier the trust. Budget for £1,000 and go from there!

If you set up the trust through a will, you'll have to fork out for the will costs, too. Other set-up costs might include valuing the asset to be put in trust, and the costs of transferring the ownership of the asset to the trust.

Once the trust has been set up there'll be occasional legal fees and the trustees' day-to-day expenses – from travel to stationery costs – to be met.

Adding the Magic Ingredient: Trustees

Without the right trustees your trust could fall flat as a pancake. The effort and common sense of your trustees combine to make the oil that keeps the wheels of your trust moving year-in, year-out.

Choosing the right trustees is explored in Chapter 3 in this Book but here, in brief, are some things to look for in a good trustee.

- ✔ **Competent and good with money.** Ideally, your trustee is a professional or someone with experience of handling money, property, or investment. If your trust includes business interests, then a background in running an enterprise would be a huge advantage.

- ✔ **The right age.** You want someone not so young that they are inexperienced, and not so old that they could soon pass away or become incapable.

- ✔ **Good relationship with the beneficiary.** A model trustee should know and care for the beneficiary but not so much that they could be tempted to break the terms of the trust if asked to by the beneficiary. The best choice is normally a family friend who is close to your loved ones but who holds you and your wishes in high regard.

You can appoint a solicitor, a bank, even, in some cases, a beneficiary to act as a trustee.

Name an alternative trustee who can take over if one of your original choices decides not to take up the job or stops performing their duties, perhaps due to ill health.

If the trustees you appoint can't act for whatever reason, then the general rule is that the trustees or surviving trustees appoint replacements. An inter vivos trust will often give this right to the settlor – it may even give the settlor the right to sack trustees.

Show Me the Money: Trustees and Assets

The trustees have a *legal interest* in the trust. The beneficiaries have a *beneficial interest* in the trust. If the trustee is also a beneficiary, then they also have beneficial interest in the trust. To explain:

Book V

Protecting
Your
Wealth for
the Next
Generation

✔ *Legal interest* means that trustees have a duty of care to ensure that the asset within the trust is looked after properly. If the asset is a house, they should make sure that it's insured and secure. If the asset is cash, then the trustees should ensure the money is invested so that it's not at risk and that a reasonable income is obtained.

✔ *Beneficial interest* is when the beneficiaries have, for example, a right to income from an asset held in trust. If the trustee is a beneficiary, he or she has beneficial interest in the trust. However, if the trustee isn't a beneficiary of the trust, he or she is not allowed to help themself to money from the trust. The only exception to this non-profit rule is if a trustee is a professional such as a solicitor or accountant. They won't do it for love – they have to be paid their fees.

The trustee must deal with the trust's assets to ensure that the terms of the trust are fulfilled. For example, you may leave property in trust for the upkeep of your spouse after your death. The trustee may decide to sell the property to provide a cash sum to invest, from which the spouse is paid an income. The trustee must pass, in legal parlance, the brilliantly named *prudent man test* in every investment choice they make. Under the terms of this test, risk should be spread and investments reviewed regularly – so no blowing it all on Sad Ken in the 3.30 at Epsom!

The trustee decides what investments he or she uses – unless the trust imposes limitations (see later) – and the beneficiary is not allowed to object. If the trustee invests the money in shares of tobacco firms and weapons' manufacturers the beneficiary can't object on ethical grounds. However, beneficiaries can ask the courts to step in if they feel the trustee is failing in his or her legal duty of care, such as letting a property in trust go to rack and ruin or investing the fortune in high-risk shares.

If the trustee, acting on his or her own behalf, purchases an asset from a trust, the beneficiary can step in and void the sale if they wish. This applies even if the price being paid for the asset by the trustee is a fair one.

A trustee is entitled to claim money from the trust to cover any expenses that arise from the execution of their duties. The trustee is duty bound to keep clear and accurate accounts, and give beneficiaries a copy.

Saving Tax Through a Trust

Some trusts have the power to reduce estate taxes. However, trusts really help save tax when they are drawn up using other tax-saving weapons such as the nil-rate band and gifting to a spouse free of IHT.

Trusts can achieve several objectives at once.

Take the example of Jackie and Paul. They're married with one grown-up son, Andrew. Jackie and Paul's estates are worth £200,000 each. Jackie and Paul own the family home – worth £250,000 – as *tenants in common*, which means they can dispose of their share of the home (each part worth £125,000) however they feel fit through their wills.

Jackie is 10 years older than Paul. She's retired and not in good health. Paul makes a will and in it he sets up a trust.

Under the terms of the trust, Paul puts his share of the family home and £50,000 in shares and cash into trust. The ultimate beneficiary is Andrew, but Paul sets up a discretionary trust (described later) and through a letter of wishes asks the trustees to allow Jackie to live in the family home during her lifetime. Paul also leaves Jackie £25,000 in the will (not written in trust).

Paul dies and a year later Jackie's medical condition worsens and she needs residential nursing care. Jackie uses her own assets to cover nursing costs, as well as the £25,000 Paul left her.

When Jackie dies two years later, Andrew inherits the £175,000 his father left for him in trust plus his mother's remaining assets – she had to pay for the nursing fees, but crucially Paul's share of the family home was kept intact – all of it free from inheritance tax.

Paul's trust achieved the following goals:

✔ Protected the family fortune from being hit too hard by Jackie's infirmity

✔ Ensured IHT wasn't due on Jackie's death

✔ Allowed Jackie to remain in the family home for as long as possible

✔ Provided for Andrew to use the income from Paul's investments held in trust to pay his way through college

✔ Enabled Andrew to acquire his substantial inheritance when he was older and hopefully wiser.

If Paul had left everything to Jackie, then her powered-up estate might have attracted IHT on her death and transferred to Andrew. If Jackie had carried on living in a residential nursing home, the family's main asset – the family home – could've ended up in the coffers of the local authority.

But the potential damage of Jackie's illness on the family's finances was ring-fenced, as was any IHT liability.

Checking Out Different Types of Trust

Book V

**Protecting
Your
Wealth for
the Next
Generation**

Plenty of trusts are out there, each doing their own thing. You must pick the right one to achieve your objectives, while all the time keeping one eye on any potential tax implications.

We explain the most common types of trust below, so that you can decide which one best fits the bill!

Bare trust

As its naughty name suggests, a bare trust is the simplest type of trust.

Under a bare trust, an asset belonging to a beneficiary is held in the name of the trustees. A bare trust is most often used when you want to give an asset to someone under the age of 18, but don't want them to have control of it until they come of age.

Bare trusts have tax advantages, too. Any income tax or capital gains tax arising from the asset in the trust is usually paid by the beneficiary. So if the beneficiary is young, it's likely that he or she can use their full tax allowances to offset some of this tax bill. After all, if the beneficiary is under 18, it's unlikely that they have a job or own any major assets that could lead to a CGT bill.

Assets held in bare trusts for your child are taxed at your tax rate if that income is over £100 a year. This is to discourage people from shielding assets from income tax by merely putting them in a bare trust in their child's name.

Discretionary trust

Under a discretionary trust, the trustees have the right to decide both what the beneficiaries receive and when. This scenario means putting your faith 100 per cent in the 'discretion' of the trustees – are you ready for that? So, it is absolutely vital that you appoint the right trustees.

A discretionary trust has *potential beneficiaries* – meaning that none of the beneficiaries have the right to anything without the trustees' say-so.

At first glance, a discretionary trust looks like a power trip for the trustees, but such trusts can be very useful in nd making sure that the real needs of the beneficiaries are met. Discretionary trusts are far and away the most flexible form of trust and are highly recommended by solicitors whose clients are looking to secure their family's financial future (Chapter 4 in this Book has more on using this kind of trust to help your family).

Knowing when to use a discretionary trust

The flexibility of a discretionary trust makes it ideal in any of the following scenarios:

- ✔ **A spendthrift beneficiary.** The trustees can judge when the beneficiary should and shouldn't receive money from the trust. This type of arrangement can help keep the beneficiary on the financial straight and narrow.

- ✔ **A disabled beneficiary.** The trustees have the power to help when a beneficiary needs a little extra help with life's expenses.

- ✔ **You're unsure who should get what.** Perhaps you don't know the financial circumstances of your potential beneficiaries. Giving the trustees the power to decide who should get what hopefully means that the trustees prioritise the beneficiary who is most in need.

Under such an arrangement your trustees have two years from your death to get their act together and decide who gets what. This two-year timescale gives your trustees real elbow-room to get their gifting in the best tax-saving shape!

- ✔ **Tax saving.** By granting your trustees carte blanche they can distribute your estate to take full advantage of your full IHT nil-rate band (the amount of money you can leave to a non-exempt beneficiary before IHT has to be paid). This is a great tactic often recommended by accountants for keeping the family home out of the clutches of the tax collector. How to best use the nil-rate band discretionary trust to protect the family home and other assets is explained more fully in Chapter 4 in this Book.

A spouse, charities, and political parties are exempt beneficiaries. Exempt beneficiary status means that you can leave whatever you like without risking an immediate IHT bill.

A discretionary trust set up for the benefit of a mentally disabled beneficiary enjoys generous tax breaks.

You can name the beneficiary of a discretionary trust as a trustee. Doing so means that the beneficiary won't have to go cap in hand to the trustees every time they want a little cash from the trust because they're a trustee themselves.

Book V

Protecting
Your
Wealth for
the Next
Generation

Saving tax with a discretionary trust

First the downside: The income received by the trustees of a discretionary trust is liable to the top rate of income tax at 40 per cent. Income from share dividends is charged at 32.5 per cent.

As if that tax liability wasn't enough, if you transfer an asset into a discretionary trust when you're alive then the sale could be liable for Capital Gains Tax. Once the trustee sells the asset for a profit, or hands it over to a beneficiary, CGT may be owed.

Now the plus side: Under discretionary tax rules you could claim *hold-over relief*. This relief means that the CGT charge is held over until the trustee sells or hands over the asset. Hold-over relief means that the asset can only attract CGT once. With other types of trusts, CGT may be due at the time that the asset is transferred, and then again when the asset is handed over to a beneficiary.

The new tax rules introduced in 2006 mean that almost all inter vivos trusts are treated in the same way as discretionary trusts. That means that there is an immediate 20 per cent tax charge on assets going into the trust over and above the nil rate band (£300,000 in 2007-08), with more tax (up to 20 per cent) liable if you die within seven years – though there's nothing more to pay on death if you survive longer than that. Then every 10 years there is a further 6 per cent charge on the contents of the trust. When the trust is wound up or assets distributed there is a further 'exit charge' of up to 6 per cent, depending on how long it is since the last 10 year charge.

Assets transferred into trusts set up to take effect on your death are subject to the same 6 per cent ongoing and exit charges, plus an immediate 40 per cent inheritance tax charge, on the value over the nil rate band.

Accumulation and maintenance trust

An accumulation and maintenance trust is a type of discretionary trust with a twist. This trust was usually used for the maintenance and education costs of someone under 25 years of age and was designed primarily to ensure future financial provision for grandchildren. They used to receive special IHT treatment, but the new rules have removed all that. Now, if you want to 'ringfence' assets for children aged over 18, you'll have to pay the charges attached to a discretionary trust. If you don't want to pay those charges, you must be prepared to hand over the assets into the child's control at the age of 18. Even those A&M trusts already in existence will lose their special status from April 2008.

Interest in possession trust

This type of trust gives the beneficiary the right to an income from the trust for the rest of their lives, or a specified period of time. However, the beneficiary does not have the right to the capital. When the beneficiary dies, or a specified period of time elapses, the asset in the trust passes to someone else. The idea of this trust is to keep the asset in the family by denying the beneficiary the right to sell it.

Using an interest in possession trust

You can use an interest in possession trust to let a beneficiary, usually a spouse, partner, parent, or sibling, live in the family home for the rest of their life but on death the property passes to someone else.

It is possible to grant your trustees a little discretion to allow them to hand out some or all of the capital from the interest in possession trust. This provision can prove useful if the beneficiary falls on hard times.

You can dispose of your main home without incurring CGT by selling it or transferring it into trust.

Interest in possession trusts vs. tax

An interest in possession trust is now treated in the same way as a discretionary trust. So when it is set up during the lifetime of the beneficiary there will be 20 per cent to pay on assets over the nil rate band going in, and when it takes effect on the beneficiary's death there will be a 40 per cent inheritance tax charge to pay. In both cases there will also be an ongoing 10-yearly 6 per cent charge.

Income tax on the trust is either paid by the beneficiary or the trust. If the income of the trust is paid directly to the beneficiary, then the trustees are said to have _mandated_ the income. In short, the beneficiary is liable for any income and can offset their personal allowance for income tax against it.

IIP trusts written into wills also become less useful for tax planning, because the new rules say that for the IHT 'spouse exemption' to apply, the spouse has to be involved in all the trustees' decisions to do with redirecting income or the passing of capital to the children. Previously, the management of the trust was in the hands of the trustees alone; they might have decided to change the way money was paid out if, for instance, the spouse remarried and no longer needed the trust income. But if the trust does not comply with the rules, the assets going to the spouse will be subject to IHT, even though there would be no tax to pay if they were passed without a trust being involved.

Any income retained by the trust is charged at a rate of either 20 per cent (if the income is from a savings account) or 22 per cent (if the income arises from another source). In turn, if the beneficiary is a higher rate taxpayer – the top rate of tax in the UK is currently charged at 40 per cent – then they must pay more tax on their income from the trust.

Interest in possession trusts could create a nasty capital gains tax bill in former days. If you created an income in possession trust to start while you were still alive, then CGT might be due when you transferred an asset into the trust. But the new rules say that capital gains on these lifetime transfers into trusts can be held over until the trustee sells them or transfers them out again. If the trust kicks in after your death, then any CGT gain your asset made during your life is cancelled. However, the tax collector may still try it on at a later date.

If the trustees subsequently sell the asset at a profit, or hand over the asset to the beneficiary, then it could be liable for CGT but only from the date of your death.

Trustees have their very own annual CGT allowance, which they can use to minimise the tax bill. Sadly, the trustees' CGT allowance is only half that of an ordinary citizen. In the 2007-08 tax year, trustees are allowed to sell trust assets for a profit of £4,600 each year before CGT is due. CGT is charged at a rate of 40 per cent.

Protective trusts

If you think the beneficiary risks going bankrupt – perhaps they're not good with money or are struggling to get a business venture off the ground – you may consider using a protective trust.

Book V

Protecting Your Wealth for the Next Generation

Revealing secret trusts

A secret trust involves leaving an asset or some money to a trusted person – such as the family solicitor – to pass on the asset to someone else. In effect, a trust is created.

But this trust is all very hush-hush, with the gift or asset not even appearing in the will. Secret trusts were often used in Victorian times to squirrel away money to an illegitimate child or a mistress. The idea of a secret trust is to keep the gift out of the public domain. After all, a will is a public document.

Secret trusts are rarely used these days, but talk to a solicitor if you want to set one up.

A protective trust pays the beneficiary a regular income – but if the beneficiary is declared bankrupt (or tries to alienate the interest in possession), it morphs into a discretionary trust. Suddenly, the trustees have the whip hand and they can halt payments to the bankrupt beneficiary to stop them being gobbled up by hungry creditors. Protective trusts are designed to protect the beneficiary and, just as importantly, the assets of the trust.

In recent years, protective trusts have fallen out of favour because they don't offer the flexibility of discretionary trusts.

You can find simpler and cheaper alternatives to setting up a protective trust. For example, you may not trust the beneficiary with money, but perhaps you can trust their spouse. You can then leave the gift to the spouse, safe in the knowledge that they'll use it to help the beneficiary.

A Potent Combination: Trusts and Insurance

Strange things can occur when you combine insurance policies and trusts. Suddenly, a mundane run-of-the-mill trust can be imbued with special powers that can be of benefit to the trust's beneficiaries and even the person setting up the trust in the first place.

Loan trust

With a *loan trust* you as settlor make a loan to the trust (obvious, eh?). The loan is used to buy a life insurance bond. Then you ask for a part of the loan back each year, which you treat as income. Meanwhile, the asset in the estate gradually runs down. A loan trust offers two key benefits:

- ✔ You can ask for your full loan back at any time, if need be.
- ✔ Any profits made from the bond are not liable to IHT.

Essentially, a loan trust is a revocable trust with a built-in tax advantage. A loan trust can help you have your cake and eat it!

Be careful. Any loan not repaid at the date of death – the second death in the case of a couple – is added back into the estate. This action rebuilds the estate you have just reduced. The exercise then becomes a bit pointless.

Split trust

A split trust sounds like a painful gymnastics accident but in fact it can help protect you and your family.

If you have an insurance policy that pays a death benefit and offers *critical illness cover* – which usually pays a lump sum if you have a life-threatening condition – you can split them up inside a trust. By splitting the two elements of the policy, your family receives the death benefits, free of IHT, when you die, while you get to hang onto the critical illness cover while you live, in case you need to call on it.

Write life insurance policies in trust to minimise your estate's IHT liability. See Chapter 4 in this Book for more on life insurance and IHT.

Using Trusts to Help Your Family

Your old family photos tell lots of stories. From the joy of new arrivals, to the sadness of parting, your family is probably not the same as it was twenty, ten, or even five years ago.

Nothing in life remains the same, especially families. Who knows what will happen in the future? You need to be prepared. Cover all the bases and plan, plan, and plan again.

The big decision is whether or not it will be useful for your family if you incorporate a trust into your will – or even start one up when you're alive.

Family trusts are usually designed to meet one of the following objectives:

✔ Saving tax

✔ Looking after a loved one with special needs

✔ Passing assets on to children and grandchildren

✔ Making sure the spouse is looked after properly while the estate is kept intact

✔ Keeping the family home

We look at each situation in turn and show how a trust can help.

See a solicitor if you want to set up a trust. Chapter 3 in this Book covers choosing the right solicitor.

Saving Tax with Trusts for Your Family

With more estates than ever before falling into the inheritance tax (IHT) trap the tax-saving advantages of trusts are sadly missed since the legislation changes of 2006. What kind of tax savings can still be achieved?

Working a discretionary trust to the tax max

You want to reduce the IHT liability of your estate, but you still want to leave your spouse with enough to live on. What can you do?

Pay the maximum amount of money you can into a discretionary trust before IHT becomes due – your nil-rate band. Name your spouse and children as the potential beneficiaries of the trust. The trustees let your surviving spouse live off the trust and when your spouse dies your children inherit whatever is left free of tax.

If the surviving spouse is given all the income throughout his or her life, HMRC might argue that it was in effect an interest in possession trust. Make payments to the children from time to time.

This type of arrangement is called a *nil-rate band discretionary trust*. This trust is a beautifully simple tax solution and now one of the main ways of beating HMRC – but just remember that special one-off charge on anything above the nil rate band in the trust for each decade that it runs (see earlier in this chapter).

Discretionary trusts invest ultimate power in the trustees. Are you and your family comfortable with this situation? If the answer is 'no', then don't go there! A great solution is to name a beneficiary, perhaps your spouse, as trustee of the discretionary trust.

The naked truth of a bare trust

A bare trust offers a partial solution on the tax front. Any income tax or capital gains tax arising from the asset in a bare trust is paid by the beneficiaries. So if the beneficiaries are young, it's likely that they can use their full tax allowances to offset some of the tax bill.

Helping a Needy Beneficiary

Trusts can help members of your family who are infirm due to age or because of mental or physical disability.

You probably have two goals in mind when looking at setting up a trust to help a vulnerable family member:

- Making sure the vulnerable person is provided for
- Ensuring the asset passes safely onto another family member when the beneficiary passes away

When setting up a trust for a vulnerable family member, it's vital to get your choice of trustees right. The wellbeing of your loved one rests on a combination of the trustees' diligence and thoughtfulness. What's more, don't scrimp! A trust of this nature has got to be perfect, so consider naming a solicitor as a trustee to work alongside a trusted family friend.

If your beneficiary has a mental disability and no one's ready, willing, and able to act as trustee, don't panic. The Mencap Trust may be able to act as trustee. However, the Mencap Trust can't act as executor and only agrees to be a trustee of a trust they have approved. For more information, contact Mencap National Centre, 123 Golden Lane, London EC1Y 0RT, Tel: 020 7454 0454, or visit their Web site at www.mencap.org.uk.

Calling on a discretionary trust

A discretionary trust is probably your best option. Firstly, the vulnerable family member can benefit from a regular income from the trust. Secondly, the trustees have the power to make any necessary payments from the trust for one-offs such as tailor-made holidays or special equipment.

If the vulnerable person is just one of many potential beneficiaries, write to the trustees stating that you want the infirm beneficiary's needs to be put first – this is called a *letter of wishes*.

Using a disabled person's trust

A *disabled person's trust* allows you to put large amounts of money – above and beyond the normal IHT nil-rate band of £300,000 in 2007-08 – into a trust free from any IHT liability. These trusts are often used when someone has become disabled due to personal injury and has received a large compensation cheque.

One proviso with a disabled person trust is that more than half the assets in it must be for the benefit of the disabled person. This type of trust is an exception to the new rules, in that there are no 10 yearly charges, but IHT is payable on the death of the disabled person.

Using the interest in possession option

An interest in possession trust grants the beneficiary the right to use an asset while still alive but states that the asset should pass to someone else on the death of the beneficiary. This type of trust offers more security for a vulnerable beneficiary than is the case with a discretionary trust, as the trustees are given a strict set of rules they are bound to follow.

The idea of an interest in possession trust is that the vulnerable person – perhaps an aged spouse – gets to live in a degree of comfort, but their circumstances cannot erode the capital of the asset, which ultimately is kept in the family.

Using Trusts for Your Little Rascals

You may want to pass on an asset to your children and grandchildren, but what if they're too young to inherit in their own right? The answer could be to place the asset into trust. Here are some scenarios where trusts can help:

✔ **Having lots of little ones.** If you have lots of children or grandchildren, then you might consider putting a pot of money into a discretionary trust and naming them as beneficiaries. Some of your children or grandchildren may turn out to be real bright sparks and a trust could enable them to go to a good university. Whatever the challenge, under a discretionary trust the trustees are free to dish out the dosh to whichever child or grandchild needs it most.

✔ **Paying for school fees.** Gifts to children and grandchildren are often made with a particular purpose in mind, such as helping them meet the costs of university. For instance, you can put the asset into a discretionary trust, asking the trustee to make payment if the child studies at university. Alternatively, you can put the asset into a bare trust. Just remember that under a bare trust the assets must pass to the beneficiary at the age of 18, come what may.

If you're married with children, it's a racing certainty that you and your spouse ultimately want your children to inherit your estate. However, gifts between parents and children are liable to IHT. Draw up your will so that when the first parent dies, a substantial part of the wealth passes to the children, making proper use of the nil-rate band. See Chapter 4 in this Book for more on using the nil-rate band.

Trusting to Look After Your Spouse

Providing for your spouse while ensuring as many assets as possible pass to your children or other beneficiaries is the holy grail of most people's trust plans. But it's not as hard as you might think to square this particular circle!

Using a discretionary trust is probably the best route – see the section on 'Saving Tax with Trusts for Your Family' earlier in this chapter.

Alternatively, you can use an interest in possession trust again. You give your spouse the right to use an asset or enjoy an income from it for life, but it passes to someone else on the death of your spouse. An important point, where the surviving spouse is not the parent of your children (that is, where there are children by a previous marriage) is that by putting the residue of your estate into an interest in possession trust, you also ensure that the surviving spouse cannot deliberately or inadvertently divert it away from your children.

This type of trust doesn't save on IHT because when the first beneficiary (say, a spouse) dies, the assets of the trust are added to their estate for IHT purposes. This can lead to estate bunching – where the assets of a married couple end up in the estate of the one surviving spouse at their death – which is a big tax no-no!

Looking after your spouse through a trust and saving tax are two sides of the same coin. For example, a nil-rate band discretionary trust achieves a double whammy of providing for your spouse and ensuring what's left passes to another beneficiary tax-free.

Home Free: Putting the Family Home into Trust

Your natural instinct is probably to ensure the family home remains just that, the family home, after you've gone. A home is such a large asset that it's worth special consideration.

The family home can come under threat from many directions when you die – many of which you can't plan for and are purely bad luck – but here are a couple that you can prepare against:

✔ **The attack of the tax collector.** An IHT bill can be so high that the house must be sold to pay it. Ways to reduce IHT liability to prevent this are explored in Chapter 4 in this Book, but you can make doubly sure by putting your home into trust.

   If you do put your home into trust, consider using a nil-rate band discretionary trust, to use your nil-rate band to the max.

   Assets above the nil-rate band are still liable to IHT, but at a reduced rate (see Chapter 4 in this Book for more).

   Whether your surviving spouse continues to live in the home is entirely up to the trustees. However, you can avoid this problem by naming your surviving spouse as a trustee.

✔ **The surviving spouse goes into residential care.** The family home may be sold to pay the local authority for care. Put your share of the family home into trust and you can protect it from being sold in this way.

   Your spouse can put their share of the home into the trust, too – if it is owned on a tenants-in-common basis. Chapter 2 in this Book goes into more detail.

   Putting a home into a bare trust is risky as the property will be considered to belong to the beneficiary and could therefore be sold to pay for residential care.

Beware of accidental trusts

In your keenness to protect an asset such as the family home, be careful not to create an *accidental trust*. For example, stating in your will that you want your spouse to have the family home but that it should pass to your son on the death of your spouse accidentally creates an *interest in possession trust*. Your spouse may not be able to sell the home if they have money worries or need to move somewhere smaller. But you were only expressing a heartfelt desire that the family home should pass between your loved ones.

If you think you're inadvertently entering trust territory with your will, seek immediate legal advice.

Ringing in Changes to Your Trust

Family circumstances change – divorce, death, and illness occur, and that's just looking on the bright side. As a result of a change, perhaps a trust you set up a couple of years ago is no longer relevant.

How you go about changing a trust depends firstly on whether it is set up through a will or kicks in while you're alive.

Altering a trust in a will

A trust set up through a will is not active until the testator – the person whose will it is – has died.

If you want to make alterations to a trust in a will, you simply go about it in the same way you would change any other aspect of your will.

Two ways to change a will and therefore a trust within it are:

- ✔ **Writing a codicil.** This is a legal document used to make additions and changes to a will.

- ✔ **Revoking and writing a new will.** When it comes to major changes to your will – and remember trusts are complex and can easily count as a major change – it's often best to start from scratch by revoking your old will and drawing up a new one.

Changing trust beneficiaries

One of the most common reasons for changing a trust is to alter beneficiaries. You can make this change quite easily under most well drawn-up discretionary trusts. You can specify beneficiary *classes* as opposed to individual names — and so leave a trust to grandchildren rather than an individual grandchild, for example. Armed with this flexibility, the trustees should be free to help the family member most in need.

To specify your wishes, write to the trustees saying which particular beneficiary you want to help.

Changing a non-will trust

Whether you're allowed to change a trust that's active while you're alive depends on whether it's a revocable or irrevocable trust (see the section 'Activating a trust before you die' earlier in this chapter for more on these types of trust).

If the trust is an irrevocable one, tough! You can't change this trust because you no longer have any legal claim over the assets held within it. However, your trustees may have the right to do so.

Under a revocable trust, you can change it by bringing it to an end and taking back your asset. Then you can start up a new trust.

Considering the Downsides of Trusts

Not all is hunky-dory with trusts. Trusts can be tricky to change and expensive to set up, and even before the tax changes of 2006 they were not necessarily the tax-saving panacea of popular imagination.

Before putting pen to paper and drawing up a trust with a solicitor, ask yourself:

- Do my beneficiaries agree with my plans?
- Am I up to speed with the tax implications of the trust?
- Am I prepared to give up the ownership and use of the asset going into trust?

> ✔ Is the trust flexible enough to take account of the challenges that my family may face in future?
>
> ✔ Can I achieve the same objective cheaper, faster, or better by using a trust alternative? (See the next section.)

Ensure that your beneficiaries are happy with your choice of trustees. If the beneficiaries and the trustees don't get on, this can lead to serious tension and claims of bias.

Book V

Protecting Your Wealth for the Next Generation

Picking Easier Options: Alternatives to Trusts

Setting up a trust can be a lot of hassle and expense. You need to consider whether there are alternatives out there that you can act on today.

Take an example. You may want to ensure that your child has his or her university fees paid for, and has enough to live off while studying (a.k.a. beer money). The trust solution would see an asset put into trust to meet studying costs, while the alternatives are:

✔ **Simply gift the child the cash.** The advantage of this action is that the gift may reduce your estate's liability for IHT. However, consider how trustworthy your child is with money.

✔ **Have money ready to pay the fees.** Simply keep the money in a savings account and meet the costs of putting your child through university as they crop up. Remember, you're allowed to make a single £3,000 large gift from your estate each year, which isn't liable for IHT. In addition, any payments for the maintenance of loved ones, and out of income, instantly leave your estate for IHT purposes (see Chapter 4 in this Book for more on gifts which are exempt from IHT).

✔ **Leave an age-dependent gift in your will.** Most people go to university in their late teens or early twenties. You can specify that your child should inherit at 21 so there's a pretty good chance (assuming that your child goes to university) that the gift is used to meet university costs, either from the start or to pay back the student loan. Under the new rules, where a gift to a child comes into their possession after the age of 18, there are 10-yearly and exit charges to pay. This caused a great stir when it was first announced, but in practice most such gifts are under the nil-rate band anyway and therefore the issue of charges is academic.

Any variant of these trust alternatives can apply to any situation you and your would-be beneficiary find yourselves in.

Chapter 6

Grasping the Basics of the Probate Process

In This Chapter

▶ Understanding probate and letters of administration

▶ Realising the work involved

▶ Tracking down the will

▶ Working with other executors and solicitors

Probate is all about dealing with the estate of someone who has died. Looking after someone's estate (being the *executor*) is a major responsibility. Whether the estate is worth a few thousand quid or millions of pounds, everyone involved pins their hopes on everything going well.

Being chosen as an executor is a real vote of confidence in your character. The person who named you in their will trusted you to do what is right. If you step into the breach and administer the estate of someone who has died without a will, then the onus is on you to get it right.

In this chapter, we show you what probate is and the processes you can expect to face when you administer someone else's estate.

Starting at the Beginning: What Is Probate?

Apparently, only two certainties exist in life: Death and taxes. But to that short list you can add probate.

The word *probate* comes from the Latin 'to prove' as probate is the legal recognition that the will is valid and the executors can deal with the estate. Nowadays, probate has come to mean the process of gathering up the property of someone who has died and then distributing it to creditors, the tax collector, and finally beneficiaries. Whether a valid will exists or not, this process is called the *administration* of an estate.

The person or people who deal with the deceased's estate are called *personal representatives*. Personal representatives come from one of three distinct groups:

- ✔ **Executor.** Someone appointed in a will to oversee the probate process by distributing the estate. The executor is duty bound to follow the wishes expressed in the will. If, for example, the will states that a beneficiary should not get a gift until a specific age, it's up to the executor to make sure this happens.

- ✔ **Administrator.** If no valid will exists naming executors, someone must come forward to take the deceased's estate through probate. More often than not a close relative volunteers to administer the estate. This person is called – wait for it – an administrator. Instead of getting *grant of probate* (explained below), an administrator applies for *grant of letters of administration*. An administrator doesn't have the terms of a will to follow. Instead, the administrator is legally bound to distribute the deceased's property under the rules of intestacy (see Chapter 1 in this Book for how intestacy works).

    If a will exists but doesn't name executors, an administrator must dole out the estate according to the terms of the will, rather than intestacy, as the will is still valid – just not perfect.

- ✔ **Courts.** If no one comes forward to take an estate through probate, then the courts step into the breach. Everything is done by the letter of the law, but without the human touch. This is the last you'll hear about this situation here, as this book presumes someone – maybe you – is willing to act as a personal representative.

If the executors appointed in a will have died or are unwilling to act, then a beneficiary steps into the breach and acts as an administrator of the estate. Under such circumstances, the would-be administrator has to apply for *grant of letters of administration with will annexed*. Many wills make provision for an executor being unable to act by naming an alternative. Alternatives have exactly the same powers as the first choice executor.

An important difference between administrators and executors is that some of the powers of an executor kick in on the testator's death. An administrator has to wait for grant of letters of administration before they can act.

Ideally a beneficiary should be paid their inheritance within a year of the testator's death. This time period is often referred to as the *executor's year* but also applies to people administering the estate under letters of administration. So get moving!

Understanding Grant of Probate and Letters of Administration

As an executor or administrator you can't fulfil your duties without first getting confirmation or permission from the courts to do so. *Grant of probate* is the official seal of approval for an executor to deal with the estate. Without grant of probate, you can't get down to sorting out much of the deceased's estate, such as selling shares and getting your hands on money held in some bank accounts.

In situations where no will exists, the person looking to administer the estate must apply for *letters of administration*. Letters of administration, like a grant of probate, is the official go-ahead to allow a person to act on behalf of the deceased.

A Highland thing

In Scotland, the terms used to describe the people involved in the administration process are different from those used in England and Wales:

✔ An executor appointed in a will is an *executor-nominate*.

✔ Someone appointed by the court to act as administrator (for example, if no will exists) is an *executor-dative*.

✔ Grant of probate is called *confirmation*.

✔ Letters of administration are called by the same name but are issued by the Commissary Department of the Sheriff Court.

In England and Wales both grants of probate and letters of administration are doled out by the High Court through a network of *probate registries*. You can find the address of your nearest probate registry in the Yellow Pages or by checking out www.hmcourts-service.gov.uk/cms/wills.htm.

You don't have to sit twiddling your thumbs until you receive the grant of probate. Typical jobs an executor can get on with prior to obtaining grant of probate include organising the funeral arrangements, getting a death certificate, and securing the property of the deceased.

Knowing When You Don't Need a Grant of Probate

If the estate is small and simple, then it may not need a grant of probate.

The following rules apply:

- ✔ No asset in the estate is worth more than £5,000
- ✔ All the property in the estate is held on a beneficial joint tenancy basis (see below for more)

Under such circumstances, the executor can crack on with the job of gathering in the assets, paying debts, and making sure the beneficiaries get what they are due. However, you must have a copy of the death certificate to take to the bank before they hand over the cash. With small estates, the administration process you need to follow involves gathering in the estate and tracking down and paying creditors; you are just relieved of the tiresome job of obtaining grant of probate or letters of administration. Now isn't that nice?

Property owned on a *beneficial joint tenancy* basis isn't subject to probate. On the death of one joint tenant, the ownership of the entire interest in the property automatically passes to the surviving joint tenants. (Chapter 2 in this Book covers leaving a home in a will.)

Even if the estate doesn't require a grant of probate, HMRC may need to see a set of estate accounts. So keep a record of all the money gathered in and paid out during the administration process.

Even if the estate doesn't have to go through probate, keep a copy of the will, or the original if you can, so that it can be produced – hey presto! – if a dispute arises.

Team Executor: Working Together

Book V

Protecting
Your
Wealth for
the Next
Generation

Most wills appoint more than one executor to share the workload and keep an eye on one another. Also, it's common for more than one person to apply for letters of administration.

Meet up with your fellow executors or administrators at the start of the process to divide up the work. One of you may have experience of dealing with tax, while another may be very close to the deceased's nearest and dearest. Talk it over and decide who is comfortable doing what – it's useful if one executor or administrator takes a leading role in the process to make sure the estate is administered as quickly and smoothly as possible.

Stay in touch with your fellow executors and administrators. Some key documents need to be signed by all the executors or administrators; for example, all the executors have to attend the probate registry when applying for grant of probate.

Treat the probate process as you would work. Agree to an agenda and follow it through. After all, it's a solemn process. Put your decisions about dividing up the work in writing and get all executors or administrators to sign. The document isn't legally binding, but it's good to set out clearly what everyone's responsibilities are.

Turning down the job of executor

Just because you are named as an executor of a will doesn't mean you have to take on the job. Perhaps you have too much on your plate to take on the job or you are suffering ill health. Be honest with yourself early on – it's better not to take on the role than to do a rushed, slipshod job.

If you want to renounce your executor status, contact your local probate registry (you can find the details in the Yellow Pages or visit www.hmcourts-service.gov.uk/cms/wills.htm). Alternatively, if you don't want to take the option of renouncing your right to act,

ask for a *power reserved letter* from the probate registry, fill it in and return it. By using a power reserved letter you retain the right to step back into the role of executor at a later date, perhaps if another executor dies.

If you believe you may have difficulty acting as an executor but don't want to go to the extreme of getting a power reserved letter, you can appoint a solicitor to do all the legwork for you. See the section 'Using a Solicitor' later in this chapter for more on this option.

Just because another executor or administrator takes on a particular area of work doesn't absolve you of any blame if something goes wrong – not a bit of it! A creditor or beneficiary doesn't care who deals with what, just as long as they get what they are due under either intestacy or the terms of a will. If another executor makes a mistake, you may be liable too.

Four is the maximum number of executors. If more than four executors are appointed in the will, an executor must renounce or reserve their rights to act. The non-acting executor can step back into the breach at a later date if one of the acting executors can no longer do the job.

Following the Duties of an Executor and Administrator

The tasks of an executor and administrator are the same (for the sake of simplicity, we just use the term 'executor' rather than 'executor and administrator' in this section).

Dealing with the deceased

An executor often takes a hand in sorting out the funeral arrangements of the deceased. For example, the will may outline the funeral wishes of the deceased or mention a pot of money to cover the expense of the funeral. How much of a role an executor plays in the funeral arrangements depends on the wishes of the next of kin. The family may want to take care of every little detail themselves. As an executor, it's best to make yourself available to the deceased's nearest and dearest, and be ready, willing, and able to take some of the administrative strain if they wish.

Registering the death and obtaining a death certificate can be dealt with by the executor or by the deceased's nearest and dearest.

The death certificate is essential to administer the estate as no one is legally dead until it has been issued – a very strange scenario!

Obtaining the legal power to act

You must get hold of the original will – if one was written – and obtain the necessary legal powers to administer the deceased's estate. You need to obtain grant of probate (if a will exists) or letters of administration (if it doesn't) from your local probate registry to assume legal responsibility.

If you are one of two or more executors, check that the other executors are willing to act. Then sort out how you are going to divvy up the work. If any trustees or guardians are named in the will, let them know the terms of the will.

Valuing the estate of the deceased

Before you're granted the power to administer the estate by the probate registry, you need to put a figure on the estate. This is necessary for working out the tax bill (explained in Chapter 4 in this Book). You must track down the deceased's bank accounts, savings, and shares. In addition, you need to work out whether the home of the deceased is subject to probate – it won't be if it's owned on a joint tenancy basis.

You then need to subtract any debts. If it is a large or complex estate you may have to advertise in the local paper to alert creditors to what has happened so that they can come forward and put in a claim.

If the estate is worth more than £300,000 and not going straight to a spouse, charity, or political party, then inheritance tax may have to be paid. See Chapter 4 in this Book for more on IHT.

Taking care of the tax collector

As executor, you must sort out any tax bill arising from the estate. Tax bills might include income tax, capital gains tax, and inheritance tax. You have the power to raise money from the sale of assets and even to borrow in your role as executor in order to meet an IHT bill. The tax collector may not just take the executor's word on how much tax is owed; it may be up to you, as executor, to submit IHT accounts. The tax collector may come back to the executor with a different figure – no doubt higher! – for what is owed in tax. As executor, you must fight the corner if the tax collector tries to take too much of the loot.

Distributing the estate

You must pay the tax collector and creditors from the deceased's estate. Don't forget, of course, to subtract your expenses from the estate. Then it's time to dish out the dosh to the beneficiaries named in the will. If no will was left, the administrator has to distribute the estate according to intestacy rules.

The final duty of an executor is to draw up a set of *estate accounts*. These give a rundown of what you've done, from paying tax to collecting and distributing the deceased's assets. Give a copy of these accounts to the beneficiaries and then keep the accounts safely for a minimum of 12 years.

With the agreement of all adult beneficiaries affected, it's possible for an executor to vary the terms of a will through a *deed of variation* to make the estate more tax efficient.

Executors are expected to make a decent fist of the job. If you are negligent, beneficiaries and creditors can take court action against you.

Good will hunting

One of your first jobs as executor is to find the will. The will is essential for proceeding to grant of probate. Hopefully, the person who made the will told you where they kept the original. However, if the whereabouts of the will is a mystery, and you can't find the document in the deceased's home, try looking in the following places:

✔ **Solicitor's office.** If the will was drawn up with the help of a solicitor, then the original may be held in the solicitor's office.

✔ **The bank.** Wills are sometimes kept safely in a bank. If a bank is named as an executor in a will they often allow the will to be deposited with them for free.

✔ **Principal registry.** The will might be deposited at the Safe Custody Department

of the Principal Registry in London, which is the granddaddy registry of them all. If the will is kept at the Principal Registry you should find a deposit certificate in the possessions of the deceased. The will can be reclaimed by sending the certificate to: Principal Registry, Family Division, Safe Custody Department, First Avenue House, 42–49 High Holborn, London WC1V 2NP.

If you can't find the original will, don't panic. In England and Wales, a photocopy of a signed and witnessed will is acceptable. The probate registry may ask for proof that the original will was not destroyed on purpose to revoke or annul it. If, for example, the will was destroyed in a house fire, the registry may want proof that the fire took place.

Using a Solicitor

Book V

Protecting
Your
Wealth for
the Next
Generation

Executors and administrators can instruct a solicitor to help them administer the estate – it's up to you whether you feel you need to call in the professionals. This All-in-One helps you through administering an estate and gives you pointers on where to go when things get more complex.

Certain situations may give you pause for thought, and make you consider calling on the help of a solicitor:

- ✔ **Missing essentials.** If you can't find a beneficiary or the original will, a solicitor can advise you on the best course of action.

- ✔ **The will is challenged.** If someone questions the terms of the will or if you think it has been drawn up incorrectly, a solicitor can utilise his or her previous experience to sort out the situation.

- ✔ **Complex financial affairs.** If the deceased owned a business or if the will contains a trust, you may want to call on the expertise of a pro.

Chapter 3 in this Book explores how to go about choosing a good solicitor.

If you use a solicitor, ask them at the outset how much they charge. Solicitors are likely to have set fees for carrying out particular work, plus an hourly fee. Keep control of costs: Some of the beneficiaries have to approve the accounts at the end of the administration process and they won't be pleased if you lavish lots of cash on legal eagles.

Let your fellow executors and administrators know that you want to use a solicitor. However, even if they disagree, the other executors or administrators can't forbid you from getting help from a solicitor or any other type of adviser.

Index

FOR DUMMIES®

Do Anything. Just Add Dummies

UK editions

PROPERTY

Buying and Selling a Home For Dummies
978-0-7645-7027-8

Renting Out Your Property For Dummies
978-0-470-02921-3

Buying a Property in Eastern Europe For Dummies
978-0-7645-7047-6

PERSONAL FINANCE

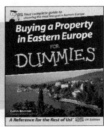

Investing For Dummies
978-0-7645-7023-0

Personal Finance & Investing All-In-One For Dummies
978-0-470-51510-5

Bookkeeping For Dummies
978-0-470-05815-2

BUSINESS

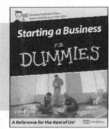  

Starting a Business For Dummies
978-0-7645-7018-6

Marketing For Dummies
978-0-7645-7056-8

Business Plans For Dummies
978-0-7645-7026-1

Answering Tough Interview Questions For Dummies
(978-0-470-01903-0)

Arthritis For Dummies
(978-0-470-02582-6)

Being the Best Man For Dummies
(978-0-470-02657-1)

British History For Dummies
(978-0-470-03536-8)

Building Self-Confidence For Dummies
(978-0-470-01669-5)

Buying a Home on a Budget For Dummies
(978-0-7645-7035-3)

Children's Health For Dummies
(978-0-470-02735-6)

Cognitive Behavioural Therapy For Dummies
(978-0-470-01838-5)

Cricket For Dummies
(978-0-470-03454-5)

CVs For Dummies
(978-0-7645-7017-9)

Detox For Dummies
(978-0-470-01908-5)

Diabetes For Dummies
(978-0-470-05810-7)

Divorce For Dummies
(978-0-7645-7030-8)

DJing For Dummies
(978-0-470-03275-6)

eBay.co.uk For Dummies
(978-0-7645-7059-9)

English Grammar For Dummies
(978-0-470-05752-0)

Gardening For Dummies
(978-0-470-01843-9)

Genealogy Online For Dummies
(978-0-7645-7061-2)

Green Living For Dummies
(978-0-470-06038-4)

Hypnotherapy For Dummies
(978-0-470-01930-6)

Life Coaching For Dummies
(978-0-470-03135-3)

Neuro-linguistic Programming For Dummies
(978-0-7645-7028-5)

Nutrition For Dummies
(978-0-7645-7058-2)

Parenting For Dummies
(978-0-470-02714-1)

Pregnancy For Dummies
(978-0-7645-7042-1)

Rugby Union For Dummies
(978-0-470-03537-5)

Self Build and Renovation For Dummies
(978-0-470-02586-4)

Starting a Business on eBay.co.uk For Dummies
(978-0-470-02666-3)

Starting and Running an Online Business For Dummies
(978-0-470-05768-1)

The GL Diet For Dummies
(978-0-470-02753-0)

The Romans For Dummies
(978-0-470-03077-6)

Thyroid For Dummies
(978-0-470-03172-8)

UK Law and Your Rights For Dummies
(978-0-470-02796-7)

Writing a Novel & Getting Published For Dummies
(978-0-470-05910-4)

FOR DUMMIES®

Do Anything. Just Add Dummies

HOBBIES

Poker
978-0-7645-5232-8

Sewing
978-0-7645-6847-3

Drawing
978-0-7645-5476-6

Also available:

Art For Dummies
(978-0-7645-5104-8)
Aromatherapy For Dummies
(978-0-7645-5171-0)
Bridge For Dummies
(978-0-471-92426-5)
Card Games For Dummies
(978-0-7645-9910-1)
Chess For Dummies
(978-0-7645-8404-6)

Improving Your Memory
For Dummies
(978-0-7645-5435-3)
Massage For Dummies
(978-0-7645-5172-7)
Meditation For Dummies
(978-0-471-77774-8)
Photography For Dummies
(978-0-7645-4116-2)
Quilting For Dummies
(978-0-7645-9799-2)

EDUCATION

Cooking Basics
978-0-7645-7206-7

The Koran
978-0-7645-5581-7

Anatomy & Physiology
978-0-7645-5422-3

Also available:

Algebra For Dummies
(978-0-7645-5325-7)
Algebra II For Dummies
(978-0-471-77581-2)
Astronomy For Dummies
(978-0-7645-8465-7)
Buddhism For Dummies
(978-0-7645-5359-2)
Calculus For Dummies
(978-0-7645-2498-1)

Forensics For Dummies
(978-0-7645-5580-0)
Islam For Dummies
(978-0-7645-5503-9)
Philosophy For Dummies
(978-0-7645-5153-6)
Religion For Dummies
(978-0-7645-5264-9)
Trigonometry For Dummies
(978-0-7645-6903-6)

PETS

Puppies
978-0-470-03717-1

Dog Training
978-0-7645-8418-3

Cats
978-0-7645-5275-5

Also available:

Labrador Retrievers
For Dummies
(978-0-7645-5281-6)
Aquariums For Dummies
(978-0-7645-5156-7)
Birds For Dummies
(978-0-7645-5139-0)
Dogs For Dummies
(978-0-7645-5274-8)
Ferrets For Dummies
(978-0-7645-5259-5)

Golden Retrievers
For Dummies
(978-0-7645-5267-0)
Horses For Dummies
(978-0-7645-9797-8)
Jack Russell Terriers
For Dummies
(978-0-7645-5268-7)
Puppies Raising & Training
Diary For Dummies
(978-0-7645-0876-9)

Available wherever books are sold. For more information or to order direct go to www.wiley.com or call 0800 243407 (Non UK call +44 1243 843296)

FOR DUMMIES®

The easy way to get more done and have more fun

LANGUAGES

978-0-7645-5193-2 978-0-7645-5193-2 978-0-7645-5196-3

Also available:

Chinese For Dummies
(978-0-471-78897-3)

Chinese Phrases
For Dummies
(978-0-7645-8477-0)

French Phrases For Dummies
(978-0-7645-7202-9)

German For Dummies
(978-0-7645-5195-6)

Italian Phrases For Dummies
(978-0-7645-7203-6)

Japanese For Dummies
(978-0-7645-5429-2)

Latin For Dummies
(978-0-7645-5431-5)

Spanish Phrases
For Dummies
(978-0-7645-7204-3)

Spanish Verbs For Dummies
(978-0-471-76872-2)

Hebrew For Dummies
(978-0-7645-5489-6)

MUSIC AND FILM

978-0-7645-9904-0 978-0-7645-2476-9 978-0-7645-5105-5

Also available:

Bass Guitar For Dummies
(978-0-7645-2487-5)

Blues For Dummies
(978-0-7645-5080-5)

Classical Music For Dummies
(978-0-7645-5009-6)

Drums For Dummies
(978-0-471-79411-0)

Jazz For Dummies
(978-0-471-76844-9)

Opera For Dummies
(978-0-7645-5010-2)

Rock Guitar For Dummies
(978-0-7645-5356-1)

Screenwriting For Dummies
(978-0-7645-5486-5)

Songwriting For Dummies
(978-0-7645-5404-9)

Singing For Dummies
(978-0-7645-2475-2)

HEALTH, SPORTS & FITNESS

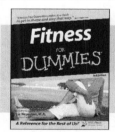
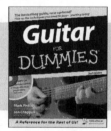

978-0-7645-7851-9 978-0-7645-5623-4 978-0-7645-4233-6

Also available:

Controlling Cholesterol
For Dummies
(978-0-7645-5440-7)

Dieting For Dummies
(978-0-7645-4149-0)

High Blood Pressure
For Dummies
(978-0-7645-5424-7)

Martial Arts For Dummies
(978-0-7645-5358-5)

Pilates For Dummies
(978-0-7645-5397-4)

Power Yoga For Dummies
(978-0-7645-5342-4)

Weight Training
For Dummies
(978-0-471-76845-6)

Yoga For Dummies
(978-0-7645-5117-8)

FOR DUMMIES®

Helping you expand your horizons and achieve your potential

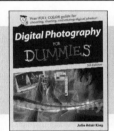

Printed and bound by CPI Group (UK) Ltd, Croydon, CR0 4YY